All the King's Horses

All the King's Horses
Vitruvius in an Age of Princes

Indra Kagis McEwen

THE MIT PRESS
Cambridge, Massachusetts . London, England

In a society in which the authority of the church is in decline, and the authority of philosophy and the state are negligible or nonexistent, it falls precisely to history to take care of ethical matters.

Joseph Brodsky, "Profile of Clio"

Prologue   ix

1   *Renaissance*   1

2   *Symmetry Takes Command*   29

3   *World Heritage, Urbino*   61

4   *Virtù-vious*   127

5   *The Architectonic Book*   177

6   *All the King's Horses*   201

Epilogue   285

Acknowledgments   293

Notes   295

References   319

Index   355

Prologue

De architectura, the treatise on architecture Vitruvius wrote for Augustus Caesar around 25 BCE, was not widely read in antiquity. The situation changed dramatically with its recovery in Italy nearly a millennium and a half later when, as the only surviving source on the topic, the work acquired virtually unchallenged authority among all who were interested in reviving the ancient art of building, and much else besides. Vitruvius, a relative unknown in his own day, became a Renaissance celebrity.[1]

His enthusiastic reception was not due solely to his status as lone survivor. Key among the reasons for Vitruvius's appeal in my view, and generally unacknowledged, is his relevance to the politics of what I have called an age of princes, the period between the mid fourteenth and late fifteenth centuries when ambitious *signori* throughout Italy were establishing control of cities that had governed themselves as free independent communes for, in most cases, the two hundred years and more preceding their

Prologue

takeover. Vitruvius's participation in the fulfillment of that autocratic agenda is the focus of this book.

Among the translations and editions of *De architectura* published during the Renaissance, one of them—or rather its frontispiece—stands out as a summation of precisely such intentions.[2] Francesco Lucio Durantino, a humanist from Casteldurante in the duchy of Urbino, claimed authorship of the translation, although he took his text from the far better-known, very lavish Cesare Cesariano translation of 1521, and his woodcut images from Fra Giovanni Giocondo's (also much better-known) first illustrated Latin edition of the work, published in 1511. Durantino's appropriations seem not to have discouraged his readers, for two editions appeared within eleven years, the first in 1524 and a second, somewhat emended one in 1535.[3] Of far greater interest than the second edition's textual emendations is its extraordinary new title page.

The ornamental floral border that had surrounded the typographically arresting title of Durantino's first edition exactly reproduced the border of Fra Giocondo's title page of 1511. In the second edition, the typography remained unchanged, but Giocondo's border of ornamental scrolls and flowers was replaced by a historiated frame, dense with images. Not one of these images evokes anything resembling a reference—direct, oblique, or even distantly symbolic—to what is conventionally understood as the topic of the work being translated, which is to say architecture.

Instead, you have Roman military trophies—shields, weaponry, armor, battle standards, and trumpets—all heaped up pellmell in the vertical panels on either side of the title. Above and below are six famous Romans, each identified by his initials. Four of them are on horseback. At the top, S.F. and A.C. charge in from the left and right respectively, their horses' hooves scattering weapons abandoned by what you assume must be fleeing enemies. S.F. is Sulla Felix ("Lucky Sulla")—Lucius Cornelius Sulla, the ruthless late republican general (138–78 BCE), famous for his brutality. A.C. is Augusto Cesare (Augustus Caesar), who needs no introduction. Nor indeed do I.C. and A.M., the world conquerors Iulio Cesare (Julius Caesar) and Alessandro Magno (Alexander the Great) who appear at the bottom of the page, riding horses that

Vitruvius, *M. L. Vitruvio Pollione di architettura* (Venice, 1535), frontispiece. Canadian Centre for Architecture, Montreal.

advance at a trot toward the center, where a third figure sits on a boulder, immobilized by his wounds and leaning on his sword.

The initials F.M. on the nameplate that lies on the ground a little to the right of the wounded warrior seem to indicate that he is Fabius Maximus, hero of Rome's third-century BCE war against Hannibal. But this would be wrong, for there is no record of Fabius Maximus being wounded in battle. There is, on the other hand, in Plutarch's *Life* of Fabius a description of his homologue and contemporary, the Roman general Aemilius Paullus, that exactly matches the image. As Plutarch tells it, Aemilius Paullus was thrown from his horse, wounded, and died in the catastrophic battle he led against Hannibal at Cannae in 216 BCE where over 50,000 Roman soldiers perished, a defeat (so Plutarch) that was due in part to the Roman troops abandoning their horses to fight on foot. "Paullus," he writes, "unable any longer to oppose the flight of his men, or the pursuit of the enemy, his body all covered with wounds, ... sat himself down upon a stone, and waited for the kindness of a dispatching blow."[4] The debacle at Cannae resulted in renewed adoption of Fabius Maximus's preferred tactics of deferral instead of the head-on confrontation with Hannibal Paullus had so disastrously favored. The success of Fabius's strategy saved Rome from conquest. The *titulus* here with its misleading "F.M." is an inferred recognition, in absentia, of the so-called Cunctator ("Delayer") and the paradoxical heroism of evasive methods that would have been difficult to represent more directly.

At the top center of the page, there is a portrait bust of a man ennobled by an encircling laurel wreath. He holds a book with the initials M.T.C. on its cover: Marcus Tullius Cicero, the only civilian among the Roman military men being honored here. Whoever decided to have Cicero preside over this unremitting glorification of horsemanship, war, and conquest must have taken Cicero at his own word when he boasted that his *virtus* as an orator was equal to the military *virtus* of Pompey the Great, and compared his (Cicero's) defeat of the traitor Catiline in the senate house with Rome's greatest military successes.[5] That eloquence is the equal in *virtus* of military prowess, if not indeed its superior, is a leitmotif in Cicero's *Brutus*, where he argues at one point that while the study of eloquence can improve the judgment required in military operations, no one has ever been made an orator by his success on the battlefield.⁶

The frame surrounding the title of Durantino's 1535 translation of *De architectura* would seem to give Vitruvius a leading role in its celebratory imperial rhetoric. In the pages that follow I will review how he performed that role, in an age of princes.

1 Renaissance

When, on Easter Sunday 1341, the senate crowned Francesco Petrarca poet laureate on the Capitol at Rome, it was not what you could call a lifetime achievement award. Petrarch was just thirty-six at the time and had so far only a limited body of work to show as evidence of his literary worth. But driving ambition and years of lobbying influential friends who included members of the powerful Colonna family at Rome as well as King Robert of Naples eventually rewarded him with the honor he craved.[1] King Robert's high opinion of a fragmentary draft of his Latin verse epic *Africa* appears to have been a deciding factor.[2]

The coronation, whose coincidence with the feast of the Resurrection was almost certainly not lost on the poet, had not taken place since antiquity. The celebration on the Capitol in 1341 seems to have unfolded following the protocol of a contemporary academic graduation ceremony, with Petrarch's carefully wrought coronation address structured much like a medieval sermon.[3]

It opens with a quotation from Virgil:

Sed me Parnasi deserta per ardua dulcis raptat amor.[4]

"But a sweet longing urges me upward over the lonely slopes of Parnassus." Only the power of such longing (such love—*amor*), he explains, could have given him the strength to surmount the untold hardships he says he endured in his solitary, unprecedented quest. You would think he means his quest for the laurel crown—the *laurea* his fervid imagination confounded with the name of Laura, the unattainable woman he loved and likewise longed for—but that is not what he says.[5] His primary goal, as he tells it, was not his own coronation but Rome's: "to garland the Roman Capitol with new and unaccustomed laurels."[6] The adversity he suffered along the way was for Rome: not for the Rome of his own time, but for the Rome of Cicero and Caesar, driven by an ardor whose motive he says was the hope to "renew in the senescent Roman republic a beautiful custom of its flowering youth."[7] The *laurea* he sought was a means to that end, with the coronation ceremony imagined as the inauguration of a new era.[8]

Petrarch despised his own time, the "dark age" he believed had begun in the fourth century and continued to his day.[9] His dim view of the centuries we now call the Middle Ages is the origin of the "darkness-into-light" metaphor underpinning the very notion of rebirth—the renewal of antiquity he longed for and was the first to invoke as an object of wishful thinking, more than two hundred years before Giorgio Vasari famously gave it the name *rinascita* in his *Lives* to make "Renaissance" a largely unchallenged commonplace of historical periodization.[10] It is as if Petrarch thought that fulfillment of personal ambition would summon this rebirth into existence.

Although, in his address, he ranks his personal ambition as secondary to his ambition for Roman renewal, Petrarch is far from denying his appetite for glory. It is an appetite present in every "common mortal," but greatest in men of "excellence and wisdom," he explains, asking his audience to recall how *in hac ipsa aula*—"here in this very hall"—Cicero once reminded Julius Caesar of his insatiable craving for glory.[11] The greatest men have the greatest ambition, for indeed their appetite is a measure of their greatness. Its just reward—the reward for excellence—is glory, and that goes for poets as well as Caesars, who indeed are nothing without poets to praise them, Petrarch argues, calling on the authority of various ancient authors in support of his claim. Who, for instance, would Achilles be without Homer to celebrate his deeds?[12] *Laurea igitur et cesaribus et poetis debita*, he concludes, "thus is the laurel the due both of Caesars and of poets."[13] This shared entitlement of poets and Caesars becomes the theme of his concluding paragraphs where he partners them as necessary and rightful laureates a further eight times.[14]

During the year immediately following his coronation, Petrarch applied himself to completion of his *Africa*, the unfinished Latin verse epic that had helped him to earn it.[15] The subject of the poem is the Roman general Scipio Africanus the Elder, hero of the second Punic war of the late third century BCE. Scipio's defeat of Hannibal in the battle of Zama in 202 saved Rome from conquest by Carthage and laid the foundations of Roman world rule. Based largely on books 21 to 30 of the third decade of Livy's history of Rome, whose text Petrarch himself had recovered and restored when he was still in his twenties, the *Africa* consists of nine books, and may have been intended to be longer.[16]

At the beginning of book 9, Scipio is on a ship, returning home after his great victory. At his side is his friend the poet Ennius, who wrote an epic account of Scipio's success, now lost. Both are to be crowned with laurel on the Capitol at Rome upon their return. While on the boat, Ennius tells Scipio of a dream in which Homer appeared to him to foretell Scipio's enduring fame. In Homer's prophecy, a poet from Florence called Francesco would, in a poem called *Africa*, celebrate the general's great deeds for posterity. Driven by his desire for glory this Florentine poet would, in the dark days of a distant future, follow in the footsteps of the ancient general and his poet to ascend the Capitoline hill once more, and there himself be crowned with laurel, to once again bestow on Rome the greatness that is its ancestral due. Ennius, known as the father of Latin poetry, was said to have brought the muses to Latium. The Florentine poet, who of course is Petrarch, will (according to the Homeric prophecy he has written into his poem) bring them back again after their long exile.[17] Scipio saved Rome. Petrarch will save Scipio from oblivion and so, once more, save Rome. At the end of the poem, the poet himself steps into his work, telling the reader, in the first person (*ipse ego*), how, after 1,500 years, he has indeed brought honor to Scipio and been crowned on the Capitol in fulfillment of Homer's prophecy.[18] To call this self-serving would be an understatement.

Petrarch's coronation, of whose perceived significance the conclusion of the *Africa* is his insistent exegesis, took place before the assembled *popolo* in the great nine-meter-high audience hall of the Senatorial Palace on the Capitol, recently renovated after an earthquake had damaged it in 1298.[19] In his address, he identified the hall as the "very one" where Cicero spoke before Caesar, but he was mistaken. The ancient Roman senate house—the *curia*—was in the Forum Romanum, below the Capitol, to the east. The room where Petrarch spoke was in the senate house first built on the Capitol in the mid twelfth century after a coup d'état in 1143 had resulted in the foundation of a free democratic commune similar to the communes whose establishment in European cities to the north had been part of an emancipatory movement begun at the end of the eleventh century.[20] Milan and Genoa, founded as communes in 1097 and 1099 respectively, were among the very first.[21]

Rome was still a commune in 1341 when Petrarch was crowned and would continue so until, crippled by factionalism and severe economic hardship, it ceded its autonomy to Pope Boniface IX in 1398. At Rome, the commune's governing body consisted of the citizenry—the *popolo*—and elected senators, whose number varied during the 250 years of its communal period.[22] At the time of Petrarch's coronation, there were two. Of these, it was his friend Orso dell'Anguillara, whose term was about to expire, who placed the coveted wreath upon his head.[23] Among the rights and privileges granted by the *privilegium* (diploma) awarded to Petrarch after the ceremony—a legal document whose text its recipient, a trained lawyer, had drafted himself—was the right to wear his crown in perpetuity, whenever he saw fit.[24] In ancient Rome, a victorious general's right to wear the laurel was normally confined to the celebration of his triumph when he received it as the ultimate

Justus van Gent, portrait of Petrarch from the famous men series in the studiolo of the ducal palace at Urbino, oil on board, 1472. Urbino, Galleria Nazionale delle Marche. Mondadori Portfolio / Electa / Bridgeman Images.

recognition of victory. But on Julius Caesar, newly appointed dictator for life, the Roman senate had, exceptionally, bestowed the unorthodox privilege of wearing the laurel at all times, as Suetonius records in a work that Petrarch knew well.[25] Surviving portraits of the poet without his wreath are rare—as indeed are those of Julius Caesar without his.

If Petrarch's coronation speech was indeed, as one scholar has called it, the "first manifesto of the Renaissance,"[26] the rebirth he was calling for was underpinned by values of status, power, and personal glory that were more than a little at odds with the ideals of the commune that was honoring him. What these ideals were is no doubt most memorably set out in the murals Ambrogio Lorenzetti painted on three walls of the Sala dei Nove in the Palazzo Pubblico in Siena and completed in 1339, just two years before Petrarch was crowned.[27]

Lorenzetti's famous fresco cycle could be read as the swan song of the communal era which had begun over two hundred years earlier as a daring experiment in civil government and was now—at Rome as elsewhere—drawing to a close. The commune's avowed ideal, which the work celebrates, was the Common Good, whose real, measurable existence was brought into being, as Lorenzetti clearly demonstrates, in the built fabric and bustling public spaces of the well-governed city: the Siena he idealized on the east wall of the Sala dei Nove. Not only did Petrarch despise his own time; he also despised cities. *Le città son nemiche* he wrote in one of his Italian lyrics. "Cities are the enemy."[28]

The commune's enemy was self-interest, which led to one-man rule. On the west wall of the council chamber, Lorenzetti has painted a corpselike female figure labeled Timor ("fear") who flies over the devastated countryside of a ruined city ruled by tyranny, personified in the horned demon he calls Tyrammides. In her right hand Timor, the flying corpse who is Tyrammides' messenger, brandishes a sword; in her left she holds a scroll bearing a legend, written in the vernacular: "Because each seeks only his own good in this city / Justice is subjected to Tyranny …"[29]

The confrontation between tyranny and the common good that takes place from opposing walls across the space of the Sala dei Nove where the Nine who ruled Siena convened to deliberate

Ambrogio Lorenzetti, *The Well-Governed City*, fresco, 1339, east wall, Sala dei Nove, Palazzo Pubblico, Siena. World History Archive / Alamy Stock Photo.

was no artistic fiction. Nor was the painter operating as a political philosopher, as one commentator (himself a political philosopher) argued at some length.[30] The drama Lorenzetti represented here was no scholarly debate.[31] The scenes of arson, pillage, and rape he painted on the west wall—a Sienese *Guernica*, in Patrick Boucheron's well-targeted formulation—were a ubiquitous, grim reality in the Italy of Lorenzetti's day where the cry for justice was urgent.[32] Roped into a shroud, Lorenzetti's Justice languishes, half-dead at the feet of Tyrammides and his court of vices. Below her the legend reads, "There where Justice is bound / no one is ever in accord for the Common Good."

The struggle in Italian cities to maintain autonomous communal governments in the face of their usurpation by powerful *signori* had been going on for decades, with ever-diminishing success.[33] Lorenzetti's fresco cycle was a late combatant in that losing battle: an impassioned plea whose argument lay bare in sheer ugliness the consequences of one-man rule as the antithesis of the well-ordered beauty of the city opposite, where the Common Good prevailed in a vision of peace. The Renaissance would teach *signori* how to bend beauty to their own ends.[34]

As I said, Petrarch hated cities, most especially the rabble who inhabited them. Communal governments, in his view, were simply an excuse for mob rule. Moreover, his passion for ancient Roman greatness was generally limited to admiration of famous men and their exploits—military men like Scipio for the most part.[35] His *De viris illustribus* (On famous men), developed in tandem with the *Africa*, consisted of twenty-three biographies of illustrious Romans beginning with Romulus. To these he later added a twenty-fourth: *De gestis Cesaris* (On the deeds of Caesar), a virtual apotheosis of the first, original Caesar—the great Julius himself. By far the longest chapter in the book, it eventually became a stand-alone work, which Petrarch continued to work on until the day he died.[36] There is no circumventing the obvious connection between Petrarch's enthusiasm for the Caesars of the past and his attachment to the princes of his own day, *signori* who became the self-styled Caesars of the Renaissance he is credited with having set in motion.[37] "The best state of a republic is the rule of one," he wrote in a letter of 1343.[38]

While working on the *Africa* during the year following his coronation, he was a guest of Azzo da Correggio, the unscrupulous warlord who ruled at Parma, whom he had befriended some years earlier and duly celebrated in verse.[39] From 1370 until his death in 1374, he was the beneficiary of another warlord, Francesco da Carrara who governed Padua. Carrara gave him a house with some land in nearby Arquà, renamed Arquà Petrarca after the poet was buried there.[40]

In November of 1373, just a few months before he died, Petrarch sent his patron an epistolary tract called "How a ruler ought to govern his state."[41] The letter begins by praising Carrara as an agent of peace "never thought possible when Padua was ruled by a communal regime": a ruler vastly superior to all others "not only in the opinion of [his] subjects, but in the opinion of the whole world."[42] It continues by enjoining him to take Julius Caesar, his heir Augustus, and the various Caesars who followed as models.[43] Self-serving to the last, he concludes with the advice that the prince honor learned men, who will "ensure the fame of your name" and even, he claims, "show you the way to heaven."[44] Some twenty-five years later, in a work called *Dragmalogia*, Giovanni di Conversino da Ravenna would take up Petrarch's argument for one-man rule, whose many benefits include patronage of the arts and letters after imperial Roman models, notably that of Augustus, while in communes "where the multitude rules, there is no respect for any accomplishment that does not yield profit."[45]

Laurea igitur et cesaribus et poetis debita, the laurel is due to both Caesars and poets. So the poet at the end of his coronation address. Petrarch's attachment to the princes of his time was a reciprocal relation. They gifted him with money, property, and status. His praise, talent, and mere presence honored them as cultivated men, notwithstanding any record of brutality. This one-on-one relationship would have been inconceivable, not to mention impossible, with the governing body of a commune, which consisted of a group of men whose elected term of office was typically of short duration—only two months for the Nine in Siena. For Petrarch, the relation of a poet to his Caesar allowed room for no intermediary.

His longest and most controversial patronage position came in mid-career, when he entered the service of the Visconti at Milan for a term that ended up lasting eight years, from 1353 to 1361.[46] Of all the *signori* vying for control of Italian cities at the time, the Visconti were reviled as the most ruthless, eventually seizing control of most of Lombardy and lands beyond, including the city of Bologna. When Petrarch's associates heard he had accepted Giovanni Visconti's invitation to Milan, they were appalled. Among the general outcry, an incredulous letter from Boccaccio inquired of his friend if he had lost his mind.[47] "They are not tyrants," Petrarch wrote testily in self-defense, "but rulers of their state." In any case, he continued, "I am *cum illis* [with them], not *sub illis* [under them as their subject], and I live in their lands, not in their household."[48] This last, in fact, was true.

The house given to Petrarch was next to the early Christian basilica of Sant'Ambrogio, at what was then the western edge of the city.[49] Among the members of his household staff was a young copyist he had brought with him to Milan to copy his own literary production, which included the letters he wrote, and also to copy, or recopy, his transcriptions of the ancient manuscripts he found. As a committed book collector, Petrarch was an eager seeker of manuscripts long before Poggio Bracciolini's well-publicized endeavors half a century later.[50] Indeed, for some, it is not Petrarch's coronation at Rome in 1341 that lights the first beacon of the Renaissance, but his discovery in Verona four years later of several manuscripts of Cicero's letters.[51] A famous letter he wrote to Cicero telling him about it is part of the disarming, one-sided correspondence he maintained with long-dead authors whose work he admired.[52]

More consequential than his find of Cicero's correspondence for shaping the world beyond the world of letters—the world of Italian cities being taken over by powerful warlords—was his discovery of a manuscript of Vitruvius's *De architectura*, the ten books on architecture later consecrated as the only surviving guide to the architectural principles of the ancients. Petrarch did not know this, of course, and may not even have known who Vitruvius was when he found the manuscript—where, exactly, is not known— since the work was unknown in prehumanistic northern Italy.[53]

The discovery, in about 1353, coincided with the beginning of his attachment to the lords of Milan.⁵⁴ Perhaps the young scribe he brought with him from Vaucluse copied the manuscript for him. There is a late fourteenth-century manuscript of *De architectura* in the Bodleian Library at Oxford, which Lucia Ciapponi identified over fifty years ago as a copy of Petrarch's own, through marginal notes, transcribed along with the text, that clearly pointed to Petrarch as their author.⁵⁵

Cum divina tua mens et numen, Imperator Caesar, imperio potiretur orbis terrarum is how *De architectura* (and the Oxford manuscript) begin.⁵⁶ In the manuscript, the initial capital "C" of *cum*—"when"—is historiated with the bust of a man, probably Vitruvius, holding an open book: "When your divine mind and power, Imperator Caesar, were seizing command of the world, and all your enemies had been crushed by your invincible strength and citizens were glorying in your triumph and victory ..." We know that the "Imperator Caesar" addressed in the opening lines of this preface is Augustus, the first Roman emperor, for whom Vitruvius wrote *De architectura* in about 25 BCE. We also know, as he writes in the next paragraph, that he had previously been attached as a military architect to Augustus's (adoptive) father, whom he does not name but who is, of course, Julius Caesar. With no previous scholarship to draw on and working on a blank slate, so to speak, Petrarch may have thought the "Imperator Caesar" Vitruvius addresses in his opening lines was his own greatest hero, the first Caesar.

In this, the marginalia are unenlightening, unfortunately, for the only note against this first preface is illegible. Nevertheless, there can be little doubt of the likely pitch of Petrarch's excitement upon opening his newly discovered manuscript to read in Vitruvius's triumphant beginning an eyewitness testament to ancient Roman grandeur at its very zenith. The key terms are all there: Caesar, power, command of the world, enemies crushed, invincible strength, glory, triumph, victory.

A letter Petrarch wrote to Pope Urban V in June of 1366 trying to persuade him to return to Rome from Avignon overtly endorses Vitruvius's view of Roman world dominion as divinely ordained.⁵⁷ Contained in the letter's appeal to the authority of "certain writers" claiming Rome's empire over the world to be naturally founded is Petrarch's complacent paraphrase of precisely the specious argument Vitruvius presents in order to validate the necessity of Roman supremacy in the first chapter of book 6 of *De architectura*.[58]

Annotation of the Oxford manuscript is most heavily concentrated on the passages in book 1 where Vitruvius writes of the required range of the architect's education and, again, in the margins of the preface to book 6, where its author once again elaborates on the importance of learning, whose incorruptible riches make it the only kind of wealth worth seeking.[59] This last must have struck a particularly responsive chord in Petrarch, for a passage from the sixth preface appears later, almost verbatim, in one of his Latin poems.[60] Whatever else it taught him, reading *De architectura* would surely have confirmed his long-held conviction concerning the necessary partnership of Caesars and their poets, a poet who, in the case of Vitruvius, happens to have been an architect.

But Petrarch's interest in building—architecture as it is commonly understood—is manifestly minimal. Indeed, that the knowledge of the architect is "furnished with many disciplines and various kinds of learning," as Vitruvius writes, was clearly of far greater interest to him than the further stipulation that this knowledge depends as much on *fabrica* (hands-on practice) as on *ratiocinatio*—the intellectual work Petrarch so warmly endorses.[61] There are virtually no notes at all in the Oxford manuscript on the six books of *De architectura* devoted to building. No manicles point from the margins to any passage concerning the rules for the planning of temples, the proportions of what would become known as the architectural orders, the building of fora, theaters, or basilicas.[62] Admittedly most of the building types Vitruvius writes about—fora, theaters, basilicas, and the like—were no longer current in Petrarch's day, but there is no evidence of curiosity about them either, as there would be a century later among readers of Vitruvius whose curiosity would verge on obsession.

So what *did* Petrarch understand about *architectura* after reading *De architectura*? What justification is there for the claim that his discovery of the Vitruvius manuscript in 1353 was more consequential for the Renaissance—at least as manifested in the political life of Italian cities—than his find of Cicero's letters eight years earlier?

When Petrarch was crowned on the Capitol in 1341 and mistakenly identified the audience hall of the Palazzo Senatorio as the "very hall" where Cicero spoke before Caesar, he was obviously unable to tell, or uninterested in telling (most probably both), a medieval building from an ancient one. What interested him was not the building as such, but the significance of the location in whose imperial aura he thought he was basking.

He had made his first trip to Rome four years earlier, in 1337, when he spent many days strolling around the city with his friend the Dominican friar Giovanni Colonna as a guide. Returning home at the end of November, he wrote a long letter to Colonna recalling their time together and the places they visited.[63] "We wandered together in that mighty city," he begins, then draws on the work of Roman authors (Livy, Suetonius, Virgil, among others) rather than on personal observation to construct a chronological survey of the city, qualified as "vast" yet strangely without spatial extent.[64] From the legends of Roman prehistory ("Here was the palace of Evander ... here the suckling wolf and ruminal fig tree, named for Romulus"), through the reign of Julius Caesar and his successors ("Here Caesar triumphed, here he died") to, at the last, the conversion of Constantine, the first Christian emperor ("Here Constantine cast off leprosy"), everything Petrarch writes of happens "here"—*hic*. But where exactly is this "here"? There is no description, and what these places actually looked like is clearly of no interest to him.[65] What did interest him, passionately, was their significance. "Who can doubt that Rome will rise up again once she begins to recognize herself?" he asks.[66]

Cicero also had a keen appreciation of the signifying power of place, expressed both in his speeches, which Petrarch knew, and in his philosophical works.[67] A passage in *De finibus*, which Petrarch refers to in another letter he wrote to his long-dead literary idol, is explicit.[68] In the course of a stroll with friends in the groves of Plato's Academy at Athens, Cicero writes, one of his interlocutors remarks that emotions are far more intense in the places associated with famous men than when we hear about them, or read their writings—Plato being a case in point here in a place which not only recalls his memory but seems even to summon up the living presence of the man. "Even the sight of our senate house at home," the interlocutor continues, referring to Rome, "brings to mind thoughts of Scipio, Cato, Laelius. ... So great a power of suggestion resides in places that it is no wonder the art of memory is based on it."[69]

"These two things are contained in all matters, but above all in architecture: that which is signified and that which signifies."[70] So Vitruvius, whose mentor Cicero also was, at the beginning of the paragraph listing all the disciplines required of an architect.[71] Although the philosophical back story here is somewhat complicated, it is possible to summarize Vitruvius's point in the following brief paraphrase.[72] The signifying power contained in all things is contained *tum maxime*, "to the greatest degree," in *architectura*. This, undoubtedly, is how Petrarch understood it. Written in the margin of the Oxford manuscript next to *tum maxime ... in architectura* is the mention "nōbn," an abbreviation, like N.B., of *nota bene*.[73] Below this, a manicle points to Vitruvius's words, placing additional emphasis on the importance their reader attached to them.

As his letter to Giovanni Colonna testifies, Petrarch knew that places were powerful locators of memory and meaning. To recognize such places (in Rome at least) would propitiate the city's rebirth: "Who can doubt that Rome will rise up again once she begins to recognize herself?" What he learned from Vitruvius was that this signifying power resided, *tum maxime*, in architecture—the lesson imparted, moreover, from the unassailable vantage of Roman grandeur at its peak: "When your divine mind and power, Imperator Caesar, were seizing command of the world ..." But unlike the already existing places that commanded learned observers' attention to the glory of days gone by, architecture could actually bring such grandeur into being, and this in a "here" not necessarily tied to the topography of Rome. Only a well-educated architect could properly manage this, of course, which is why Vitruvius follows up his claim about architectural signification with the formidable list of required disciplines Petrarch so approved of.

Petrarch read and annotated *De architectura* in Milan where, from 1353 to 1361, he was a guest of the Visconti lords of the city, for whom he frequently acted as a diplomat. Giovanni Visconti, the archbishop and iron-fisted ruler of Milan who had invited him, died in 1354 and was succeeded by his three nephews, Matteo, Galeazzo II, and Bernabò. Matteo was murdered by his brothers a year later, leaving Galeazzo II and Bernabò as corulers of the city and its ever-expanding territory. They consolidated their joint reign with the institution of the notorious 40-day regime of unspeakable torture known as the *quaresima* reserved for traitors, which no traitor was expected to survive.[74]

Milan had been one of the very first communes, founded in 1097, as already mentioned. Nearly 200 years later in 1288, Bonvesin della Riva wrote *De magnalibus urbis Mediolani* (On the marvels of Milan), an encomium of the city as an ideal commune—a picture in words, you might say, of a city very like the well-governed city Ambrogio Lorenzetti would idealize on the east wall of the Sala dei Nove in Siena fifty years later. After praising Milan's natural riches, water most especially, and drawing up an enthusiastic inventory of human and man-made "marvels" that include 6,000 fountains for drinking water, 300 public ovens, 440 butchers, 1,500 lawyers, 130 bell towers, 12,500 *portoni* (large front doors), and much, much more, Riva moves to a rapturous account of the public place in the middle of the city, surrounded by its civic buildings.[75] Such a place, the *platea communis*, accessible to all, was where the communal era's notions of public utility and the common good shed the imprecision of rhetorical commonplace to take concrete shape in the unambiguous reality of shared inhabitable space at the center of an ideally open city.[76] Lorenzetti made this place the incandescent source of the light that brings his entire painted city to life. In Milan (as elsewhere) the public place was called the Broletto, from which the main streets led to the city gates.

Azzo Visconti, considered the founder of the Visconti dynasty, took control of the city in February of 1329 in order, ostensibly, to put an end to the factionalism that, in Milan as elsewhere in Italy, was undermining communal viability. Just over a year later, in March of 1330, the commune's general council proposed that Azzo be elected "perpetual and general *dominus rector et gubernator* [lord and governor] of the city and district of Milan," a move that led the new ruler to assume an absolute authority that was essentially above the law—the authority to grant favors and give pardons, for instance, or issue decrees and seize properties.[77] Consolidation of this power freely bestowed on him, as he believed, by his subjects entailed an extensive building program that included a lavish urban palace built on the site of the Broletto, as well as religious buildings that would be testaments to his piety.[78]

In about 1344 Galvano Fiamma, a Dominican chaplain in the Visconti household, wrote a chronicle of the deeds of Azzo and his uncles, Luchino and Giovanni.[79] Chapter 15, "De magnificentia edificiorum" (On the magnificence of buildings), combines an account of Azzo's building activity with the ideological justification for it. This is how the chapter begins:

> Azzo Visconti, considering himself ... to be freed from all his enemies, resolved in his heart to make his house glorious, for the Philosopher says in the fourth book of the *Ethics* that it is a work of magnificence to construct a dignified house since people seeing marvelous buildings stand thunderstruck in fervent admiration ... and from this they judge a Prince to be of such power that it is impossible to attack him. ... In addition, it is required of a magnificent prince that he build magnificent, honorable churches, for which reason the Philosopher says in the fourth book of the *Ethics* that the honorable expenses which a magnificent prince should defray pertain to God. For this reason Azzo Visconti began to work on two magnificent structures, the first for the purpose for divine worship, that is, a marvelous chapel in honor of the Blessed Virgin, and a magnificent palace, fitting to be his dwelling.[80]

The reference here is to the *Nicomachean Ethics* where Aristotle ("the Philosopher") discusses the ancient virtues of *megalopropeia* (magnificence) and its corollary *megalopsychia* (magnanimity) which underwrite the expenditure, both public and private, that he says is required of great men.[81] Fiamma's is the first recorded vindication of such expenditure ("magnificence") as a yardstick of princely virtue which, sanctioned by the authority of none other than "the Philosopher," would become a commonplace of Renaissance thought in the course of the ensuing century.[82] A detailed description of the palace follows Fiamma's introductory paragraph: of its chapel, cloisters, multistoried tower, workshops, gardens, menagerie, aviary, and, opposite the aviary, "a most splendid great hall, in which are depicted Vainglory and the illustrious princes of the Gentile world, such as Aeneas, Attila, Hector, Hercules and many others." Also Azzo Visconti, of course. He and Charlemagne are the only two Christians among the heroes represented, Fiamma notes.[83] Giotto, leading painter of the age, is thought to have painted the murals in this hall with intentions that were, to say the least, a far cry from those that underwrote the murals in the hall of the Palazzo Pubblico in Siena where Ambrogio Lorenzetti was working at virtually the same time.[84] Nevertheless, Fiamma insists, once again invoking the authority of "the Philosopher," the considerable outlay all this and more entailed was for the common good.[85]

But *where* at this point was the common good to be found? Now occupied by a palace built, as Fiamma declares, to keep the *popolo* at bay, its time-honored locus, the Broletto, was of course no longer accessible. With the usurpation of the *platea communis*, the common good as a shared, inhabitable space lost its vital factuality, to leave only the empty air of a time-worn formula in its stead. The trend would become irreversible.

Azzo Visconti died in 1339, not long after completion of his palace. Petrarch arrived in Milan fourteen years after that. The palace was demolished, possibly as early as the mid 1350s; if so during the reign of Galeazzo II and his older brother, the notoriously brutal Bernabò.[86] Galeazzo and Bernabò were joint rulers of Milan itself, while each had separate charge of different cities in the Milanese territory.[87]

In 1359, after a campaign of almost four years, Galeazzo seized control of the neighboring commune of Pavia, some thirty kilometers away. The takeover took longer than expected because of the leadership of one Giacomo Bussolari, an Augustinian friar of humble birth who, through his exceptional skill as an orator, had rallied the citizens of Pavia to fierce, unyielding resistance.[88] A long excoriating letter Petrarch wrote to Brother Giacomo in March of 1359 reveals much about the Visconti lords' expectation of their resident scholar-poet in such circumstances.[89] Drawing on the resources of his vast erudition, Petrarch musters an army of ancient authorities, from "the Philosopher" to St. Augustine, in support of his attack on Brother Giacomo's political activism, demanding in the strongest possible terms that he give it up and return to a life of prayer. "I thought you were a friend of peace, but I was deceived," Petrarch writes, accusing the friar of using his eloquence to undermine the common good. "It would have been more fitting to chew your tongue up with your teeth, and spit it out, doing good to dogs and crows instead of doing harm to men," he continues in a bare-knuckle assault delivered here on no authority save his own and the authority, evident if undeclared, of his Visconti lord. It is Brother Giacomo himself, he writes, who with his own hands has drawn the enemy force to the city. The Visconti claim, like that of their marauding counterparts all over Italy, was that they were bringers of peace, who waged war only when provoked by a failure to capitulate. Eight months later Pavia finally surrendered, and on 13 November Galeazzo's troops entered the city.

In March of 1360, less than six months after conquering Pavia, Galeazzo began construction of a great square castle by first clearing the site through expropriation of the densely populated area he had chosen for it near the wall at the city's northern limit.[90] The castle, whose splendor inspired the contemporary chronicler Bernardino Corio to call it "the first palace of the universe," was part of a program of urban renewal meant to enhance the city's ancient Roman origins.[91] In one of its four towers, Galeazzo set up a library, soon to become famous.[92] The new castle became his principal residence, while his brother Bernabò stayed in Milan as in effect its sole ruler. In 1361, Galeazzo founded the University of Pavia with a charter granted by the emperor Charles IV. Petrarch left Milan in 1361, not for any political motive, but because of an outbreak of the plague. Between 1363 and 1369 he returned often, not to Milan but to Pavia for extended stays as Galeazzo's guest.[93]

Among the now lost frescoes in the castle, there was an equestrian portrait of its lord, as well as one of Petrarch himself portrayed in an incident where Galeazzo's infant son Giangaleazzo allegedly pointed him out as the most learned man at court.[94]

An enthusiastic letter Petrarch wrote to Boccaccio from Pavia in 1365 lists all the things his friend would see if he visited the city, which for Petrarch owed its fame, first and foremost, to its past as a "pious and devout concourse of illustrious men," whom he enumerates, beginning with Augustus Caesar who he says once set up camp there.[95] Another connection to Pavia's imperial past which he greatly admires is "an equestrian statue in gilded bronze (that) stands in the middle of the market place and seems to be just on the point of reaching, with a spirited bound, the summit of an eminence." This statue of ancient Roman origin, destroyed by Jacobins as a symbol of the monarchy in 1796, is the so-called *Regisole* ("sun king"), which had been brought to Pavia as war booty from Ravenna. More than the famous equestrian statue of Marcus Aurelius, which of course does survive, the *Regisole*—the horse, especially, not its rider—was taken as a matchless paradigm for many of the equestrian monuments set up as emblems of princely power throughout the cities of Renaissance Italy and beyond.

"Lastly," writes Petrarch to Boccaccio, concluding his account of Pavia's attractions,

> Lastly in order of time, though not of importance, you would see the huge palace, situated on the highest point of the city, an admirable building, which cost a vast amount. It was built by the princely Galeazzo, the younger of the Visconti, rulers of Milan, Pavia, and many neighbouring towns, a man who surpasses others in many ways, and in the magnificence of his buildings fairly excels himself. I am convinced, unless I be misled by my partiality for the founder, that, with your good taste in such matters, you would declare this to be the most noble production of modern art.

In the twenty or so years since Galvano Fiamma wrote his chapter on Azzo Visconti's magnificence, the notion of sumptuary excess as a measure of princely virtue had obviously taken hold, at least in the circuits traveled by poets and their Caesars. Galeazzo II Visconti was Petrarch's patron and also his friend, no doubt a consequence of their shared interests, scholarly and other. Indeed, Petrarch is thought by some to have played a role in developing the collection in Galeazzo's library.[96] It is surely likely, therefore, given the poet's warm appreciation of the Visconti lord's surpassing excellence in the magnificence of his buildings, that their conversations would have sometimes turned to discussion of Vitruvius and his *De architectura*, still fresh in Petrarch's mind if the letter he wrote in 1366 to Pope Urban V, referred to earlier, is anything to go by. And Vitruvius's claim, should it have arisen, that the power of signification resided *tum maxime* in architecture would just as surely have met with undisputed agreement, considering the imposing presence of Galeazzo's castle "on the highest point of the city" that was its affirmation. Even missing one of its four wings, destroyed with the *Regisole* in the revolutionary upheavals of the late eighteenth century, the Castello Visconteo dominates Pavia's historic center to this day. Shortly after building the castle at Pavia, Galeazzo began construction of the fortified Castello di Porta Giovia, also square on plan, at the northwestern edge of Milan, later replaced by the Castello Sforzesco, which still stands.[97]

Sometime in the late fourteenth century a manuscript of *De architectura*, copied like the Oxford manuscript from Petrarch's own, entered Galeazzo's new library in Pavia.[98] It was probably made especially for the collection, possibly at Petrarch's suggestion. The recto of the first of the 39 folios that make up the manuscript is illuminated and contains Vitruvius's opening address to Augustus Caesar ("When your divine mind and power Imperator Caesar ...") followed by the first paragraphs of book 1, chapter 1 ("The knowledge of the architect is furnished with many disciplines and various kinds of learning"). The initial capital *C* of the first word on the page (*cum*—"when") frames the bust of a man, portrayed against a blue ground, whose scarlet robe, ermine collar, and matching fur-trimmed headdress crested with a white feather clearly identify him as a prince, possibly Galeazzo II himself, whose portraits invariably show him with a feathered

Fourteenth-century Vitruvius manuscript at the Bibliothèque nationale de France, Paris, BN Ms. Lat. 7228, Paris, fol. 1r. Photo: Bibliothèque nationale de France.

headdress. He holds a closed book, which he seems about to open: *De architectura*, the book which itself opens with the letter that frames his image.

In a tondo below the first column of text on the left, a man painted in profile against a gold leaf ground is dressed in a plain gown and hood very much like what Petrarch himself might have worn. The man reads aloud from an open book, also *De architectura*. An intricate barbed quatrefoil with a human face in the center separates this reader from his audience of one, rather as in paintings of the Annunciation a column or other device separates the Virgin Mary from the angel delivering God's message. On the other side of the quatrefoil, at the right, an imposing white-haired personage portrayed frontally listens attentively from his own encircling gold leaf tondo, his head turned slightly to the left, his eyes looking toward the reader opposite. Bearded, caped, and crowned in ermine, this regal figure is obviously of higher rank than the prince in the initial *C* at the top of the page. In keeping with medieval tradition, their gold leaf backgrounds signal these figures as not of the living world but of some otherworldly realm, of which the prince above, whose background is blue, is not a part. Thus, for all that he looks like Petrarch, the reader on the bottom left is clearly meant to be Vitruvius, and the regal personage listening to him the Imperator Caesar for whom Vitruvius wrote *De architectura*, denizens both of the ancient Roman world their gold leaf haloes render transcendent in an apotheosis that is a perfect reflection of Petrarch's own enthusiasms.

The point of these images is obvious—so obvious, you might think, as not to be worth special attention. Vitruvius's address to Imperator Caesar is at the same time a dedication to the reigning prince of the present day, who here presides over the opening of the work from his blue window in the initial *C* of the "when" (now!) at the upper left of the manuscript page. But this is incidental, you say, and not really what *De architectura* is about. Perhaps not to you, but to Petrarch whose ambition was to bring Rome back to life—"to garland the Roman Capitol with new and unaccustomed laurels" as he put it in his coronation address—it was fundamental.[99] The two gold leaf portrait medallions at the bottom of this page, together with the quatrefoil that separates them, form the centerpiece of a bright foliage border—a conventional motif, admittedly, but still—that weaves a colorful garland around the opening paragraphs of Vitruvius's text. There are no more illustrations in the manuscript after this.

The conceit of rededication, if rarely formulated with such concision and elegance, would become commonplace in future dedications of *De architectura*. Fra Giocondo's of his illustrated 1511 edition to Pope Julius II, the "warrior pope" who named himself after Julius Caesar, is one instance. Claude Perrault's of his 1673 edition to Louis XIV another: *Voicy la seconde fois que l'Architecture de Vitruve a l'honneur d'estre dediée au plus grand Prince de la Terre*.[100] Notwithstanding its eventual reduction to a matter of convention, the dedication page of the Pavia manuscript brings into sharp focus the perceived importance of the continuity between imperial Rome and the present, renascent age of princes styling themselves as its rightful heirs in the face of increasingly futile attempts by Italian communes to maintain their viability.

Petrarch's call for Roman rebirth, first recorded in his coronation address, is the background for his discovery of *De architectura*. Visconti rule at Milan and Pavia is its immediate context, a circumstance pregnant with the possibility for Vitruvius to become a player in renewal of the imperial project. Poggio Bracciolini's much-vaunted discovery of a Vitruvius manuscript at the monastery of St. Gall in 1416, reported not by Poggio himself but by his companion Cencio de' Rustici, was far less consequential than Petrarch's in making Vitruvius an accomplice in that project's realization.[101] Besides the copy in the Pavia library, other copies of Petrarch's manuscript, known to have belonged to prehumanist contemporaries Giovanni Dondi dall'Orologio, court astrologer to Galeazzo II Visconti, and Niccolò Acciaiuoli, an influential figure at the Angevin court in Naples, testify to Petrarch's eagerness to share his discovery and the importance he attached to it.[102] Petrarch's friend Boccaccio, who became a scholar at the Neapolitan court, also had a copy. The ambitious building program undertaken by Galeazzo II's son and heir, Giangaleazzo Visconti, included the Certosa at Pavia as well as Milan's cathedral. Though neither work is ostensibly "classical," it is possible to see Vitruvian rhetoric in their underpinning. Drawings of the cathedral would figure prominently as illustrations for Vitruvius's terms *ichnographia, orthographia,* and *scaenographia* (plan, elevation, perspective) in Cesare Cesariano's 1521 Milanese edition of *De architectura*.[103]

Pier Candido Decembrio, secretary at the Visconti court during the reign of Galeazzo II's grandson Filippo Maria in the early fifteenth century, was a committed reader of *De architectura*, listing Vitruvius, along with Plato and others, as "greatly necessary" to any scholar wishing to put together a proper library. Pier Candido's promotion of the work resulted in its acquisition by bibliophiles as diverse as Duke Humphrey of Gloucester, the youngest son of the English king Henry IV, Francesco Pizzolpasso, archbishop of Milan, and Cardinal Branda Castiglione, who through connections in Hungary brought Vitruvius to Budapest.[104] Between 1420 and 1440, Cardinal Branda transformed the tiny village of Castiglione Olona just north of Milan into a personal fiefdom by rebuilding it in keeping with what he took to be Vitruvian principles, over a generation before Pope Pius II's analogous transformation of Corsignano, the Tuscan village he then renamed Pienza.[105]

The arrival of the manuscript copy of Petrarch's Vitruvius in the library of the would-be scholar-prince and warlord Galeazzo II Visconti was a signal event for the *fortuna* of *De architectura* in Renaissance Italy.[106] It coincided with the beginning of an alternative Renaissance, rather darker than the *rinascita* Vasari would later celebrate, entailing as it did in the rise of the *signori* who were Caesar's heirs the eclipse of the daring experiment in self-rule known as the free democratic commune. In this, Milan where Petrarch gave Vitruvius a new lease of life was paradigmatic.[107] With their deliberate focus on what the Renaissance destroyed rather than on what it brought into being, the chapters that follow examine various iterations of this darker Renaissance and the role *De architectura* played in it.

2 Symmetry Takes Command

Aerial view of the Piazza del Campidoglio, Rome. Photo: Folco Quilici, 1975. © Fratelli Alinari. © Alinari Archives / Folco Quilici / Art Resource, NY.

A bronze equestrian statue of the Roman emperor Marcus Aurelius stands at the center of the Campidoglio, capitol and civic center of Rome where Petrarch was crowned in 1341: the celebrated urban square that reached its current state of perfect symmetry between 1450 and 1650.[1] In ancient Roman times the site was the saddle between the peak known as the Arx (citadel) where the Roman mint was located in the temple of Juno Moneta and the Capitoline hill proper, from whose summit the great temple of Jupiter Optimus Maximus, the "greatest and best," overlooked the Roman Forum to the east, below. *Pignus imperii* was how the historian Tacitus once referred to the temple in the first century CE: "the guarantee of empire."[2] It was in imperial Rome that the symmetrical principles, revived in the architecture of the Italian Renaissance to shape the design of the Campidoglio, were first articulated by Marcus Vitruvius Pollio with theoretical intentions that were also, arguably, imperial.[3]

Written in Latin for Augustus Caesar, the first Roman emperor late in the first century BCE, Vitruvius's *De architectura* is, as we know, the only work on the topic to have survived from classical antiquity. The second of its 10 constituent books—10 *volumina*, or "scrolls" in Latin—opens, as each book does, with a preface addressed to the treatise's dedicatee, new ruler of the Roman world. Immediately following this preface, the first chapter of book 2 presents an account of the origins of building, Vitruvius's story of the so-called primitive hut.[4]

"In their old way of life," Vitruvius writes, people lived in forests and caves, eating wild food and breeding like animals. When, as a result of a violent storm, trees in a certain place caught fire, the people nearby were terrified at first and fled. In time, however, they came to appreciate the benefits of the fire's warmth, drew closer to feed it with fuel and, through repeated attempts to communicate with one another, eventually acquired the faculty of speech. Once able to speak, they set about building shelters. From these primitive huts, which Vitruvius describes in considerable detail, they eventually advanced to houses with foundations, tiled roofs, and walls of brick or stone. Finally, he concludes, "by applying themselves to their studies, they were led from wayward and uncertain opinions to the certain calculations of symmetries."[5]

Vitruvius's story about the origins of building is an account, concurrently, of the origins of civilization itself, a riff you could say on similar accounts by his older contemporaries Cicero and Lucretius who both stress, as he does, that leading the *vaga multitudo*, the "wayward multitude," from its savage ways into "one place" and the subsequent establishment of civic order are what define the civilizing process. But neither Lucretius nor Cicero discusses building, which for Vitruvius is key. For him, the story of civilization culminates with builders being "led from wayward and uncertain opinions to the certain calculations of symmetries." Because such principles are no longer "vague" but "calculated," architecture governed by them can become the incontrovertible evidence of civic order, the very *proof* of civilization—and also of Roman conquest. For the aim of conquest, as Romans told it, was precisely to lead people from their savage ways and bestow on them the benefits of Roman civilization.[6] It was quite natural for Vitruvius to share this conviction: as a Roman, of course, but more specifically as a military architect in the service of Augustus's adoptive father Julius Caesar, whose devoted henchman he had been during the great general's conquest of Gaul in the 50s BCE, and possibly right up to his assassination in 44.[7]

Caesar's conquest of Gaul (one million killed, another million enslaved) was followed by its urbanization under Caesar's heir, Augustus. "When I realized," Vitruvius declares to Augustus in his first preface, "that ... even as through you [Rome] was increased with provinces, so public buildings were to provide eminent guarantees for the majesty of empire, I decided not to hesitate and took the first opportunity to set out for you my writings on these matters."[8] Such "matters" include the "certain calculations of symmetries" that testify to his hut-builders' attainment of the civilized state which, given the context, would of course mean their becoming Roman. In France, close to nothing remains of pre-Roman Gallic settlements, whereas the traces of Roman conquest have proven to be virtually indelible. In this—in Gaul as elsewhere—symmetry can be said to have played a significant role.

Symmetry, for Vitruvius, included, but was not limited to, bilateral symmetry. Similar to what today is referred to as proportion, Vitruvian symmetry (from the Greek *symmetria*) referred more generally to the harmonious correspondence of parts to each other and to the whole, of which his "Vitruvian man," memorably rendered in Leonardo da Vinci's famous drawing of the late fifteenth century, is generally taken as the quintessential avatar.[9] In this, the body of what Vitruvius calls a "well-shaped man," each part bears a proportional relation to every other part (four fingers to a palm, four palms to a foot, etc.), as well as to his overall configuration (six feet add up to his height, which is also his arm span). The symmetry of this body is such that, with height equal to arm span, it can produce a square. It is also such that when the man lies on his back with arms and legs outstretched and a compass point is placed on his navel at the center, he can be made to produce a circle. Its perfect symmetry, of which the circle and square so produced provide geometrical proof, renders this body perfectly coherent and inviolable, making it, for Vitruvius, the architect's ideal template.

That, pared down to its very barest essentials, is Vitruvius's argument about symmetry in architecture. It was an internally coherent system that in his case had more in common with ideology than with any specific or verifiable design method, while throughout the real built Roman world the symmetrical correspondences between schematically identical towns, temples, theaters, and fora would become the guarantee and palpable proof of Roman perennity.

Among the many cultural strands woven into Vitruvius's thinking about architecture was the Stoic philosophy that was much in vogue during the early Augustan principate. Augustus himself had a series of philosophical advisers, all Stoics.[10] Stoicism was also an internally coherent system: "Nothing is more finished ... so well constructed, so firmly jointed and welded into one. ... Where is lacking such close interconnection of the parts that, if you alter a single letter, you shake the whole structure?" So Cicero, writing of the Stoic system's coherence, which as he wrote elsewhere was the coherence of the cosmos (also a body) as of all bodies.[11] The symmetry whose template is "Vitruvian man" is the embodiment of cosmic order, and its perpetration in the built world a matter (you might even say, if you were Vitruvius) of cosmic necessity.

A millennium and a half later, in the mid fifteenth century, this is what the Florentine architect and humanist polymath Leon Battista Alberti wrote in his *On the Art of Building in Ten Books*, the first Renaissance treatise on architecture: "Beauty is the reasoned harmony of all the parts within a whole, so that nothing may be added, taken away, or altered, but for the worse."[12]

Whether "beauty" or "symmetry," its defining criteria—perfection, coherence, and inviolability—remain the same. It was the apparent inviolability of such perfection, its daunting power to intimidate, that made beauty a weapon of choice among the Renaissance princes for whom Alberti wrote.[13] Fixity made it invulnerable and, in theory, impervious to change.[14]

This brings me back to the Campidoglio. Alberti wrote much of his treatise on architecture when he was living in Rome as a member of Pope Nicholas V's entourage.[15] Nicholas V's oracular deathbed "testament" of 1455 records the pope's conviction that to ensure submission of the illiterate Roman rabble he considered his enemy, the power and authority of the Holy See was to be made visible "in majestic buildings" and "imperishable memorials." "Noble edifices combining taste and beauty," his testament continues, "would immensely contribute to the exaltation of the chair of St. Peter."[16]

Nicholas V had been elected in 1447, and it was around this time that Alberti undertook a topographical survey of Rome, published in 1450 under the Latin title *Descriptio urbis Romae*. It is a very short work, essentially a list of polar coordinates for drawing a map of the city, tabulated by means of sightings taken from a fixed point. The point Alberti chose was, as he puts it, "the center of the city, that is the Capitol."[17] The phrase deserves attention because at the time the Capitol was not in fact at "the center of the city" at all. It was located at the edge of Rome's relatively small inhabited area—the densely populated *abitato*, so called, confined throughout the Middle Ages within a bend in the Tiber, while the rest of the territory circumscribed by the ancient Aurelian wall—the *disabitato*—was largely occupied by vineyards and other small agricultural holdings.[18] Moreover, at the time, the "center" of power at Rome was the Lateran from which popes ruled the city.[19] That the Capitol *had been* the center of the city in antiquity no doubt influenced Alberti's choice of words, passionate as he was in his admiration for ancient Roman grandeur. But there was more at issue than humanist enthusiasm for antiquity.

In July of 1143, the coup d'état that one historian has called "one of the most decisive events in the history of Rome" had resulted in the foundation of a free democratic commune, a municipality with a popular government, similar to those in northern Italy, as discussed in the previous chapter of this book.[20] In Rome the populace was further impelled to revolt by long-standing intolerance of papal domination, a mutual hostility that would fuel conflict for centuries to come.[21] A contemporary chronicle by Otto of Freising tells how, on that day in July of 1143, Romans assaulted the Capitol, then proceeded to a *renovatio senatus*, a "revival of the senate" on the ancient Roman republican (rather than imperial) model.²² Much later, unable to resolve internal divisions between its constituent factions, or endure the economic hardship that had become chronic without the infusion of papal funds, the commune ceded its autonomy to Pope Boniface IX in 1398, bringing to an end an audacious experiment in participatory democracy that had lasted for over 250 years.

By 1150, within just seven years of the refoundation of the senate, the senators had built a senate house on the hill that had once been, as the contemporary guidebook known as the *Mirabilia urbis Romae* reminded its readers, the *caput mundi*—"head of the world." The area to the west of this building—the area that became the present-day Campidoglio—and its southern slope had been, and would continue to be throughout the communal period, the place where the city's vast Saturday market was held.²³ Regular occupation of the area by the merchants, craftsmen, and their clients who together formed an emerging middle class established there a ready-made public realm whose vitality wove the memory of the Capitol's ancient greatness into the rhythms of everyday life. The commune's senatorial palace opened onto the marketplace to confirm the new political reality. SPQR, *senatus populusque romanus* was how the commune styled itself, reviving the ancient acronym. North of the senate house, higher up on the left, and facing it at an angle of approximately 60 degrees, stood the tenth-century Benedictine abbey church of Santa Maria in Capitolio, rebuilt around 1150 with steps in front of it leading down to the marketplace. Sometime in the twelfth century, or possibly in the early thirteenth, the upper segment of an ancient obelisk supported on the backs of four lions was raised between the church and the senate building as a symbol of the free senate.²⁴ The open loggias of a market building and the urban militia's barracks faced each other on the right-hand side of the unpaved open area between them and the church.²⁵ It was all something of a jumble symmetrically speaking, yet eloquent as a narrative that united the senate, convent church, and market in the shared space of a common project.

In 1250, the Benedictine convent and its church were ceded to the Franciscans, the monastic order whose commitment to the urban poor led to even closer ties to the commune. The earlier

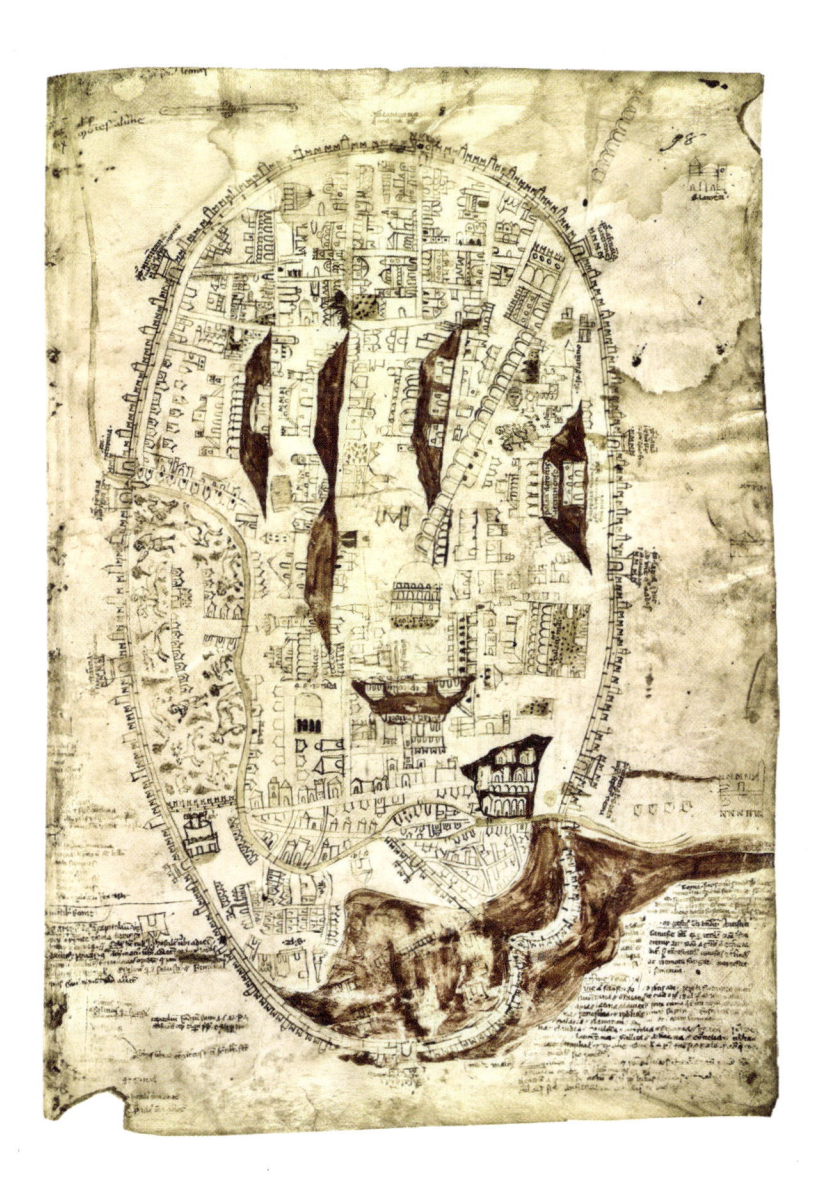

Plan of communal Rome, c. 1320. Biblioteca Nazionale Marciana, Venice, Ms. Lat. Z, 399 (=1610), fol. 98r. By permission of the Ministero della Cultura—Biblioteca Nazionale Marciana. Reproduction prohibited. East is at the top, with the Capitol and the Palazzo Senatorio (viewed from the east) at the lower center of the plan.

church was incorporated into the transept of the new west-facing church of Santa Maria in Aracoeli, which the Franciscans built on the peak to the left of the senate house.[26] The immense basilica continued to be connected to the lower area in front of the senate house by a stair on its south side, and was a frequent venue for audiences, popular assemblies, and council meetings. With the steep marble staircase of 124 steps added to its west front in 1348, the Aracoeli is by far the most eloquent of surviving witnesses to Rome's largely forgotten communal period.

The senate house itself underwent many changes over the centuries that followed the construction, initially, of a single-story building (the *porticus camellariae*, so called) with its public portico open to the market.[27] Over time, while continuing to retain the ground-floor portico, it eventually grew to three stories, topped by a crenelated parapet and flanked by two towers of unequal height. In the tallest of the two hung the great bell known as the Patarina, which rang to summon the entire citizenry to the hill for parliamentary assemblies where attendance was required by law.[28] In the 1440s when Alberti took the sightings for his survey, he probably worked from the top of this bell tower, since it was the highest point on the Capitol.

The building would never have met his criteria for beauty, of course, nor indeed would it have conformed to Vitruvius's definition of symmetry, axial or other. Even less satisfactory would have been the random asymmetry of the piazza itself, where no identifiable geometry governed the spatial relationships among the various buildings on the site. There is no surviving record of what Alberti thought, but his friend the historian Flavio Biondo recorded the sentiment that prevailed among humanists of the day when he wrote in his *Roma instaurata* (Rome restored) of 1448, "I am ashamed, beginning with the Capitol, to show such a beautiful place in such a formless and forlorn condition ... *nihil habet is captolinus* [there is nothing on the Capitol]."[29] Nothing there to see.

From the early fourteenth century, the front of the senate house included the especially awkward feature of two parallel *cordonate* (ramped stairs) of different sizes built next to each other on the right side of the façade. The longer of these led up to the

The Palazzo Senatorio in the late Middle Ages, after Pietrangeli 1964, 193. Canadian Centre for Architecture, Montreal.

first-floor *piano nobile* and its nine-meter-high audience chamber, the shorter one to the open ground-floor portico. At the top of the shorter *cordonata* stood the fragment of an ancient marble sculpture, Hellenistic of the fourth century BCE, which represented a lion savagely attacking a horse, its teeth and claws sunk deep into the flesh of the horse's flank.[30]

It was one of several lions connected to the Capitol at the time. These included the four that supported the obelisk mentioned earlier, as well as living lions kept there in a cage, for the lion was the symbol of communal Rome, with the city itself being (so it was claimed) *in forma leonis*, "in the shape of a lion."[31] Lion heads ornamented hollowed-out sections of certain ancient columns used at the market as official measures, known as *rugitelle*, for wine, oil, and grain.[32]

The lion attacking a horse was of particular importance as the emblem, specifically, of municipal justice, for it was before this sculpture, *allo luogo del leone*—"at the place of the lion"—that death sentences were pronounced and carried out. The lion, as noted, was the commune's chosen symbol, but what is there to say about the appeal of the poor, savaged horse?

The center of papal power at Rome was the Lateran basilica and palace, seat of the bishop of Rome, who was of course the pope himself. The pope claimed in fact to *own* the city, as the triumphal procession known as the *possesso* was meant to confirm when it threaded its way through the Roman streets after the election of each new pope.[33] How could a pope claim to "possess" the city? "We give over," reads the document known as the Donation of Constantine allegedly written by this, the first Christian emperor shortly before he died in 337 CE, "to the most blessed pontiff and universal Pope, our father Sylvester and to ... his successor pontiffs not only our palace [i.e., the Lateran] ... but the city of Rome and all the provinces, places, and cities of Italy or the western territories, and ... grant that they should remain under the law of the Holy Roman Church."[34] The Donation of Constantine was the basis of the popes' claim to political power. It was of course a forgery, but not unmasked as such until the mid fifteenth century.[35]

The document is thought to have been concocted in the eighth century, which would be around the same time the

Amico Aspertini, Lion attacking a horse, pen and brown ink on paper, 1496. bpk Bildagentur / Kupferstichkabinett, Staatliche Museen, Berlin / Volker-H. Schneider / Art Resource, NY.

Maarten van Heemskerck, Remains of the Lateran Palace, with the bronze equestrian statue of Marcus Aurelius, pen and brown ink, from the Roman sketchbook II, c. 1535. Kupferstichkabinett, Staatliche Museen, Berlin, Inv. 79 D 2, fol. 71 verso. bpk Bildagentur / Kupferstichkabinett, Staatliche Museen, Berlin / Jörg P. Anders / Art Resource, NY.

bronze equestrian statue of the emperor Marcus Aurelius was first brought to stand in front of the Lateran Palace where it would remain until 1538 as an emblem of the temporal authority the Donation was claimed to guarantee. Throughout the Middle Ages, the rider of the horse was identified as Constantine himself. Even as late as the sixteenth century, after its proper identity had been established, the famous ancient bronze continued to be referred to as *caballus Constantini*, "the horse of Constantine."[36]

The first recorded *possesso* took place in 795 to inaugurate the reign of Pope Leo III. Not surprisingly, this late eighth-century date overlaps both the date of the spurious Donation's fabrication and that of the installation at the Lateran of "Constantine" on his horse. Pope Leo and his successors did not ride in a carriage during the ceremony of taking possession, but horseback and, in keeping with the details of the Donation, mounted on a white horse.[37] A mid-thirteenth-century fresco cycle in the chapel of St. Sylvester at the monastery of the Santi Quattro Coronati in Rome celebrates Constantine's alleged transfer of his authority. Among the emblems of imperial power Constantine hands over to Sylvester in one of the panels is a white horse, while in the next panel the horse, which the pope has now mounted, is led into the city by the emperor who has become the pope's "squire," once again in keeping with the text of Donation. From the fourteenth century on, a telling ritual performed as the commemorative *possesso* approached the Lateran on the last lap of its itinerary involved the *popolo*'s attempt to remove this horse from under its newly elected rider before he reached his destination.[38]

It is obvious to me that the bronze horse ridden by "Constantine" at the Lateran, and the white horse the *popolo* tried to take out from under Constantine's purported heir during the last lap of the *possesso*, were symbolically one and the same—an identity surely shared, in the mind of the *popolo*, with the fragmentary marble horse being savaged on the Capitol. It is not difficult to imagine the degree to which the commune intolerant of papal rule would have relished how neatly the horse under attack *allo luogo del leone* epitomized its own struggle for power whose legitimacy the antiquity of the marble fragment could be claimed to underwrite, just as the ancient bronze horseman at the Lateran underwrote the pope's.

To return to Alberti. What exactly was afoot when, in the 1440s, he called the Capitol the "center of the city"? A friend of Pope Nicholas V, Alberti's sympathies were probably not with the commune, whose power had in any case been seriously hobbled by its concessions to Pope Boniface IX fifty years earlier in 1398. The changes Nicholas V made at the Capitol soon after the completion of Alberti's survey are instructive.

The two towers flanking the then rather lopsided Senatorial Palace were, as noted, of unequal height. I suggested earlier that Alberti probably took his sightings from the taller of the two, on the left. Between 1447 and 1453, Nicholas had these towers supplanted by a single, very tall tower built at the center of the other side of the building, not facing the market but overlooking the ruins of the Forum Romanum to the east. Further enhancement of the east face of the senate house, crowned by its new central tower, created a majestic, symmetrical backdrop for papal ceremonies now staged in the forum below, as well as for any traditional *possesso* making its way eastward through the forum along the ancient *via sacra* toward the Colosseum and the Lateran beyond.[39]

Nor did Nicholas neglect the open area on the west side of the senate house. Until the time of Alberti's survey, two parallel loggias, one a market building, the other a barracks, faced each other (as already noted) on the south side of the piazza, more or less at right angles to it. These the pope united under the single roof of the Palazzo dei Conservatori, which was not a municipal building but the seat of a governorate upon which devolved administrative functions not covered by the senatorial judiciary and housed the offices of "conservators" responsible for questions concerning commerce and craft. Its symmetrical façade, which faced the marketplace at an 80-degree angle to the senate house, consisted, according to a 1535 drawing by Maarten van Heemskerck, of nine bays, four equal ones on either side of a wider bay at the center. With arcades supported on classical columns—Corinthian, or possibly Ionic (the drawing is not explicit)—it was very much in keeping with the classicizing *goût du jour* favored by Alberti.

Led by Constantine, Pope Sylvester rides the emperor's white horse into Rome, thirteenth-century fresco, west wall, chapel of St. Sylvester, Santi Quattro Coronati, Rome. Hirmer Fotoarchiv / Bridgeman images.

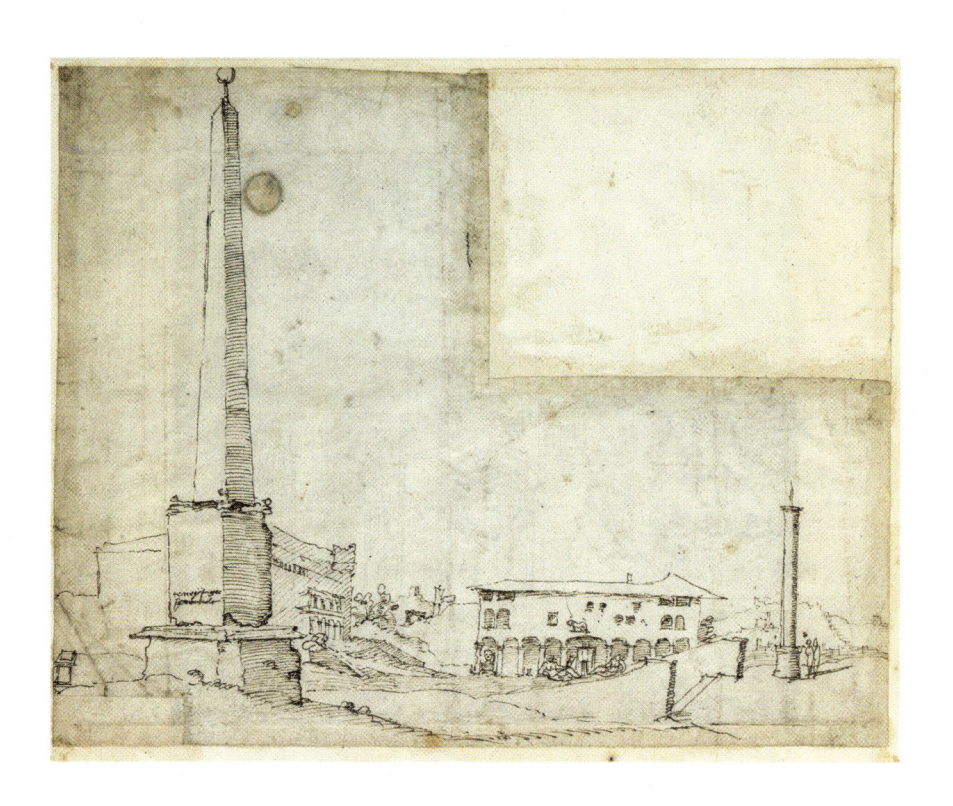

Maarten van Heemskerck, View of the Campidoglio from the Aracoeli looking south toward the Palazzo dei Conservatori, pen and brown ink, from the Roman Sketchbook II, c. 1535. Kupferstichkabinett, Staatliche Museen, Berlin, Inv. 79 D 2 a, fol. 72 recto. bpk Bildagentur / Kupferstichkabinett, Staatliche Museen, Berlin / Volker-H. Schneider / Art Resource, NY.

Construction of the conservators' palace coincided with Nicholas V's withdrawal in 1453 of the municipality's right to collect all duties on imports as well as the salt tax, both of which were henceforth to be paid to the Apostolic See.[40]

Twenty years later, in December of 1471, a few months after his election, Pope Sixtus IV donated to the *popolo romano* a collection of ancient statuary which had been at the Lateran, bringing it to the Capitol. The bronzes included the statue known as the *spinario* of a boy pulling a thorn from his foot, a colossal bronze head, later identified as that of the emperor Constantius II, and the smaller but ideologically loaded bronze she-wolf, *mater Romanorum*—the mother of all Romans—symbol of the city itself.[41] If the *caballus Constantini* was the emblem of the pope's temporal authority, the *lupa* had been the emblem of papal justice, in whose presence at the Lateran crimes were punished.[42] The wolf, mounted (again according to the Heemskerck drawing) over the central opening of Nicholas V's new Palazzo dei Conservatori, clearly defined the axis of the building's symmetry. The other sculptures were placed on public view in the portico of the palace.

There is some difference of opinion as to how much, or even whether, the *popolo* wanted these gifts, whose donation marked the founding, it is claimed, of the Capitoline Museums.[43] Be that as it may, it is surely significant that six years after making the donations, Sixtus IV banished the market from the place it had occupied for over 300 years and relocated it to Piazza Navona, in a move that irreversibly compromised the Capitol's role as a place of public assembly.[44] A museum, it seems, could not be expected to accommodate the hubbub of a marketplace.

More papal donations followed in the 1480s when Innocent VIII brought to the Capitol a larger-than-life-size gilded bronze Hercules wielding his club, where it was raised on a high plinth at one side of the piazza. Innocent's donation also included the fragments of a colossal marble statue of Constantine now on view in the Conservatori palace courtyard. Whatever the rhetoric that accompanied such papal gifts, and whether or not they were actually welcomed by their designated recipients, their accumulation on the Capitol was unequivocal evidence of the site's gradual appropriation by the Holy See and of the *popolo*'s increasing irrelevance in the public place that had once been their own—the beating heart of communal Rome.

The gift-giving continued. Among Pope Leo X's donations to the *popolo* in the early sixteenth century were two colossal statues of river gods, and three large marble reliefs with scenes from the reign of the emperor Marcus Aurelius: Marcus Aurelius performing a sacrifice in front of a temple; Marcus Aurelius upright in a quadriga, celebrating a triumph; Marcus Aurelius on horseback subjugating Germanic peoples with a commanding gesture of his raised right hand. Author of a text of Stoic philosophy known as the *Meditations*, Marcus Aurelius was also a conqueror—the bearer, in the best Roman tradition, of *pax romana*, with all the ambiguities that entailed.[45]

And so back to the *caballus Constantini* and its rider, now no longer "Constantine," but correctly identified as the emperor Marcus Aurelius. The bronze horseman's raised right hand virtually duplicates the authoritative gesture of the other Marcus Aurelius, the one subduing vanquished Germans in the marble relief just mentioned. Of all the antiquities various popes brought to the Capitol, the equestrian statue was in every way the most significant, sealing as it did the fate of the Campidoglio.

It was at the behest of Pope Paul III Farnese that Marcus Aurelius and his horse were transported in separate pieces from the Lateran to the Capitol on 12 January 1538. The transfer was made over the objections of the canons of the Church of St. John in the Lateran as well as those of Michelangelo, who had been made a citizen of Rome just over a month earlier and who said that the horse should stay where it was.[46] Michelangelo was charged with the design of a new marble base for the statue, which bears the Farnese arms on the front and an inscription giving details of the statue's transfer on one side.

"Today on the *piazza del Campidoglio* you can see the bronze equestrian statue of Marcus Aurelius the Philosopher, in the dress and gesture of *pacificatore* [*in habito e gesto di pacificatore*]."[47] So wrote the antiquarian Lucio Fauno in a work of 1548 on the antiquities of Rome, where he adds that it is the most beautiful ancient work in the whole city. For centuries, from the early Middle Ages on, the statue had stood for the temporal power of the pope. But now

Marcus Aurelius receiving the submission of German captives, marble relief from a triumphal arch dedicated to Marcus Aurelius, 176–180 CE, Capitoline Museums, Rome. Peter Horree / Alamy Stock Photo.

Gilded bronze equestrian statue of the Roman emperor Marcus Aurelius, 176 CE, Capitoline Museums, Rome. Photo c. 1870, taken on the Campidoglio. © Alinari Archives /Art Resource, NY.

that the horseman was no longer "Constantine" and the spurious Donation unmasked as a fake, the symbolism was in need of an update. Far more relevant in these humanist times was the alias of philosopher prince and *pacificatore*, bearer of *pax romana*. It was an identity with obvious appeal to Pope Paul III, himself the product of a humanist education and the first native-born Roman pope to be elected in over a century.[48] Indeed, the pope claimed the designation *pacificatore* for himself after he brokered the Truce of Nice between the French king Francis I and the emperor Charles V in 1538, with subsequent representations of him reproducing the bronze horseman's "pacifying" gesture. Moreover Paul III, elected after the sack of Rome in 1527, was also the first post-Reformation pope, leaving him with much (including Germans) to "pacify." From the time of his reign, the city was entirely subject to the papal court, living in a state of constant economic dependence on it. It was a condition of which a symmetrical Campidoglio would over time become the architectural proof, with the bronze horseman at its center the ultimate affirmation of papal supremacy.

But when the statue arrived at the Capitol and was placed in front of the Senatorial Palace, some distance from its façade, its position could not yet be called the center of the piazza. In 1538 the buildings around it were far too randomly asymmetrical for the place to have, properly speaking, any center at all. What occurred with the installation of the statue on the Capitol was the *creation* of a center—a reference point that, with adjustments, would determine development of the site for the next 100 years, rather as if the perfectly symmetrical body of "Vitruvian man" were to be generated from his navel.

A body is a bounded entity. A center can only be the center of a delimited area. In 1538, the Capitoline piazza had no clear limit, extending as it did northward to the higher ground of the Aracoeli church to which it was linked by a broad staircase, and spilling westward down the bumpy slope of the hill to the Piazza dell'Aracoeli below. Between 1540 and 1542 the umbilical cord joining the church to the communal area was severed when the ancient stair was demolished and a retaining wall raised next to the church, effectively excluding the venerable monument from the piazza. The new retaining wall was built at an angle of 80 degrees relative to the Palazzo Senatorio, mirroring the 80-degree angle of Nicholas V's Palazzo dei Conservatori on the other side. A niche in the middle of the new wall corresponded to the entrance bay at the center of the palace façade directly opposite. In the course of these operations, the obelisk that since the twelfth century had stood next to the Aracoeli as a symbol of the free senate was removed to the Caelian hill.[49] With the beginnings of a perimeter and transverse axis, the Campidoglio was acquiring serious symmetrical potential.

In 1546 Michelangelo, who at 71 had just been named architect at St. Peter's, also began work at the Capitol, charged by Pope Paul to deal with the next challenge: the Palazzo Senatorio, more lopsided than ever since the addition in the 1520s of a loggia on its right-hand side. Work began with the elimination of the loggia and enlargement of the right-hand tower so that it matched the tower on the left. This was followed by the architect's most important and lasting intervention at the palace: a double-flight monumental staircase—the *scalone*—on the front that extended almost its entire width and led directly to the audience chamber on the piano nobile. The *scalone* culminated in an entrance portal at the exact center of the now symmetrical façade, on axis with the statue of Marcus Aurelius.

The marble fragment of the lion attacking a horse, still in place on the old palace stair in 1535 according to a van Heemskerck drawing of that date, had of course to be moved to make way for the new construction. An engraving in a book on Roman antiquities of 1565 shows it located at the side of the piazza, on the ground near the niche in the middle of the Aracoeli retaining wall.[50] In 1594, a Milanese sculptor, one Ruggiero Bescapè, a student of Michelangelo, "restored" the sculptural group, adding the head, neck, legs, and tail of the horse and the hind legs and tail of the lion.[51] At this time, it was moved inside the Palazzo dei Conservatori. Afterward, and until 2012, it was part of a rather sad, nonfunctioning fountain in the garden behind the museum.

In 1554, the municipal council decided to transform the piazza into a terrace, bounded by a balustrade overlooking the city and opening onto a grand *cordonata* that would descend to the Piazza dell'Aracoeli below, creating a stage, as it were, elevated above

Maarten van Heemskerck, the Capitoline Hill seen from the portico of the Palazzo dei Conservatori, pen and brown ink, from the Roman sketchbook I. The marble fragment of a lion attacking a horse appears at the top of stairs (pre-Michelangelo) to the Palazzo Senatorio, c. 1535. Kupferstichkabinett, Staatliche Museen, Berlin, Inv. 79 D 2, fol. 61 recto. bpk Bildagentur / Kupferstichkabinett, Staatliche Museen, Berlin / Jörg P. Anders / Art Resource, NY.

The Campidoglio c. 1560, wood engraving from Bernardo Gamucci, *Libri quattro dell'antichita della citta di Roma* (Venice, 1565), 18, showing Michelangelo's *scalone* and, on the lower left, the marble fragment of a lion attacking a horse, identified as "E." Canadian Centre for Architecture, Montreal.

the pit of a theater. To achieve this, a second retaining wall was built along the front of the Campidoglio, establishing the precise western limit that completed its perimeter. Michelangelo contributed to the project, but the *cordonata*, designed by Giacomo della Porta, was not completed until 1581–1582. With its completion, the longitudinal axis that bisected the Palazzo Senatorio and passed through the Marcus Aurelius statue (now raised on an enlarged base and framed by a recessed oval in the piazza's brick pavement) extended down the center of the *cordonata*, terminating only when it reached its base in the square below.

In the 1530s Tommaso de' Cavalieri, a strikingly beautiful young Roman nobleman, had been Michelangelo's muse and the love of his life. The episode was followed by a close friendship that endured until the artist's death. Named deputy to the *fabbriche* (offices in charge of construction) at the Campidoglio in 1554, and later appointed commissioner of antiquities by Pope Pius IV, Cavalieri was key in determining the eventual shape of the piazza whose overall design is generally attributed to Michelangelo alone.[52] In fact, no original drawing of Michelangelo's for the Campidoglio survives, nor does any other record of his ever formulating such a design during his lifetime. He seems not, in other words, to have projected the Campidoglio in its familiar final shape, in spite of countless claims that he "must have done."

What do survive are three engravings, all published after his death: an anonymous plan of 1567, attributed to Michelangelo; an elevation of three bays of the Palazzo dei Conservatori published in 1567–1568; and a bird's-eye perspective view of the piazza by Étienne Dupérac, published in two versions, one in 1568 and another the following year. The deceptive finality of these renderings belies the fact that when he died in February of 1564, Michelangelo's finished work at the Capitol consisted of the base of the Marcus Aurelius statue, the partially completed *scalone* of the Palazzo Senatorio whose façade he rendered symmetrical but seems to have wished to remain medieval in character, and a single bay of the projected seven bays of a new front for the Palazzo dei Conservatori on the right-hand side of the piazza. The bay was Michelangelo's last work.

Its grandeur, and the powerful harmony of its constituent parts—giant Corinthian pilasters extending over two stories; between them, a smaller order of freestanding Ionic columns framing the deep void of the ground-floor portico; first-floor windows framed by still smaller columns carrying broken pediments; the play of these gray tectonic elements (all of porous native Roman travertine) against the smooth rose-colored brick of the wall surface—were a crucial model for everything that happened next.

But it was not Michelangelo who directed the course of subsequent developments. It was Tommaso de' Cavalieri, the artist's respectful moral heir.[53] As commissioner of antiquities appointed by Pope Pius IV—a position created by Pope Paul III—Cavalieri was de facto artistic consultant to the pope. It was he who appointed Giacomo della Porta as Michelangelo's successor at the Capitol.

In 1566, rather than just stop at the foot of the Capitol as had, until then, been the custom, the *possesso* of Pius V climbed all the way to the top of the hill where, on the ground of the piazza itself, the new pope received the homage of the *popolo* and Capitoline magistrates, inaugurating thereby the precedent for all subsequent processions.[54] Papal "possession" of the Campidoglio was complete. It required only its final, symmetrical confirmation.

There is good reason to believe that the finished Campidoglio presented in the engravings published during the two years that followed Pius V's *possesso* is the work of Cavalieri and his collaborators.[55] The upper left of Dupérac's bird's-eye view of 1568 bears the arms of Pius V, over an inscription that reads "Dedicated to the generosity of his Holiness Pius V, Supreme Pontiff." On the upper right, a cartouche frames a Latin text crediting "the eminent architect Michelangelo Buonarroti" with creating the *exemplar* or "model" for "restoring the Capitol to its ancient splendor, as can be seen in the image." A shield with a banner bearing the acronym SPQR appears to the right of the cartouche. On the balustrade, statues of Julius Caesar and his heir Augustus frame the entrance to the piazza.[56]

It is questionable whether Michelangelo, who seems to have liked the medieval allure of the old Senatorial Palace façade and

Étienne Dupérac, bird's-eye view of the Campidoglio, with design credited to Michelangelo, engraving, 1568. Rijksmuseum, Amsterdam, RP-P-1999-85.

who, thirty years earlier, had objected strenuously to the transfer of Marcus Aurelius from the Lateran, was all that interested in "restoring the Capitol to its ancient splendor." But his friend Tommaso de' Cavalieri, papal commissioner of antiquities, most certainly was. Recesses in the vestibule walls of the Conservatori palace, just inside its entrance portal, display twin inscriptions, dated 1568, which name two deputies, Tommaso de' Cavalieri and his colleague Prospero Boccapaduli, as having restored the Capitol, victim of the ravages of time, to its ancient grandeur.[57] The inscriptions, which make no mention of Michelangelo, record a "restoration" whose completion still lay a century ahead. All that was finished in 1568 was the engraving that projected it.

In the 1569 version of the engraving, some details have changed, including the replacement of Caesar and Augustus by statues of the mythical twin horse-tamers, Castor and Pollux, who occupy the position to this day. But the architecture remains the same: the Palazzo Senatorio, with a façade copy-pasted from that of the Palazzo dei Conservatori on the right whose front, in turn, is duplicated wholesale on the left by what would become the Palazzo Nuovo. Eventually built to a depth of only 11 meters so that the distance from its entrance to Marcus Aurelius at the center would exactly match the distance to the statue from the entrance of the Conservatori palace opposite, the Palazzo Nuovo had no real name (besides being designated as "new") and no real purpose either, other than to mirror its model.[58] It took another hundred years for it all to be built, and there were changes along the way, but during the whole of that time the engravings continued to function as a kind of master plan. The starburst pavement these images show radiating from the bronze horseman in insistent emphasis of its central position was not executed until 1940 under the fascist government of Benito Mussolini, who seems to have grasped better than anyone their peremptory imperial discourse.

For Vitruvius, the "certain calculations of symmetries" made architecture the ultimate proof of civilization and, with it, of Roman conquest. From 1450 on, the Campidoglio was a construction site for the imperial ambitions of the Roman papacy for whose supremacy its perfect symmetry would likewise stand as incontestable evidence. Once complete, its beauty—the "reasoned harmony" of its coherence—was such that (to recall Alberti) nothing could be "added, taken away or altered but for the worse."[59] The communal government the papacy supplanted had been experimental, disorderly, at times chaotic, and eminently flexible.[60] From the early fifteenth century the popes, as lords of the city, sought to bring this "wayward multitude"—the Roman *popolo*—under its control. The perfect symmetry of the Campidoglio was lasting proof of their success.

Papal rule of Rome ended on 20 September 1870 when the Italian army breached the Aurelian wall surrounding the city at the Porta Pia. The following year, the city was named capital of the newly unified nation ruled by the Piedmontese king, Victor Emmanuel II. When Victor Emmanuel died on 9 January 1878, it was unanimously agreed that there should be a monument honoring both him and the *patria* unification had brought into being.

Competitions were held, and various sites considered, including the Piazza Termini at the railway station, and the Pantheon where the king was buried.[61] The site eventually settled on was the Capitol—a choice meant, above all, as an unequivocal assertion that Rome belonged to the nation now, and not to the pope.[62] There was, of course, no question of violating the perfect symmetry of the Campidoglio itself. But it could be upstaged, as indeed it was. The blazing white marble Vittoriano was built between 1885 and 1921 against the north flank of the Capitol, which the monument's staggering bulk obliterates from view entirely. Oversized and overstated, with a 12-meter-high bronze horseman (Victor Emmanuel) at its center, its hyperbolized, neoclassical symmetries are those of the Campidoglio it was meant to supplant, blown out of all reasonable proportion by the magnitude of the challenge this presented.

3   World Heritage, Urbino

Aerial view of the Vittoriano and the Campidoglio, Rome, 1929. Photo supplied by Istituto Luce Cinecittà Historical Archive (A00015575), Rome:

The Victor Emmanuel monument at Rome, evoked at the end of the previous chapter, has been vilified more or less continually since it was completed in 1921: for its whiter-than-white whiteness, its inordinate size, its overweening pomposity—in sum, for its monumental bad taste. Critics, including myself, decry as worst of all its violation of the urban fabric and the annihilation, by occluding them from view, of such essential markers of the great city's identity as the imperial fora, the Capitol itself, and the Aracoeli church in order to celebrate the unassailable fact of its own overwhelming presence. It is a shamefully easy target.

    The ducal palace at Urbino in the Marches of northeastern Italy was built by its ruling warlord, Federico da Montefeltro, between 1462 and 1482. It dominates its hilltop site with mass measurably larger than that of the Vittoriano and at the time of its construction was just as destructive of the city it came to occupy.

But it is beautiful and, given the general enthusiasm for its perfections, an easy target it is not.

When you visit Urbino and make the steep ascent along the path below the west façade of the palace, famous for the two slender towers or *torricini* that soar skyward to frame a series of superimposed loggias to herald in a distant view the triumphal, if fictive, entrance to the city, you will notice a large black metal plaque fixed to the retaining wall on your right, centered directly below the turrets that rise above.[1] On this plaque, a citation in Italian, French, and English identifies Urbino as a UNESCO World Heritage Site, on whose list you are told the city's historic center was inscribed in 1998. The reasons given are a brief summary of the conventional view.

> Urbino represents a pinnacle of Renaissance art and architecture, harmoniously adapted to its physical site and to its medieval precursor in an exceptional manner. During its short cultural pre-eminence, Urbino attracted some of the most outstanding humanist scholars and artists of the Renaissance who created there an exceptional urban complex of remarkable homogeneity, the influence of which carried far into the rest of Europe.

Implicit in the praise of how "harmoniously adapted" the Renaissance art and architecture of Urbino are to its site is admiration for the shared identity of palace and city (interwoven to the degree that to name one is to name the other), first recorded even before the palace was completed. A Latin verse encomium of the Montefeltro lord, written in 1471 by a humanist, one Mabilio da Novate, includes the lines "Whoever sees your dwelling, Federico / declares in amazement: this is no house but a city"—*non domus ista sed urbs*.[2] Much better known is Baldassare Castiglione's virtually identical observation made some fifty years later in his *Book of the Courtier* where he famously declared the ducal residence at Urbino to be *una città in forma di palazzo*—a city in the form of a palace.[3]

The house that is really a city, the city that is shaped like a palace. Leon Battista Alberti, whose participation in the design

Aerial view of the ducal palace at Urbino, fifteenth-sixteenth centuries. Photo: Folco Quilici, 1968. © Fratelli Alinari, with permission. © Alinari Archives / Folco Quilici / Art Resource, NY.

of the Urbino palace now appears to have been much more extensive than previously thought, promoted precisely this reciprocal relation when discussing *partitio* ("compartition" or planning) in book 1 of his *On the Art of Building in Ten Books*, a work he began in 1443 and may still have been working on at the time of his death in 1472.[4] "The city is like some large house," he wrote, "and the house in turn like some small city."[5] The directive was something of a watchword when I was in architecture school in the early 1980s, transcribed into a hardbound notebook along with similar guiding maxims and sketches that might eventually prove useful. No one ever questioned that a city should be like a house, a house like a city, nor asked why Alberti might make such a claim. I am raising the question now. This chapter is an attempt to answer it.

For all that Alberti often exhibits a rather lofty impatience with Vitruvius and his treatise which, as he wrote in a well-known passage, was incoherent, poorly written, and full of "many omissions and many shortcomings," *De architectura* is nevertheless the very *fons et origo* of Alberti's own treatise on the subject.[6] From its chosen subject and overall form—who, other than Vitruvius, had ever written a treatise on architecture? in ten books?—to countless details of its content, *On the Art of Building* is unimaginable without its ancient Roman precedent, to which, moreover, Alberti refers at least 150 times.[7] A request from Pope Pius II for the loan of his (Alberti's) copy of *De architectura* when both he and the pope were in Mantua in 1459 is evidence that the work must have accompanied him on the long voyage there from Rome, and no doubt on his many other trips as well, further pointing to its importance as a *vademecum*.[8]

Vitruvius wrote *De architectura* for Augustus Caesar around 25 BCE, at the beginning of an unprecedented worldwide building boom that coincided with the inception of the period of one-man rule known as the Empire whose ultimate vindication Vitruvius meant architecture to be.[9] His opening address to the new ruler of the Roman world could not be more explicit.

> When I realized that you had care not only for the common life of all men ... but also for the fitness of public buildings—so that even as through you [Rome]

was increased with provinces, so public buildings were to provide eminent guarantees for the majesty of empire— I decided not to hesitate and took the first opportunity to set out for you my writings on these matters. ... It is because I noticed how much you have built and are now building, both public and private buildings in keeping with the greatness of your achievements so that these might be transmitted to the memory of posterity ... that in these scrolls, I have set forth complete and detailed rules ... [and] laid out all the principles of the discipline.[10]

During the thirteenth and fourteenth centuries, heads of powerful families (Visconti, Gonzaga, Este, della Scala, Carrara, and others) who sought control of Italian cities ruled by progressively weaker communal governments were all confronted by the same hurdle—their lack of legitimacy.[11] Communal governments were legally constituted, with constitutional recognition granted them under the terms of the Peace of Constance of 1183.[12] *Signori* seeking control of the cities so governed were warranted by little other than their ambition. The power they sought demanded ratification. Becoming a *comes* ("companion" or "count") by being named imperial vicar if you were a Ghibelline, or named papal vicar if you were a Guelf, was a help. Nonetheless, at some point negotiating agreement with the commune itself became unavoidable. Azzo Visconti became the founder of the Visconti dynasty that ruled Milan only after the Milanese commune conceded his election as "perpetual and general *dominus rector et gubernator* [lord and governor] of the city" in 1330.[13] Even after being named imperial vicar in 1312, the legendary strongman Cangrande I ("Big Dog") della Scala of Verona was obliged, as self-appointed *podestà* or chief magistrate, to operate within the commune's institutional structures and to consider (or at least appear to consider) its citizens' needs and interests.[14] Such shows of respect may have been a façade, but even if they were, that the pretense of deference was considered necessary is itself significant. It was a precarious situation where no *signore* could claim full control of a state whose municipalities still considered themselves self-governing, and whose autonomy demanded recognition by a superior sovereign power—the emperor or the pope.[15]

Until the early fifteenth century, signiorial residences, sometimes including several interconnected buildings, were referred to as *domus*. Though larger than the average burgher's and often fortified, these "houses" were integrated into the fabric of the city, whose communal institutions, on the other hand, remained visibly prominent in buildings called *palazzi* (palaces)—the *palazzo del comune, del podestà, dei priori*—which, along with the cathedral, framed the shared public space of the *platea communis* at the city's heart.[16]

The early decades of the Quattrocento brought consolidation of signiorial power, beginning with the pope's. Following the election of Martin V in 1417, the papacy returned definitively to Rome after a century of exile at Avignon, to find, according to the prevailing view, "a city desperate for rehabilitation."[17] Rehabilitation began in earnest thirty years later with the election of Nicholas V, the humanist pope whose work at the Campidoglio I discussed in chapter 2. Complementing his interventions in this, communal Rome's own *platea communis*, was his relocation of the papal residence from the Lateran to the Vatican, and construction there, next to old St. Peter's basilica, of a vast, fortified *palatium papae* for himself and his hugely expanded court, which included his former university classmate Leon Battista Alberti, who had been a member of the papal entourage since the reign of his predecessor, Eugenius IV.[18]

As *signori* in northern Italy became more firmly established in their states, with some, as Giangaleazzo Visconti of Milan was in 1395, unassailably legitimized by investiture with the sovereign title of duke, their expanding courts, not to mention their heightened self-regard, demanded appropriate accommodation. In the fifty years between 1400 and 1452, the year Borso d'Este became duke of Modena, the Este court at Ferrara increased tenfold, from about fifty domestic retainers and administrative staff to some five hundred.[19] Similar conditions came to prevail at Mantua and Urbino, among other cities, whose lords during the second half of the fifteenth century would preside over what can only be called a construction boom, building lavish new residences—now called *palazzi*—and further enhancing their power and prestige with new churches, monuments, fountains, and, as at Milan and Mantua, hospitals.

Alberti, adviser to the pope and also, at different times, to the rulers at various of these courts (Ferrara, Mantua, Urbino), saw this coming and became its advocate. He had been a reader of *De architectura* since at least the mid 1430s and, finely tuned as he was to his time, could not but have recognized in Vitruvius's opening address to Augustus Caesar ("because I noticed how much you have built and are now building …") a mission statement of such striking resonance with contemporary circumstances that he made it his own.[20] Thus, taking *De architectura* as his model and, as he tells it, at the request of Leonello d'Este, marquis of Ferrara, he went on to write his *On the Art of Building*.[21] "And what is this we now see," Alberti asks, "the whole of Italy competing for renewal? How many cities," he continues in a paraphrase of Augustus's famous boast concerning Rome, "which as children we saw all built of wood, have now been turned to marble?"[22]

Unlike *De architectura*, however, Alberti's treatise has no dedication. He may have meant to dedicate it to Leonello d'Este who died in 1450, or to Pope Nicholas V to whom he showed a draft in 1452, or perhaps to Federico da Montefeltro, as indeed two contemporary sources suggest.[23] But no dedication survives, not even in the manuscript copy Federico commissioned for his famous library at Urbino.[24] In any case, it is at once quite clear and entirely fitting that the person to whom Alberti addresses his work (the "you" he enjoins in so many of his directives) be not just one Caesar, as it had been for Vitruvius, but any or all of the would-be Caesars of the Italian Quattrocento.

Like *De architectura* which inspired it, *On the Art of Building* is a profoundly political work.[25] This is what Alberti writes in his prologue.

> When you erect a wall or portico of great elegance and adorn it with a door, columns, or roof, good citizens approve and express joy for their own sake, as well as for yours, because they realize that you have used your wealth to increase greatly not only your own honor and

> glory, but that of your family, your descendants, and the whole city.[26]

Alberti's reformulation of Vitruvius's praise of Augustan building activity (care for the common life of all men, glorification of the builder) is also as unequivocal an affirmation as you are likely to find of the princely virtue of magnificence. The notion of lavish spending as evidence of virtue, which first surfaced as a component of signiorial ideology in Petrarch's day, had hardened into dogma by the mid fifteenth century, with Alberti, one of its most articulate defenders, making the case for architecture as the magnificent prince's best, unbeatable means of self-aggrandizement.[27] To build is to project greatness, even if you are not really a great man. Thus, Alberti continues,

> Thucydides did well to praise the ancients who had the vision to adorn their cities with such a rich variety of buildings as to give the impression of having far greater power than they really had. Has there been one among the greatest and wisest of princes who did not consider building one of the principal means of preserving his name for posterity?[28]

The buildings that would stand as evidence of princely power were to include more than just the signiorial residences Alberti writes about in the fifth and ninth books of his treatise, under the headings respectively of "Works of Individuals" and "Ornament to Private Buildings." Indeed, his scope is nothing less than the overhaul of entire cities.[29] It was in remaking a city that the "art of building" would equip its lord not only with unrivaled means to magnificence but, even more crucially, with incontestable proof of his legitimacy—beginning, once again, with the pope.

Nicholas V was crowned in 1447. His predecessor Eugenius IV had spent nine years in exile in Florence, from 1434 to 1443, after fleeing Rome in disguise when an uprising of citizens besieged his house, demanding civic autonomy.[30] Just over five years into Nicholas's reign, in early January of 1453, republican insurgents led by the humanist nobleman Stefano Porcari went so far as to plot the pope's assassination.³¹ The conspiracy was foiled and Porcari hanged along with his fellow conspirators. There were, in other words, ongoing challenges to the legitimacy of the pope's claims to temporal authority and many who sought a civic alternative, as indeed Alberti recalls in a long letter he wrote about the Porcari conspiracy to an unknown recipient shortly after the events in question.³² Such challenges were, by Nicholas's own account, precisely the reason for conceiving the vast, deliberately intimidating building program that included construction of his own palace already mentioned, work at the Campidoglio, new fortification walls, a new St. Peter's, and major restructuring of the entire west bank of the Tiber to create the new curial city—never completed—that Giannozzo Manetti describes at length in the second book of his biography of the pope.³³ Book 3 of the biography records Nicholas's deathbed testament, where he answers criticism of his aedilatory excesses with claims that "everlasting monuments" are essential for keeping the *popolo* properly respectful, and fortress walls for keeping it at bay.

> Not ambition, not pomp, not vainglory, not a longer perpetuation of our name, but the greater authority of the Roman church, the more complete dignity of the Apostolic See among Christian peoples, and the more sure avoidance of the familiar persecutions—these are the reasons we conceived so many great buildings in our mind and heart.³⁴

Though most of Nicholas V's projects remained unrealized, it was from his time onward that Rome was represented as a papal city, as a well-known woodcut view published in the Nuremberg Chronicle of 1493 attests. ROMA printed in capitals against the sky on the top left identifies the image, the upper two-thirds of which is occupied by the pope's domain on the west bank of the Tiber which divides the plate diagonally into two unequal triangles. Against the sky on the right, the legend *palatium papae* appears as the typographical counterpart of ROMA opposite and identifies the papal palace, which dominates the panorama. Next to it, rising with greatly exaggerated prominence in the upper right-hand

Panorama of Rome, woodcut by Michael Wolgemut or Wilhelm Pleydenwurff for the chronicle of Hartmann Schedel, Nuremberg, 1493. Interfoto / Alamy Stock Photo.

corner, is the Belvedere, the small papal villa Pope Innocent VIII added to the Vatican complex in 1487 not long before the plate was made. All of what might be called nonpapal Rome on the opposite, east bank of the Tiber is crowded into the small triangle at the lower left bounded above by the river and below by the long stretch of the Aurelian wall in the foreground at the bottom of the plate. A scant quarter of the pictorial space is devoted to this part of the city, dominated by imperial monuments (the Pantheon, the Colosseum, the Monte Cavallo and Trajan's Column) which encircle and lend undue distinction to an overscaled rendering of the half-built church of Santo Stefano Rotondo whose rebuilding had been part of Nicholas V's intended urban renewal. The contentious Capitol, erstwhile heart of communal Rome, is nowhere to be found in this image, where the identities of the pope, his palace, and the city have become notionally interchangeable.

The extent of Alberti's role in planning Nicholas V's projected overhaul of the city has been contested, with some scholars arguing that he disapproved of its excesses, going so far as to mock them in his dark comedy *Momus* of 1450.[35] But that he advised the pope on architectural matters and that he showed Nicholas a draft of *On the Art of Building* in 1452 are matters of record.[36]

Alberti's enthusiasm for Nicholas V's architectural ambition may have been mitigated, but not so that of Aeneas Silvius Piccolomini, the pope's friend and unequivocal advocate, who took the name Pius II when he was elected pope in 1458 after the three-year papacy of Calixtus III which followed Nicholas's death in 1455. "Nicholas adorned Rome with many buildings on a grand scale. If his projects could have been completed, they would have rivaled in magnificence any erected by the ancient emperors," Pius wrote in his *De Europa* of the same year, adding with regret, "But the buildings and their mighty looming walls still lie unfinished."[37]

Yet Pius showed no interest in completing Nicholas V's grand scheme, limiting his own projects at Rome to relatively minor interventions at the Vatican.[38] Although his publication in 1462 of a bull aimed at preserving Rome's ancient ruins was significant for the city's surviving architectural identity, it was not a building project as such.[39]

It is important to keep in mind the obvious fact that, as a papal city, Rome belonged to no single pope or family, but to an institution in which the pope was essentially a placeholder. Popes were elected; the papacy was not dynastic. A pope was not a hereditary ruler, for all that he might behave like one. Thus, if Alberti was right in claiming building as the best way "to increase greatly not only your own honor and glory, but that of your family, your descendants, and the whole city," the very nature of the papacy made any one pope's architectural activity at Rome ultimately self-defeating as a vehicle of personal magnificence.[40] It was an impasse that goes a long way to explaining Pius II's shift of architectural focus from the eternal city where he reigned as pope to the Tuscan village where he was born.

Corsignano, as the village was called, had been a small agricultural community in the territory of nearby Siena. An *estimo* or municipal census of 1320 that catalogued properties and their values records a total of 350 houses and huts with about 1,600 inhabitants, most of them very poor, whose number was later reduced to around 1,000 by the plague that also claimed several members of the future pope's own landowning family.[41] Aeneas Silvius Piccolomini lived there until he was eighteen, working with his father on the family farm.[42] In the fourteenth century, the village had a *piazza del comune* and a priors' palace but as part of Sienese territory was not autonomous, nor did it qualify as a *civitas*—a city.[43]

Pius's autobiographical *Commentaries*, written like Julius Caesar's in the third person, record his first return to Corsignano as an adult in February 1459, six months after his election. The visit was a stopover in a triumphal progress as the newly crowned pope and his court traveled north from Rome to Mantua, where in May he was to lead a congress he had convened to plan a crusade against the Ottoman Turks who had taken Constantinople six years earlier. Alberti, as papal abbreviator, may have been one of the party.

Reminded, the pope writes, of his own mortality by the death of his boyhood friends and the decrepitude of the few still living, he "decided to build a new church and palace in the town as a lasting memorial of his birth, and to this end he hired architects and workmen at no small expense."[44] The architect was Bernardo Rossellino, a Florentine who had worked for Nicholas V at Rome, and the entire project eventually consisted of four main buildings, not just two. Together these frame a small trapezoidal piazza and constitute the new city's monumental center: another UNESCO World Heritage Site, added to the list in 1996 two years before the nomination of Urbino.

In the effusive praise of its UNESCO citation, Pienza represents

> the first application of the Renaissance humanist concept of urbanism, giving it a defining role in the development of the "ideal city" project which played a significant part in subsequent urban developments in Italy and elsewhere. The application of these principles at Pienza, and in particular to the group of buildings surrounding the central piazza, has resulted in a masterpiece of human creative genius.[45]

While to label it the prototype in the "ideal city project" raises more questions than it answers, there is no questioning that the center of Pienza is beautiful, perfect to a degree that the Campidoglio, for all its laboriously calculated symmetry, fails to achieve. Perfect, indeed, to a degree that makes questioning its intentions seem churlish. No doubt that was the point. Contributing greatly to the perfection of the ensemble is the expert deployment of what Alberti called "refined variety," which makes it tempting to assume that his exquisite sensibility played a part in its overall development.[46] But here, as for Nicholas V's Roman projects, the extent of Alberti's involvement remains more than a little uncertain.[47] Moreover, Pius mentions Alberti only once in the whole of his *Commentaries*, and this in a completely different context, qualifying him not as an architect but as a learned man, expert in the study of antiquity.[48]

The Palazzo Piccolomini, first of the buildings to be completed, was raised on the foundations of the house where Pius was born, to which were added those of seven other houses he expropriated and demolished in order to assemble a building site to match the size of his ambition.[49] The resulting palace, built of warm golden travertine and square on plan, measures just under 40 meters to a side.[50] The stylar façade, with three superimposed tiers of pilasters, that wraps around three of these sides is often taken as evidence for Alberti's participation in the project. Columns, in Alberti's view, were de rigueur for the ornament of public buildings. For the façades of private buildings belonging to men of standing he recommends what he calls the "representation of stone colonnading"—fictive colonnades, which would make these residences analogues of public buildings and so "represent" the role of their owners in public life.[51] Such is the revetment of the Palazzo Piccolomini, but also that of Palazzo Rucellai in Florence, whose stylar façade of about 1455 most claim predates the former. If so, this would make the Palazzo Rucallai the first use of such a motif in the Renaissance, and its design is generally credited to Alberti, making the Rucellai façade the source for that of the Piccolomini palace, which Alberti may also have designed. But the evidence remains inconclusive, with an alternative scenario being that the Florentine palace came *after* the one in Pienza and that Bernardo Rossellino (not Alberti) was the author of both.[52]

There is no such controversy concerning the plan of the Palazzo Piccolomini, which most agree derives from that of Cosimo de' Medici's recently completed palace in Florence, designed by Michelozzo.[53] With its square interior courtyard bounded on all four sides by colonnaded porticos formally reminiscent of a convent cloister, its axial plan set the style for late fifteenth-century princely residences everywhere in Italy, and beyond.[54] After his visit to Corsignano and his decision to build there, Pius stopped at Florence where he saw Cosimo's new residence. "A palace fit for a king," he writes in his *Commentaries*, from which he says the immensely rich and powerful banker ruled as "master of the city." A tyrant, no less, "who, as illegitimate lord, kept the city and its people in cruel servitude."[55] Pius's unflattering opinion of Cosimo did not stop him from adopting the plan of Cosimo's palace as a template for his own. Indeed, the appeal of the banker's "regal" residence was entirely in keeping with the pope's own monarchic project and the kingly role he increasingly sought to play.[56] In the course of a lavish Corpus Christi celebration, observed with *magnificentissimus apparatus* at Viterbo in 1462, Pius writes with satisfaction in his lengthy description of the event, "two boys, singing as sweetly as angels" hailed the pope repeatedly as "King Pius, lord of the world."[57]

And it was not the convent cloister that gave the palace courtyard the pedigree that made it, in the late fifteenth century, the single most sought-after requirement in a new princely residence. Its prestige derived from the atrium which, Alberti was the first to grasp, was not the entrance space commonly called "atrium" in the Middle Ages.[58] The ancient (and therefore authentic) atrium was, as Alberti came to appreciate, the inner courtyard of a Roman house, described by Vitruvius in book 6 of *De architectura* as the *atrium* or, alternatively, the *cava aedium*, of a patrician's *domus*.[59] Alberti calls it the *sinum* or "bosom" of the house, and declares it to be the most important part of all, because it is "like a public forum, toward which all the lesser members converge."[60] In Cosimo de' Medici's palace, this analogous "forum" became in actual fact an alternative seat for the government of Florence—a court, greater than that of any king, the Florentine poet Alberto Avogadro eulogized in his panegyric of Cosimo, where all roads lead.[61]

The small trapezoidal piazza on the east side of the Piccolomini palace—a *forum*, as Pius calls it in the *Commentaries*—is actually smaller than the generously dimensioned "bosom" of his house.[62] In this interior courtyard, described as "a lofty peristyle [*peristylium altum*]," 16-foot columns are said to have appropriate bases and capitals and thicknesses proportionate to their height. It is flanked by summer dining rooms (*triclynia*) and chambers fit for kings (*cubicula digna regibus*).[63] Conspicuous in this, with its mindfully correct Vitruvian terminology, is an almost verbatim echo of what Vitruvius says is required in the house of a Roman aristocrat—a house whose magnificence, he says, should rival that of a public building because public business is often conducted in it.[64]

Pius's description of his new residence can, on many further points, be matched with prescriptions in *De architectura*, book 6, on private building, making the Piccolomini palace, as Georgia Clarke has argued, a paradigm of the filial relation between the Renaissance palace and the Roman house.[65] Not that the palace actually resembled what we now know a Roman house looked like. In the mid fifteenth century, with archaeology in its infancy and the excavation of Pompeii still 300 years ahead, the filiation was, perforce, largely text-based: that of Vitruvius, overwhelmingly, with Pliny, both elder and younger, and others contributing.[66] Most important in this context is Vitruvius's apparent endorsement of the aristocratic *domus* as a place for the conduct of public business—and thus, by extension, of the princely palace as a seat of government.

This, without a doubt, is what led Fra Giovanni Giocondo to choose the plan, elevation, and perspective of a Renaissance palace to illustrate Vitruvius's terms *ichnographia*, *orthographia*, and *scaenographia* (plan, elevation, perspective) in his, the first illustrated edition of *De architectura*, published in 1511 and dedicated to Pope Julius II.[67] Giocondo's plan is of a palace with a colonnaded courtyard, while his elevation and perspective give the palace exterior a stylar façade like that of the Piccolomini palace, the Rucellai palace, or the more recently completed Cancelleria at Rome.[68]

Now, plan, elevation, and perspective are, of course, generic terms referring to the images—"what the Greeks call *ideai*"— Vitruvius says serve to represent the *dispositio* (arrangement) of a building. This could be any building at all, needless to say, which the absence of illustrations in the original *De architectura* of c. 25 BCE left appropriately unspecified.[69] To choose, as Giocondo does, images of a specific building or building type to illustrate generic methods applicable to the design of all buildings is to reveal not only what the chooser considers a typical building to be, but also to whom he thinks the practice of architecture (typically) belongs. This in turn points to certain political assumptions. The most fundamental of these is the assumption of where power resides.

The Piccolomini palace was built between 1459 and 1462. The same short period of intensive construction saw the completion of the church of Santa Maria Assunta, a light-filled three-bay hall church built on the German model, immediately to the east of the palace, facing the "forum" onto which both palace and church open. The church is smaller, both in surface area and in height,

PRIMVS. 4

ad artis grammaticæ regulam fuerit explicatum, ignoscat. Namqǔ non vti summus pſius, nec rethor disertus, nec grāmaticus summis rōnibus artis exercitatus, sed ut architectus, his litteris ibutus, hæc nisus sum scribere. De artis uero potestate quæqǔ insunt in ea rōcinationes, polliceor (uti spero) his uoluminibus, non modo ædificātibus, sed etiam omnib⁹ sapientibus, cum maxima autoritate me sine dubio prestaturum.

Ex quibus rebus architectura constet. Caput. II.

Architectura autē cōstat ex ordinatione, quæ græce τάξις dicit, & ex dispositione, hāc autē græci διάθεσιν uocāt, & eurythmia, & symmetria, & decore, & distributiōe, quæ græce οικονομία dicit. Ordinatio est modica membrorum operis cōmoditas, separatim, uniuersæqǔ proportionis, ad symmetriā comparatio. Hæc componitur ex qātitate, quæ græce ποσότης dicitur, Quantitas autem est modulorum ex ipsius operis sumptiōe, singulisqǔ membroꝝ partib⁹ uniuersi opis cōueniēs effectus. Dispositio autē est reꝝ apta collocatio, elegāsqǔ in cōpositiōib⁹ effectus opis cū qſitate. Spēs dispositiōis;iq græce dicunt ιδέαι, hæ sunt, ichnographia, orthographia, scenographia. Ichnographia e circini regulǣqǔ modice cōtinēs usus, ex q̄ capiūt formæ i solis areæ descriptiōes.

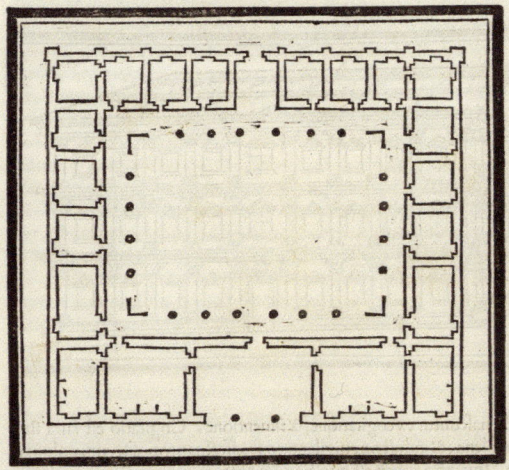

Orthographia autem est erecta frōtis imago : modiceqǔ picta rationibus operis futuri figura.

A iiii

Ichnographia, from Vitruvius, *M. Vitrvvivs per Iocvndvm solito castigatior factvs cvm figvris et tabvla vt iam legi et intelligi possit*, ed. Fra Giovanni Giocondo (Venice, 1511), fol. 4r. Canadian Centre for Architecture, Montreal.

LIBER

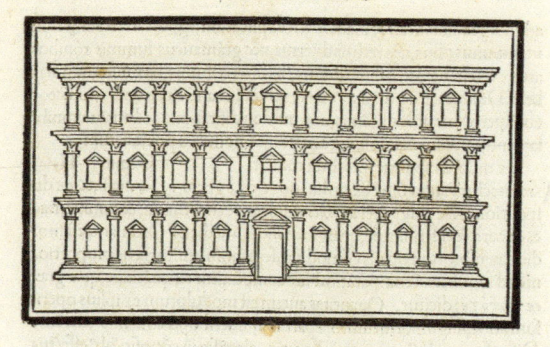

Item scenographia est frontis & laterum abscedentium adumbratio, ad circiniq; centrum omnium linearum responsus.

Hæ nascuntur ex cogitatione, & inuentione. Cogitatio est cura studii plena, & industriæ, uigilantiæque, effectus propositi cum uoluptate. Inuentio autem est quæstionum obscurarum explicatio, ratioque nouæ rei, vigore mobili reperta. Hæ sunt terminationes dispositio

Orthographia and *scaenographia*, from Vitruvius, *M. Vitrvvivs per Iocvndvm solito castigatior factvs cvm figvris et tabvla vt iam legi et intelligi possit*, ed. Fra Giovanni Giocondo (Venice, 1511), fol. 4v. Canadian Centre for Architecture, Montreal.

than the palace that dominates it. Pius calls the church a *templum* which he meant it to resemble, all shining white stone in contrast to the golden travertine palace next to it and crowned by a high triangular pediment where papal and Piccolomini arms, set off in an encircling stone wreath, are prominently displayed.[70] Churches are invariably "temples" for Alberti too.[71] Building *all'antica* depended on your choice of vocabulary as much as anything else.

The year the palace and the church were completed Pius made two interconnected, not strictly architectural moves with important consequences for his native village. In June 1462, he proposed to the papal consistory that Corsignano (as it still was) be elevated to the status of a city (*civitas*) and given the new name Pienza, to which, he reports, the cardinals unanimously agreed.[72] Two months later, on 13 August, he issued a bull declaring Pienza a bishopric, ratifying a proposal he had made to the consistory several months earlier in February of the same year. The decree was essential, because both the title of "city" and the name "Pienza" were directly dependent upon it.[73] To qualify as a city, in other words, a municipality had to be the seat of a bishop. At the end of the month, on 29 August, during a visit to the newly minted city to view his buildings, Pius consecrated its recently completed "temple" as a cathedral to which he subsequently appointed a bishop. The visit was the first of three he made to Pienza during the remaining two years of his life.[74]

Pius was often ill and knew he would not live much longer, which put him, as we have already seen, in legacy mode. "He could not help but admit that he was an old man whose demise was looming," he acknowledged, writing of his visit to Corsignano in 1459 and his decision to build there.[75] But the new church and palace he says he projected at the time "as a lasting memorial of his birth" were just part of the far more ample legacy he would seek to transmit—one that required a city. When he became aware of this requirement is not clear, but the realization probably came after that first visit since, at least according to his own testimony, his project at the time had consisted of just two buildings.

If building the church could be justified as a testament to the pope's piety, it is difficult to grasp the point of building a vast palace in a small farming village populated by peasants, whatever Pius may have claimed about wanting to honor his birthplace. In Italy at this historical juncture, princes built palaces in cities to consolidate their control of them, overturning or assimilating or subordinating existing communal institutions, which in one way or another continued to be part of the equation, because such institutions, along with the cathedral, were ultimately what made a city a city. The foundation of Pienza and the building activity that followed reproduced that urban dynamic and affirmed its new signiorial norms. But not as a part or in conclusion of any historical process; rather, with no preexisting city, Pius created one as it were out of thin air, in a kind of time-lapse abridgment of far more complex and much lengthier processes under way elsewhere.[76] An ideal city, you could say.

The ancient Roman world had been studded with such foundations, many bearing the names of their imperial founders, Caesar and Augustus most notably. Vitruvius devotes more than half of his first book to the foundation of cities and their layout, a topic which also preoccupied Alberti.[77] In founding Pienza as a legitimately constituted *civitas* named for its founder, Pius followed in the footsteps of Caesar and Augustus. Its foundation was indispensable for the consolidation of his legacy.

The next two years saw completion of the monumental center around the "forum" Pius says he wished "to be surrounded by four noble buildings," as well as the construction of several palaces built along the main thoroughfare by various nobles and prelates the pope bullied into establishing residences in his new city.[78] East of the square, across from the Piccolomini palace, the bishop's palace, travertine like the pope's, replaced "an old house" where the priors had lived. With three stories of diminishing height separated by stringcourses and plain rectangular windows framed in white stone, its astylar sobriety is an elegantly proportioned foil for the highly articulated façade of the papal residence opposite.

On the north side of his "forum" across from his "temple," the pope's purchase and demolition of several citizens' houses cleared the site for the fourth of his "noble buildings." It was intended, he writes, "to be the residence of the magistrates of the city and

Pienza, view of the piazza and façade of the cathedral from the portico of the Palazzo Comunale (1459–1462). Photo George Taige, 1997. © Alinari Archives / George Taige / Art Resource, NY.

a meeting place for councils of citizens": a *palazzo comunale*, no less, and an essential acknowledgment that citizen participation in city government—or at least a semblance thereof—was being allowed for.[79] "He called his city Pienza, which had been the town Corsignano," wrote the court scholar and encomiast Giannantonio Campano in his biography of the pope, "with urban magistrates appointed to give it the proper appearance of a city [*speciem iuste civitatis*]."[80] Of the four buildings, the town hall, whose open ground-floor loggia conformed to the medieval convention for such structures, was the one that above all underwrote the new foundation's status as a city. At just two stories, it is by far the smallest in a palatial hierarchy that nonetheless depended on its scaled-down presence to both lay down the chain of command and endow it with legitimacy.

Subtended by an entablature, the arched, biforate windows of the council chamber on the upper floor of the *palazzo comunale* virtually duplicate those of the Palazzo Piccolomini, to which it is thus annexed. Looming through these windows to peer in, as it were, over the shoulders of the councillors and reinforce the town hall's annexation to the palace are the papal/Piccolomini arms in the pediment of the cathedral opposite, displayed in their circular wreath.

There are three parts to the heraldic motif. In the bottom half of the encompassing circle is the stemma of the Piccolomini family—a cross emblazoned with five crescent moons. In the top half is the tall papal headdress with its triple crown. Between them, linking upper and lower halves, the crossed keys of the Church complete the papal insignia, which also, in this ultimately ambiguous representation, crown the family's coat of arms. There is more at stake here than a celebration of the pope's origins. Rather the reverse. Reading from top to bottom—that is, from the papal tiara on down—what the heraldry celebrates here is at once the pope's foundation of a dynasty and papal endorsement of its power.

This brings me back to the question of legacy. The "ideal city" Pius brought into being in just five years was the perfectly harmonious proof of a rather less tangible institutional legacy whose beneficiary and principal legatee was the *famiglia* of Aeneas

Silvius Piccolomini. The papal bull proclaiming Pienza a bishopric, issued on 13 August 1462 to underwrite its status as a *civitas*, was followed two weeks later by another bull, issued at Pienza itself on 28 August. This last gave exclusive *ius patronatus* or the hereditary authority of patronage rights over all the institutions the pope had founded—the cathedral, cathedral chapter, *opera* (buildings), and bishopric, which meant the person of the bishop himself—to members of the Piccolomini family.[81] From then on, the diocese was considered family property, even if the details of Pius's arrangements took some time to be ratified.[82] Giuseppe Chironi's study of the Pienza diocesan archive includes a diagrammatic representation of these arrangements: a complex spider web of relations all of which ultimately refer to the authority of the family at the center, guaranteeing its control of the city's ecclesiastical institutions, and of the city itself.[83]

In 1463, Pius ordered the building of twelve small two-story row houses at the edge of the city, four by eight meters on plan, with workshops on the ground floor and living quarters above.[84] These *case nuove* are usually taken as evidence of the Pope's attempt to mitigate his erasure of Corsignano by providing accommodation for some of the villagers he dispossessed.[85] The new houses were rental properties, whose revenues were meant to provide an income to the cathedral chapter, over which the Piccolomini exercised direct patronage rights, further enriching the pope's *famiglia*.[86]

The papacy, as I said, was not hereditary. Pius II used his authority *as pope* to circumvent that impasse, creating, through a series of bulls, a city with a ruling dynasty whose founder was a pope, but whose continued existence was entirely independent of the Holy See. The result of this extraordinary legerdemain—a farming village transfigured, Cinderella-like, by papal fiat—was an "ideal" city that took its place beside the dynastic centers of the day and even, in certain cases, served as their example: Mantua, Ferrara, and Urbino among others.

On 27 May 1459, three months after his first visit to Corsignano earlier that year, Pius at last arrived at Mantua to lead the congress he had convened to plan war against the Turks. There had been many stops along the way, including Florence where, as already mentioned, he saw Cosimo de' Medici's new palace, Bologna whose republican leanings he took issue with, and Ferrara where Borso d'Este, then papal vicar, petitioned him for a dukedom of that city but was refused.[87] The decision to hold the congress in Mantua, made seven months earlier in October 1458, reached its ruling marquis, Ludovico II Gonzaga, in early November, and propelled him to a frenzy of activity in preparation for the pope's arrival, beginning with improvement of water access to the lake-bound city.[88]

Attendance at the congress was to include (besides the pope) sixteen cardinals, papal allies from all over Europe, and the rulers of the cities just mentioned: Borso d'Este of Ferrara, Francesco Sforza of Milan, and Federico da Montefeltro of Urbino. Proper accommodation of such guests presented no small challenge to a princely host sensitive to the competitive pressure of magnificence.

The congress, which lasted eight months but produced no crusade, is generally taken as the impetus for Ludovico's undertaking the *renovatio urbis* of Mantua meant to "renew" his city along ancient Roman lines.[89] And if it is difficult to pin down Alberti's involvement in Nicholas V's plans for Rome or in Pius II's creation of Pienza, there is no doubt whatsoever about his contribution to Ludovico's overhaul of Mantua where, as part of the papal cortège and armed with his copy of *De architectura*, he remained during the long months of the pope's war council, with ample time to cultivate the marquis's patronage and discuss with him the desirability of urban renewal *all'antica*.[90] Alberti's design of two major "temples"—the churches of San Sebastiano and Sant'Andrea—was key in Ludovico's *renovatio* of the city, whose reconfiguration the architect's advice shaped in other crucial ways as well.[91] The eventual outcome, intended no doubt from the outset, was *una città in forma di palazzo*: an entire city that became, in effect, the Gonzaga family palace.[92]

Unlike the transformation of Corsignano, Mantua's transformation did not occur overnight, because unlike Corsignano, a no-account village onto which the autocratic pope's dream of dynastic power was easily grafted with little fear of pushback, Mantua had been a properly constituted city for centuries. Celebrated for its

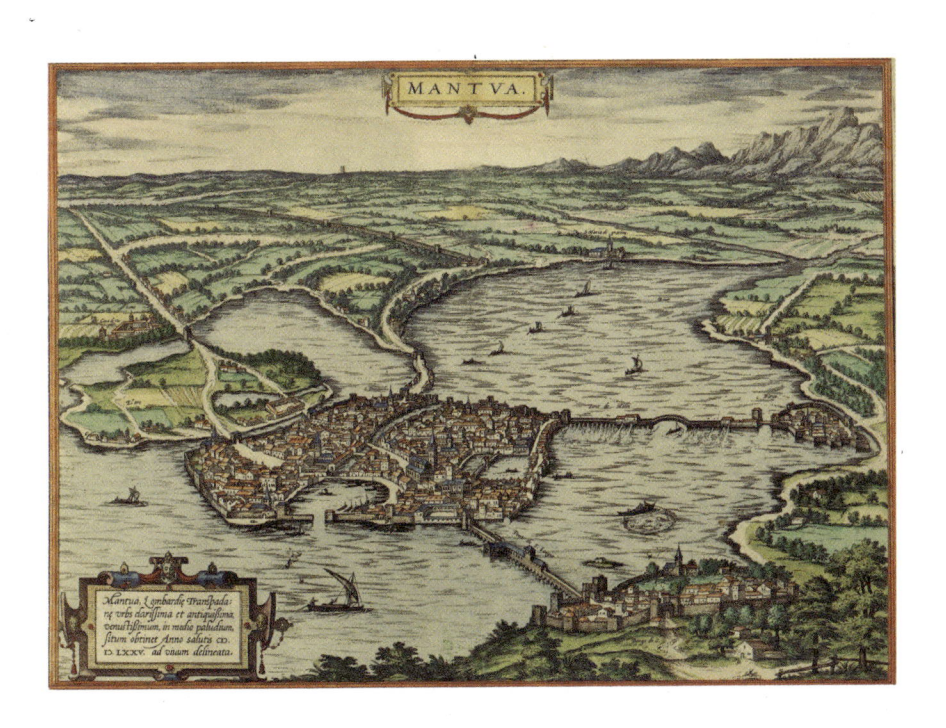

Bird's-eye view of Mantua, from Georg Braun and Franz Hogenberg, *Civitates orbis terrarium*, vol. II (1575). Private collection. Album / Art Resource, NY.

Etruscan origins by Virgil who had been born nearby and who was considered the city's presiding genius if not its patron saint, Mantua's civic status dated from the time it became a Roman colony in the late second century BCE.[93]

The life of the medieval city began with Charlemagne in 804 and the discovery of a relic that seems to have figured as something like the Carolingian foundation's cornerstone.[94] The relic in question, whose presence there contributed to Pius II's choice of Mantua as the venue for his congress, was the blood of Christ, collected at Calvary, according to legend, by the Roman soldier Longinus (later saint) who had pierced the saviour's side with his spear and scooped the blood-soaked earth at the foot of the cross into a box which he then brought to Mantua, where he buried it.[95] In 804, St. Andrew appeared to an unidentified believer, telling him where to find the relic, subsequently authenticated as the most Precious Blood of Christ by Pope Leo III who traveled from Rome to Mantua for the purpose at Charlemagne's request, and declared it genuine.

The Holy Blood was the agent of salvation at the very heart of Christian belief. Moreover, because Christ ascended bodily to heaven forty days after Easter, this blood was all that was left in the world of the saviour's earthly existence and therefore doubly precious. Possession of the relic would become an immeasurable enhancement of the city's Etrusco-Roman pedigree, adding to it a direct link to the founding event of the Christian story. For a would-be magnificent prince, ownership of sacred matter so incontestably numinous was a potential vehicle of prestige well beyond the reach of all competition, impervious to challenge. But the prince was not the relic's owner, and I am getting ahead of myself.

Tradition has it that the ninth-century discovery of the relic was followed by its disappearance and subsequent rediscovery two centuries later, in 1048.[96] This time, God himself revealed the relic's presence to a blind man, one Adelberto, whose sight was restored when he unearthed it in the Benedictine abbey of Sant'Andrea, founded ten years earlier in 1037. The rediscovery occurred when Mantua was ruled by Bonifacio di Canossa, margrave of Tuscany, assassinated in 1052, succeeded by his widow

Beatrice and afterward by their daughter Matilde, known as the *gran' contessa*. The Canossa venerated the relic, enshrined in the crypt of the abbey church, but they did not control the monastery nor claim ownership of its treasure. A bull issued by Pope Leo IX in 1053 approved the cult and fixed its celebration on the feast of the Ascension.[97]

The longest account of the relic's rediscovery is an anonymous source called *De inventione Sanguinis Domini* (On the discovery of the Blood of the Lord), thought to have been written about a century after the event in the mid twelfth century. Mantua was by then a free democratic commune, established after the *gran' contessa* died in 1115.[98] According to this somewhat imaginative reconstruction of events, Bonifacio di Canossa, Pope Leo IX, and Emperor Henry III were all present at the moment of the relic's rediscovery, with the pope's alleged attempt to abscond with the relic he feared would make Mantua a new Rome foiled by the brave resistance of the local citizenry.[99] The twelfth-century author of *De inventione* was a partisan of the new civic order, recalling the discovery of 1048 as a political drama in which the relic is cast as the commune's champion and the Benedictine monastery its shrine, the capitol as it were of the *civitas nova* that rose around it after the fall of the Canossa.[100]

The suburban *civitas nova* was "new" as opposed to the "old" *civitas vetus*, beyond whose walls, next to the monastery of Sant'Andrea and around a *platea communis*, the Piazza delle Erbe, buildings devoted to communal institutions were raised: the Palazzo del Podestà, the Palazzo della Ragione, the Torre Salaro for salt storage, and the Domus Mercati or home of the merchants' guild.[101] The *civitas vetus* northeast of the *civitas nova* was the small fortified nucleus on whose Roman foundations the early medieval city had been built. Here were the cathedral of San Pietro and its baptistery, the Canossa palace, and the tower houses of the old aristocratic families, which together made it the seat of feudal power supplanted by the commune in 1116.[102]

The emergence 160 years later of an ambitious strongman and his eventual dominance of the communal oligarchy conformed to a familiar pattern. Pinamonte Bonacolsi, founder of the Bonacolsi dynasty, took control of Mantua in 1274, with family members monopolizing various positions in the city's communal institutions, notably that of *podestà* and *capitano del popolo*.[103] Pinamonte's rise entailed his transfer back to the *civitas vetus* where the family acquired properties adjacent to the cathedral, tearing them down to build first a fortified tower house, then a crenelated palace, the Domus Magna, and later still a *palazzo del capitano* next to it, designed to resemble the institutional buildings of the *civitas nova* in an attempt to represent the *signoria* as the commune's legitimate heir.

The real estate ventures that barricaded Bonacolsi power behind the walls of the old city were balanced by, among other measures, the effort to win popular support through patronage of the cult of the Holy Blood, whose celebration on Ascension Day unified the people in a major expression of what had become virtually a civic religion. In 1311–1312, after attempts to play a role in the Ascension Day celebration proved unsuccessful, Rinaldo Bonacolsi, known as Passerino, sought an alternative path to popular favor by ordaining that every 1 July a mass was to be offered at the monastery on behalf of the commune.[104] Shortly afterward, in 1313, Passerino's son Giovanni became abbot of Sant'Andrea. But Bonacolsi dominance was short-lived.

On 16 August 1328, a violent uprising led by Luigi Gonzaga and backed by the troops of Cangrande della Scala of Verona stormed the city, overthrew the Bonacolsi, murdered Passerino, and inaugurated the rule of the Gonzaga dynasty, which would last nearly four hundred years.[105] Passerino's embalmed corpse was kept as a trophy of the victory, and in the early seventeenth century was part of a display in the cabinet of curiosities at the Gonzaga palace.[106] The Gonzaga, who had themselves been quietly acquiring significant real estate leverage in the old city during the Bonacolsi years, seized the defeated family's holdings and added them to their own to form the nucleus of what would eventually grow into the vast walled city within a city that was the Ducal Palace.[107] *Un palazzo in forma di città*.

In the first century of Gonzaga rule, the most significant addition to the palace complex was the Castello di San Giorgio, built as an unmistakable attestation of the family's dominance by Francesco I Gonzaga between 1395 and 1405 on the shore of the *lago di*

Domenico Morone, *Expulsion of the Bonacolsi by Luigi Gonzaga*, oil on canvas, 1494. Palazzo Ducale & Museo, Mantua / Bridgeman Images.

Andrea Mantegna, north wall, *camera picta*, 1467–1474, Palazzo Ducale, Mantua. Album / Alamy Stock Photo.

mezzo, or "middle" of the four lakes that surround Mantua, at its northern edge. A fortress (not a residence), it was designed by Bartolino da Novara, architect of the contemporaneous, very similar fortress at Ferrara (for Niccolò II d'Este), built of brick, square on plan around a square courtyard, with square towers at each of its four corners, impregnable and menacing. The looming presence of the new castello notwithstanding, Gonzaga authority in the early fifteenth century did not extend to the Benedictine monastery and its precious relic—nor, by implication, to the *popolo* in the *civitas nova* devoted to its cult. With Alberti's help, the century would end in resolution of the problem.

When Pope Pius II and his retinue arrived at Mantua at the end of May in 1459, their host Ludovico arranged for their accommodation in his own palace: the Domus Magna and its adjacent *palazzo del capitano*. In the meantime, the marquis and his court moved to the Castello di San Giorgio, in an arrangement that would become permanent with the Florentine architect Luca Fancelli engaged to take charge of converting the fortress into a residence, domesticating, as it were, its inherent menace.[108]

Providing suitable accommodation for the marquis in the castello included the transformation, most famously, of a small room in the northeast tower into a nearly cubical space measuring 8.05 by 8.07 by 6.93 meters, which was decorated between 1465 and 1474 by Andrea Mantegna to create the so-called *camera picta*, or *camera degli sposi*—a room Zaccaria Saggi, the Mantuan ambassador to Milan would praise shortly after its completion as *la più bella camera del mondo*, "the most beautiful room in the world."[109] In the absence of a cortile, impossible in any case to retrofit into such a building, it was the *camera picta* with its fictive colonnade of painted pilasters that, thanks to Mantegna's genius, came to represent the "bosom" of Ludovico's repurposed castle, where "like a public forum ... all the lesser members converge."[110] If you look, you will find them there.

It is New Year's Day of 1462. On the north wall of the painted room, facing you as you enter, you see the marquis being given a letter, informing him that Francesco Sforza, duke of Milan is ill, and that matters concerning the Milanese succession require his immediate attention. Casual, in slippers with the sleeves of his loose rose-colored gown pushed up and his favorite dog, Rubino, under his chair, Ludovico relaxes at home surrounded by his impeccably attired *famiglia*—his wife, Barbara of Brandenburg, resplendent in cloth of gold, three of their ten children, servants, leggy courtiers pressing forward with petitions, a court dwarf, and even, arguably, Leon Battista Alberti himself standing, eyes lowered and deferential, in black at the rear.[111]

A great white horse—a warhorse known as a courser—and four huge mastiffs crowd your left shoulder as you enter the room from the east wing of the castle.[112] The horse, left in the care of a groom, belongs to the marquis who, now fully dressed with his sword buckled to his side, stands further along the west wall, in conversation with his two oldest sons: his heir Federico, and Francesco, a new cardinal at just 17, who holds the letter his father was given on the north wall, in front of you. The "Encounter" (as this episode in the two-part narrative is usually called) takes place at Bozzola later on that same New Year's Day. Its all-male company includes the marquis's youngest son, also named Ludovico and a future bishop of Mantua, two small grandsons Francesco and Sigismondo, as well as the emperor Frederick III, to whom his wife was related, and Christian I of Denmark who was married to his sister-in-law. Their presence shows how well connected the marquis was, and how well-assured his dynastic succession, although historically none of these last five—young Ludovico, the emperor, the Danish king, the two grandsons—were, or indeed could have actually been, at the scene here depicted.[113] In the vault above, a trompe-l'oeil oculus—a circle in a square—surrounded by faux-relief busts of the first eight Caesars beginning with Julius, opens on a vaulted blue heaven to bless the dynasty and confer on the events of that (or any) day in the life of Ludovico II Gonzaga the weight of cosmic-imperial necessity.

But "weight" is not quite the right word. Invoking Virgil, Mantegna's dedicatory inscription presents the work to his patron as *opus hoc tenue*, "this slight labor," which of course it is not.[114] Yet slightness as the kind of light touch Castiglione would later advocate in his *Book of the Courtier* as *sprezzatura* or "nonchalance" pervades the intricate, brightly painted narrative, in perfect reflection of the careless ease with which the truly powerful affect to take charge.

The room is a spousal bedchamber—a *camera degli sposi* where the sleepy-eyed marquis, postcoital father of ten, still in slippers, is seated in an upholstered chair where the curiously suggestive knob-topped finial of the chair's armrest rises stiffly in front of the hands that hold the letter. More babies are about to tumble down from the trellis that frames the circular sky above. This room is also an audience chamber: simultaneously very private and very public, a brilliant spatial analogue of the ruler's own person and an affirmation of the new signiorial norm where the seat of government could now be a bedroom in the prince's castle.

"You have seen how the spider arranges the threads of his web in rays," Alberti advised near the end of his *Della famiglia* in the 1430s.

> Each one of them, no matter how long, finds its
> beginning, its root, its point of origin in the center, where
> that most industrious animal dwells. Once it has spun
> its web, it dwells there alert and diligent, so that if any of
> the threads, no matter how minute or distant, is touched,
> it feels it immediately, rushes there, and takes care of
> everything. This is what the head of a family should do.[115]

Concurrent with his work in the Castello di San Giorgio at the northern edge of Mantua in the *civitas vetus* were the marquis's extensive interventions in the *civitas nova* to the south. These entailed work on the civic buildings of the Piazza delle Erbe for the most part, but also extended as far as the southern city gate, the Porta Pusterla, where Alberti's project for the church of San Sebastiano, proposed in February 1460, was already under construction less than a month later.[116] Alberti designed it as a centralized church on a Greek cross plan, with a dome over the crossing and a Gonzaga family mausoleum in the crypt.[117] Completed long after Alberti's death in 1472 with no dome and the purity of its austere geometry compromised, the church was never used as a mausoleum either. It did remain family property, however, and its site near the Porta Pusterla firmly anchored Gonzaga presence at the southern limit of the city, which anchor, taken together with the work in the Piazza delle Erbe, lay down the initial trace of the *asse gonzaghesco*, as it would become known—the "Gonzaga axis" that bound Mantua to the castle and its lord.[118]

Major work in the region of the Piazza delle Erbe began in 1461, with the leveling and paving of streets and the building of a new portico on the Palazzo della Ragione.[119] Lack of documentary evidence makes Alberti's involvement in much of the work here difficult to pin down, especially since none of the specific proposals he made in 1460 for interventions on the site were ever carried out.[120] This of course does not preclude his having advised Ludovico on matters of urban renewal, which he undoubtedly did. *On the Art of Building* is full of such advice.[121] But it was mostly Luca Fancelli who, while working on the renovation of the Castello di San Giorgio, also directed much of the building activity in the area: the renovation, with Giovanni Antonio da Arezzo, of the Palazzo del Podestà (1462–1464); the rebuilding of the Casa del Mercato (1462); the construction of the clock tower next to the Palazzo della Ragione (1470).[122]

The zeal with which Ludovico applied himself to improving the city's civic center had little to do with any alleged degradation of its buildings. His father Gianfrancesco had launched an urban renewal project of his own in the area just twenty years earlier, involving many of the same buildings—the Palazzo del Podestà and the Palazzo della Ragione, for instance—which would still have been in good condition in 1460.[123] But the Piazza delle Erbe and its adjacent Piazza Broletto were the remit, so to speak, of the Benedictine monastery of Sant'Andrea, home of the relic of the Holy Blood and time-honored capitol of the *civitas nova* and its communal institutions. Embedded in the marquis's evident wish to surpass the requirements of mere serviceability and make the city's civic center a showcase for the classicizing humanist standards he espoused—to endow it with the *decor* and *ornamentum* for which Alberti claimed nothing less than ethical worth—was the desire to mark this ambit of alternative power with incontestable signs of his own and so to claim it for himself and for his family.[124] Absolutely crucial in this was control of the abbey church of Sant'Andrea, the relic, and the celebration of its cult.[125]

Sant'Andrea was top priority. In June 1459, during the very first month of the papal congress and well before any of the projects just enumerated were set in motion, Ludovico commissioned a model for a new church of Sant'Andrea from the Florentine architect and woodworker Antonio Manetti Ciaccheri.[126] Manetti died in 1460, soon after completing the model in question, which the marquis no doubt discussed with the pope. While in Mantua, Pius appealed to the Holy Blood for relief from his crippling gout, was cured, and would go on to reaffirm the relic's authenticity.[127] But Ludovico II Gonzaga had no authority over the monastery, which was an ecclesiastical institution ruled by its abbot, Ludovico Nuvoloni. And Nuvoloni had no interest in demolishing the abbey church, which he considered still perfectly adequate. Had it not just served as a venue for several sessions of the papal congress? The pope could have issued a bull, of course, but seeing no justification for doing so, advised the marquis to wait it out until the abbot died. In any case, what Ludovico II really wanted was dissolution of the entire monastery, and its replacement by a collegiate community of secular clergy, under Gonzaga patronage and directed by a Gonzaga family member. This he ultimately obtained, but not without a struggle.

In June 1472, two changes of pope later, shortly after the election of Sixtus IV which (not coincidentally) Ludovico's son, Cardinal Francesco Gonzaga, had just helped to effect, the new pope finally issued a bull ordering demolition of Sant'Andrea. The marquis's protracted attacks on the monastery and its recalcitrant abbot during the intervening years had included claims that Abbot Nuvoloni was insane, that the monks were woefully negligent in the care of their relic, and that the church itself was about to collapse and in desperate need of replacement. More than forty years after its publication in 1977, David Chambers's article detailing the whole sequence of vulpine maneuvers remains as darkly compelling as a film noir.[128]

When Abbot Nuvoloni finally died in March of 1470 and the marquis's cardinal son became titular abbot of the monastery,

Leon Battista Alberti, rightly anticipating the direction matters would very soon take, set about formulating his own proposal for a new Sant'Andrea. Six months later, Ludovico Gonzaga received the following carefully worded letter from him.

> I have also learned recently that Your Lordship and certain of your citizens have been considering building here at Sant'Andrea. And that the chief concern was to have a great space where many people could see the Blood of Christ. I have seen Manetti's model. I liked it. But to me, it did not seem suited to your purpose. I have thought out and imagined this, which I am sending you. It will be more capacious, longer lasting, nobler, and more fitting [*più capace, più eterno, più degno, più lieto*]. It will cost much less. The ancients called this kind of temple sacred Etruscan [*etruscum sacrum*]. If you like it, I will see to drawing it up in proportion. I recommend myself to Your Lordship. Your servant, Baptista de Albertis.[129]

Implicit in Alberti's claim that his design will make for a more capacious, longer-lasting, nobler and more fitting temple than Manetti's is an appeal to the criteria of the so-called "Vitruvian triad," the best-known directive in all of *De architectura*. When executing works of architecture, Vitruvius wrote, you must take three things into account: *firmitas* (strength—Alberti's *più eterno*), *utilitas* (use—his *più capace*), and *venustas* (beauty—manifested in the combined qualities of *più degno* and *più lieto*).[130] Alberti used virtually identical terms in his *On the Art of Building* where he also rephrased Vitruvius's *firmitas, utilitas, venustas*, to invoke the principles that Richard Krautheimer claimed were the organizing criteria for the whole of the Albertian treatise.[131]

"What we construct," Alberti writes at the beginning of book 6, the first of his four books on ornament, "should be appropriate to its use, lasting in structure and graceful and pleasing in appearance."[132] The third of these, "the noblest and most necessary of all," is the vehicle of beauty whose power, he goes on to claim, will not only tame the savagery of the illiterate rabble, but also deflect attack by enemies. "No other means is as effective in protecting a work from damage and human injury as dignity and grace of form."[133] Such advice, advocating intimidation rather than brute force as the preferred means of exerting control over potentially subversive subjects, was obviously formulated with the concerns of *signori* like Ludovico II Gonzaga in mind. For all that Vitruvius conferred on *venustas* a decisive role in his argument for architecture as the ultimate guarantee of Roman world rule, he was never as explicit as this.[134]

Alberti invariably refers to beauty as *pulchritudo* (a word Vitruvius never uses), and not as *venustas*, which is Vitruvius's preferred term and a vehicle of *voluptas* or pleasure. In his *De officiis*, a work Alberti knew well, Cicero distinguished between two kinds of *pulchritudo*: *venustas*, which he says is feminine beauty, and *dignitas*, which is masculine.[135] Recoiling from the implied sensuality of *venustas* to favor *dignitas*, Alberti opts for the manlier standard.

A temple is the chief ornament of a city, he writes in book 7 of his treatise, and must therefore be beautiful beyond compare: of such beauty that all who enter will be stupefied (*stupefacti*)—speechless with awe and admiration for a place so clearly worthy of God.[136] The great vaulted interior of Alberti's Sant'Andrea can still affect you that way. Your stupefaction, however, should not preclude your appreciating that the church was built as a dynastic temple, with intentions not so very different from those that underwrote temples of the imperial cult, built to honor Caesars and their descendants in cities all over the ancient Roman world. Writing at the very beginning of the imperial period, Vitruvius describes a so-called *aedes Augusti*, or temple of Augustus, he included in his design for a basilica at Fano on Italy's Adriatic coast.[137]

After some initial confusion (*etruscum sacrum*?), Ludovico Gonzaga gave Alberti's project for Sant'Andrea his approval and was straining with impatience for papal permission to begin construction when he wrote to his cardinal son Francesco at Rome on 2 January 1472, urging him to speak to the pope in person without delay. Demolition of the old church must begin immediately, he writes, for his heart is set on rebuilding as a matter of prime importance: for the cardinal's, for his own, and for the city's honor. When, God willing, the church is finished it will be very, very beautiful—*una bella bella cosa*—he continues, pausing briefly in his insistent directive to allow God this single offhand mention.[138] If the marquis did not share Alberti's view that God's honor was the principal concern when it came to the beauty of temples—at least not this one—he obviously had no quarrel with the architect's advocacy of architectural magnificence in general which, as Alberti wrote in the prologue to his treatise, increases "greatly not only your own honor and glory, but that of your family, your descendants, and the whole city."[139] Sant'Andrea would be the most magnificent of Ludovico's achievements, the climax of his rewritten urban narrative.

For over three hundred years, active participation in Mantuan public life by the monastery had made it a contributing author of that narrative, with engagement in the political culture of its *civitas nova* making the abbey church far more of a city church than the cathedral, San Pietro, ever was. While, from the end of the twelfth century, their cathedrals were cities' most spectacular manifestation of civic religion, in Mantua the role belonged to Sant'Andrea.[140] Its appropriation by the Gonzaga meant the erasure of what was left of communal Mantua and final dynastic appropriation of the entire city. Alberti's proposal for a church designed as an "Etruscan temple" was his most brilliant contribution to that purpose.

More than fifty years earlier, Ludovico Gonzaga's father Gianfrancesco had commissioned an account of Mantua's origins from the Florentine humanist Leonardo Bruni, leading historian of the day.[141] Bruni obliged with *De origine urbis Mantuae*, a compilation of literary evidence from an impressive range of ancient sources (Livy, Virgil, Pliny the Elder, and Plutarch among others) assembled to prove that Mantua had originally been an Etruscan city. This was clearly a matter of importance to a prince who, in seeking a pedigree meant to enhance the prestige of his city, was looking to enhance his own. Taking a passage from Virgil, whose testimony as Mantua's most celebrated native son was unexceptionable, Bruni established that the city had been founded before the Trojan prince Aeneas arrived in Italy which, he extrapolated, meant a foundation date at least 300 years prior to Rome's.[142] Mantua was *old*, older than Rome itself and possibly the oldest city in all of Italy: a claim not lacking in clout among humanist elites who revered the antique. Needless to say, Alberti also revered the antique, whose surviving texts and monuments were the bedrock of his theory and practice, especially when it came to architecture.[143] "In our opinion," he writes, "age will give a temple as much authority, as ornament will give it dignity."[144]

Hence his *etruscum sacrum*. If the old church of Sant'Andrea was to be torn down—without waiting for written confirmation, Ludovico began demolition on 6 February 1472 as soon as he heard from his son of the pope's verbal assent—then the new church that replaced it would be older:[145] an Etruscan temple whose great authority tapped the inveterate wellspring of the city's origin, worthy at last of the precious relic it enshrined and (far more to the point) of the dynasty now in charge of its cult.

The Etruscans were Italy's first builders, Alberti writes, and first to formulate rules for the building of temples.[146] To these Etruscan temples he attributes proportions transcribed more or less verbatim from Vitruvius's account in book 4 of *De architectura*, but adding "side chapels," which Vitruvius does not mention.[147] Vitruvius's proportions, which Alberti misinterpreted, were the literary source for the plan of Sant'Andrea. Its monumental source, on the other hand, is generally agreed to have been the hulking brick skeleton of the Basilica of Maxentius/Constantine in the Forum Romanum, a late antique building whose flanking spaces he mistook for the "side chapels" of what he thought had been an Etruscan temple.[148] From the intersection of these learned misunderstandings, Alberti "thought out and imagined" the *etruscum sacrum* he proposed to Ludovico Gonzaga in his letter of October 1470, a majestic, single-nave, barrel-vaulted brick church with six vaulted side chapels, as startlingly new for its time as it was authoritatively old.[149]

Also startling was the deep entrance porch of the church, with which construction unconventionally began on 12 June 1472, two months after Alberti's death in April of that year, with Luca Fancelli as trusted on-site architect.[150] Alberti's pedimented façade, with giant Corinthian pilasters flanking the arched opening to a lofty barrel-vaulted passage leading from the piazza to the door of the church, is an unprecedented fusion of two different antique

Elevation, Sant'Andrea in Mantua, rendered by Chris Bearman, 1988. Bearman / Alberti Group.

motifs: temple front and triumphal arch. By itself, a temple front for a would-be Etruscan temple would not of course have been surprising. Alberti had already experimented with the triumphal arch as façade at the Tempio Malatestiana in Rimini ten years earlier. But there it appears as an essentially two-dimensional motif. He had never combined the two, nor had he (or anyone else) ever elaborated the triumphal arch as church front in full three-dimensional depth as he does here.

More startling still is the anomalous superstructure that rises above the peak of Alberti's triumphal arch. Known as the *ombrellone*, this high barrel-vaulted canopy arches over a pavilion-like chamber which originally opened not only onto the piazza in front of the church as it still does, but also—the triumphal porch being considerably lower than the nave—onto the church interior from which a circular glass window now separates it.[151] It could be reached inside the church by spiral stairs integrated into the pillars on either side of the entrance.[152] What was this strange excrescence *for*?

One answer is that it was meant for ritual display during Ascension Day celebrations of the *sacri vasi*, the sacred phials containing the Holy Blood.[153] This would be thematically consistent with a fresco, now much damaged and in the diocesan museum in Mantua, that Mantegna painted in the large central tondo on the pediment of the triumphal porch. In the fresco, St. Longinus, who collected the Blood at the foot of the cross, and St. Andrew, titular saint of the church responsible for its discovery, appear together in the act of presenting the *sacri vasi* to the city under their protection.[154] According to this hypothesis, yearly display of the Holy Blood on a platform under the *ombrellone* would have backed up Mantegna's representation with its real, salvific presence.

Another more convincing hypothesis, far more consistent with the consolidation of Gonzaga power that was the overriding aim at Sant'Andrea, is that the high chamber under the *ombrellone* was part of something like a *Westwerk*, in keeping with the tradition of such structures built on the west fronts of churches in the European north.[155] Charlemagne's late eighth-century palace church at Aachen was an early prototype.[156] At Aachen, there is a tribune over the west door of the church, reached by spiral stairs inside the pillars flanking it, where the emperor, mediator between heaven and earth, sat on an ivory throne overlooking the vaulted octagonal nave during religious celebrations. This Carolingian *Westwerk* also opened to the exterior, with a window above the church entrance where Charlemagne and his successors would appear to the people assembled below.

The analogous elevated space at Sant'Andrea in Mantua would thus have been a tribune or chapel meant for similar occupation by the city's lords, dramatically haloed in light flooding in from the opening behind them. Accordingly, the *ombrellone* arching over the triumphal porch outside would have presented the city with the unassailable fact of Gonzaga rule, whether or not any Gonzaga was actually present. Inside, on Ascension Day, as documentary evidence affirms, the Holy Blood was displayed on a podium in the apse at the eastern end of Alberti's Etruscan temple, which is to say far below the prince's elevated tribune at the opposite, western end of the church.[157] Spatial affirmation of signiorial control could not have been more explicit.

As Alberti tells it, a city gate is essentially a triumphal arch and, of course, vice versa.[158] Every triumphal arch is also a gate. At the beginning of his long account of this "the greatest ornament to the forum or crossroads," Alberti instructs that a triumphal arch be located where the royal road (*via regia*), as he calls the most important road in a city, meets a square or a forum.[159] The architect appears to have followed his own advice when it came to the triumphal porch fronting the church of Sant'Andrea, as Robert Tavernor observed in his monograph on Alberti, for the church does indeed terminate the main road into the city from its southern gate at the Porta Pusterla, veering slightly to the right as it enters the Piazza delle Erbe at the crossroads in front of the church.[160]

But the question of the royal road becomes somewhat chicken-and-egg if you remember that Pius II's triumphal entry into the city on 27 May 1459 was at the Porta Pradella, west of the Porta Pusterla, and followed an entirely different route to the cathedral of San Pietro, where it terminated. Carpeted, its flanking buildings hung with gold hangings, this papal route into the city was its incontestable *via regia* on that particular day at least.[161] With

Section, Sant'Andrea in Mantua, rendered by Chris Bearman, 1988. Bearman / Alberti Group.

Anonymous eighteenth-century view of Sant'Andrea in Mantua, oil on canvas. Technische Universität Plannsammlung, Berlin, inv. 18244.

this in mind, Alberti's triumphal porch becomes more the *creator* of a royal road into the city—the famed "Gonzaga axis" discussed earlier—than the post factum enhancement of an existing one. Similarly, the antique grandeur of the porch was less an ornament to a preexisting "forum"—the adjacent Piazza delle Erbe and erstwhile *platea communis*—than a key contributor to the creation of such a forum in confirmation of the ruling marquis's dominance.

The first triumphal arch/gate of postclassical times was the Capua gate built between 1234 and 1239 by the emperor Frederick II Hohenstaufen. The gate was a bridgehead on the Volturno river, just north of Capua on the Via Appia, and one of the clearest expressions of the Swabian emperor's proto-Renaissance ambition to bring about an imperial Roman revival led by himself as Caesar.[162] The bridgehead consisted of two massive crenelated towers on either side of an arched passageway that passed under a tall "triumphal" superstructure which featured classical ornament, statuary, and Latin inscriptions.[163] The gate was dismantled in 1557, leaving only the bases of the flanking towers in place. Its original appearance survives in sketches made of it before its demolition, one by the multitalented architect and theoretician Francesco di Giorgio Martini in about 1480 and another anonymous one, possibly by Fra Giocondo, in the early sixteenth century, as well as in three written descriptions of it.[164]

The Capua gate faced north and marked the boundary between the Papal States and the *Regnum Caesaris*—the "Kingdom of Caesar" to the south. Salient features of the north face of this triumphal entrance to the Kingdom of Sicily, where Frederick ruled unchallenged, included first of all the archway itself, framed in a broad band of moldings that seem to have intrigued Francesco di Giorgio, who took pains to record their complex profile. Three circular niches framed the upper part of the arch. At the summit of the arch, the largest of these niches contained a colossal female head of Justice, with an inscription CESARIS IMPERIO REGNI CUSTODIA FIO—"by Caesar's command I am guardian of the kingdom." The smaller tondi to the left and the right held busts of Frederick's chief jurists, Pier delle Vigne and Taddeo da Sessa, with further admonitory inscriptions severely enjoining fealty (or else) in all who crossed into his domain.[165]

World Heritage, Urbino

In the middle of the register above this—the piano nobile—an arched aedicule enshrined the monument's visual focus and its raison d'être: a seated statue of the very young-looking emperor wearing a toga and a crown and originally holding, it is thought, insignia of imperial power.[166] The statue's head and other details are now missing, but known thanks to a drawing made of the statue before it was vandalized by invading French soldiers in 1799.[167] On either side of this central niche were smaller ones containing statues of unidentified figures, one of them, it has been suggested, an ancient statue of the Roman goddess Diana.[168] The attic above appears to have been articulated in a mixture of gothic and classical details, with small niches that may have contained additional statuary, as Cresswell Shearer's reconstruction of the gate suggests.[169]

Alberti must have known the gate, for he could not have avoided seeing it on the road south from Rome to Naples when he traveled to that city in the spring of 1465.[170] He has, moreover, been credited with contributing to the design of the Capua gate's closest and most famous Quattrocento emulation, the triumphal arch at the Castel Nuovo in Naples, begun by Alfonso of Aragon in 1451 and completed by his heir Ferrante in 1475.[171] According to Alfonso's biographer, Antonio Panormita, the new king's decision to rebuild the castle was accompanied by a command to be brought a copy of *De architectura* for consultation.[172] Vitruvius has nothing to say about triumphal arches, which mostly postdate the time of his writing. But be that as it may, in the mid fifteenth century Vitruvius was ever the ultimate authority for princely builders seeking architectural affirmation of their right to rule, whatever the projected monument.

Alberti may also have been aware of one of the three known written sources concerning Frederick II's Capua gate, a description that appears in Giovanni Antonio Campano's life of the famous early fifteenth-century condottiere Braccio ("Strong Arm") da Montone, written in 1458. Widely read and much appreciated by the condottiere's warmongering homologues, the biography made Campano's reputation, earning him a place in the papal entourage at the Mantua congress the following year and countless literary commissions, including a life of Pius II, whose

Triumphal gate of Frederick II Hohenstaufen at Capua, thirteenth century, after Cresswell Shearer, *The Renaissance of Architecture in Southern Italy* (Cambridge, 1935), fig. 38. Canadian Centre for Architecture, Montreal.

encomiast he became. He also wrote a biography of Federico da Montefeltro, who had it in his palace library at Urbino, along with a very beautiful manuscript copy he commissioned of Campano's Braccio biography.[173]

Campano's description of Frederick II's triumphal gate appears in his account of how the warlord seized Capua in 1421. The passage through the city gate is narrow, writes Campano, who was a native of the region. "Between the two towers," he continues, "above the extremely high arch that overhangs the road, there is a *regium cubiculum* opulently furnished with marble statues and ancient images."[174]

This *regium cubiculum* is not the "royal chamber," which is to say an actual room overhead, that scholars have never been able to square either with Campano's account of it or with the archaeological evidence. It was the representation of something analogous yet different.[175] As ancient Roman sources attest, and as Campano obviously knew, a *cubiculum* was another name for the raised and canopied dais, also called a *pulvinar*, where a Roman emperor sat with his court in what you might call a "royal box," at the theater, the games, or the racetrack.[176] That is what Campano meant by "*regium cubiculum*." As he understood it, the entire triumphal superstructure above the Capua arch was a royal dais high above the roadway, where its crowned and togate emperor sat enthroned in the company of his ministers.

How exactly, if at all, the Capua gate helped shape Alberti's thinking about Sant'Andrea and its triumphal porch—or indeed about triumphal arches in general—must remain speculation. But the possibility of Alberti's failure to make such connections should not preclude our doing so. Frederick II's monument can still throw light on what is at issue here. The *ombrellone* over the triumphal porch in Mantua sheltered what was also, in effect, a *regium cubiculum*—the "royal box" that overlooked the church interior—whose exterior expression was the high arch over the pediment outside. As such, and bearing the Capua gate in mind, the *ombrellone*, clearly integral to the porch it crowns, is the ultimate fulfillment of the church front's intentions and the very summation of its discourse—its architectural punch line, as it were. For what is a triumphal arch without a triumphator?

View of Mantua, c. 1550, from Philippo Orsoni, *Liber Philippi Ursonis manu* (Mantua, 1554), vol. II, detail of title page. Victoria and Albert Museum E1725-2031-1929. © Victoria and Albert Museum, London.

Although the importance of the city's precious relic was prominently acknowledged by Mantegna's circular fresco in the pediment of the porch, the triumph did not belong to the Holy Blood represented there. The triumph belonged to the occupants of the *regium cubiculum* overhead—the dynasts who now owned it.

Alberti wrote that a triumphal arch is also a gate, and so obviously is its porch the gate to the church of Sant'Andrea. But more important is what, as a gate, it stood for. Just as the triumphal arch at Capua had once been the point of entry to the kingdom of its Caesar, so, in its essence, did Alberti's porch now stand as the gateway to the city of Mantua, the whole of it at long last under complete control of the Gonzaga lord and his family. Not coincidentally, when construction of Sant'Andrea began in 1472, it began with construction of that triumphant declaration.[177]

During the sixteenth century, and throughout the years of Gonzaga rule, views of Mantua tended, understandably, to focus on the magnificent great church at the city center, never failing to give prominent, often greatly exaggerated acknowledgment to its crowning *ombrellone*. In a woodcut of Mantua from about 1550 the view looks north from the vantage of an east-west line that cuts through the middle of the city, running right in front of Sant'Andrea as if this, the front edge of the image, were in fact the city limit where the church entrance appears, with its disproportionately high *ombrellone*, on the left.[178] Not knowing any better, and with nothing to identify it as a church, you might very well think it a gate to the Gonzaga city.

Mantua and the nearby "ideal city" of Sabbioneta, founded *ex nihilo* in the late sixteenth century by Vespasiano Gonzaga, a junior family member eager to make his own mark, received joint nomination to the World Heritage list in 2008. The UNESCO citation reads, in part, as follows.

> Mantua and Sabbioneta, in the Po valley, in the north of Italy, represent two aspects of Renaissance town planning: Mantua shows the renewal and extension of an existing city, while 30 km away, Sabbioneta represents the implementation of the period's theories about planning the ideal city. ... Mantua and Sabbioneta offer

exceptional testimonies to the urban, architectural and artistic realizations of the Renaissance, linked through the visions and actions of the ruling Gonzaga family.[179]

And so back to Urbino where I began this chapter and where, from the time of its completion at the end of the fifteenth century, Federico da Montefeltro's palace—like Sant'Andrea, but more insistently given its hilltop site—fixed the viewpoint of all subsequent representations of the city. It is indeed a captivating view, where the two tall watchtowers of the *torricini* façade frame three superimposed loggias to create a triumphal, if fictive, gate to the city, skewed at a 30-degree angle from the west front of the palace for maximum visibility from the south.[180] Its most famous antecedents are the Aragonese gate at Naples already mentioned and the Capua gate that inspired it.[181] Spiral stairs inside the flanking towers climbed to the summit of this multitiered declaration of supremacy, where, crowned by the eagle that was his emblem, the top loggia gave an unmistakable sign to those below of the ruling lord's presence, unseen and watchful, high above in private quarters whose inner sanctum—the famous studiolo—was another iteration of what you would not be wrong in recognizing as a *regium cubiculum*, a room at the top of a triumphal arch built as the mirror of its occupant's supposedly teeming inner life.[182] Tiny (3.5 by 3.6 meters), badly lit, with no place for books, it was not a real study at all, of course, but a consummately crafted image of immense learning presented by a would-be philosopher king as a voucher for his right to rule.[183]

As already intimated, the question of legitimacy was an enduring preoccupation among *signori* seeking power. In this, architecture played a key role. Buildings staked claims to territory; their immutable factuality proved, so to speak, the legality of might as right. Alberti's understanding of the issue gave him an entrée into the princely courts of the day and motivated his writing of *On the Art of Building*, as indeed it had motivated Vitruvius's writing of *De architectura* at the time of Roman imperial expansion a millennium and a half earlier. The American philosopher John R. Searle argued that you are free, in theory, to reject institutional reality but not free to reject what is physically real.[184] Buildings

View of Urbino, late sixteenth century, fresco after drawings by Ignazio Danti. Gallery of Maps, Vatican. Chris Heller / Alamy Stock Photo.

are physically real; you cannot "reject" them. But they are not (being physical) immune to physical attack, as the historical record relentlessly attests.[185] The challenge for a builder, Alberti knew, was to build in a way that would deflect such attacks.

Alberti was keenly aware of the issue of legitimacy. He begins the fifth book of his treatise, on the works of individuals, by distinguishing between two kinds of rulers. The first is "the sort who governs reverently and piously over willing subjects." The second rules against his subjects' will.[186] The distinction, in effect, is between a legitimate ruler who rules with the people's consent—which is to say after obtaining the kind of negotiated settlement with the ruling commune I wrote about earlier—and an illegitimate one who does not. The first "pious" ruler Alberti calls a king. The second is a tyrant. The seat of a king (*regum aedes*), he continues, "should be sited in the city center, easy of access, and gracefully decorated, elegant and refined rather than ostentatious." A tyrant, on the other hand, dwells in an *arx*—a menacing fortress or citadel—at the edge of the city where its position allows for defense against insurgent subjects as well as against external enemies. But even a legitimate ruler should have an escape route to some nearby fortress, Alberti cautions, because you never know.[187] The multitude is perfidious, unpredictable.[188] Better safe than sorry.

What Alberti means is that in order to appear legitimate, princes should build palaces, not citadels. Given his parameters, and as he stops short of openly suggesting, there is nothing to prevent a tyrant from building a "gracefully decorated, elegant and refined" royal palace at the city center in order to persuade potentially seditious subjects of his legitimacy—to persuade them with a beautiful palace in the middle of town that he is, in fact, a good prince. Worth the risk, you might say. There would, in any case, be an escape hatch should a quick getaway prove necessary. Moreover, Alberti is a forceful proponent of beauty as an arm against insurgency, arguing in book 6 that "no other means is as effective in protecting a work from damage and human injury as dignity and grace of form."[189]

Born in 1422, Federico da Montefeltro was the illegitimate son of Guidantonio da Montefeltro, count of Urbino. His father recognized him as his heir until Federico's legitimate half-brother Oddantonio, born in 1427, displaced him in the line of succession. Accordingly, when Guidantonio died in 1443 it was the sixteen-year-old younger son, not Federico, who became the new count, elevated to a dukedom by Pope Eugenius IV shortly after his accession.[190] Federico would have to wait 30 years before receiving the coveted ducal title.

Oddantonio ruled for just over a year until, on 22 July 1444, he was brutally assassinated in a coup, justified in contemporary accounts by his licentiousness, greed, and the punitive taxes he imposed. On 23 July, the morning after the murder, Federico, who had been waiting at the city gate, made a triumphal entry into Urbino and was acclaimed its lord on condition that he sign a pact with municipal leaders, drawn up the day before.[191] Although his biographers exonerated him of any collusion in these decidedly murky doings, his involvement in the conspiracy is beyond doubt.[192] It is possible, moreover, that Federico was not even the son of Guidantonio, as indeed his enemies claimed—an accusation that would further undermine his claim to legitimacy.[193]

The first article of Federico's pact with the commune was agreement to unconditional impunity for Oddantonio's assassins. Twenty more articles of agreement followed whose demands for political and fiscal concessions were aimed at restoring the rights citizens had enjoyed before the death of Guidantonio, Federico's father. These included rebuilding the priors' palace, seat of municipal government on the Piazza Maggiore, as well as the reduction of taxes, to which Federico responded cagily, "*Fiat, nisi in casa necessitatis*"—"So be it, except in case of need."[194] The pact was duly signed, but agreement on paper did not, needless to say, guarantee that Federico would walk the walk. In fact, his reign entailed the same gradual incapacitation of the last vestiges of communal autonomy as was under way elsewhere—in Mantua, for example—during the second half of the fifteenth century. Yet his obvious ability to talk the talk, and above all his enrichment of the city through the staggering wealth he accumulated as a mercenary captain, led to a relatively trouble-free reign that lasted until his death nearly forty years later—"a reality based on an initial fiction," as Jane Stevenson has remarked recently.[195]

Documentary evidence of what the people of Urbino forfeited when they acclaimed Federico as their lord is the telling change, under his regime, of their traditional designation as *cives* (citizens) to that of *subditi* (subjects) in the city's official records.[196] Confirmation of that lost autonomy (its architectural proof) was the *torricini* façade of the palace that placed the lord at its summit and erstwhile citizens far below in the *mercatale*—the marketplace, moved from the *pian di mercato* so called that had been located at what is now the Piazza della Repubblica at the city center, to a vast new site developed for the purpose just outside the southern gate, well within the sight lines of Federico's lofty perch.[197]

Although this triumphal gate defined at once the city, its palace, and the relations between the two, the real entrances to both city and palace were in fact elsewhere. Until the late Middle Ages and up to the time of Federico's reign, you would in all likelihood have approached Urbino from the north, as indeed had been the case from its earliest days as Urvinum Mataurense, "the little city on the Mataurus river," first mentioned during the Punic wars of the third century BCE.[198] Until the fifteenth century you would have entered Urbino through one of its northern or eastern gates—most probably the Porta Lavagine, which became the main entrance to the city and led to the Via Flaminia, the road north to Rimini and Ravenna. Topography played a major role in determining this orientation, for the northern approach to Urbino's hilltop site is relatively flat, whereas from the south the climb to the city center is steep and difficult, as anyone who has ever visited knows well.

Federico da Montefeltro quite literally turned the city around. Its forcible reorientation, a full 180 degrees from the north to the south—from Rimini to Rome—went in tandem with construction of the palace, begun in earnest in 1464 with the first of Alberti's many visits to Urbino and the beginning of the Dalmatian architect Luciano Laurana's tenure as architect of the project.[199] As a result of this about-face, you now entered Urbino from the south through the Porta Valbona, the new main city gate, located at the edge of the new *mercatale*, which was itself an integral part of the signiorial program. No longer a deterrent, the steep southern ascent that in earlier times had resulted in the choice of an easier approach from the north now became an asset, brilliantly

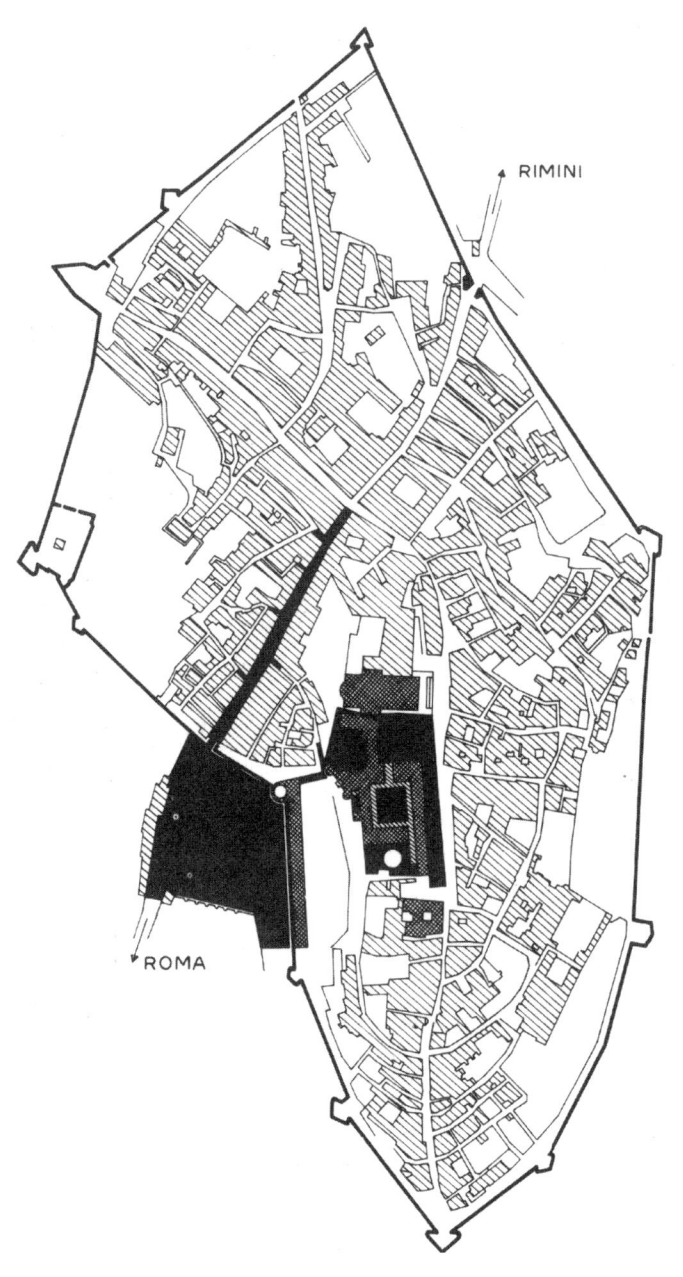

Plan of Urbino, after Leonardo Benevolo, *The Architecture of the Renaissance* (London, 1978), 167. The spaces developed by Federico da Montefeltro appear in black. Canadian Centre for Architecture, Montreal.

exploited as a naturally occurring, topographical enhancement of the prince's exalted position.

Toward the end of Federico's reign, the Sienese architect Francesco di Giorgio Martini designed an ingenious helicoidal ramp that permitted rapid ascent on horseback straight up from the *mercatale* to the foot of the *torricini* above. This private access to the palace allowed Federico to bypass the public thoroughfare he would otherwise have had to share with his subjects, something like the fifteenth-century equivalent of a presidential helicopter, but in reverse. The stout brick tower that enclosed the ramp was designed as a cylindrical bastion, complete with gun emplacements, meant to secure the marketplace and give the palace its own defensive system.[200]

The palace faced two ways. On the opposite side from the south-facing, fictitious *torricini* gate and its rhetoric of dominance, the real entrance to the palace faced north and was meant to tell a different story. Here, when you came through the door famously said to have always stood open, you entered a palace "sited in the city center, easy of access, gracefully decorated, elegant and refined"—the dwelling, allegedly, of a good prince.[201] Alberti would surely have recognized it as such had he not died in 1472 before this part of the palace was completed, when Francesco di Giorgio was project architect in the late 1470s.

Through this open door, framed by Corinthianizing marble pilasters at the sides with a high, richly carved entablature overhead, you follow a passageway, too dark and narrow to be a vestibule, to step into the bright light of the large square palace courtyard—the *atrium* or "bosom" of Federico's house, and the sine qua non of any princely dwelling from the time Cosimo de' Medici built his palace more than twenty years earlier in Florence as an alternative seat of municipal government.[202] At five by six bays, Federico's courtyard is grander than either Cosimo's or Pius II's emulation of it in Pienza, where each is only three bays square. Federico's has greater elegance too, with finer proportions, more skillfully carved imperial Roman column capitals, and a famously happier resolution of the corner detail.[203]

Above the porticos that frame the space, inscriptions on two levels celebrate the achievements, both military and moral, of

FEDERICUS URBINI DUX in crisp Roman capitals, declaring him the builder of this, the house he "raised up from its foundations for his own glory and that of his descendants." Limited perhaps by lapidary constraints, the inscription leaves out any mention of the palace being meant to enhance the glory of the city. Otherwise, it is another iteration of the by now commonplace appeal to the virtue of magnificence Alberti endorsed in On the Art of Building.[204] Ludovico Gonzaga pushed for the rebuilding of Sant'Andrea in Mantua on precisely the same grounds.[205]

HANC DOMUM A FUNDAMENTIS ERECTAM. The inscription says the duke raised his house from its foundations. What exactly does this signify? Are you meant to believe that there was nothing there before he began to build? This is easy enough to accept, given the sober elegance and seeming inevitability with which the palace wraps around the square then known as the *piazza grande*. Even the cathedral, which Federico reoriented and rebuilt with Francesco di Giorgio as architect to close off the square like a third palace wing, was given a supporting role in the single-minded narrative that now defined the city center.

In 1476, Giovanni Sulpizio da Veroli ("Sulpicius Verulanus"), who ten years later would edit the first printed edition of Vitruvius, was resident at Urbino when he wrote the following Latin epigram praising the ducal palace, then still under construction. *Aemula Caesaris et postibus aemula priscis / Urvini trivio stat veneranda domus*—"Challenging Caesar and rival to the portals of the ancients / at the crossroads of Urbino your stately house stands firm."[206] Julius Caesar had given Urbino, then known as Urvinum Mataurense, the formally constituted civic status of a *municipium* (city) in 46 BCE, and Sulpicius seems to have known what archaeological evidence now confirms—that the site of the *piazza grande* around which the duke wrapped his palace had once been the forum of that Roman city, located at the crossroads of its two main streets, its *cardo* and its *decumanus*.[207] Federico probably knew it too, acquiring in this ancient crossroads a genuine Roman *fundamentum* for the house he built in keeping with the principles of Vitruvius and the ancients.

There were two copies of *De architectura* in Federico's palace library: a twelfth-century manuscript of German origin, and

Courtyard entrance to the ducal palace, Urbino. Photo Fratelli Alinari, 1915–1920. © Alinari Archives / Fratelli Alinari / Art Resource, NY.

another more elegant one, made to order for him some time before 1474.²⁰⁸ Federico was the equal of Vitruvius himself, according to the praise bestowed on him by his young secretary, Federico Galli, in a letter of 1466 which contains the earliest known description of the palace.²⁰⁹ What Vitruvius has to say in book 6 about the aristocratic Roman *domus* would, of course, have been of special interest, as indeed it had been to Pius II when he built his palace in Pienza a decade earlier. The distinction Vitruvius makes between the public and private spaces of a high-ranking person's house is key to understanding the source of Federico's vaunted accessibility. Unlike ordinary people, Vitruvius writes, men of rank who conduct public business in their dwellings need them to be open, with rooms anyone can enter even without being invited.²¹⁰ Such a person's house, Cicero advised in his *De officiis*, must be an ornament to his dignity.²¹¹ Vitruvius goes on to specify the kind of rooms required: royal entrances, lofty atria, spacious peristyles, libraries, picture galleries, and basilicas like those of public buildings.²¹² Endorsed by Leon Battista Alberti, this precisely was Federico da Montefeltro's ancient Roman model.

Vitruvius's preferred walling method was ashlar, the *saxa quadrata* or "squared stones" he discusses in book 2 of *De architectura*, on building materials. For him, the prevailing Roman walling methods collectively known as *opus caementicium* (exterior surfaces of stone or brick, with infill of rubble mixed with concrete) were all intrinsically flawed. Besides brickwork, or *opus testaceum*, there were two kinds of *opus caementicium*: *opus reticulatum*, whose facings of crisply cut pyramidal stones made for regular, reticulated wall surfaces, and *opus incertum* whose rough surfaces of uncut stone were highly irregular. *Reticulatum* tends to crack, Vitruvius points out, while admitting that it is attractive. *Incertum*, he says, is solid enough, but downright ugly. Ashlar masonry, on the other hand, is at once solid, good-looking, and long-lasting. Only squared stones satisfied all three Vitruvian criteria for architectural excellence: *firmitas, utilitas, venustas*—solidity, use, and beauty.²¹³

The passage was transcribed almost verbatim in Raffaele Maffei Volaterrano's chapters on architecture (largely devoted to palaces) of his *Commentatiorum rerum urbanorum*, an encyclopedic digest of ancient studies published in Rome in 1506 and dedicated to Pope Julius II.[214] Volaterrano concurs with the opinion of *dulcius Viturius* (sic) concerning the superiority of ashlar, declaring all masonry excepting that of squared stones to be "irrational," and pointing to its exemplary use in the recently completed Palazzo Riario (the Cancelleria) at Rome as well as the Palazzo Strozzi in Florence. He might very well have also mentioned the Montefeltro palace at Urbino where, in the white marble ashlar revetment applied to the basement of its brick façade in a late phase of construction, its badge of Vitruvian authenticity is knowingly displayed.

The site, Caesar, Vitruvius, and imperial Rome all contributed to the Roman foundations of Federico's house. Also essential as a *fundamentum*, in view of his questionable paternity and the fratricide that had secured his position, was the Montefeltro ancestry on which depended the claim to legitimacy that the overwhelming, immutable presence of his palace would eventually "prove." Federico makes explicit reference to the matter in the famous *patente* or brief he drew up in 1468 on behalf of the architect Luciano Laurana, where he writes of his decision to build "in our city of Urbino a beautiful residence worthy of the rank and illustrious reputation of our forefathers, as well as of our own stature."[215]

In 1235, the emperor Frederick II Hohenstaufen, builder of the Capua gate discussed earlier, had conferred the title of count on the Montefeltro brothers Buonconte and Taddeo.[216] But forebears of more recent date—Federico's grandfather Count Antonio (1348–1404) and his father Guidantonio (1377–1443)—built what he adopted as ancestral ground for his *domus*. As elsewhere in Italy, signiorial residences at Urbino during the Middle Ages had tended to be dispersed throughout the city. One of these, larger than the others, was the so-called Palazzetto della Jole that Count Antonio built in the last quarter of the fourteenth century on the *poggio* or crest of the hill that defines the city. The *palazzetto* became part of the east wing of Federico's sprawling pile, facing what is now the Piazza Rinascimento. According to recent research, Antonio's successor Guidantonio was the first to build a residence on the site Federico chose for the northern, entrance wing of his palace.[217] Freestanding, at right angles to the latter, was a defensive structure known as the *castellare*, also Montefeltro property, built against a section of the medieval city wall. This Federico incorporated into the palace wing on the west side of the *piazza grande*, where he installed the apartments of his wife Battista Sforza, married to him in 1460 when she was thirteen.[218] It was, by all accounts including Federico's, a happy marriage, though there is of course no firsthand record of what Battista thought about it.[219] She died at 26 after giving birth to a longed-for male heir, Guidobaldo, having already borne eight daughters, six of whom survived. It was her ninth pregnancy in 12 years—a testament, a recent biographer has remarked without apparent irony, to her "extraordinary vitality."[220]

Other than Count Antonio's Palazzetto della Jole which survives almost entire, knowledge concerning which of Federico's ancestors built exactly what, where, and when tends to be uncertain. Nonetheless, it is unambiguously clear, thanks to a surviving bill of sale, that by 1461 two sides of the *piazza grande* belonged to Federico, while on the other two sides there were ecclesiastical properties belonging to the bishopric of Urbino. The document, written in Latin, identifies the square as *platea magna dicte civitatis*—the "great square so-called of the city."[221] *Civitatis*, "of the city."

This "great square," Urbino's *piazza grande*, had been its *piazza comunale* during the communal period. And if, like the exact location of the Montefeltro ancestral residences, the precise sites occupied by the *palazzo del poedstà*, priors' palace, and other civic buildings remain controversial, it is uncontested that these, along with the cathedral, had stood on the perimeter to define this shared civic space.[222] None of these buildings were "fundamental" for Federico's palace, which on the contrary became the agent of their erasure, with the *platea magna* "of the city" transformed into what was essentially the prince's private *cour d'honneur*.[223] *Una città in forma di palazzo*. The ducal monogram FE DUX emblazoned on the lintels of the windows that overlooked this palatial entrance court after 1474 left no doubt as to who now controlled the erstwhile *platea communis*. Even its brick pavement was laid to exactly match the radiating pattern of the palace courtyard inside.[224] It was as if, between the time of the piazza's appropriation by

Federico and that of its existence as a Roman forum in Caesar's day, there had never been anything there at all—or certainly nothing worth mentioning.

Consolidation of signiorial rule rendered such elision commonplace. In his chapters on architecture, tellingly sandwiched between one on gems and another on clothing, Raffaele Maffei Volaterrano, mentioned earlier in connection with the Vitruvian bona fides of ashlar masonry, includes a very brief overview of the history of cities, *De urbium aedificatio*.[225] There once were colonies, and monasteries, he writes, both in Italy and elsewhere. Some of these places were abandoned. Others were founded anew by a *vir maximus*—a very great man—with a citadel, or arranged with palaces, villas, and temples which the great man then marked with his insignia because he built them at his own expense. And that is all Raffaele Maffei Volaterrano has to say about cities in his encyclopedia of 1506.

Recent scholarship notwithstanding, conventional histories of the Renaissance have tended to collude with the world heritage take on "ideal" cities like Urbino that makes a *vir maximus* their hero. Throughout the Middle Ages and even after Federico's appropriation of it, the square in front of the palace he built was always known as the *piazza grande*, or alternatively *piazza maggiore*. At the beginning of the twentieth century, in belated affirmation of its takeover more than 500 years earlier, it was renamed Piazza Duca Federico, corralling collective memory into a place with no exit and no room left for anyone but the duke.[226]

4   Virtù-vious

On 10 June 1468, Federico da Montefeltro, count and later duke of Urbino, was in Pavia staying in the *castello* built by Galeazzo II Visconti a century earlier. He was a guest of Galeazzo Maria Sforza, then duke of Milan, the city where, as discussed in chapter 1, Francesco Petrarca gave Vitruvius a new lease of life. "Pavia" and the date appear at the end of a letter the count wrote on behalf of the Dalmatian architect Luciano Laurana, resident in Urbino, where Federico had ruled since seizing power 24 years earlier. Written in Italian, the letter—a *patente* or brief—was not a letter of hire, as Luciano had already been working on the count's new residence in Urbino for several years.[1] Addressed, as it were, "to whom it may concern" among the overseers of Urbino's building trades with the intention of confirming the architect's contractual authority over them, the letter's abiding interest lies in its author's commanding pronouncement on what Federico took to be the defining condition of architecture. "We deem most worthy of honor and commendation," he begins,

> those men who are endowed with talent and *virtù*, and greatest among the *virtù* unfailingly prized by ancients and moderns alike is the *virtù* of architecture, because it is founded in the arts of arithmetic and geometry which are chief among the seven liberal arts and possess the highest level of certainty, and thus [architecture] is an art of great knowledge and great talent and held by us in the very highest regard.[2]

Architecture, an art of *gran scienzia* (great knowledge) and *grande ingegno* (great talent), is to be prized, as it always has been (so Federico), for being of surpassing *virtù*, a quality famously tending to evade definition, but which you could take in this context, at least for now, as having to do with excellence and innate value. As Federico would have it, this *virtù* derives from architecture's foundation in mathematics—in arithmetic and geometry, chief among the seven liberal arts because they stand at the highest level of certainty (*in primo gradu certitudinis*).

That the truth of mathematics was immutable and stood at the "highest level of certainty" had long been axiomatic in the western cultural tradition. Tradition had it that no one ignorant of geometry was to enter Plato's Academy.[3] The creation myth Plato presented in the *Timaeus* fixed the created world's ideal template, mathematically, in five regular geometric solids.[4] St. Augustine's writings on mathematics and music repeatedly drew for corroboration on the Old Testament text that declared God to have ordered "all things by measure and number and weight."[5] Closer to home, and with the uncanny reverberation of an echo, in 1498 the mathematician Luca Pacioli, sometime member of the Urbino court in later years, wrote in the dedication of his *De divina proportione* to Ludovico Sforza, duke of Milan, that "as Aristotle and Averroes confirm, among those things that are true, mathematical truths are the most true of all, and stand at the highest level of certainty [*nel primo grado de la certezza*]."[6]

Federico da Montefeltro first acquired his own appreciation of mathematics in his early teens, when his intensive training in the arts of war was interrupted by two years of study at Ca' Zoiosa, Vittorino da Feltre's famous school for young aristocrats in Mantua where Vittorino's curriculum gave mathematics exceptional emphasis.[7] Federico's exact contemporary Ludovico Gonzaga, future marquis of Mantua, was also a student at the school, which had been founded by his father Gianfrancesco in 1423. Federico would later honor their former schoolmaster in the gallery of famous men that presided over his studiolo, pairing the portrait of Vittorino, his "most sainted preceptor," with one of Euclid.[8]

But it was undoubtedly Leon Battista Alberti, himself a mathematician of considerable repute, who ultimately helped shape Federico's opinion concerning the *virtù* of architecture as mathematical certainty, expressed with such conviction in the *patente* of June 1468. Alberti first visited Urbino in 1464 just as work on the then count's new residence was getting under way, and returned often.[9] "Nothing was closer or more loving than the bond of friendship between Battista and me," Federico would later recall in a letter he wrote to their mutual friend, the humanist Cristoforo Landino, in 1475, three years after Alberti's death.[10] It may well have been Alberti who convinced Federico to have a copy of *De architectura* made for his library, a work that together with Alberti's own treatise (still in progress at the time) was undoubtedly a major informant of their exchanges over the years.[11]

"To follow a consistent theory [*certa ratio*, or 'certain calculation'] is the mark of a true art," Alberti writes, recalling in this the "certain calculations [*certae rationes*] of symmetries" that for Vitruvius made architecture the ultimate proof of civilization, as I discussed in chapter 2.[12] "Of the arts the ones that are useful, even vital, to the architect are painting and mathematics," Alberti asserts, pausing to scoff at his (here unnamed) ancient Roman predecessor for advocating that the architect have knowledge of no fewer than nine different disciplines, not just these two.[13]

Nonetheless, the grounding of architecture in mathematics is fundamental for both Vitruvius and Alberti.[14] Each appeals to the Pythagorean tradition in his exploration of the relation of music to architecture, and Alberti famously affirms that the very same numbers are the source of harmony (*concinnitas*) in both.[15] For each, mathematics is celestial, endowing architecture with the dimension of cosmic necessity—a notion sure to appeal alike to the emperor Augustus for whom Vitruvius wrote and to humanist *signori* such as Federico who were Alberti's intended audience.[16]

As we have seen, the palace at Urbino was built, above all, as incontestable evidence of its ruler's legitimacy. The unbendable truths of mathematics were, for Federico, its immanent theoretical stiffening. The marble ashlar revetment applied to the basement of the palace façade discussed in the previous chapter was not just an attestation of Vitruvian authenticity. The evident rationality of these perfectly fitted squared stones was also a billboard for the countless unseen calculations whose mathematical certainties permeated every aspect of the palace design: the set-square precision, for instance, of the 30-60 right triangle that determined, on plan, the angle at which the *torricini* façade (its hypotenuse) skewed southward from the west front of the palace and whose fixed triangular boundary exactly circumscribed the architect-prince's private apartments behind it;[17] the near-cubical dimensions of the sudiolo contained therein; the carefully calculated proportions of other rooms, stairs, column orders, entablatures, doors, window openings, and more. The ashlar of the palace entrance was a cipher for the *virtù* of mathematical certainty embedded in all of this.

But in his own lifetime, Federico's main claim to fame was neither as a mathematician nor as an architect. The two years of schooling with Vittorino da Feltre that introduced him to humanistic studies and ignited his appreciation of mathematics had in fact been but a short break from the far more serious business of his training in the arts of war in which he would eventually excel. For Federico da Montefeltro's main claim to fame was as a condottiere, a warlord with a private army for hire, the most celebrated, the most successful, and hence the wealthiest mercenary captain of his day—one of the richest men in fifteenth-century Europe.[18] The Latin inscription on the walls of his palace courtyard declared that he had never lost a battle. Bronze medals

Elevation, courtyard façade, ducal palace, Urbino, after Roberto Papini, *Francesco di Giorgio architetto* (Florence, 1946), vol. 3, plate XXXIII. Canadian Centre for Architecture, Montreal.

bearing his portrait were stamped with legends proclaiming him *invictus*. For Giannantonio Campano he was a new Hercules, as inseparable from his military glory as Hercules from his club.[19] Eager for a share in the bounty that swelled the warlord's coffers, biographers and court poets competed to outdo each other in praise of the loyalty and iron will with which, along with courage and military genius, this man of inauspicious beginnings bent fortune to his own ends and rose to exceptional prominence.[20]

Their praise, in sum, was of Federico's surpassing *virtù*: the quintessential attribute of a Renaissance prince later celebrated by Machiavelli as the chief means to his having and holding onto power. "I hold the Fates bound fast in iron chains / And with my hand turn Fortune's wheel about," boasts Christopher Marlowe's Tamburlaine in a Machiavellian moment that reads like an epitome of *The Prince*, chapter 25.[21] *Fortuna* was notoriously fickle. A successful prince would master her and make his own luck. In the cutthroat world of Quattrocento politics, the aim ideally was for his *virtù* to operate in the same unambiguous realm of incontestable certainty as mathematics.[22]

The entrance wall of Federico's palace was a representation of that shared realm. For there, subtending the ashlar revetment, a frieze made up of 72 travertine panels carved in relief with images of civil and military machinery evoked the successes that underwrote the warrior prince's rule—a declaration, given its architectural context, of *virtù* equivalent in certainty to the mathematical *virtù* advertised in the perfectly squared stones directly above. Neither truth was to be challenged; might was as right as mathematics. As a reminder, the open door of the palace, which interrupts the frieze at the eastern end of the north section of the façade, exactly frames the word DEPUGNAVIT ("he fought ferociously") at the center of the courtyard inscription celebrating Federico's undefeated record.

Removed in the eighteenth century, the 72 panels were carved in the 1470s under the guidance of the duke himself by the Milanese sculptor Ambrogio Barocci after designs, initially by Roberto Valturio, author of the fifteenth-century treatise *De re militari* and later by Francesco di Giorgio Martini, palace architect and acknowledged expert in the machinery of war and peace.[23]

Luca Pacioli singled the frieze out for praise in his dedication to Ludovico Sforza of *De divina proportione* where, on the previous page, he had extolled the immutable truth of mathematics that, as he points out here, underwrites the fabrication of such machinery as the frieze depicts.[24]

Just under a meter high, it was over 40 meters in length. Like the ashlar masonry above it, it also attested to Vitruvian authenticity. For if the masonry affirmed adherence to Vitruvius's "certain calculations of symmetries," the frieze below it was essentially an updated transcription of *De architectura*, book 10, the last and longest of the ten books whose topic, *machinatio*, included the machinery of war and was the third of the three parts of architecture, after building and gnomonics.[25]

Machinatio had been Vitruvius's own specialty as a military architect in Caesar's army, designing the scorpions, catapults, ballista, and other artillery that were indispensable tools in the war, among others, where Caesar, moving with breathtaking speed (so Caesar), seized Gaul for Rome in the 50s BCE—tools that, along with contemporary iterations such as cannon, are represented in the frieze at the ducal palace at Urbino.[26] As the preface to book 1 of *De architectura* recalls, Vitruvius had occupied a ringside seat at the spectacle of Roman conquest. Its testament to imperial grandeur had been a principal source of the work's appeal to Petrarch in the fourteenth century.[27] It would continue to play a major role in the appeal of *De architectura* to Quattrocento *signori* like Federico, who revered Caesar and Augustus, but especially Caesar, as role models.[28]

There are countless illustrations of the appeal to imperial Rome, the emperors and Julius Caesar in particular, as legitimating precedent for affirmations of power during the Renaissance. Portraits of the Caesars were a consistent feature of architectural ornament: examples include the arch of the entrance to the family palace in Castiglione Olona, the town near Milan that cardinal Branda da Castiglione had redesigned as his personal fiefdom in the 1420s; the pillars with reliefs of the emperors that supported the balcony Ercole d'Este added to the ducal palace at Ferrara in the 1470s; and the faux reliefs of the same date that Mantegna painted in the fictive vault of the *camera picta* in the Gonzaga castle

Andrea Mantegna, *Triumphs of Caesar 2: Bearers of Standards and Siege Equipment*, 1484–1492, tempera on canvas, Hampton Court, UK. classicpaintings / Alamy Stock Photo.

at Mantua.²⁹ Beyond Italy, the terra-cotta roundels of imperial portraits Cardinal Thomas Wolsey commissioned from Giovanni da Maiano for the central courtyard of his new palace at Hampton Court in 1520 were likewise an attestation of his exalted (if, as it turned out, precarious) position.³⁰

Painted in Mantua for the Gonzaga at the end of the fifteenth century as a brilliant, extravagantly theatrical celebration of the prevailing cult of Caesar, and on view at Hampton Court near London since 1630, nine giant canvases, each over eight feet square, make up what was long considered Mantegna's masterpiece, that "great festive movement of warriors, prisoners, weapons and plundered treasure" (Stephen Campbell) that is the *Triumphs of Caesar*.³¹ Mantegna, who adopted Julius Caesar's portrait as his personal seal and whose antiquarian zeal underwrites the work's extraordinary illusion of verisimilitude, was himself a passionate devotee of the cult.³²

Caesar played a leading role at the wedding of Federico da Montefeltro's daughter, Isabetta, to Roberto Malatesta, son and heir of Federico's late, erstwhile archenemy Sigismondo Pandolfo Malatesta in Rimini in June 1475.³³ Gaspare Broglio di Tartaglia records the eight days of festivities in his late fifteenth-century *Cronaca universale*.³⁴ "The most illustrious duke of Urbino" and "the illustrious lady," his daughter, entered Rimini at the eastern limit of the city through the ancient Roman Arch of Augustus on which, Broglio writes, stood men "dressed like good ancient Romans," proclaiming verses in their honor.

> And the whole street leading to the forum [today's Piazza Tre Martiri] was covered with cloths and at the entrance of that noble square another triumphal arch was built. This square is where Imperator Caesar stopped and spoke to his captains to announce his [intention to] triumph over Rome by force, which was forbidden to him and so became a rebel against his republic. And there is also the stone on which he climbed to speak. ... At the top of the triumphal arch stood a statue of Caesar in armor holding a book and on the other side was the strongman Hercules with his club in his hand.³⁵

What Broglio is recalling here is that the Roman forum at Ariminum, as Rimini was known in antiquity, was where Julius Caesar stopped to harangue his troops in January of 49 BCE in preparation for his lightning descent on Rome, after crossing the Rubicon just north of the town.[36] What Broglio also recognizes is that crossing the Rubicon with his army had been a treasonous act, for the Rubicon marked the southern boundary of Cisalpine Gaul, the point at which, after his Gallic conquest, Caesar was bound by law to give up his *imperium*, disband his troops, and return to Rome, no longer *imperator* but a private citizen. This Caesar did not do, and in resolving to "triumph over Rome by force" became, as Broglio observes in clear recognition of the general's fundamental illegality, "a rebel against his republic."

The armed statue of Caesar holding a book set atop the triumphal arch at the Montefeltro-Malatesta wedding was obviously placed there to flatter Federico, the soldier-scholar about to become Roberto Malatesta's father-in-law, with the statue of the strongman Hercules included as rhetorical amplification of the same encomiastic intent. But what about Broglio's odd, somewhat misplaced reference to Caesar's illegality? Did that also refer to Federico—a veiled hint at the murky circumstances that had initiated the warlord's own reign?[37] This is entirely possible. Broglio had been the loyal companion and sometime ambassador of Sigismondo Pandolfo Malatesta who, until quite recently, had been Federico's enemy.[38] The marriage uniting the children of these two legendary foes was one of pure political expediency.[39] Broglio may well have used his text as a chance to express, albeit obliquely, his continued hostility to Federico in the face of changing times.

But be that as it may, and whatever Gaspare Broglio's reason for bringing the matter up, it is an important reminder that Caesar's rule had been illegal, founded in treason. Even Petrarch, whose admiration for Caesar knew no bounds, recognized this, making much in his *De gestis Cesaris* of Caesar's hesitation at the Rubicon "lest in crossing the boundary of his province he appear to be acting openly against the Republic."[40] He also mentions Caesar's speech to his troops in the forum at Rimini, and the stone on which he stood to speak, saying he had seen it himself as a boy—probably in about 1320. A most effective speech, writes Petrarch, delivered with tears and rent clothing, as he pleaded with his soldiers to keep faith with his greatness in the face of his enemies' envy, promising prodigious rewards.[41] Donated by Mussolini and still in place, a bronze statue of Caesar commemorating the event was installed there in 1933, where it was dedicated as "a tribute in memory of the Founder of the Roman Empire ... to the Founder of the new imperial Italy."[42]

Opposition to Caesar as Petrarch tells it was due to his enemies' envious failure to acknowledge the man's greatness which, when it came down to it, reduced objection to the transgression that was the empire's foundation to a matter of small-minded legalistic quibbling. Before being expanded as a stand-alone work, *De gestis Cesaris* was a chapter of *De viris illustribus*, which included the lives of twenty-four famous Romans, beginning with Romulus.[43] In a letter of the early 1350s outlining his intentions, Petrarch wrote that he was "not concerned with physicians, poets or philosophers, but only those distinguished through military power or great attention to the state who achieved glory for their deeds."[44] *Virtus* was what made these men famous, he writes in the preface to the work. *Virtus* was the key to Caesar's astounding success. *Virtus* alone brought him to the pinnacle of glory, and never mind mundane concerns like legitimacy which preoccupy the senseless masses (*insanienti vulgi*), as Petrarch calls the enemies of *virtus*.[45] Caesar's fundamental illegality and its ultimate irrelevance when measured against the immensity of his *virtus* throw considerable light on his appeal to *signori* facing their own issues of doubtful legitimacy.

Vitruvius had been with Caesar in Gaul and may very well have crossed the Rubicon with him to stand among the ranks of legionaries swept away by the great general's rhetoric in the forum at Rimini.[46] After Caesar's assassination in 44 BCE, he transferred his unwavering support to Caesar's heir, Augustus. The Latin word *virtus* appears twice in his dedication of *De architectura* to the new ruler of the Roman world: once in the very first sentence, and again in the second paragraph. "When your divine mind and power, Imperator Caesar, were seizing command of the world and all your enemies had been crushed by your invincible *virtus* ..." is how he begins.⁴⁷ In the next paragraph, recalling his attachment to Augustus's adoptive father, he goes on to say that his continued devotion to Caesar's memory (*studium ... in eius memoria*) after the latter's death was what led him to support the son. As Vitruvius tells it, his knowledge of architecture was what had made him known to Caesar (*eo fueram notus*). This knowledge, he claims, had been what bound him to Caesar's *virtus* (*eius virtutis studiosus*).⁴⁸ Not to Caesar the man, note, but to the great man's *virtus*.

It would be difficult to find a better illustration of what *virtus* signified in Vitruvius's world—its primary meaning, that is to say—than these two instances of its use right at the beginning of *De architectura*. *Virtus*, as Cicero pointed out, derives from *vir*, the Latin word for man, and for a man, he says, courage is the most essential thing, demanding the greatest scorn for both pain and death.⁴⁹ *Virtus*, which Myles McDonnell in a recent study has styled as "Roman manliness," was primarily a military virtue, as Petrarch clearly recognized.⁵⁰ Manifested in the refusal to accept defeat, it was the quality to which, above all others, Romans attributed their success as conquerors.⁵¹ Personified as a goddess, *Virtus* was represented as an Amazon, in a short tunic with one breast bared, usually armed with a dagger and a spear.⁵² Significantly enough, the goddess Roma—Rome personified as a supernatural being—was usually represented in exactly the same way. Although it is difficult to establish which of the two, Roma or Virtus, was the first to appear in this guise, their shared iconography could not make plainer the interchangeable identities of Rome itself and the manly courage to which Romans said they owed their ascendancy.

Personified as a goddess, Virtus, like Roma, was an armed Amazon. But the preeminent *symbol* of *virtus* (as opposed to its personification) was a mounted warrior, his horse often trampling a fallen enemy.⁵³ In imperial times, only the emperor could be represented in this way as the unique and essential representative both of *virtus* and of Rome itself.⁵⁴ The famous bronze equestrian statue of Marcus Aurelius brought to the Capitol in the sixteenth century discussed in detail in chapter 2 is a case in point. The melting down of ancient bronzes for their metal destroyed many other such statues, leaving Marcus Aurelius an all but lone survivor. Yet emperors on horseback continue to exist in marble reliefs and in countless instances of Roman imperial coinage, the latter much imitated by Renaissance princes.[55] Suetonius tells how Caesar honored his own horse with a statue raised in the Forum Julium in front of the temple of Venus Genetrix, the shrine he built to affirm his divine ancestry.[56] The horse, it is said, had hoofs split like the toes of human feet, and the soothsayers had predicted that whoever owned this exceptional horse would rule the world. No doubt. But less, perhaps, due to simple ownership of the horse than to the *virtus* the horse epitomized.

The reappearance of the equestrian monument in the fifteenth century is a well-known phenomenon, which H. W. Janson went so far as to claim "demonstrated the fundamental unity of the Renaissance," observing further that the quality common to equestrian figures "is the emphasis on *virtù*, the prowess of the individual hero."[57] I will have much more to say about horses, equestrian monuments, and the light they shed on the Vitruvian revival in chapter 6.

While there are 38 known fifteenth-century Italian manuscripts of *De architectura*, over five times as many—a total of 220—copies of Caesar's commentaries were produced during the same period: the great general's own self-aggrandizing accounts of his conquest of Gaul and of the civil wars from which he emerged victor and sole master of Rome.[58] Federico da Montefeltro had three copies of Caesar's *De bello gallico* in his library.[59] The commentaries that first appeared in print in 1469 were among the earliest books printed in Italy, followed by eleven more editions before the century was out—further evidence, if any is needed, of Caesar's overwhelming popularity.[60] *De architectura* did not appear in print until 1486, with a second edition, now with illustrations, in 1511.[61] My own view, as I have already intimated, is that Vitruvius's success followed on Caesar's and that his attachment to Caesar's *virtus* underwrote his appeal to the lords of city-states, seized for the most part by force of arms, in northern Italy where *De architectura* made its first major comeback.

It is important to keep in mind Vitruvius's claim that his knowledge of *architecture* was what had bound him to Caesar's *virtus*—and the implication, crucial to the Vitruvian afterlife, that the great man's *virtus* had needed an architect. His expertise in the machinery of war was his most obvious tie to Caesar's manliness, of course, but not just *machinatio*: the rest of what Vitruvius qualifies as architecture as well, including, especially, building.[62]

From the time Petrarch first introduced Vitruvius to the Visconti court at Milan in the 1350s, any prince who took the time to read the first pages of *De architectura* would have surely found the assertion regarding the link between architecture and Caesar's *virtus* far more compelling than Vitruvius's claim, a few paragraphs further along, that the knowledge of the architect depends on *fabrica* and *ratiocinatio*.[63] And if a prince was not yet aware that proper deployment of his *virtù* required architectural support, it is safe to assume that any ambitious architect who had read his Vitruvius would have been more than happy to point it out to him. Or, to put it another way, if Caesar showed the way to ambitious warlords, so too did Vitruvius, ever at the ready as Caesar's loyal henchman, show the way to ambitious architects, ultimately uniting prince and architect in a common project whose avowed purpose, now, was *di risucitare le virtù*, as Filarete would write in his treatise on architecture of about 1460—"to bring the ancient virtues back to life."[64]

Book 1, chapter 1 of *De architectura* deals with the education of the architect, who (as Vitruvius claims and Alberti would later deny) is to be something of a polymath.[65] One of the nine disciplines with which he says the architect must be familiar is history so that, if called upon, he can justify the use of certain ornaments. Two stories illustrate his point. The first explains the use of caryatids.

As Vitruvius tells it, Carya, a city in the Peloponnese, was sacked by the Greeks for collaborating against them with the Persian invaders—in the early fifth century BCE you naturally assume, when the great king, Xerxes, overran much of Greece. Permanent admonitory chastisement of the Caryans' treachery is why caryatids, statues of widowed Caryan women wearing their finest clothes, are put in the place of columns to support entablatures. "So that they might be led in triumph not just once but enslaved forever as a lesson."[66]

"Porticus Persica insigne virtutis constituta," from Vitruvius, *Di Lucio Vitruvio Pollione De architectura libri dece: traducti de latino in vulgare affigurati*, translation and commentary by Cesare Cesariano (Como, 1521), fol. 7r. Canadian Centre for Architecture, Montreal.

Vitruvius's second story is also drawn from the Persian wars. At the battle of Platea, the Greeks, led by the Spartans, won their final, decisive victory over the Persian invaders. Vitruvius says that, once back home in Sparta, the Spartans used their war booty to build what he calls a "Persian portico" as a trophy of their victory and "a sign" as he puts it, "of the glory and *virtus* of their citizens."[67] As punishment for the Persians' insolence, statues of Persian captives clad in "barbarian" attire were used to support the roof of this portico which, Vitruvius writes, was meant to strike terror in the hearts of Sparta's enemies, and to stand before Spartan citizens as an *exemplum virtutis*—a paradigm of *virtus*.

Thus, in the first ten paragraphs of *De architectura* the word *virtus* appears four times: twice as the attribute of victorious generals (Caesar and Augustus), and twice in the description of a building whose attestation of victory Vitruvius declares an "exemplum" of *virtus*.

The word occurs forty-seven times in *De architectura*, where it is used in ways, for the most part, not obviously related to the primary meaning just reviewed.[68] The highest concentration of occurrences is in books 2 and 8 where *virtutes* refer to the "virtues" of building materials and of water: their innate natural qualities and potential use in building.[69] The machines described in book 10 can also have *virtutes*, the "virtue" of a machine—whether a crane or a battering ram—being a question of how effectively it performs, particularly in warfare.[70] As already noted, it was Vitruvius's knowledge of war machinery that had forged his bond with Caesar's *virtus*.

Machines can have "virtue," then, but does an architect possess *virtus*? Not at this point in the history of the profession. What made an architect praiseworthy, and distinguished a good one from a bad one, is what Vitruvius called *sollertia*: his skill, or cunning, or both.[71] *Sollertia* is a question of craft, not of artistic talent as inspiration, the latter being a gift, independent of skill. In war, the *sollertia* of an architect will outmaneuver even the most effective machinery, Vitruvius boasts at the conclusion of his treatise, after recalling various situations in the past where an architect's clever strategy saved the day.[72] Fifteen hundred years later, Alberti would make a similar claim for the worth of architects, but what he writes in his preface to *On the Art of Building* is that the *virtus* (not the *sollertia*) of architects has won more victories than the leadership of generals.[73]

Yet Vitruvius seems to have believed that architecture as such possessed *virtus*, even if the architect himself did not. Architecture understood as the knowledge of the architect at any rate—*architecti scientia*, the self-proclaimed subject of *De architectura*.[74] In his third preface, Vitruvius writes that because it has so far been hidden, this knowledge has remained unappreciated, claiming nonetheless that once his treatise is published, "the *virtus* of our knowledge" will become evident.[75] The theme resurfaces again in the preface to book 9, where he declares that in bestowing the benefit of his knowledge upon mankind, a writer (such as himself) deserves more than just the palms and crowns bestowed on victorious athletes.[76] Such a person should, like a victorious general, be awarded the ultimate accolade of a military triumph and judged worthy of a seat in the dwellings of the gods. Present, if unmentioned, are the deified Caesar, his successor Augustus, and the underlying implication that the knowledge of the architect is their equal in *virtus* and deserving of the same rewards.[77] Athletes' fame grows old with their aging bodies, he continues, but thanks to their writings, the thoughts of Plato and Pythagoras among the Greeks, of Lucretius, Cicero, and Varro among the Romans, will live forever.[78]

A similar trope regarding the nature of architectural *virtus* is the subtext of Vitruvius's second preface. There he tells the story of Dinocrates, an exceptionally well-built architect famous for his *sollertia*, who is trying to attract the attention of Alexander the Great.[79] When all else fails, Dinocrates strips naked, rubs his magnificent body with oil and approaches Alexander in the immediately identifiable guise of Hercules, complete with lion skin and club, introducing himself as "Dinocrates, the Macedonian architect who brings you ideas and designs worthy of your renown." Although Alexander does not approve Dinocrates' project to transform Mount Athos into the statue of a man, holding a city in one hand and a bowl of water in the other, he is nonetheless won over by the architect's ruse, and hires him. Now Hercules, slayer of monsters and *victor invictus*, was of course the very paradigm of *virtus*, as Vitruvius himself acknowledges in another context where he says that "because of their *virtus*" Hercules and Mars should have temples built in the Doric order and be free of frills.⁸⁰

Unlike Dinocrates, Vitruvius is old and ill. Or so he says. Thus, with no Herculean physique to recommend him, what he offers instead is *architecti scientia*, the knowledge of the architect. The rhetorical structure of the anecdote makes it obvious that Vitruvius means this knowledge to be understood as equivalent in *virtus* to that of the invincible, monster-slaying demigod impersonated by the muscle-bound Dinocrates. Equivalent also to the *virtus* of the emperor whom he addresses at the end of his story: "As for me, Imperator, ... it is with the help of knowledge and writings that I hope to gain recognition."⁸¹

Among Renaissance architects who drew on the Dinocrates story as a paradigm for figuring the architect as "the king's double" (to invoke my own coinage) is Francesco di Giorgio Martini, who wrote an adaptation of it in the early 1470s when he was not yet working for Federico da Montefeltro but eager to do so.⁸² His application for the duke's patronage was an album of drawings of mechanical devices and fortresses, known as the *Opusculum de architectura*, which he dedicated to Federico in a fulsome if somewhat awkwardly written Latin preface.⁸³

Even as Alexander the Great delighted in Dinocrates as a man of genius expert in the attack and defense of cities and other matters essential for the preservation of sovereignty (*imperium*), Francesco writes, so too did Julius Caesar honor Vitruvius. Likewise, he hopes, will Federico da Montefeltro, who has "lighted up all Italy with his immortal exploits," allow the brilliance of his (Federico's) own genius (*ingenium*) to recognize the genius of others, meaning, of course Francesco's own. Evidence of this *ingenium* is the book of drawings its author here presents to the duke. As Martin Warnke has shown, an increasingly popular term for the "genius" shared by both patron and artist was the word *virtù*.⁸⁴

Francesco di Giorgio has deliberately styled Dinocrates in his own image, making the Macedonian architect, like him, an expert in the machinery of war, a claim for which there is no known source. Also noteworthy is his insistence on Vitruvius's being honored by Caesar, not Augustus, to whom *De architectura* is dedicated and whom, in his first preface, Vitruvius gratefully acknowledges for *commoda* (stipends) received.[85] As already discussed, it was Caesar Renaissance princes idolized, more than Augustus, and it had been, specifically, Vitruvius's expertise in artillery and siege machinery that had first bound him to the great general's *virtus*. Francesco di Giorgio's strategic rewriting of the story lends the weight of antique authority to his bid for his own Caesar's patronage, while burnishing his (Francesco's) claim to a "genius" the famous warlord cannot, he intimates, afford to ignore if he is to maintain *imperium* over his territory.

Whatever the role, if any, the *Opusculum* played in securing his position, Francesco began working for Federico in 1477, becoming in fact a principal agent in the preservation of the duke's *imperium* and as such a key instrument of his prince's *virtù*. Writing in 1490, eight years after Federico's death, he records having received 136 commissions from the duke who he claims "loved him tenderly like a son."[86] Of these commissions, more than half were fortification projects. A map of the dukedom's defense system at the end of the fifteenth century shows Urbino at the center of its territory, ringed by no fewer than twenty-three fortresses, mostly designed by Francesco. Exotic and inventive, those that survive—Cagli, Costacciaro, Mondavio, San Leo, Sassocorvaro, among others—have lost little of their fascination or indeed their menace over the centuries.[87]

Francesco di Giorgio appears to have been captivated by the story of Dinocrates, which he translated in his fragmentary Italian translation of *De architectura*, the first such in any language.[88] Tellingly the translation omits the story's conclusion, where Vitruvius makes the rhetorical point that his own "knowledge and writings" have a Herculean potential at least the equal of, if not superior to, that of the Macedonian architect's physique. When Francesco invokes Dinocrates in his theoretical work, as he does on two further occasions, it is principally to dwell on the Mount Athos project, which had been unmentioned in the preface to his *Opusculum*.

The well-known drawing of Dinocrates that appears in the Magliabechiano manuscript of the second of Francesco's two treatises conflates Dinocrates and his project in a single graceful image. The text next to the drawing outlines the Dinocrates story

The architect Dinocrates, from Francesco di Giorgio Martini, *Trattato di architettura II*, c. 1495. Biblioteca Nazionale, Florence, Codex Magliabechiano II.1.141, fol. 27v (detail). By permission of the Ministero della Cultura—Biblioteca Nazionale Centrale, Firenze.

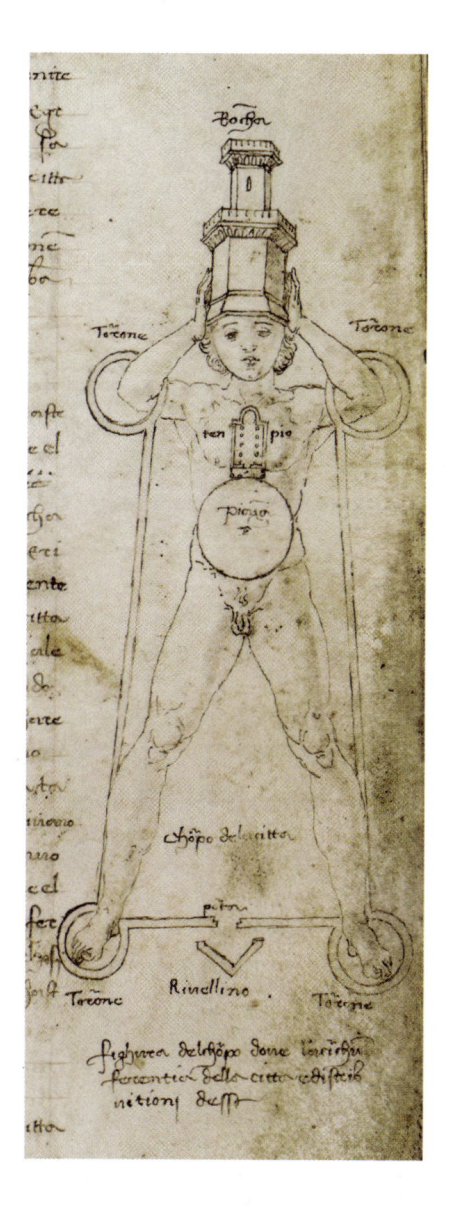

Anthropomorphic representation of a fortified city, from Francesco di Giorgio Martini, *Trattato di architettura I*, c. 1486. Biblioteca Reale, Turin, Codex Saluzziano 148, fol. 3r (detail). © MIC—Musei Reali, Biblioteca Reale di Torino.

much as Vitruvius tells it, minus Vitruvius's concluding message. Preparing the ground for his own conclusion, Francesco says that what Alexander admired in Dinocrates' project was *la similitudine della città al corpo umano*.[89] This is Francesco's own interpolation and does not appear in Vitruvius. Moreover, it is from Alexander's alleged admiration of the city's resemblance to the human body that Francesco draws the conclusion that all the principal parts of cities and other buildings should reflect some part of a man's body, and that each should have the same proportional relation to the city overall as the parts of the body have to the body overall.

Francesco had drawn similar conclusions from an earlier reference to the Dinocrates story, which appears at the beginning of his first treatise.[90] Here, however, it is not Dinocrates who appears in the margin, but a charming boyish figure whose body parts are made to correspond to the different parts of a fortified city. On his head is a *rocca*, or fortress (because, Francesco explains, the head rules the body), at his elbows and feet appear round bastions labeled *torroni*, and beyond the city gate between his feet, a defensive outwork known as a ravelin. In his chest there is a church and, in the center at his stomach, a circular piazza. And so, Francesco's text concludes, "just as in the body all its members relate to one another ... with perfect proportions, so must the same be observed in the composition of temples, cities, fortresses and castles."

The boy with the *rocca* on his head presents the reader with an appealing graphic abridgment—a theoretical vindication, if you will—of precisely what the fortresses Francesco built for the duke of Urbino were meant to do, which is to say, to preserve his sovereignty.[91] But of course there was nothing charming or boyish in the built reality of such *rocche*, nor indeed was there meant to be. Introducing the chapter on fortifications in his second treatise, Francesco argues passionately and at some length that the divine order of things has ordained that some must dominate, and others be dominated.[92] That is why a prince needs fortresses, he concludes—instruments, by implication, of the natural hierarchy and its divine decree.

Thus, on the two occasions Francesco invokes the Dinocrates story in his treatises, the architect and his project appear as justification for the prescription that "the composition of temples, cities, fortresses, and castles" be based on the proportions of the human body. For Francesco di Giorgio, whose pages overflow with images of lovely boys and girls, the body metaphor is a panacea.[93]

If the body-based principle of commensurability cannot be derived from Vitruvius's version of the Dinocrates story as Francesco di Giorgio has it be, it most certainly does derive from Vitruvius. But for Vitruvius the principle is relevant, above all, to the design of temples. Otherwise, it is mentioned only twice in *De architectura*.[94] "Vitruvian man," who is its epitome, appears at the beginning of *De architectura* book 3, right after the assertion that, just as in a well-shaped man, "in sacred dwellings, the symmetry of the members ought to correspond completely, in every detail and with perfect fitness, to the entire magnitude of the whole."[95] In Vitruvius's day, Roman world rule—the virtually limitless power Virgil styled as *imperium sine fine*—was universally assumed to be underwritten by Rome's privileged relation to the gods, which made the temple, in turn, the privileged locus of that power.[96] With the fall of the Republic and the advent of one-man rule, Augustus Caesar, the tireless temple-builder who stands behind Vitruvius's well-shaped man, became the exclusive channel of that privileged relation and, through his temples, the locus of the power it conferred.[97]

Francesco di Giorgio's almost verbatim citation of Vitruvius on the corporeal referent for proportion runs alongside his fortress man with only a passing reference to temples. The image, and the chapter on *fortezze* it introduces, leave no doubt that the overriding preoccupation of this late Quattrocento reader of Vitruvius was, as he puts it, *città, rocche e castelli*. A few pages further along, at the beginning of his chapter on cities, right next to a drawing of a menacing quadrangular fortress is where Francesco di Giorgio places his drawing of a pretty naked youth, arms outstretched, poised with insouciant elegance inside Vitruvius's circumscribing circle and square. Reiterating the prescription that cities must have the *ragion, misura e forma* of the human body, the text that accompanies this, Francesco's take on "Vitruvian man," says that where there is no *rocca*, a cathedral and the *palazzo signorile* will face each other across the principal piazza at the city center.⁹⁸ The description, with no mention of any public building, could very well be of the center of Urbino, with its palace facing the cathedral with the *piazza maggiore* between. Writing in a fiercely competitive age of unremitting contests for dominance, Francesco di Giorgio identifies *città, fortezze e castelli* (not temples) as the chief architectural loci of a prince's power.

But what about the ethical component of *virtus* which, after all, is where the English word "virtue" comes from? Vitruvius advocates honesty and high-mindedness in his architect, but such qualities, for him, are not linked to *virtus*, and his use of the word appears to be without ethical content.⁹⁹ Effectiveness is the common denominator linking the *virtus* of the emperor and of Hercules, the "virtues" of building materials and machines, and the "virtue" of architecture itself. Success is the measure of effectiveness: desirable of course, even admirable, but not normally linked to moral goodness.

Yet the Latin word *virtus* was also the word Romans used to translate the Greek word *aretê*—innate excellence in general, including ethical integrity. Romans' increasing contact with the Greek world appears to have played a role in expanding the semantic field of *virtus* from the military into the ethical realm.¹⁰⁰ One of the principal agents of that expansion was Vitruvius's contemporary Cicero, who translated many Greek philosophical works for a Latin-reading public.¹⁰¹ The project was not disinterested.

It is well known that Cicero was extremely ambitious politically. But in republican Rome, a successful military career was the prerequisite for a political one, and the road to political eminence was, without exception, via a reputation for military *virtus*. Cicero, a self-made man, orator, and intellectual who had had a less than stellar military career, was unlikely to rise to prominence in the usual way. Yet if he wanted to succeed in public life, he still had to be seen as a man who possessed *virtus*. His tactic, to make a long story short, was not so much to redefine *virtus* as to redefine the arena of its deployment—to redefine war, in other words.

His detection of the Catilinarian conspiracy, in which Catiline and his supporters had attempted to overthrow the Republic, gave him his window of opportunity. When this great public service was duly acknowledged by the Roman senate with honors traditionally awarded for military success, Cicero hastened to proclaim that if Pompey the Great's *virtus* had defeated foreign enemies, his (Cicero's) war was not against the armed barbarian but against decadence, madness, and vice itself.[102] The Republic had been saved by his *virtus*, he boasted, and to the end of his career he compared his defeat of Catiline with Rome's greatest military victories.[103]

In 1339, just ten years before Petrarch revived the ancient Roman ideal of military *virtus* with his *De viris illustribus*, Ambrogio Lorenzetti completed his so-called allegory of good government painted on three walls of the Sala dei Nove in the Palazzo Pubblico in Siena as a celebration of the communal ideal and a warning against its enemies. As discussed in chapter 1, the ideal celebrated there was the Common Good brought into existence by the built fabric and the shared public spaces of the well-governed city represented on the east wall of the room. On the west wall, opposite, you see the devastation wrought by the commune's archenemy, the self-interest demonized as one-man rule.

It would be easy, but both hasty and inaccurate, to point complacently to the east wall of the Sala dei Nove as the "virtue of architecture" in its medieval incarnation. First of all, it is well known that the terms "architect" and "architecture" were not current at the time, for building activity in the medieval commune, initiated collectively by communal governments, was carried out and controlled collectively through a tightly regulated and cumbersome guild structure in which master builders (not yet "architects") in charge of building sites deferred to the collective will of corporations.[104] And if the terms *architectus* and *architectura* ceased to be current with the eclipse of the Roman world, so too did the term *virtus*—*virtus*, that is to say, as virtue-in-general: the military *virtus* already discussed at some length, but especially *virtus* as the moral excellence equivalent to the "virtue" signified by the Greek word *aretê*.[105]

Thus, in Lorenzetti's allegory, the "goodness" of *buon governo* is nowhere shown to be dependent on *virtus* or virtue as such. In this complex narrative, the rule of Siena by the Sienese is presented as *Buon Governo* itself, figured in the imposing bearded man who appears at the right of the north wall of the room, wearing black and white, Siena's heraldic colors. The superhuman female figures on whose interaction good government is shown to depend are all carefully labeled in gold letters: wisdom, justice, concord, peace, fortitude, prudence, magnanimity, temperance, and then justice once again, on the far right. Above the bearded man's head fly three more women, winged and partially disembodied: faith, hope, and charity, the three theological virtues.

My point is that, as Erwin Panofsky demonstrated eighty years ago, the Middle Ages acknowledged only multiple, individual virtues: the cardinal ones of temperance, fortitude, prudence, and justice; the theological ones of faith, hope, and charity.[106] These plural virtues were represented as women, which is how they appear in the Lorenzetti frescoes, although the artist has swelled their conventional ranks somewhat by the addition of wisdom, magnanimity, concord, and peace. In the Christian Middle Ages, God was the only (unrepresentable) embodiment of virtue in general. That is why, in this context, it would be inappropriate to ask about the "virtue of architecture."

What you could say, however, is that just as virtues of all kinds, and not a single *virtus*, contribute to good government in this brilliantly imagined scene, so does the city brought into being by the common good depend not on the virtue of architecture but on the multiple virtues of many different trades and *crafts*: something that Lorenzetti is at pains to demonstrate in his rendering of the well-governed city on the east wall of the Sala dei Nove. Nobody in Italy was reading Vitruvius yet.

Petrarch, the so-called father of humanism, did a few years later, as discussed at length in chapter 1, and so did Leon Battista Alberti some eighty years after that.

Alberti, a prominent member of the humanist lineage founded by Petrarch, was an illegitimate orphan and a personal victim of the vicissitudes of fortune.[107] His preoccupation with *virtù* appears to have preceded his interest in architecture and may even have decided it. One of the things *virtù* was for Alberti—the main thing, in fact—was the combative quality of will demanded by the continual struggle to overcome *fortuna*: the quality needed to determine one's own fate, in other words. The prologue he wrote for his *Della famiglia* of about 1430 leaves no doubt that his model was, as Petrarch's had been, Roman military *virtus*.

Harking back to Italy's imperial past, Alberti writes, "Can it be said that our marvelous, boundless empire, our dominion over all peoples obtained through our Latin virtues, acquired through our industry and might, was granted us by Fortune? Shall we say that we are indebted to Fortune for what we acquired through *virtù*?"[108] As Alberti tells it, the loss of empire was the direct result of a failure of *virtù*. For him, its recovery is simply a question of willpower. "We must deem *virtù* sufficient for accomplishing the greatest and most sublime deeds, for creating mighty empires, gaining the highest praise and eternal fame and glory. We must not doubt that *virtù* is as easy to acquire as anything else, provided we desire and cherish it."[109] What, you may well ask, is this sort of thing doing in the introduction to a work on the family?

As his admirers never tire of pointing out, Alberti was good at everything—*the* original universal man of the Renaissance.[110] This view, first popularized by Jacob Burckhardt in the nineteenth century, is based on the image Alberti himself promulgated in the tireless self-praise of his allegedly anonymous *Vita*, the third-person autobiography he wrote in 1438 at the age of 34.[111] According to this autobiography, he was "devoted to the proper and skillful handling of arms, horses and musical instruments, as well as to literature ... and all recondite and difficult knowledge [and] embraced with diligence and thought every art that brings glory."[112] Aware, no doubt, of the link between *virtus* and horses, he places particular stress on his horsemanship and makes a point of mentioning his "skillful handling of arms" while adding that "as a youth he excelled in military exercises." Nonetheless, there is no disguising the fact that Alberti was not a soldier. There is no record of any military engagement fought or won, as there assuredly would have been had any existed. That time-tested path to glory, victory in the field, is the one accomplishment that cannot be numbered among Alberti's countless successes.

His homologue in this is Cicero, who as we just saw had not cut much of a figure on the battlefield either. Indeed, as Martin McLaughlin has noted, Cicero was at the top of Alberti's personal canon of classical authors, as he had been of Petrarch's.[113] A copy of Cicero's *Brutus*, a work Alberti especially admired, became something of a *livre de chevet* in which, over the years, he recorded the births and deaths of family members, as you might in a family Bible.[114] That eloquence is at least the equal in *virtus* of military prowess, if indeed not its superior, is something of a leitmotif in that work, for while the study of eloquence can improve the judgment required in military operations, Cicero argues at one point, no one has ever been made an orator by his success on the battlefield.[115]

Cicero's tactic had been to relocate the arena of *virtus* from the battlefield, where he had been a failure, to the floor of the Roman senate, where he was a success. Alberti's tactic is similar. In his prologue to *Della famiglia*, he takes the prodigious capital accumulated by the *virtus* of Roman world conquerors and reinvests it, as it were, in the family home, where education for a life of *virtù*, imparted by the family, supplies the knowledge essential for its deployment.

Thus, in one of his gloomier dinner pieces called *Fatum et fortuna*, written around the same time as *Della famiglia* but in Latin, a philosopher relates a dream vision of the hardships entailed in navigating the turbulent river of life.[116] Desperate swimmers can save themselves by climbing aboard one of the boats Alberti calls *Imperia* which translators render variously as "Empires" or "States": which is to say, by participating in public life. But the drowning man's surest *planche de salut* is, quite literally, a plank—a *tabula* in Latin. As Alberti certainly knew, *tabulae* can also be writing tablets, books, and paintings. Indeed the name he gives to the life-saving planks of his fable is *bonae artes*—the "good arts" which, according to some translators, are the liberal arts; according to others, the "useful" or "noble" arts. The point of Alberti's story is that knowledge—particularly "useful," active knowledge—supplies more of the *virtus* needed for life's struggle than anything else. He would go on to promote precisely such knowledge in his books on sculpture, painting, and architecture.

His *On the Art of Building*, the treatise discussed at length in chapter 3, was also written in Latin. Not unexpectedly, a survey of how Alberti uses the word *virtus* in this work turns up much on the *virtus* of learning, as for instance one passage where he insists that almost as much care be devoted to the construction of the family home as to the cultivation of *virtus*, since the home is the incubator of "noble studies."[117] Knowledge of "noble disciplines" is essential for architects, whose *virtus*, as mentioned earlier, is declared to have won more victories than the command of any general.[118] Christian *virtus*, also allied to learning, is likewise of a combative nature, as when temples are called the battleground for *virtus* against vice.[119]

And the "virtue of architecture"? In one important passage, Alberti is explicit in naming Roman building an extension of Roman military *virtus* and of the *virtutes* bestowed by Roman conquest.[120] That, he insists, is why Roman architecture is to be taken as exemplary. Alberti often gave Vitruvius short shrift in his treatise, but he was closer to his Roman predecessor than he cared to admit, notably in the *virtus* they both claimed for an architect's knowledge. Not surprisingly against this background, indeed predictable to the point of inevitability, is Alberti's very first project as a practicing architect.

Writing of the Montefeltro-Malatesta wedding of 1475, the chronicler Gaspare Broglio declared the Arch of Augustus at Rimini through which Federico da Montefeltro and his daughter entered the city "one of the most beautiful in Italy."[121] Some 25 years earlier, Alberti had taken this same triumphal arch as the model for the façade of San Francesco in Rimini, the medieval church Sigismondo Pandolfo Malatesta, lord of the city, commissioned him to remodel as a dynastic monument—the church at the city center that since the nineteenth century has been known as the Tempio Malatestiano.[122] The triumphal arch is generally considered a brilliant choice of architectural motif, one that itself would become a model for generations of architects to come. It was Alberti's first exploration of it, and was, at the time, completely original—a choice entirely without precedent, which he would elaborate further some years later in the façade of Sant'Andrea in Mantua.[123] A finely judged choice indeed, but not just of a formal motif, as Alberti, learned humanist partisan of Roman *virtus*, would have grasped better than anyone.

The Arch of Augustus at Rimini had been built at the eastern edge of the city at the end of the civil wars in 27 BCE, the year

Augustus became Rome's first emperor.[124] It was built, that is to say, during precisely the triumphal period Vitruvius evokes in the address with which he begins *De architectura*: "When your divine mind and power, Imperator Caesar, were seizing command of the world and all your enemies had been crushed by your invincible *virtus* ..." Every triumphal arch celebrated *virtus*, of course, but the one at Rimini did so with special emphasis.

There is another Roman monument in Rimini, the so-called bridge of Tiberius, begun by Augustus at the end of his reign in 14 CE, a fine, five-arched stone structure that still crosses the Marecchia River to lead westward out of the city.[125] As Sigismondo's loyal retainer Gaspare Broglio recalls in his chronicle, between the arch and the bridge, the center of Rimini had been, as it were, the birthplace of empire where, after crossing the Rubicon, Julius Caesar mobilized his troops and coordinated his seizure of power.[126]

Hence, by taking the triumphal motif of the Arch of Augustus as a template for his design, what Alberti's project did was to refigure the medieval church of San Francesco as a monument to Roman *virtus*, specifically (and indeed paradigmatically) that of Caesar and Augustus, in order to celebrate the *virtù* of the city's lord, Sigismondo Pandolfo Malatesta. The reverse of Matteo de' Pasti's foundation medals (there were several) show the building, with its triumphal façade and the dome Alberti had originally planned for it. On the obverse, Sigismondo appears in profile, crowned, like Caesar, with laurel. Inside the church, in the chapel so called of the planets, on one of Agostino di Duccio's twelve zodiacal reliefs a giant crab hovers over an aerial view of Rimini, showing the city bounded by its two Roman monuments, the arch and the bridge, and dominated by an overscaled representation of Sigismondo's magnificent new castle, the Castel Sismondo. The enormous crab (Cancer) that floats above was Sigismondo's birth sign, but also Julius Caesar's, its presence here confounding the Malatesta lord's identity with that of his hero, and his hero's with the city over which their shared birth sign looms.

Like Ludovico Gonzaga and Federico da Montefeltro, Sigismondo was a condottiere, one of the most brilliant and daring of his day. His military prowess had astonished contemporaries

Leon Battista Alberti, Tempio Malatestiano, Rimini, begun 1450. Photo credit: Scala / Art Resource, NY.

Agostino di Duccio, *Cancer*, marble relief, chapel of the planets, 1449–1456, Tempio Malatestiano, Rimini. © Alinari Archives / Art Resource, NY.

from the time he first took to the field at the age of just thirteen to arrest the advance of papal troops against Rimini in September of 1430, a feat he repeated two years later with even more brio against Pope Eugenius IV's invading army after he (Sigismondo) succeeded his older brother Galeotto Roberto as lord of Rimini.[127]

The succession had been messy and was contested. Sigismondo and his two brothers, one older, one younger, were the illegitimate sons of Pandolfo Malatesta of Brescia, who died in 1427. Their uncle, Pandolfo's brother, Carlo Malatesta lord of Rimini, adopted the three orphaned boys, then aged fifteen, nine, and eight, who succeeded him when he in turn died without issue two years later in 1429. The papacy did not consider the succession legitimate, whence the repeated attempts to annex Riminese territory to the Papal States. Sigismondo's military resistance, together with his stubbornly haughty refusal to bend to papal fiat, nourished a vendetta that lasted through the reign of five popes and culminated in Pius II's vicious public condemnation of him at Rome in January of 1461. There Sigismondo was accused of, among other things, treachery, murder, horrific sexual crimes, and, worst of all, heresy.[128] A year later, the pope enjoined all the princes in Italy to unite in a crusade against the monster. Shortly afterward Pius had life-sized effigies of Sigismondo immolated on three separate pyres, one at St. Peter's, another on the Campidoglio, and a third in the Campo dei Fiori, in a macabre celebration of his canonization of the miscreant as a citizen of hell. Pius left a record of Sigismondo's "unspeakable crimes" in his *Commentaries*, pronouncing him "the worst of all men who have ever lived or ever will live, the shame of Italy and the disgrace of the age."[129] His condemnation had the desired effect of sealing the warlord's fate and ruining his reputation for centuries to come, but who can say, under the circumstances, how much of it was true?

But even Pius acknowledged Sigismondo's intelligence, his learning, his strength of character, and, above all, his military prowess.[130] When the project to remodel San Francesco was conceived in about 1450, a decade before his downfall, the warlord's star was at its zenith.[131] In 1455, the court poet Basinio da Parma celebrated Sigismondo's victories in the epic *Hesperis*, calling him a national hero.[132] A description of the remodeling of San Francesco concludes the work, where the church appears almost as if the last of Sigismondo's military successes—or at the very least, his victory monument which, with its triumphal façade, of course it was. Basinio calls this *mirabile Templum* the conquering hero's votive offering to the gods, confirmed in Sigismondo's dedication "to God immortal and the City" inscribed in Greek on panels fixed to both sides of the church.[133] The manuscript of *Hesperis* now in the Bodleian library at Oxford includes a well-known miniature of the *tempio* under construction: a monument to princely *virtù* but also, like so much else built for *signori* during those hectic decades, a project of legitimation.

If you adhere to the taxonomy laid down in book 5 of Alberti's *On the Art of Building*, Castel Sismondo, the eponymous castle its lord built against the western wall of Rimini between 1437 and 1446, was not the dwelling of a legitimate ruler, but the fortress of a tyrant who rules against the people's will.[134] The bristling defenses of his citadel, stronger on the city side than on the side facing outward toward the country, appear to confirm this, suggesting that Sigismondo's fear of insurgency by a hostile populace was greater than his fear of attack from external enemies.[135] Thus, on the evidence, while the castle was obviously an affirmation of Sigismondo's unassailable dominance, it was not, as Federico's palace at Urbino would be a generation later ("at the city center ... easy of access"), a declaration of legitimacy.[136]

At Rimini, the legitimating role was assigned to the church of San Francesco, first built in 1259 and adopted as a family church by the Malatesta at the end of the thirteenth century, after they consolidated control of what had been an independent commune. Family members were buried there from that time forward.[137] Contested by the papacy, Sigismondo's accession in 1432 had not been smooth. Moreover, as Marco Folin has pointed out, Sigismondo was neither a count nor a duke nor a king, which is to say, he had no proper title.[138] On what did his authority rest? What or who gave him the right to rule? The *tempio* was his answer. Taking its triumphal façade from the Arch of Augustus at the eastern entrance to the city, and its arcaded flanks from the arches of the Roman bridge to the west, Alberti's genius was to wrap San Francesco in an austere mantle of *romanitas* that not only gave the old family church the dignity of an ancient mausoleum, but also made it, in a sense, an analogue of the city itself. Its emphasis on dynastic succession gave legitimacy to Sigismondo's disputed inheritance. Because of this, and thanks to the *virtus* he shared with Caesar, the city rightly belonged to him. There was no arguing with the solemn grandeur of the temple façade, with the imperial pedigree it actively called forth, or indeed with the self-justifying Latin inscription, crisply chiseled in elegant Roman capitals onto the cool Istrian stone of the frieze: SIGISMUNDUS PANDULFUS MALATESTA FECIT ANNO GRATIAE MCCCCL. The legend declaring that Sigismondo Malatesta "made this" in 1450 is repeated in smaller letters over the door and in various locations inside the church.

Alberti, who died in 1472, was still alive when Antonio Averlino, better known as Filarete, wrote his treatise on architecture between 1461 and 1464. It was the second architectural treatise, after Alberti's, since Vitruvius, but the first written in the vernacular. Filarete's case is especially relevant to the issues raised in this chapter, for as everyone knows the pseudonym "Filarete" means "lover of virtue." "Such as it is," Filarete writes of his book in its dedicatory preface, "take it not as written by Vitruvius nor by other worthy architects, but as by your virtue-loving architect [*come dal tuo filareto architetto*], Antonio Averlino the Florentine."[139] But does Filarete love *aretê* or *virtus*? The answer takes a little unraveling.

As will soon be obvious, what Filarete in fact professed to love was indeed *virtù*—full-strength Roman-style manliness. But because of the pseudonym, you are encouraged to believe (as indeed most architects who are aware of Filarete still like to think) that what he loves is ethical integrity. Thus, for Filarete who in fact loves *virtù* while claiming to love *aretê*, Roman *virtus* and Greek *aretê* have become essentially the same thing.

The pseudonym "Filarete" was bestowed on him by the eminent scholar Francesco Filelfo, his Hellenist friend at the court of Milan where both were employed.[140] And for Filelfo, the terms *aretê* and *virtus* were interchangeable, at least as he deploys them in an epigram he wrote for the architect around 1465 entitled *Ad Antonium Averlinum philaretum architectum*.[141] The first two lines read:

*Philarete Antonii, studium virtutis et archi-
Tecturae, danda est Gloria prima tibi.*[142]

"High praise is yours, *areté*-loving Antonio, for devotion to *virtus* and architecture." In addition to the implied equivalence of *areté* and *virtus*, particularly arresting here is the echo of the phrase *studium virtutis* with Vitruvius's declaration of his attachment to Caesar in his first preface, where he says he was devoted to Caesar's *virtus* (*eius virtutis studiosus*) as well as to Caesar's memory (*studium ... in eius memoria*) after his death.[143] Further, even as Vitruvius says that his knowledge of architecture was what made him known to Caesar (*eo fueram notus*) and bound him to Caesar's *virtus*, so, further along in his epigram, Filelfo has Filarete "*bene notus*" by "*dux Franciscus Sphortia*." Filarete knew Latin, but not very well. It was the immensely learned Filelfo who helped him read *De architectura*, whose first preface is reflected in these lines.[144]

Filarete wrote his treatise on architecture for Francesco Sforza, who of course is the "Franciscus Sphortia" Filelfo here casts as Caesar to Filarete's Vitruvius. Sforza was a condottiere (again) who seized Milan by force in 1450, overthrowing the existing Ambrosian Republic, so called, which had made a doomed attempt to restore communal government at Milan after the last Visconti duke, Filippo Maria died without an heir in 1447.[145] Sforza's sole claim to the dukedom rested on a tenuous connection through his marriage to Bianca Maria Visconti, Filippo Maria's illegitimate daughter. It was a claim, in other words, strictly without legal foundation, which made him perhaps the least legitimate among the *signori* of questionable legitimacy discussed in these pages.[146] Sixty years later, Machiavelli, who begins *The Prince* by distinguishing between hereditary and "new" principalities, would single out Sforza as the paradigm of a "completely new" prince, writing further that "Francesco, using the right means, and by his own great *virtù* from being a private citizen became duke of Milan."[147]

Filarete's friend Filelfo had been a court humanist at Milan since 1439 when he entered the service of the then duke, Filippo Maria Visconti.[148] Famously adept at negotiating the tortuous corridors of power, Filelfo nimbly transferred his immense erudition to the service of the Sforza warlord more or less immediately after Visconti's death. His prodigious literary output was particularly rich in philosophical works, but it also included poetry—ecstatic Latin encomia, written in the classical style, addressed to virtually every known person of importance, among them Francesco Sforza to whom he dedicated the entire collection in the mid 1450s.[149] "Your poet Francesco Filelfo honors you, Francesco Sforza, with gifts worthy of your rank," he begins; "kings are praised and princes honored because of their lofty deeds. Among these men your noble Sforzan *virtus* gleams and seeks the highest stars."[150]

When Filippo Maria Visconti died in 1447, the first action taken by the Milanese populace was to tear down the Visconti castle, the Castello di Porta Giovia, menacing emblem of a reviled tyrant's rule that had dominated the city from its northwestern edge for nearly a hundred years. Afterward, liberated citizens of the newly founded Ambrosian Republic used the stones from the demolished castle for the cathedral under construction, and to repair the city wall.[151] Francesco Sforza took the city three years later. Filelfo recalls these tumultuous times in his ode "To Francesco Sforza: The City of Milan Narrates the Fall of the Republic and the Triumph of Sforza," where he writes how the city itself pours forth its thanks to the heaven-sent liberator who freed it from the tyranny of the mob.[152] Similarly, in what he calls a "hymn for Sforza's triumphant entry into Milan," he writes, "Now true liberty has been instituted for the people. Gone is the arrogance of the cowardly plebs, the reign of terror and crime and rape. ... Our hero, the noble Francesco Sforza lifted our hearts and bodies from the foul disease deep within the city."[153] Sforza, Filelfo continues, is an Apollo who "spreads his ruddy rays, looks down on us with shining eyes ... restores the downcast with his sweet light and refreshes the weary."[154]

Before taking Milan, Francesco Sforza had sworn to the Milanese he was holding hostage in a cruelly protracted blockade that he would never rebuild the hated citadel if they accepted him as lord. In July 1450, just four months after entering the city he had at last starved into submission—a "heaven-sent liberator" distributing cartloads of bread—Sforza went back on his word. It was to work on rebuilding the castle that Filarete arrived at Milan from Rome a little over a year later, in September 1451, where "Filarete's tower" (destroyed in the sixteenth century, rebuilt in the early twentieth) became the dominant feature of the southeast entrance wing of the fortress, thereafter known as the Castello Sforzesco.[155] Before arriving at Milan, Filarete had been known principally as a sculptor, author of the famous bronze doors of St. Peter's and also of the very first of the countless Renaissance copies of the bronze equestrian statue of Marcus Aurelius in Rome.[156] He was also a medalist, one of the earliest fifteenth-century practitioners of the art, who specialized in portrait medals of the Roman emperors. The reverse of one he made of Julius Caesar has its subject armed, on horseback, and includes an image of Caesar's birth sign, an oversized crab, under the horse's belly.[157]

The central theme of Filarete's treatise on architecture is the project for a city, named Sforzinda for his patron. This alone sets him apart from his forerunners. Although Vitruvius and Alberti had both dealt extensively with urban issues, neither had made it their principal aim, as Filarete did, to build (on paper) a single city from scratch: the first ideal city of the Renaissance, it has been claimed.[158]

Also completely new is the image of virtue Filarete presented in his work—one he says he took considerable pains to devise, and which is unequivocal in confirming the essentially warlike nature of the *aretê* for which this *filareto architetto* was professing his love. He first describes the figure in book 9 of his treatise as a "beautiful invention" meant to stand at the door of the Ducal Palace of his imagined Sforzinda.[159] It appears again, with images this time, in book 18 as a bronze statue standing on the summit of the House of Virtue, a gigantic building Filarete refers to interchangeably as "Casa della *virtù*" and "Casa Areti."[160]

His *Virtù* is a winged man in full armor, his bare head haloed in a sunburst, his feet balanced on the point of a diamond. Adopted as a family emblem by Francesco Sforza's condottiere father,

Mucio Antendolo Sforza, the diamond, as Filarete explains in another context, ranks first as the hardest, most intransigent and most transparently "virtuous" in the hierarchy of stones: *diamante* in Italian, in Latin *adamanta*—from *adamas*, the Greek word for "invincible."[161] "A figure of Fame flies above," he writes, expressing some pride in his invention and claiming—quite rightly, as we saw earlier—that to represent Virtue *in general* as a single figure was an entirely original undertaking at the time. Filarete reminds his reader that, until now, there had only been multiple, individual virtues: the four cardinal virtues, the three theological ones.

Thus, without precedent, has our virtue-loving architect figured the object of his affection as an armed man crowned with glory. Relevant in this context is how, in book 1 of his treatise, Filarete idealized the architect's relation to his *padrone* as the intimate, sexual bond between an uxorious lord and his submissive wife, with the architect, famously, becoming the "mother" of designs fathered by his (her?) lord and master.[162]

In the real life hyperbolized here, the architect of course is Filarete himself, and the lord is the condottiere Francesco Sforza, who is also the model for the iron man at the top of Filarete's Casa Areti.[163] His head, with its sunburst, recalls Francesco Filelfo's encomiastic portrayal a decade earlier of Sforza as an Apollo who "spreads his ruddy rays, looks down on us with shining eyes," and adds to the evidence for collaborative teamwork between the man of letters and his architect friend.[164] If you look closely at Filarete's image, and recall the bald-pated condottiere's official portraits, you will see the resemblance.

Also hyperbolized by Filarete as sexual intimacy is the emerging status of the court artist whose ability is now called *virtù* as well.[165] The artist's *virtù* is a gift, inborn talent rather than skill, whose deployment depends on precisely that one-to-one relation between artist and prince Filarete eroticizes, instead of a craftsman's rather less glamorous task of negotiating the cumbersome medieval structure of guilds and corporations, which indeed both Filarete and his prince were busy trying to circumvent at Milan.[166]

Moreover, the pool of honey at the feet of Filarete's iron man is a direct reference to how the prince should reward artistic *virtù*, something he discusses in some detail elsewhere in his treatise.[167]

The figure of *Virtù*, from Filarete, treatise on architecture. Biblioteca Nazionale, Florence, Codex Magliabechiano II.I.140, fol. 143r (detail). By permission of the Ministero della Cultura—Biblioteca Nazionale Centrale, Firenze.

The matter, dear to his heart, was made explicit in the personal motto that appears on the reverse of the portrait medal he devised for himself, where the legend reads UT SOL AUGET APES SIC NOBIS COMODA PRINCEPS: "As the sun feeds the bee, so the prince lavishes his favor on us."[168] Filarete may very well have had in mind the princely favor Vitruvius says he enjoyed, claiming in his first preface that his gratitude for the benefits Augustus bestowed on him was why he began to write *De architectura*.[169] Vitruvius used precisely the same word—*commoda*—to refer to gratifications received as Filarete does in the motto on his medal.[170]

What interests me is how the interdependence of princely and artistic *virtù*, so clearly set out in Filarete's image, brings into focus the politics of antique revival and Vitruvius's role in it. The ancient ways of building Filarete draws from Vitruvius, and his scorn for what he calls *la maniera gotica*, are not just an expression of a stylistic preference for "ancient" over "modern." They are also a rejection of the cumbersome corporate bureaucracy that inhibited the free play of *virtù*—both the artist's and that of his prince.[171] The ancients, Vitruvius seemed to attest, had not been hampered in this way.

As Filarete describes it, the sprawling Casa Areti includes not only the huge coliseum-like structure drawn in section and in elevation in the margins of his manuscript pages,[172] but also a temple, a theater, and a house for the architect, one "Onitoan Noliaver" which is an anagram for Antonio Averlino—Filarete himself.[173] One significantly recurring motif in this mammoth construction of princely and artistic *virtù* is Filarete's obsessive use of what he calls "figures in the place of columns," which support the bronze roof of the uppermost story of the House of Virtue. Over them towers the figure of Virtue just described.

"Figures in the place of columns" reappear on three levels as the internal supports for the dome of the Temple of Virtue, as well as paired up on two levels of a portico outside the same temple. At the top of the theater, for which there is no drawing, the roof, Filarete writes, is "supported by columns in the shape of human figures and made like certain peoples who had rebelled and were then forced into subjugation. They were made in this form in order to increase contempt for them."[174] Vitruvius's lesson concerning the role of caryatids and Persian prisoners as the architectural sign and very paradigm of *virtus* has been taken enthusiastically to heart.

In addition to the armies of such figures deployed throughout the Casa Areti of book 18, Filarete also uses extensive caryatid/Persian underpinning in two monuments he describes elsewhere in his treatise. Both are monuments to one "King Zogalia." In book 14, one of them has the king seated on a throne balanced on a sphere at the summit of an obelisk.[175] The obelisk itself with its sphere and supporting lions is a fairly close rendering of the Vatican obelisk at Rome, as it appeared before it was moved to the front of St. Peter's at the end of the sixteenth century. In Filarete's day, the bronze sphere at the top of the obelisk was thought to contain the ashes of Julius Caesar. The two ranks of human figures lifting the obelisk from below are, of course, Filarete's own addition to the assembly. There is no victory without evidence of submission.

King Zogalia reappears in book 21, fully armed this time, brandishing a sword, and sitting astride a rearing horse. This second statue stands on the top of a revolving tower clad in no fewer than five levels of "figures instead of columns."[176] John Spencer, Filarete's English translator, notes rather primly that this structure "is quite impractical and seems to serve no definite function in the city but to demonstrate the abilities of the architect."[177] Joint celebration of princely and architectural *virtù* could hardly be more flagrant. But who is King Zogalia?

In book 14, just over halfway through his treatise, excavation for the port of Sforzinda turns up a long-buried, mysterious stone chest, discovered to contain an ancient so-called "Golden Book," written in Greek. In Filarete's story, it is the court scholar, one Iscofrance Notilento—an approximate anagram for Francesco da Tolentino which is to say the Hellenist Filelfo—who translates the book.[178] "I, King Zogalia … leave this treasure in your guardianship," it begins. "No one will ever be able to touch this treasure until there comes a man who will rise from a small principate and through his own *virtù* acquire a substantial kingdom. Because he will be magnanimous, his state will be at peace. He will have large buildings built."¹⁷⁹ Needless to say, the prophecy here is of the reign of Francesco Sforza.

King Zogalia is the ancient king of this very land where once flourished a magnificent city called Plusiapolis. The narrative continues with a history of Zogalia's dynasty—how his heroic father, "by *virtù* of battle and through celestial grace acquired the signoria," and so on.¹⁸⁰ The account is an instantly recognizable, if epically enhanced, history of the Sforza themselves and their rise to power, with "Zogalia" a rough anagram for Galeazzo, Francesco Sforza's eldest son and heir.

The Golden Book also contains accounts of the many splendid monuments and buildings in Plusiapolis, including the two just described, built under the direction of the virtuoso architect "Onitoan Noliaver" (Filarete), who forthwith takes these ancient models to rebuild them in the fictional present for the lord of Sforzinda. The role of the Golden Book in Filarete's treatise is to create a past that legitimates the present, in keeping with the practice, common in traditional societies, of invoking imperishability, autochthony, and the greatness of ancestors as justification for present claims.¹⁸¹ Filarete takes the tactic a step further, making the fictions of the Golden Book *identical* to his invented present. The principle of antiquity as legitimator, embedded in the stories about King Zogalia et al., is another impetus driving Filarete's argument for the virtue of architecture, and his preference for "ancient" over "modern."

As almost every commentator on the treatise has noted, Sforzinda is to a large extent identifiable with the real city of Milan.¹⁸² To this idealized Milan Filarete has given the name *Sforzinda*—"Sforza-town"—a city which is like Milan, only much better, thanks to the revival of ancient tradition through the tandem deployment of princely and architectural *virtù*. Thus Filarete's treatise lays out a picture of "Sforza-town" (Milan under Sforza rule) which demonstrates, hyperbolically of course, how *as* Sforza-town the city propitiates the common good.

But many people thought Sforza rule of Milan was doing just the opposite: that it was *undermining* the common good. Many—particularly the oligarchs of the Ambrosian Republic Sforza

Monument to King Zogalia, from Filarete, treatise on architecture. Biblioteca Nazionale, Florence, Codex Magliabechiano II.I.140, fol. 102v (detail). By permission of the Ministero della Cultura—Biblioteca Nazionale Centrale, Firenze.

Revolving tower with equestrian monument, from Filarete, treatise on architecture. Biblioteca Nazionale, Florence, Codex Magliabechiano II.I.140, fol. 172r (detail). By permission of the Ministero della Cultura—Biblioteca Nazionale Centrale, Firenze.

overthrew in 1450—contended that the condottiere's claim to the dukedom was founded on nothing but raw ambition and brute force; that he had no legal right to rule the city. For his numerous critics, Francesco Sforza was a usurping warlord.[183]

As Gary Ianziti has shown, one consequence, among others, was the new regime's mobilization of literary and scholarly talent, charged with generating propaganda in praise of Sforza and defending him as the strongman who saved Milan from certain collapse into chaos. In 1450, Francesco Filelfo began a verse epic called the *Sforziad* (or *Sphortias*), a heroic chronicle in verse of the warlord's military triumphs, modeled on the *Iliad*, which he followed up with an attempt to write a prose history of the life and deeds of Francesco Sforza, never completed.[184] "I have learned to repay my benefactors," Filelfo wrote to Giovanni Simonetta, chancellor at the Sforza court, in January 1451, "by transforming them—to the best of my ability—from men into gods by conferring upon them the immortality that eternal praise and glory are wont to bestow."[185]

Between 1461 and 1463, Lodrisio Crivelli, Sforza's secretary and Filelfo's protégé, wrote *De vita rebusque gestis Francisci Sfortiae* (On the life and deeds of Francesco Sforza).[186] With no possible appeal to constitutional or dynastic legitimacy, Crivelli's book justified the condottiere's claim to Milan on the grounds of sheer personal merit; on the grounds, exclusively, of the Sforza lord's *virtus*, which, so went the argument, had *earned* him the right to rule. Recent precedents for this kind of partisan historiography included Bartolomeo Facio's biography of Alfonso of Aragon (1455), for instance, and Giannantonio Campano's life of Braccio da Montone (1458), discussed earlier in chapter 3, works which, according to Ianziti, Crivelli subverts to his own purpose. Where Campano, for instance, wrote of the clash between *virtus* and *fortuna* as abstract forces, Crivelli has *virtus* triumph as the very person of Francesco Sforza.

Filarete, who wrote his treatise during the same years as Crivelli did his biography, presented architecture—through the statue, of course, but also through Sforzinda and Plusiapolis and the staggering gigantism of their buildings—as the ultimate representation of the Sforza lord's *virtù* and thus the ultimate justification of his claim to Milan.[187] Filarete, in other words, was part of the same propaganda machine as Filelfo and Crivelli. Filelfo's epigram of 1465, addressed to Filarete shortly after he completed his treatise and casting the "virtue-loving" architect as Vitruvius to Francesco Sforza's Caesar, points to precisely this, while revealing Filarete's intentions as a mirror of Vitruvius's own: to present architecture as the legitimator of conquest and consolidator of the conqueror's seizure of command.

5   The Architectonic Book

On the one hand you had Filelfo's *Sforziad*, on the other Filarete's Sforzinda. Given the context just discussed, there can be no doubting that the collaboration between the Florentine architect and his learned friend which, in the early 1460s, produced the second Renaissance treatise on architecture, after Alberti's, was shaped by the same project of legitimizing Sforza rule at Milan as the one that underwrote Filelfo's *Sforziad*, Lodrisio Crivelli's *Vita*, and other works of humanistic propaganda with similar aims. Any attempt to make sense of the work Vasari dismissed in his life of Filarete as "perhaps the stupidest book ever written" without taking these intentions into account is bound to fall short of the mark.[1]

In 1450, Francesco Sforza seized Milan, defeating the Ambrosian Republic, so-called, founded three years earlier when Filippo Maria Visconti died without an heir. Initially, the Republic was an oligarchy ruled by its founding elites, but elections in 1449, won by the popular faction, ushered in a government of common people whose leading members were a weaver, a craftsman, and a notary.[2] The transition was, to say the least, not smooth, resulting in violent confrontation and ongoing civil unrest, greatly exacerbated by the famine that resulted from Francesco Sforza's blockade of the city.

Filarete would not arrive at Milan until 1451, but Filelfo, who had lived there since 1439 as a dependent on Visconti patronage, suffered the distress of those years keenly and at first hand. Choleric at the best of times, his rage against the Republic, especially the "plebs" he said had enslaved it, is recorded in his *Odes*:

> Look, the rabble, girt with their moneybelts, have taken over our noble magistracies—the chicken farmer, the auctioneer, the adulterer, the pimp. The perjurer and his accomplice now put on airs. What should I praise of theirs? ... If the illustrious nobility crushes the incompetent plebs, how strong and eloquent my Muse will make my poems. ... With the plebs I'll have nothing to do.[3]

Underlying Filelfo's invective was acute anxiety over the loss of the aristocratic patrons who were his only source of income. Unlike Alberti, for instance, he had no other. Even the famine caused by the Sforza blockade he blamed on the popular government:

> No tyranny is more vile that that of the feckless plebs and the angry rabble. ... Look, the people are rioting. The repeated cries "Bread! Bread!" strike the very poles of the earth. Death to the scoundrels. Away with false liberty, more evil than any tyrant, more cruel than death and more savage than the dog who guards the underworld.[4]

Filelfo's horror at the collapse of civil order that was the result, as he saw it, of rule by the very dregs of society throws his enthusiasm for Francesco Sforza as a "heaven-sent liberator" into sharp relief, and with it Filarete's wildly fanciful representation, discussed in the previous chapter, of the warlord as *Virtù* triumphant, standing atop the monumental *casa della virtù* in book 18 of his treatise on architecture. In its attempt to restore the commune of pre-Visconti times, the Ambrosian Republic had overturned a monarchical hierarchy that had been the norm at Milan and elsewhere for over a hundred years. And monarchy was not simply a political norm—an arbitrary convention of habitual usage. As many, including Filelfo himself, would argue, one-man rule was the only *natural* form of government. Which, of course, condemned the rule of many as *un*natural.

In the mid 1460s, Filelfo translated Xenophon's fourth-century BCE *Cyropaedia*, a work on the education of a prince, from Greek into Latin, and dedicated it to Pope Paul II.[5] The dedication is a vigorous plea for monarchical rule as the sole defense against political instability. Only through Julius Caesar, the most virtuous man nature ever produced, Filelfo claims, had the ravages of civil war been brought to an end. Modern exemplars of one-man rule include his former patrons Filippo Maria Visconti and the "peacemaker" Francesco Sforza, as well as his (Filelfo's) dedicatee, the pope himself. The rule of one is both natural and necessary, he continues, drawing on ancient Greek sources for his argument. Is not there just one God who rules the cosmos, one authority—the father's—in the household? Is not the body ruled by the soul, and the soul by the mind? Are not all numbers generated from the number one?[6] Kingship is grounded in mathematical certainty.

Such arguments became commonplace in the decades that followed. The figure of the *paterfamilias* as a political paradigm is explicit in Alberti's last work, *De ichiarchia* (On ruling the household) of about 1470, where he argues that the city, like a household, is best governed by a single ruler "with an authority that enables him to rule his fellow citizens in an honorable life and the ability to punish those who disobey the laws of the fatherland."[7] A decade later, Francesco Patrizi, bishop of Gaeta and Filelfo's former student, wrote a widely read and often reprinted work, *De regno et regis institutione* (On kingship and royal education), which enlarged on Filelfo's monarchic polemic and invoked justification, as Filelfo did, in the unitary rule of God in heaven, of the father over his household, of the mind over man, and so on. Man is called a *parvus mundus*, or "small world," because mind rules the body just as God rules the world. Men are brutes, Patrizi observes, but for the rule of the mind.⁸ Brutish too (not to mention godless), but for the rule of one, is the body politic, for in cities ruled by many, there is sedition and intestine hatred, he writes, concluding that *naturale imperium unitas esse hominis*—unity is the natural form of sovereignty over men.⁹

A defense of natural hierarchy also appears in Francesco di Giorgio's second treatise of approximately the same date.¹⁰ Some years earlier, the drawing at the beginning of Francesco's first treatise of a boy as a city with a fortress on his head ("because the head rules the body") had made precisely the same point.¹¹

There is, of course, no question that Filarete's treatise was meant to celebrate one-man rule, or—at the very least—one man's rule. His political intentions far exceeded that single purpose, however, and resulted in a thoroughgoing architectural vindication of monarchic hierarchy, which needs to be seen against the recent memory of natural order overturned by three years of ill-fated republican rule. In the real built world, restoration began with Francesco Sforza's rebuilding of the Visconti *castello* at the northwestern edge of the city, torn down by the insurgent *popolo* when Filippo Maria Visconti died. As already noted, Sforza brought Filarete to Milan to work on its reconstruction, "the proudest and strongest castle existing on level terrain in the whole universe," according to the fifteenth-century Milanese historian Bernardino Corio.¹²

In the virtual reality of his treatise, Filarete's fable of restored order begins with Adam who, created by God in his own image, was the most beautiful man who ever lived. Adam was a giant, according to Filarete, for whom size, along with ornament, is a determinant of what he calls *qualità*. *Qualità*, like "qualities," could apply to classes of people and their social rank or to classes of objects and their relative value; or indeed, as Filarete presents it, to both at once. Through the consistent attachment of social rank to the "qualities" of objects, most notably the elements of architecture, Filarete builds a world in the image of a rightful hierarchy which, as John Onians has convincingly shown, is the unifying theme of the entire treatise.¹³

The giant Adam was of the very highest *qualità*. He was also the first builder, and his own body, in whose perfect proportions all of architecture is founded, became the first building when, as Filarete tells it, he was caught in a rainstorm and lifted his hands over his head to make a roof.[14] From this elemental model came the first huts, described much as Vitruvius describes them, for indeed *De architectura*—in the matter of huts, human proportions, and much else besides—provides Filarete with the warp into which he weaves his own highly idiosyncratic narrative.

It is well known that, according to Vitruvius, building originated when people were brought together around a fire to form a community whose members became the first hut-builders. This community reached its ultimate expression in architecture and the "certain calculations of symmetries" that guaranteed its perennity.[15] Fire is altogether absent from Filarete's treatise and plays no part at all in the genesis of the huts he describes. For him, these huts and architecture itself originate in Adam as of course does the entire human race. Architecture and people share a common ancestor; their "qualities" overlap. It is not surprising that Filarete omits the fire. His interest is to rank people in their proper order, not bring them together into what could all too easily turn into an uncontrollable mob. Adam stands at the pinnacle and origin of the desired hierarchy, rather as Francesco Sforza does, as *Virtù* personified at the top of the *casa della virtù*.[16]

Like Vitruvius, Filarete treats of three principal architectural orders: Doric, Ionic, and Corinthian, which Vitruvius called *genera* or "kinds."[17] For Filarete the orders are *qualità*, which he ranks, like men, according to size—large, medium, and small (*grandi, mezzani, piccoli*). *Grandi* refers to size, but also to status. In Italian *i grandi* are the members of the upper crust the French call *les grands*; aristocrats qualified in English as "grand" or "people of quality." Shuffling Vitruvius's taxonomy to suit his own ends, Filarete gives the name "Doric" to the largest and most ornate of the column orders—the one with the leafy capital conventionally known as "Corinthian"—and calls it Adam's column, because it is the tallest and finest of the three.[18] These grand, foliated Adamic columns are like *signori*, he writes in a later chapter and, just as lords need servants to support them, such columns must always stand at the tops of buildings, sustained below by the lesser *qualità*. "*Signori* need these kinds of persons in order to be lords," he explains.[19]

Elsewhere, as discussed earlier, statues of kings enthroned or on horseback crown impossibly overscaled monuments whose structural support consists of multiple tiers of what Filarete calls "figures in the place of columns." These, it is worth repeating, "are made like certain peoples who had rebelled and were then forced into subjugation. They were made in this form in order to increase contempt for them."[20]

Filarete measures men in heads, not in feet as Vitruvius did, "because the head is the handsomest and noblest member," and presents Adam's "most beautiful" head as the paradigm.[21] The same goes for columns, whose heads are their capitals. His Corinthian lookalike, the Adamic Doric, is nine heads high. The *mezzani* of eight heads in height he calls "Corinthian," giving this *qualità*, in his manuscript drawing, a somewhat less ornate but still recognizable Corinthian capital. The *piccoli* are his Ionic, the smallest and stockiest at seven heads, with capitals that do indeed look somewhat conventionally Ionic.[22] It is all rather confused and not a little confusing, but the rhetorical point is hard to miss.

Heads rule. Many portraits were drawn of Francesco Sforza, because he had a noble and handsome head, Filarete writes in a claim which surviving portraits might lead you to question.[23] When he shows the young lord (a stand-in for Sforza's heir, Galeazzo Maria) to whom he is giving lessons in how to draw a head, the exemplar that appears in the manuscript margin is the drawing of a laureate head which, given its appearance, you assume must be meant to be Caesar's.[24] Moreover, while for Vitruvius the Doric is male and the other two *genera* female, all three of Filarete's *qualità* are masculine. It is a man's world, with no room for women in its ranks.

The gathering around a fire that opens Vitruvius's primitive hut chapter derives from anthropologies of Greco-Roman origin.[25] Adam, of course, belongs to the Judeo-Christian tradition. His presence, as others have noted, adds a Christian dimension to Filarete's essentially classical aetiology.[26] But the need or desire to acknowledge the Christian world he lived in is, alone, not nearly

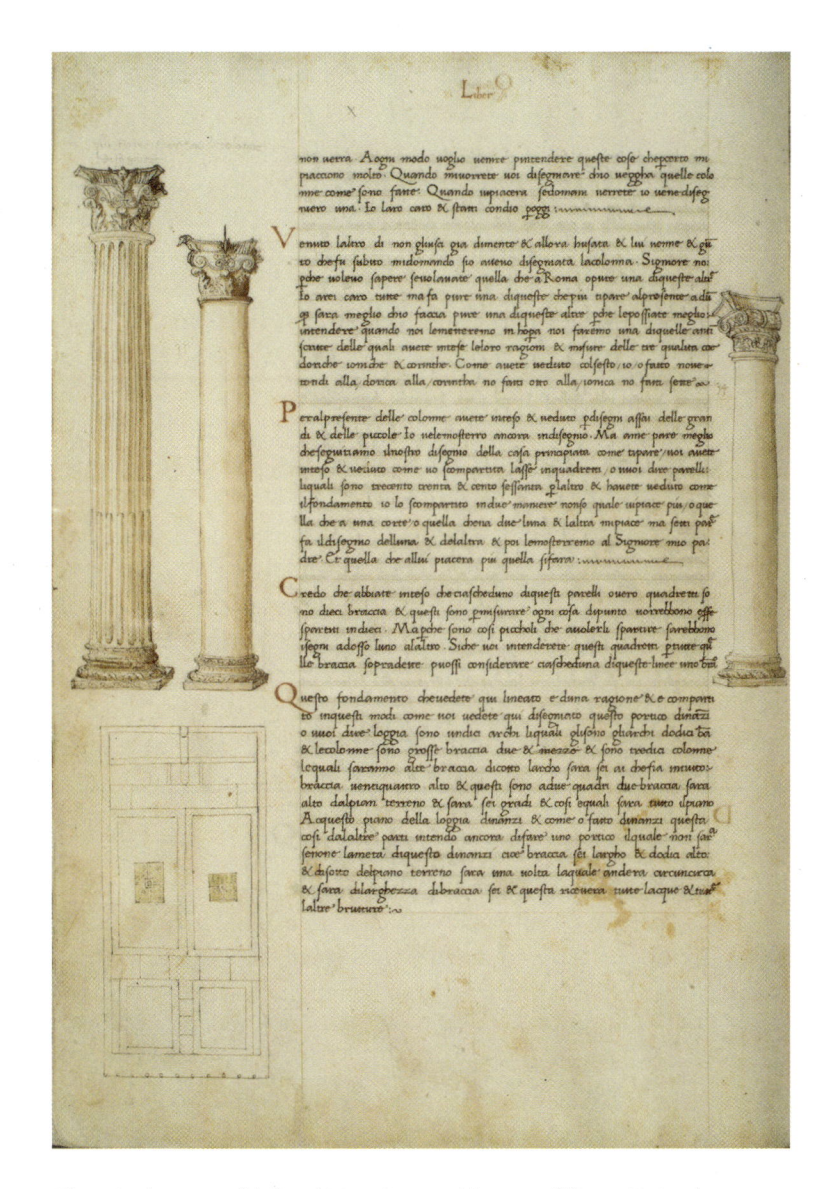

Filarete's columnar *qualità*, from his treatise on architecture. Biblioteca Nazionale, Florence, Codex Magliabechiano II.I.140, fol. 57v (left to right: Doric, Corinthian, Ionic in his nomenclature). By permission of the Ministero della Cultura—Biblioteca Nazionale Centrale, Firenze.

enough to explain the exalted position he confers on Adam at the summit of his socio-architectural hierarchy. This was, without a doubt, the first time Adam was made a contributor to a theory of architecture. It was not the first time he was called upon to underwrite an imperial agenda, however.

The emperor Frederick II Hohenstaufen (1194–1250), who built the triumphal Capua gate with its crowning *regium cubiculum* discussed in chapter 3, was a fervent exponent of imperialism on the Roman model.[27] He was also an implacable scourge of the communes, not only in the kingdom of Sicily where he ruled as absolute monarch, but also in the Italian north where his imperial forces regularly clashed with communal armies. His victory over the Lombards, cut to pieces at Cortenuova on 27 November 1237, became legendary, with the Milanese *carroccio*, its standard-bearing battle cart, seized as a trophy for display on the Capitol at Rome.[28]

The Constitutions of Melfi, laws governing the Kingdom of Sicily that Frederick promulgated as a self-styled "Augustus" in 1231, were especially concerned with preserving a strict social hierarchy.[29] In article 50 of its 107 clauses pertaining to public law, "Augustus" abolishes as illegal usurpation the performance of governmental functions by anyone elected by the people, ordaining that "throughout the kingdom there should be only those officials established by our majesty or by our command." Any commune ruled by elected officials he condemns to perpetual desolation, its men held forever as forced laborers and the elected officials themselves put to death.[30]

The prologue to this code of laws, also known as the *Liber Augustalis*, begins with Adam whom, the text declares, God made in his own image and likeness, "put in charge of all the other creatures ... and had crowned with a diadem of glory and honor."[31] Adam, in other words, was not only first man. He was also the first king—the first just world ruler before the fall. But fall Adam did, of course, which is why (following the logic at work here) lawgivers were created—"princes of nations ... through whom the license of crimes might be corrected. And these judges of life and death for mankind might decide ... how each man should have fortune, estate, and status."[32] Reflected in this is what Frances Yates called a form of Adam mysticism, which made every prince a prelapsarian Adam with a divine mandate to restore the earthly paradise Adam ruled before he sinned.[33]

Such Adam mysticism persisted in the following century and beyond, as for example in Dante's *De monarchia* of 1313, where the poet argues for the world monarchy of an emperor tasked with leading mankind back to the Eden of its Adamic origin.[34] Yates has suggested that the ideal of universal monarchy lived on, "if only as a rhetorical appendage," in Frederick II's spiritual descendants, tyrants like Sforza and the Medici who claimed to be the restorers of the golden age in their dominions.[35] Of this Filarete's Adamic rhetoric is a striking corroboration. The light Frederick II's imperial theology sheds on the treatise, especially on the role it assigns to Adam, makes it impossible not to see in the "ideal" city of Sforzinda the earthly paradise the architect imagines his prince—an Adam to his Eve—as having been mandated to restore. There, at the top of the *casa della virtù*, Sforza-as-*Virtù* stands balanced on the point of a diamond, ancestral emblem and gem of the very highest *qualità*—the stone, as I said, called *adamas* in Greek.[36]

Filarete dedicated the first version of his treatise to his patron Francesco Sforza in about 1464. The dedication survives, but the manuscript itself, destroyed in an Allied bombing in 1944, does not. Shortly thereafter, he dedicated a second version of the work to Piero de' Medici in Florence, enjoining his dedicatee to read or have read to him *questo architettonico libro*—"this architectonic book."[37]

Most readers—John Spencer, Filarete's English translator among them—have assumed this rather unusual turn of phrase to be the obvious equivalent of "book on architecture."[38] For me, however, the expression points to certain intentions implicit in the Vitruvianism of architectural theory in early Renaissance Italy—intentions which, as I have repeatedly insisted, are intrinsically political. If, to quote the American visionary architect Lebbeus Woods, "architecture is a political act," so too is its theory.[39] Beginning, of course, with Vitruvius.

Indeed, Vitruvius's is the first recorded use of the word "architectonic" in Latin. It appears in *De architectura*, book 9, on gnomonics—the construction of clocks, which is the second part of Vitruvius's tripartite rubric of architecture. It is a transliteration of the Greek *architektonikos*, a word that appears most frequently in Aristotle, who uses it mainly in nonarchitectural contexts to which I will return shortly. This is what Vitruvius writes at the beginning of book 9.

> The analemma is the pattern obtained from the course of the sun and discovered by observing the shadow of the gnomon as it lengthens to the solstice. It is by means of architectonic principles [*rationes architectonicas*] and the tracings of the compass that the analemma discloses how the universe operates.⁴⁰

Simply put, what Vitruvius is describing here is the two-dimensional projection of spherical solar order onto a flat surface in order to create the analemma or "face" of a sundial, with the analemma thus becoming a reflection of universal order. In the next paragraph, he goes on to assert that celestial order is in turn "architected" (*architectata est*) by the power of nature.⁴¹ Such natural powers are themselves (presumably) governed by "architectonic principles," which would therefore direct even the "architecting" activity of nature itself.

These passages appear to distill the very essence of that faith in the cosmic dimension of architecture generally taken as a key feature of orthodox Vitruvianism, as advanced by Rudolf Wittkower and his followers.⁴² But was crediting architects with cosmic agency Vitruvius's primary intention? I think not, at least not primarily.

Vitruvius wrote his treatise for Augustus Caesar, the first Roman emperor, whose very name Augustus, a name never before given to any human, was an epitome of divine order. I have argued elsewhere that the work's ultimate purpose was to show how architecture was the privileged means of giving the "divine" imperial power that now commanded the world real measurable extent through the buildings, gnomonics, and machines that together made Roman world dominion palpable and incontestable.⁴³ This world dominion, Vitruvius insists at the beginning of book 6, was itself decreed by the "divine mind."⁴⁴

Thus, to name as "architectonic" the principles that guide the projection of heavenly order onto the earthly realm in the construction of sun clocks is indeed potently metonymical, but not altogether as generally assumed. Heavenly order is, simultaneously and interchangeably, the order of Augustus and Rome, and its earthly deployment through the application of "architectonic principles" is the endowment of such principles with crucial political clout. And this, as a result, assigns an equally crucial political role to the person with knowledge of them and of how to apply them—*architecti scientia*, the knowledge of the architect.[45]

Knowledge is key. As Aristotle famously put it in the *Metaphysics*, the master craftsman he calls *architekton* is more estimable than the artisans over whom he exercises authority, because the *architekton* knows the reasons for doing things—superior in wisdom through his possession of *logos* and his knowledge of causes.[46] The artisans he names *cheirotechnai* or "hand-workers" are classified as mindless *things* whose mechanical activity is guided by the thought of a higher power.

The authority of thought, of reason, of knowledge, brings me to Aristotle's use of the adjective *architektonikos*, the Greek word transliterated by Vitruvius as "architectonic" in the passage just discussed.

To the "architectonic" arts, Aristotle writes in the *Metaphysics*, are attributed origins, causes, beginnings (*aitia, archai*).[47] Architectonic arts are arts to which other arts are subordinate, he explains in his *Nicomachean Ethics*, where bridle-making is said to be subordinate to horsemanship, and horsemanship, along with every other military pursuit, subordinate to strategy.[48] In this example, strategy, the art of the *strategos* or military commander, is an architectonic art because, like the *architekton*, the *strategos* knows the reasons why things are done.

But for Aristotle, the supremely "architectonic art" to which all the other arts refer is not architecture, although Vitruvius, later, seems to present it as such, when he begins his first book with the declaration that, judiciously exercised, the "knowledge of the architect ... demonstrates everything the other arts achieve."[49]

There was in any case no word for architecture in Aristotle's day, and the art of the *architekton*, whose thoughts directed the activities of artisans—this as yet nameless art, though doubtless architectonic, was not, for Aristotle, the *principal* architectonic art.

This is how Aristotle, famously, begins his *Nicomachean Ethics*. "Every art and every inquiry, and similarly every action and pursuit, is thought to aim at some good; and for this reason the good has rightly been declared to be that at which all things aim."[50] And the *supreme* good, the good toward which all arts and inquiries must ultimately be directed, is not individual, but collective: it is the common good.

Thus, Aristotle argues, the common good is the end to which the most truly *architectonic* of arts is directed: the good aimed for by the master craft to which every other art and discipline is subordinate. For Aristotle this, the most authoritative, preeminently architectonic of disciplines is *hé politiké*: "the political"—the knowledge or science of politics.[51] In the Greek context of Aristotle's day, knowledge of political matters, *hé politiké*, had, of course to do specifically with the rule of cities—the good governance of the *polis*, from which needless to say the term *politiké* derives.

Keeping in mind the radically architectonic role Aristotle assigns to politics, let me return to Filarete's fifteenth-century "architectonic book." As I said earlier, Filarete's principal theme is the building of a city he names Sforzinda, after Francesco Sforza, and of its port, Plusiapolis.

Taken in context, and in the light of the Adamic agenda just reviewed, Filarete's reinvention of Milan as Sforzinda is clearly a political project, and his book, while indeed about architecture, is also "architectonic" in precisely the Aristotelian sense just discussed. Is this just a little too neat to be true?

Many years ago, Nikolaus Pevsner pointed to thirteenth-century readings of Aristotle's *Politics* and *Metaphysics* by Aquinas and Albertus Magnus as sources for the appearance (or reappearance) in the fourteenth and fifteenth centuries of the then novel notion of an *architectus* as the master mind that conceived and designed new buildings, for, as we just saw, Aristotle had qualified the *architecton* as the person who, because he knows *why* things are done, is the person with authority over craftsmen.[52] Pevsner did not mention the *Nicomachean Ethics*, whose opening passages seem particularly relevant to Filarete's *architettonico libro* and its project for an "ideal" city.

But how well would Filarete, with his little Latin and less Greek, have known Aristotle? Moreover, the phrase *architettonico libro* does not appear in Filarete's original dedication to Francesco Sforza, but rather in the dedication of the slightly reworked version he later presented to Piero de' Medici. There is nothing exceptional in an author's grasping the import of a work's intentions only after it is written—it happens all the time. But where did Filarete get the idea?

The dukes of Milan owned one of the most important libraries in Quattrocento Italy. By Filarete's day, it contained well over a thousand manuscripts. Located in the ducal castle at Pavia, its holdings counted multiple copies of Aristotle, including several of the *Nicomachean Ethics*.[53] If anyone knew the contents of this library, it was Filelfo, who had served the dukes of Milan as court scholar and panegyrist since 1439.

Some forty years ago, John Onians argued for Plato as the primary source for Filarete's book—especially for the port of Plusiapolis.[54] His claim was that Filelfo, an eminent Hellenist, worked from a manuscript in the Pavia library and mediated Plato's *Republic* and his *Laws* for Filarete's benefit. Other identifiable sources (besides Vitruvius), to which Filelfo must certainly have provided Filarete with the key, include Diodorus Siculus, Aesop, Virgil, Ovid, Statius, Pliny the Elder, Plautus, Isidore of Seville, Suetonius, Plutarch, Dante, and, of course, the Bible, as already discussed. And it was Filelfo, you could venture, who suggested to Filarete that his book on architecture was "architectonic" in the political sense just discussed: Filelfo whose early letters record a preoccupation with the correct Latin translation of the *Nicomachean Ethics*, and who gave a course of lectures on the same work in Florence in the 1430s.[55] Later, in the 1470s, he wrote a book, *On Moral Doctrine*, in which he discussed the ethics and metaphysics of Aristotle.

As I said, use of "architectonic" in Latin is not attested before Vitruvius. After Vitruvius, the word appears as a noun whose referent, it must be acknowledged, can only be meant as the equivalent of what we call architecture. Such is the case in Pliny the Elder and Quintilian, as it is when the fifth-century poet Sidonius Apollinaris writes that where dialectic argues and astrology predicts, *architectonica* builds.[56] When Servius in his commentary on the *Aeneid* refers to Vitruvius *qui de architectonica scripsit*, he obviously means "Vitruvius, who wrote about architecture." But in each instance *architectonica* is a noun, not an adjective, as it had been in Aristotle's "architectonic discipline," Vitruvius's "architectonic principles," and is, indeed, in Filarete's *architettonico libro*.

"Architectonica" also appears as a noun in Cetius Faventinus's third-century abridgment of Vitruvius, a work limited to the treatment of private building. Its title, literally translated, is "A shortened book on the arts of *architectonica* for private use by M. Cetius Faventinus."[57] As it happens, one of the twenty-two surviving manuscripts of Faventinus's abridgment is in the Biblioteca Ambrosiana in Milan, bound with a copy of *De architectura*.[58] Both the Vitruvius and the Faventinus were copied by the same Milanese scholar Boninus Mombritius, and the copy is clearly dated 1462, which coincides precisely with the time when Filarete was writing his treatise.

But before we allow ourselves to dismiss Aristotle and decide to favor the less demanding role of Faventinus's abridgment in Filarete's decision to call his book "architectonic," it is well to recall that Faventinus's little book was, emphatically, a book on *private* architecture. Indeed, as he writes in his conclusion, "And so for this little book of mine I have gathered in order all the prescriptions relevant to private use. I have left public institutions [*civitatum institutiones*] and everything of that sort to be related by a writer of outstanding wisdom."[59]

Whether or not Filarete can be considered "a writer of outstanding wisdom," it is obvious that his book, with the staggering gigantism of its buildings' celebration of princely power, concerned public institutions almost exclusively. And to pin Filarete's source on Faventinus is to forget the architectonic ambitions of Filarete's friend and mentor, the panegyrist and Aristotle scholar Filelfo, whose contribution to the ideology of the treatise was major.

Frontispiece to Antonio Bonfini's Latin translation of Filarete's treatise on architecture (1488–1489), dedication to Matthias Corvinus. Biblioteca Nazionale Marciana, Venice, Ms. Lat. VIII.2, fol. 1r (detail). By permission of the Ministero della Cultura—Biblioteca Nazionale Marciana. Reproduction prohibited.

The political potential of Filarete's treatise was taken to a new level when, just twenty years after it was written, King Matthias Corvinus of Hungary commissioned the Italian humanist Antonio Bonfini to translate it into Latin. The translation, in large, lavishly illuminated manuscript format, was intended to join other similar volumes in the king's famous library at Buda, which included an ornate manuscript of Alberti's treatise commissioned at about the same time.[60] The reason for translating Filarete into Latin could not have been that Matthias knew no Italian. He had been educated in Italy, and his Italian wife, Beatrice of Aragon, spoke no Hungarian—was criticized, in fact, for refusing to learn the language.[61] The explanation lies elsewhere.

Elected in 1458 to the Hungarian throne at the age of fourteen against stiff opposition, Matthias, like Francesco Sforza, was considered by many to be a usurper.[62] Bonfini addresses the issue when he writes in his dedication to the invincible *Divo Matthia* that the sword had chosen Matthias king—not "niggardly votes and cheap electioneering." Overtly dismissing the electoral process, Bonfini is claiming that the king's contested election was irrelevant: *virtù* alone had earned him his coronation.[63]

Matthias's father, Janos Hunyadi, a condottiere famous for his victories against the Ottoman Turks, had no pedigree worth mentioning. Moreover, Matthias was without legitimate offspring. He had only one bastard son, Johannes Corvinus, whom he declared his successor in 1485 when all hope for a legitimate heir had been abandoned. In 1488 he made Johannes co-proprietor of his library in what has been taken as a legitimating move to further the youth's chances of succession.[64]

Almost exactly contemporaneous with Antonio Bonfini's Filarete translation is a political treatise written for Matthias by the Florentine humanist Aurelio Lippo Brandolini, called *De comparatione rei publicae et regni* (Republics and kingdoms compared). Presented as a debate between the king and a Florentine knight, one Domenico Giugni who has been set up as a straw man in the proceedings, it also entails the participation of the king's son Johannes, for whose instruction the debate is being conducted, and whose legitimacy the work was meant to confirm.[65] The argument runs along predictable lines, reaching a foregone conclusion concerning the superiority of kingdoms. Even Giugni, the king's republican interlocutor, is persuaded. Republics are corruptible because they are ruled by many corruptible men. A king is incorruptible because he is rich and answers to no one. Republican liberty is an illusion. Monuments are "marks of virtue and nobility necessary for distinguishing one man from another."[66] And, of course, one-man rule is the only natural form of government. "What else is a city but a large household, or a king and city leader but a great head of a household?"[67]

Antonio Bonfini had earlier proven himself an able courtier when he gave the king the Roman name "Corvinus" and a fine Roman pedigree to go with it. Prominent among the personal emblems Matthias adopted was a raven (*corvo*), bird of divine prophecy.[68] In 1488, a few years after Matthias gave Bonfini the Filarete commission, the king asked him to trace Hungary's history from prehistory to the present day—an immense work called *Rerum ungaricarum decades*, which took the scholar ten years to complete. Its aim was to redeem the nation's barbarian origins in what Patrick Baker has seen as an artistic crafting of the past to meet the needs of the present.[69]

The latinization of Filarete's *architettonico libro* belongs to this context. As Maria Beltramini has shown, the translation entailed what she calls a Vitruvianization of the text, with passages where Filarete diverges from his Vitruvian source not translated but replaced wholesale with the "correct" version from *De architectura* itself.[70] Digressions are cut, and references to the work's original Milanese context suppressed. In sum, the highly reductive Latin translation of Filarete's treatise is an attempt to strip the work back to its Vitruvian warp, to make both it and the man who commissioned it Roman and therefore universal.

Also universal of course, is Adam, whom Bonfini has allowed to retain a position of prominence in his translation. Matthias's prophetic raven was often represented with a diamond ring in its beak and is figured in the upper right-hand corner of the illuminated border that frames Bonfini's dedication to the king he addresses as *Divo Matthie*. Matthias, like Francesco Sforza, was "adamantine," and adopted the diamond as another of his personal emblems. In a poem entitled *De adamante Matthie* a court

Matthias Corvinus as *Virtù*, from Antonio Bonfini, Latin translation of Filarete's treatise on architecture (1488–1489). Biblioteca Nazionale Marciana, Venice, Ms. Lat. VIII.2, fol. 137v (detail). By permission of the Ministero della Cultura—Biblioteca Nazionale Marciana. Reproduction prohibited.

poet praises the king's *vires adamas* (invincible strength); in another poem, his *adamantina virtus*.[71] In Bonfini's translation it is Matthias Corvinus, not Francesco Sforza, you see balanced on the point of a diamond as the personification of *Virtù*.[72]

Diamonds were a warlord's best friend, apparently, for besides Francesco Sforza, warrior princes among the Este, Gonzaga, and Malatesta all favored them as emblems. Their Adamic resonance may well have enhanced the appeal of Filarete's "architectonic book" to the allegedly invincible Hungarian monarch, whose embrace of Italian Renaissance ideals could be taken as evidence of a dream of restoring the earthly paradise in his own kingdom.[73]

Matthias had been quick to recognize Filarete's "architectonic" intentions, thanks to the grandiose buildings projected in the images of the Magliabechiano codex, which was the manuscript Bonfini worked from. "What did you say as soon as you saw this book which you asked me to translate into Latin?" Bonfini asks the king in his dedication. "Seeing the plan of a bridge, did you not immediately think of throwing a marble bridge over the Danube, as Trajan did, and of building many cities in Pannonia?"[74]

And yet the phrase "architectonic book" does not even appear in Bonfini's translation. When he translates Filarete's preface, he renders *architettonico libro* as *opus*: "It therefore gives me pleasure to dedicate this *opus* to you," he writes.[75] An *opus* no less architectonic, for all that.

In the end, I do not think it really matters who in fact supplied Filarete with the troublesome word. Whether it was Vitruvius, Aristotle, Pliny, Cetius Faventinus, Filelfo, or all (or even none) of the above, it is, as Bonfini's suppression of it demonstrates, not the word *as a word* that counts.

The word "architectonic" is consequential, rather, in pointedly naming a confluence of architecture and *hé politiké*, which brings into sharp focus a key dimension of the Renaissance love affair with Vitruvius. Like *De architectura* itself, Filarete's *architettonico libro* and other architectural treatises of the Renaissance were conceived and written in political circumstances which cannot be overlooked if you are to appreciate the full range of their theoretical import. Inasmuch as they were political, and whether or nor they were in fact called "architectonic," all such works were, like Filarete's, architectonic books.

In 1465, the year he dedicated the revised version of his manuscript to Piero de' Medici, Filarete also presented Piero with a bronze statuette, a copy he had made in Rome some 20 years earlier of the equestrian statue of the Roman emperor Marcus Aurelius, still at the Lateran at the time.[76] *Hé politiké* is the obvious thematic link between these two offerings, made in the hope of securing the Florentine prince's patronage, with rulership on the imperial Roman model (the emperor on horseback) reinforcing the rhetoric of the "architectonic book" and vice versa. Equine participation in this convergence is the topic of my next and final chapter.

6 All the King's Horses

A marble fragment of a horse struggling to escape the assault of a lion once stood as an emblem of municipal autonomy in front of the Palazzo Senatorio on the Capitol at Rome, where for more than 200 years it presided over the *platea communis* that had been the beating heart of the communal city. The lion had symbolized municipal Rome, while in the eyes of the *popolo* the mangled horse, as I argued earlier, invoked the papal power that popular government (the lion) fought to overcome. In chapter 2, I reviewed the papacy's appropriation of that shared public place through the deployment of symmetries meant to revive the imperial Roman grandeur Renaissance popes claimed as their rightful inheritance. Central, literally, to these symmetries, and the ultimate affirmation of papal supremacy, was the gilded bronze equestrian statue of the ancient Roman emperor Marcus Aurelius, transferred to the Capitol by Pope Paul III in January of 1538 from the Lateran, where it had stood as an emblem of the pope's temporal authority for nearly 800 years.

The horse that emerged triumphant from the struggle for control of the Campidoglio is a powerful cipher for the outcomes of political confrontations endemic to much of early Renaissance Italian history. From such conflicts, horses and their lordly riders invariably rode away victorious, so to speak, to be celebrated in equestrian statues that eventually emerged as monumental constants in many early modern cities.[1] The *popolo* did not ride, of course. It never had.

For all that the hoplite infantry has been routinely credited with saving Hellenic civilization from destruction by foreign invaders in the fifth century BCE, in ancient Greece as indeed through much of human history until the advent of mechanized transport, it was the horse that conferred nobility, power, and status on the man who rode one, seated as he was well above anyone on foot who had, perforce, to look up to him. Even without a horse, the man who sits (king, general, president, or CEO) wields inherent authority over the person who stands before him. A man on a horse is seated and has the added advantage of being some five feet above the ground on the back of a powerful living creature he alone controls. Reactions to such a presence can vary and may include not only intimidation and fear but reverence, respect, and deference as well as admiration and the thrill of being in the presence of greatness. Thundering cavalcades of Athenian horsemen, not hoplites, excite our admiration and even now confer above all else their uncontestable glory on the Parthenon frieze, outclassing every person who proceeds on foot. It is not for nothing that "pedestrian" is often used as a synonym for "dull." And it is not for nothing that in commemorative representations, in equestrian statues most particularly, the horsemen—never horsewomen—being celebrated are not poets, philosophers, painters, architects, accountants, or farmers, but conquering heroes and leaders of men.

In the frontispiece of the earliest known manuscript of Petrarch's *De viris illustribus*, winged and haloed *Gloria* rides high in a two-horse chariot, heralded by small, winged spirits who trumpet her descent from the empyrean.[2] Looped over her left

Frontispiece, Francesco Petrarca, *De viris illustribus*, mid-fourteenth-century Italian manuscript. Bibliothèque nationale de France, Paris, BN Ms. Lat. 6069, fol. 1r. Photo: Bibliothèque nationale de France.

forearm is a bundle of bright green laurel wreaths, which she bestows on the deserving few among a crowd of men jockeying for position below. Every one of these eager petitioners for her favor is on horseback. Not one stands on his own two feet. To be a candidate for glory, you had to have a horse.

The preeminent symbol of *virtus* among Romans had been a mounted warrior. Petrarch's *De viris illustribus* revived that Roman military ideal. The miniaturist who illuminated this manuscript, originally the property of its author's last patron, Francesco da Carrara, understood this well:[3] not only the ideal of military *virtù* as such, but the virtually indispensable contribution of horses both to its representation and to its actual deployment on the battlefield in the endless real-world conflicts of those years. The skillful handling of a horse alone was evidence of manliness, and the possession of fine horses the source of great prestige.[4]

All the warrior princes discussed in these pages were expert horsemen, and all maintained large stables. Many were involved in the complex and costly business of horse breeding. Half buried into the hillside under the ducal palace at Urbino, the stables known as the *Data*, designed for the duke by Francesco di Giorgio along with the famous helicoidal ramp leading up to them, had room for 300 horses. It is said that up to a thousand could be accommodated in the immense *scuderie* built at the Sforza palace in Vigevano near Milan by Francesco Sforza's successors, Galeazzo Maria and Ludovico il Moro, between 1473 and 1492. Bramante contributed to the design of Ludovico's 94-meter-long addition to this stable complex, whose cross-vaulted interior may be the one represented in a sectional drawing of stables Leonardo made in about 1490.[5]

Borso d'Este, marquis of Ferrara, is reported to have had 700 horses in his stable, while the Gonzaga in neighboring Mantua owned 650.[6] The Gonzaga were famous horse-breeders, who imported bloodstock from Sicily, North Africa, Turkey, and Eastern Europe for the purpose.[7] Suppliers of horses to European nobility, including Henry VIII of England and Francis I of France, the Gonzaga used horses as a medium of diplomatic exchange. When, in 1514, Henry VIII sent Francesco Gonzaga a return gift of horses with precious caparisons and trappings, the delighted marquis wrote in his thank-you to the king that nothing conferred on him "by nature, fortune or military skill had so raised [his] esteem in Italy as this."[8]

The Sala dei Cavalli, largest of the reception rooms at the Palazzo Te in Mantua, was where, in the sixteenth century, the Gonzaga held their most lavish ceremonies and welcomed their most distinguished visitors, including in 1530 the emperor Charles V.[9] Designed and decorated in the late 1520s for the then marquis Ludovico Gonzaga's great-grandson Federico II by the Roman painter and architect Giulio Romano, this "Hall of the Horses" is uniquely explicit in affirming the essential role of horses in shaping and representing their owners' *virtù*. Life-sized portraits of six prize Gonzaga studs give the room its name, where the horses stand as if on a narrow ledge a small distance away from the wall behind them, some eight feet above the floor, one at either end of the room, two against each of its long side walls. Each horse was a unique favorite, originally identified by name. Four of their names survive: Dario, Morel Favorito, Battaglia, and Glorioso.[10] Directly behind each, a window appears to open onto a Lombard landscape. Above the landscape and the champion horse, a faux relief rendered as bronze shows the strongman Hercules, undefeated paradigm of ancient *virtus*, performing one of his heroic exploits.

Alternating with the horses, painted niches enshrine faux marble statues of Roman divinities, while in recesses over the windows portrait busts of Gonzaga princes present them as scions of some unidentified imperial Roman dynasty, reinforcing the narrative of ancient Roman grandeur of which Dario, Battaglia, and the rest have here been made a part. Most eloquent, powerful, and indeed authentically Roman in all of this are the giant trompe-l'oeil Corinthian pilasters whose rhythmical deployment confers the dignity, coherence, and architectural order of a fictional colonnade on the disparate elements of the frescoes that crown the room. Two of these pilasters frame each paired landscape and Herculean relief to create a richly ornamented niche—or stall—for the stallion standing in front of it. The flutings of the lower third of the pilaster shafts are cabled, their concavities filled with reinforcing convex "cables," not twisted here but smooth, an ornament typically meant to protect the edges of flutings from

Giulio Romano, the horse Morel Favorito, 1528, fresco, Sala dei Cavalli, Palazzo Te, Mantua. Photo Raffaello Bencini. Roman Beniaminson / Art Resource, NY.

Giulio Romano, the horse Dario, 1528, fresco, Sala dei Cavalli, Palazzo Te, Mantua. Photo: Raffaello Bencini. Roman Beniaminson / Art Resource, NY.

Giulio Romano, horse, 1528, fresco, east wall, Sala dei Cavalli, Palazzo Te, Mantua. Photo: Raffaello Bencini. Roman Beniaminson / Art Resource, NY.

Giulio Romano, horse, 1528, fresco, south wall, Sala dei Cavalli, Palazzo Te, Mantua. Photo: Raffaello Bencini. Roman Beniaminson / Art Resource, NY.

Giulio Romano, horse, 1528, fresco, north wall, Sala dei Cavalli, Palazzo Te, Mantua. Photo Raffaello Bencini. Roman Beniaminson / Art Resource, NY.

Giulio Romano, horse, 1528, fresco, southwest wall, Sala dei Cavalli, Palazzo Te, Mantua. Photo: Raffaello Bencini. Roman Beniaminson / Art Resource, NY.

damage in areas of heavy traffic. Each of the horses is tethered by his reins to this sturdier lower segment of the pilaster in front of him, as if to a hitching post.

It is a telling detail. For it is not as if these vibrant animals were free to move, and thus in need of restraint. Their confinement to narrow ledges precludes the possibility of even the slightest change in position. Perhaps the artist tethered them as a way of highlighting this enforced immobility, a reminder, paradoxically, of their extraordinary potential for speed. Still as statues, yet full of life, they are like the statues made by the legendary Greek sculptor Daedalus, which were so lifelike that they had to be bound in chains to prevent them from running away.[11] But more important here than simply being tied up is what these studs have been tethered *to*. Being tied to the majestic Corinthian pilasters that frame them ties the animals to the power of architecture—and architecture, in turn, to their vitality. For their presence animates not only the fictive architecture of the Corinthian colonnade, but that of the entire room. Surrounded by inert statuary rendered as marble or as bronze, only the horses are alive and in color.

In the mid 1440s, eighty years before Giulio Romano decorated the Sala dei Cavalli at Mantua, Leon Battista Alberti wrote a short work called *De equo animante* (On the living horse) dedicated to Leonello d'Este, marquis of Ferrara, whose humanist interests he shared and with whom he had been in contact for several years.[12] The Este were major contenders in the competitive culture of horses, and had made horse races a preferred venue for public rejoicing from the time Azzo VII Novello d'Este inaugurated the first ever palio in Italy to celebrate his defeat of Ezzelino III da Romano at the battle of Cassano d'Adda in 1259.[13] When Azzo died in 1264 the Ferrarese commune (established, as at Mantua, in 1115) elected his grandson Obizzo II d'Este *gubernator et rector et generalis et perpetuus dominus* (perpetual and general lord and governor), conferring on him what amounted to absolute lordship over Ferrara, where the dynasty would rule for over 500 years.[14] With this formula, identical to the one that would give the Visconti the same power over Milan in 1330, Ferrara surrendered its autonomy to become the most short-lived of northern Italy's independent communes. What, if anything, did horses have to do with it?

In the dedication of his *De equo animante* to Leonello, Alberti explains that the marquis had invited him to help judge a competition for an equestrian statue honoring his (Leonello's) father, the condottiere Niccolò III d'Este. Judging the entries to Leonello's competition, Alberti writes, led him to undertake a more thoroughgoing reflection not only on the beauty and lineaments (*lineamenta*) of horses but also on their nature and habits. Although he begins by calling attention to the indispensability of horses to all men, in all spheres of endeavor, he quickly makes it clear that the living horse that interests him most is the horse belonging to a prince: the noble steed ridden into battle, devoted to the single rider he carries home in triumph after victory, as for example the horses ridden by Julius Caesar, the "divine" Augustus, and Alexander the Great, who honored their animals with monuments. The dedication concludes with Alberti's reminder to readers, his dedicatee in particular, that he has written not for laborers or herdsmen, but for a prince of great erudition, and has therefore been more concise than the ignorant masses might like.[15]

The treatise proper begins with the all-important issues of lineage and breeding. As Alberti tells it, the ancients recommend that the ideal stud be endowed with, inter alia, a small head, long neck, mane falling to the right, broad chest, well-hung testicles of equal size, perfectly proportioned thighs, slender legs, and that he be crowned with glory when victorious in battle. A mare is most appreciated if she resembles the male in both appearance and character, he advises somewhat laconically, before going on to devote his attention to her breeding potential. Mating a stallion with a mare—what Alberti calls "the work of Venus"—is a topic of intense concern. If the mare resists, she is to be restrained; if too ardent, you should cut her mane.[16] A young colt is to receive the tenderest of care until comes the time, in his third year, for training him to *virtus*. Besides teaching him to take the bridle, the bit, and eventually the saddle, this means, among other things, keeping him away from "Venus" to prevent enslavement to desires that will cause him to age prematurely.

Once schooled in the basics, the young horse is ready to be trained in other "noble arts," which is to say "to suffer hardship for the honor and glory of his *patria*, to serve its citizens, annihilate its enemies, and other glorious matters of the kind." The rigorous training, in short, to ready a warhorse (always a stallion) for the "work of Mars."[17] The uncompromising discipline required includes judicious recourse to the use of spurs, the bit, and the crop in order to inculcate in a fearful or mutinous animal the habit of unhesitating response to the bidding of the man on his back. The fury and unforeseeable conditions of battle demanded above all that horse and rider perform as one, with the horse a flawless emanation of its rider's will. In this, the living horse was the unrivaled expression of a prince's power.

In his fourth-century BCE treatise on horsemanship Xenophon, who tops Alberti's list of sources, explains how to make a stallion rear up on its hind legs, and why this is such an effective move.

> Now, if when he is planting his hind legs under him you pull him up with the bit, he bends his hind legs on his hocks and raises the forepart of his body, anyone facing him can see the belly and the sheath [of his penis]. When he does that you must give him the bit so that he may appear to the onlookers to be doing willingly the finest thing a horse can do. ... This is the attitude in which artists represent the horse on which gods and heroes ride, and men who manage such horses have a magnificent appearance.[18]

Giordano Ruffo (listed as *Calaber*—"the Calabrian"—in Alberti's bibliography) was another important source among the many listed.[19] Ruffo was squire to the thirteenth-century emperor Frederick II Hohenstaufen for whom he wrote an influential treatise on horses called *Maniscalcia liber*. The focus of this "blacksmiths' handbook," like that of *De equo*, is princely horses, warhorses most especially. Without them, writes Ruffo, it would be impossible to control an empire. When Alberti boasts of his own horsemanship in his autobiography, he expresses special pride in his ability to subdue even the fiercest animals which, he claims, "would shudder violently when he mounted them and tremble beneath him as if in terror."[20]

The sculpture competition that brought Alberti to Ferrara and inspired his essay on horses was, as I said, for an equestrian statue honoring Leonello d'Este's father, Niccolò III. There had been equestrian statues before, of course. One of Cangrande I della Scala in Verona (1330) was the earliest in postclassical times, followed 50 years later by Bernabò Visconti's funerary monument in Milan. Paolo Uccello's trompe-l'oeil fresco (1436) of the condottiere Sir John Hawkwood in Florence's cathedral was another.[21] But Cangrande della Scala and Bernabò Visconti and their respective mounts were carved in stone while Hawkwood's painted funerary monument is rendered as marble.

The equestrian statue of Niccolò III was to be cast in bronze: the first such since antiquity, of which only three were known at the time: Marcus Aurelius, of course, the no longer extant *Regisole* which stood raised on a column in front of the cathedral at Pavia, and a statue of Justinian near the hippodrome in Constantinople, also no longer extant and also raised on a column.[22] All were imperial Roman, emblems of ancient authority transmitted by the rarity and unassailable resilience of the metal alloy of their facture as much as anything else. *Exegi monumentum aere perennius*, the Augustan poet Horace famously boasted of his poetry. "I have raised a monument more lasting than bronze"—the most lasting thing he could think of.[23] Of Donatello's equestrian bronze of Erasmo da Narni, the condottiere known as Gattamelata, and Verrocchio's of Bartolomeo Colleoni, also a condottiere, that followed a few years later, Niccolò III's equestrian statue was the forerunner.[24]

Thoroughly schooled in the classics by his preceptor the illustrious humanist Guarino Veronese, Leonello d'Este was an especially avid reader of Pliny the Elder's *Natural History*, of which he owned two copies.[25] Pliny devotes more than half of book 34, on metals, to the topic of bronze. Esteemed for being as ancient as the city of Rome, he begins, bronze was more precious than silver; more precious even than gold, if the bronze were Corinthian. Bronze not gold, he adds, was the original standard in ancient

Roman currency. Included in the chapters that follow is a detailed account of all the things that are cast in bronze, with particular emphasis on bronze statues and the famous sculptors (366, all listed by name) who made them.[26]

The complexity of bronze casting had led to its virtual disappearance in Europe during the intervening centuries. Cast from a clay model, not chiseled from unyielding stone, bronze is a very supple material. Furthermore, it expands slightly just before it sets, filling in the finest details of the mold, then shrinks a little as it cools, making it easy to extract the finished work from its casing. "Breathing" bronze, Virgil called it, in what is no doubt the best-known passage in the *Aeneid*—the passage that concludes with a prophecy of Rome's mission to rule the world.[27] "Others will draw from breathing bronze more supple lines," he writes, invoking at once the protean quality of the alloy itself and the work in bronze whose "supple lines" it animates as if with life-giving breath.[28] *Arma virumque cano*, the epic began, "of arms and the man I sing." The man, of course, is Aeneas, whose name, "man of bronze," makes his story, the *Aeneid*, a book of bronze: a celebration of Roman greatness more "bronze" than bronze itself.[29]

The marquis of Ferrara's novel project of having the equestrian statue of his condottiere father cast in bronze and Alberti's *De equo animante* converged in a shared understanding of the living horse as a testament of authority and the most lastingly appropriate means of its representation.

Like so many of the princes discussed in these pages, Leonello d'Este was plagued by questions of legitimacy. He was the third of Niccolò III's eleven illegitimate children, and had a younger full brother, Borso, born of the same mother. Their births were followed, late in Niccolò's life, by the birth of two legitimate sons Ercole and Sigismondo. Leonello was Niccolò's favorite and was named his heir, but his position was precarious, contested by, among others, Ricciarda da Saluzzo, mother of his legitimate half-brothers, on behalf of her two young sons.[30]

Niccolò III died unexpectedly in Milan on 26 December 1441. Leonello's investiture took place in Ferrara just two days later. The haste in having his position ratified, obviously aimed at forestalling any attempt to usurp it, points to the new marquis's awareness of its questionable legality.³¹ According to the chronicles, the investiture included both public acclamation and a solemn episcopal mass where he was presented with the baton of command in confirmation of his titles. These ceremonies were followed by the new lord's apparently customary ride throughout the city on horseback, "taking possession" of it, Charles Rosenberg has put it, in a final affirmation of sovereignty that closely resembled the *possesso* of a newly elected pope at Rome, which it may have been meant to emulate.³² In this, the rider's mount was indispensable as presenter of the man now in control. His victory lap would have been unimaginable—pedestrian and utterly meaningless—without a horse.

The bronze equestrian monument of Leonello's father made the declaration of legitimacy permanent, as indeed the marble inscription on its base insists when it records in Roman capitals that the statue was executed at the command of Niccolò III's rightful successor (GERMANO ET SUCCESSORE PERFICI IMPERANTE).³³ The inscription is dated 1450, the year Leonello died, but the work was only installed on its base on the feast of the Ascension in June of the following year, when it was dedicated by Leonello's younger brother and (illegal) successor Borso in another affirmation of dynastic continuity.³⁴

The first mention of the project had occurred eight years earlier in the minutes of a meeting of the Ferrarese municipal council known as the "Twelve Sages of Ferrara," or *Savi*, on 27 November 1443, where the two finalists in the competition for the sculpture, both Florentines, were named.³⁵ It is generally agreed that Alberti's involvement followed soon after.

Initially competitors, the two finalists, Niccolò Baroncelli and Antonio di Cristoforo, ended up sharing the commission, with the latter put in charge of the rider and Baroncelli—thereafter known as "Niccolò del Cavallo"—in charge of the horse. The finished statue was installed to the right of the archway leading to the marquis's urban residence, the Palazzo di Corte or Corte Vecchio, facing the cathedral, where it stood on a base that projected into the *piazza comunale*, which it came to dominate. Its five-meter-high support consists of two somewhat mismatched Composite columns under a semicircular arch surmounted by an entablature whose frieze is carved with laurel wreaths. One of the columns, an engaged half-column attached to the brick wall of the palace behind, is of friable limestone known as *pietra d'Avesa*. The freestanding column is of higher-grade Istrian stone with a capital appreciably different in its details from those of its counterpart. Just under the capital of the freestanding column, at the top of its shaft, a small inscription reading OPUS NIC. BARUNCELI FIORENTINI, attributes its facture to Niccolò del Cavallo.[36]

Marco Folin has recently challenged as misguided the long-standing tradition of crediting Alberti with involvement in the design of the statue's architectural underpinning, as well as the even more tenacious and equally erroneous view of its being conceived as a triumphal arch.[37] The basic requirement of a triumphal arch is that it is meant to be passed through, which is clearly not the case here, Folin points out, while also noting that contemporary accounts invariably refer to the statue as standing on a *column*, not an arch, as indeed did both the *Regisole* and the equestrian statue of Justinian in Constantinople.[38]

Be that as it may, and whatever the anomalous typology of the statue's support, there is no question that—consisting as it does of two columns, an arch and an entablature—this underpinning is, quintessentially, architectural. It is equally undeniable that the architecture in question, articulated *all'antica* in keeping with the canons of a renascent classical tradition, was meant to heighten (literally) the importance of the man represented in the statue above. "Statues were raised on columns so that the persons represented might be elevated above other mortals," writes Pliny the Elder in one of his chapters on bronze statuary—a passage with obvious bearing on the shape of the Este monument, given Leonello's known interest in the *Natural History*.[39] "In a work of building," Alberti would write in his treatise on architecture, "the column is the principal ornament."[40]

The architecture under the statue multiplies what, in the horse, was an emanation of its rider's power, lifting him to even greater heights. United in their shared rhetorical purpose, the architecture becomes equine, the horse, of which its underpinning is as it were an extension, architectural. When Borso d'Este, Leonello's brother and heir, raised a monument to himself in the

Bronze equestrian statue of Niccolò III d'Este, Ferrara, 1450 (restored). LLUXX / Alamy Stock Photo.

Pellegrino Prisciani, "The inauguration of Obizzo d'Este as first lord of Ferrara in 1264," pen and ink, *Historiae Ferrarienses liber VII* (late fifteenth/early sixteenth century), Archivio di Stato, Modena, ms. 131, fol. 79v. By permission of the Ministero per i Beni e le Attività Culturali e per il Turismo—Archivio di Stato di Modena prot. no. 2710.

1450s, he dispensed with the horse and had his statue seated on the top of a column. With its tall, multitiered entablature, elaborately carved by the same Niccolò del Cavallo, the Composite column Borso sat on served a similar equine purpose.[41]

The equestrian statue of Niccolò III has the horse pacing forward, its right hoof raised, its left hind leg moving ahead of the other. The rider, outfitted like the condottiere prince he was, holds the horse's reins in his left hand, and carries the baton of command in his right. The cylindrical beret he wears identifies him as a military commander.[42] But the representation is, to a certain extent, conjectural, for the original statue was toppled and melted down, along with the statue of Borso d'Este, during the revolutionary upheavals of 1796—the same that led to the destruction of the *Regisole* in Pavia.[43] The statue that now stands in front of what was once the Palazzo di Corte (now Palazzo del Comune) in Ferrara is a reconstruction, the work of one Giacomo Zilocchi who restored both it and the one of Borso during the Mussolini era, in 1926.[44]

Possible sources for the restored equestrian statue include Paolo Uccello's virtually contemporary portrait of Sir John Hawkwood, which the restored Niccolò III closely resembles, as well as three surviving drawings of the monument that date from the fifteenth, seventeenth, and eighteenth centuries respectively.[45] The earliest of these is by Pellegrino Prisciani (1435–1518), librarian, historiographer, and theoretician of architecture at the Este court during the reign of Ercole d'Este, and appears in one of two drawings on a manuscript page of his late fifteenth/early sixteenth-century *Historiae Ferrarienses*.

The drawing occupies the left-hand side of a diptych and illustrates the inauguration of Obizzo II d'Este installed, as I mentioned earlier, as the first lord of Ferrara in 1264. His investiture, which marked the end of Ferrara's communal period, is dominated by the figure of one Aldighiero Fontana, a powerful Ferrarese nobleman and kingmaker, who harangues the crowd assembled in the *piazza del comune* from a high wooden podium raised between the cathedral on the left and the Palazzo di Corte on the right. The small figure seated at the foot of the podium is Obizzo d'Este, just seventeen at the time, whose acclamation as *signore* by the assembled Ferrarese is being assured by the cordon of armed pikemen who hem them in.[46] The inclusion of the equestrian monument of Niccolò III, shown in position in front of the Palazzo di Corte at the upper left of the image, is an anachronism, of course. It was raised two hundred years after the foundational event the drawing records, something the drawing's author, Pellegrino Prisciani, who would have been in his teens when the statue was erected, knew perfectly well. Its inclusion is an affirmation of unbroken dynastic continuity between the first hereditary Este lord and Prisciani's own patron, Ercole, current ruler and legitimate son of the bronze horseman in question whose anachronistic presence in this context is the epitome of the signiorial power that brought Ferrara's brief communal period to an end.

The drawing of Obizzo II's investiture is set in the middle of the city in a piazza crowded with people. The scene in the drawing on the other, right-hand side of the folio is rural: an open field where the figure of a man in full armor sits astride a prancing warhorse he guides with reins held in his left hand. In his right he brandishes a sword above his head. Counterpart of the bronze horseman in the image opposite, this celebrant of victorious signiorial power is Obizzo later in life, shown conquering his territorial domain, with three young sons included in the foreground as a testament to dynastic continuity.[47]

Dynastic continuity was key in maintaining a trouble-free autocracy. As Machiavelli observes, citing Ferrara by way of example, "in hereditary states, accustomed to their prince's family, there are far fewer difficulties in maintaining one's rule. ... And in the antiquity and persistence of [a hereditary prince's] rule memories of innovations and the reasons for them disappear, because one change always leaves a foothold for the next."[48]

The statue of Niccolò III anticipated an explosion of building activity in Ferrara during the decades that followed, most notably during the reign of Pellegrino Prisciani's patron Ercole d'Este, who ruled the city from 1471 to 1505.[49] Principles formulated by Alberti and Vitruvius guided much of it, with Prisciani their enthusiastic intermediary.[50] And if Alberti was, at best, only indirectly involved in determining the shape Niccolò III's equestrian monument eventually took, the time he spent in Ferrara in the mid 1440s was career-defining nonetheless. For it was at Leonello d'Este's request that he wrote his *On the Art of Building*, and in Ferrara that his architectural journey began with (as Pauline Morin has pointed out) a reflection on horses.[51]

Vitruvius was not interested in horses, which he mentions just once, in book 9, where he gives the name Equus to the constellation now better known as Pegasus, in a rather awkward description with no discernable relevance to the issue here at hand.[52] Proportion was the bedrock of Vitruvius's architectural theory and horses had nothing to do with it. *Symmetria*, he called it, using the Greek term that had no Latin equivalent. It referred, as discussed in chapter 2, to the harmonious correspondence of parts to each other and to the whole. Its proper deployment in a work of architecture resulted in what he called *eurythmia* or eurhythmy, "the beautiful appearance and fitting aspect of the parts once they have been put together." Vitruvius's referent for the proper deployment of *symmetria* in architecture was the proportions of a man's body.[53]

It is well known that Renaissance theoreticians of architecture, Filarete and Francesco di Giorgio among others, took Vitruvius's corporeal referent as axiomatic and with it the implication that an architect's work must be grounded in a relationship, analogical or other, between human bodies and buildings. Francesco di Giorgio was particularly enthusiastic about the idea, which he took to a more literal level than most.

Alberti, on the other hand, was ambivalent. Not about the importance of proportion, nor indeed about a necessary relation between architecture and body, both of which he subscribed to. His hesitation, rather, was about the exact nature of the body in question. In book 7 of his treatise, where he writes about ornament to sacred buildings, he interrupts his account of the correct proportions of a temple portico with the following:

> Just as the head, foot, and indeed any member must correspond to each other and to all the rest of the body in an animal [*in animante*] so in a building, but especially a temple, the parts of the whole body must be so composed that they all correspond one to another, and

any one, taken individually, may provide the dimensions of all the rest.⁵⁴

The passage is a digest of the first four paragraphs of the first chapter of *De architectura*, book 3, which was the first of Vitruvius's two books on temples. In his abbreviated account of what is essentially Vitruvian *symmetria*, Alberti's emendations and omissions are as instructive as what he chooses to retain. In the third of the four paragraphs Alberti paraphrases here, Vitruvius tells how you can circumscribe the body of a "well-shaped man" with a circle and also enclose it in a square, supplying therein the geometrical proof of the body's symmetry in the image that would later become known as "Vitruvian man."⁵⁵ Although obviously interested in the requirement for what Vitruvius calls *symmetria*, Alberti shows not the slightest interest in Vitruvius's "geometrical proof" of the principle in question. The description of the man in the circle and square remains unmentioned, here or anywhere else in Alberti's treatise. For Vitruvius, the point of Vitruvian man was to "prove" that the well-shaped male body was to be taken as the ultimate referent for the perfect correspondence of parts on which he says *symmetria* depends. This Alberti was clearly reluctant to do.⁵⁶ His referent for the perfect correspondence of parts in a building is not the body of a well-shaped man; it is the body of an *animans*, an animal.

This is not to suggest that Alberti was uninterested in human proportions. Knowledge of human proportions is essential for any artist wishing to represent the human figure, he wrote, initially in his treatise on painting and later in *De statua*, his treatise on sculpture, with exhaustive *Tabulae dimensionum hominis*—"tables of human measurements"—presented at the end of the work.⁵⁷ It goes without saying that when (for the sake of readability) I write "human figure," "human proportions," and "human measurements," the reference is to the figure, proportions, and measurements of a man. As Cennino Cennini, author of the widely read *Craftsman's Handbook* that was one of Alberti's sources for *De statua*, assured his readers, women had no set proportions.⁵⁸

Another source for the proportions Alberti tabulates in *De statua* is the proportions Vitruvius details in *De architectura* 3.1.

But a building, obviously, does not represent a man as a statue does. For Alberti it did not and could not. For Vitruvius, on the other hand, it could and did, or at least was meant to. Vitruvius wrote *De architectura* for Augustus Caesar, and his overriding purpose was to persuade the new world ruler of architecture's indispensable role as consolidator of Roman power throughout what, during Augustus's reign, would become known as *corpus imperii*, the "body of empire." The unifying agent of coherence that permeated this imperial world body was the person of its ruler, the "body of the king" whose presence everywhere was assured not only by statues, inscriptions, and coins bearing his image, but also and especially (so Vitruvius) by architecture: by the temples and other buildings that cohered and were beautiful thanks to proportional relationships grounded in the perfect symmetries of the well-shaped man whose transcendent avatar was none other than the emperor himself.[59]

That, to make a very long story short, is why for Vitruvius a building could "represent" a man, or rather, to be honest, *the* man. A temple in a Roman colony in the province of Lusitania, say, would be an attestation of the man's presence through the proportional relationships of his perfect body, which were physically enshrined not, as in a statue, in the contingencies of portraiture, but abstracted in the eternal and ideally changeless forms Vitruvius itemized and sought to render canonic in *De architectura*. Ubiquitous, highly idealized statues of the ever-youthful Augustus and his heirs were meant to tell the same story, but, as Vitruvius knew well, the story told by architecture was by far the more powerful narrative.

De architectura, including Vitruvian man and all the rest, was grounded in the imperial Roman circumstances of its composition. Also grounded in its own time, needless to say, was Alberti's *On the Art of Building*. Like his contemporaries, Alberti was in awe of imperial Rome. In what amounts to an open endorsement of might as right, he even suggested that Roman world rule alone was reason enough to demand the adoption of Roman architectural models.[60] He read *De architectura* carefully, at times critically, and understood the importance Vitruvius attached to architecture as proof of command, invoking in his prologue "the imperial authority and fame that Latins got by their building."⁶¹ He embraced wholeheartedly the concomitant requirement concerning the correspondence of parts that conferred on a work the beauty of an ideally unassailable whole. This whole he often (not always) refers to as a *corpus* or body, as in "a building is a kind of *corpus*," but rarely if ever as that of a man much less that of a woman, sidestepping for instance the gendered anthropomorphism of Vitruvius's column orders, two of which are female.⁶²

In book 6 of *On the Art of Building*, right after pledging that beauty in architecture has the power to cow the ignorant and deflect potential enemies, Alberti sets down his well-known claim that "beauty is the reasoned harmony of all the parts within a whole, so that nothing may be added, taken away, or altered, but for the worse."⁶³ *Concinnitas*, translated here as "harmony," is a key term of Alberti's aesthetics. It has been said to correspond, roughly, to a combination of Vitruvian *symmetria* and *dispositio*— the proportional correspondence of parts combined with their proper arrangement—while at the same time transcending both.⁶⁴ "Spouse both of the soul and reason," Alberti elaborates with some lyricism in book 9, *concinnitas* entwines a man's entire life and everything he does. It permeates the whole of Nature who, concerned that everything she produces be absolutely perfect, produces nothing not governed by its law. Reformulating his famous dictum, he continues:

> Beauty is a form of sympathy and consonance of the parts of the whole in which it is found, according to definite number, outline, and position as dictated by *concinnitas*, the absolute and fundamental rule in Nature. *Concinnitas* is the main object of the art of building, and the source of her dignity, charm, authority and worth.⁶⁵

Grounded exclusively in the proportions of a man's body, Vitruvius's *symmetria* was too restrictive for Alberti, with the word itself too Greek for an author self-consciously seeking at all points to make his language Latin.⁶⁶ Vitruvian man, however perfect, was too fixed and static a referent. Tied as it was to the world rule of a single all-powerful man, the figure was of little practical relevance in the Quattrocento circumstances of Alberti's own day where would-be Caesars were legion.

Alberti eschews *symmetria* (both as a Greek term and for its perceived unsuitability to his purpose) to choose instead *concinnitas*, a word rarely used in classical Latin, never by Vitruvius. Yet for all that Alberti considers it a "law" and "absolute rule," there is no suggestion that its dictates can ever be tied to a single proportional system, just as it never is in the infinitely varied productions of Nature herself. *Concinnitas* governs the perfect correspondence of parts that constitutes *any* whole or "body." Cicero, who topped the list of writers Alberti most admired, was one of the very few Latin authors to use the term.[67] A well-formed speech, Cicero writes, following Plato in this, is like the figure of a man, or indeed of any living creature (*animans*), whose "body has no part added to its structure that is superfluous, and whose whole shape has the perfection of art, not accident."[68] The body of an *animans*, not of a man, is Alberti's exemplar for the *concinnitas* he instructs an architect to seek as the object of his work.

Quemadmodum in animante, Alberti writes in a passage I examined a little earlier, "just as in an *animans*," all the members must correspond to each other and to the whole body, "so too in a building, especially a temple." *Animans* is the present participle of the Latin verb *animo*—"to fill with breath, quicken, animate, endow with life"—and can be either a substantive, as here, or a modifier, as it is in Alberti's *De equo animante*, "On the living horse."[69] As a substantive, *animans* could refer to an animal (not human), or to any living creature, which is how Cicero used it in the passage just referred to, where he goes on to invoke the beauty of trees by way of example.

The life of this *animans* is obviously a primary concern. A corpse, it goes without saying, would have had little appeal as a paradigm for the body either of a well-formed speech or of a well-formed work of architecture. Indeed, setting aside the Leonardo drawing, there is something decidedly corpselike, not to say unnatural, about the essentially two-dimensional, splayed-out figure Vitruvius describes in book 3 of *De architectura*, a lifelessness which may have contributed to Alberti's reluctance to have anything to do with it. And although he draws on Vitruvius for the proportions he tabulates in *De statua*, he is far from limiting himself to these, expanding them into a thoroughgoing numerical account of the fully three-dimensional figure through coordinates established by measuring the bodies of living men.

Earlier, I observed that Alberti begins *De equo animante* by calling attention to how indispensable horses are to all men in all spheres of endeavor, but soon makes it clear that what really interests him is the horse of a warrior prince. Leonello d'Este, the prince for whom he wrote the essay, was unlikely to have been interested in any other kind.

There is a comparable shift in *On the Art of Building*. Alberti begins by declaring architecture a "wholly indispensable" art that "gives comfort and the greatest pleasure to mankind, to individual and community alike."[70] It is not long, however, before his focus narrows to frame it as an art of power and magnificence in a view that mirrors the interests of the *signori* he is writing for—men like Leonello d'Este at whose request he took the project on. Citizens applaud with joy when you erect a fine new building, Alberti writes addressing his chosen audience, because "you have used your wealth to increase greatly not only your own honor and glory, but that of your family, your descendants and the whole city." Building gave Romans fame and imperial authority, he continues.[71] Architects should "deal only with eminent princes of cities who are enthusiasts of such matters," he advises at the end of book 9.[72] "Enthusiasts of such matters" were also more likely than not to be enthusiasts of horses.

Concinnitas, the main object of the art of building, is the source of its "dignity, charm, authority and worth." The perfect correspondence of parts it entails is that of a living creature and confers on a work of architecture the immutable beauty of unassailable truth. Among the myriad creatures informed by *concinnitas*, the living horse is the one which members of Alberti's public, horsemen to a man, would most probably have thought of when they read, for example, that "Nature was so thorough in forming the bodies of animals, that she left no bone separate or disjointed from the rest," the point here being that the "bones" of a building must be bound fast with "muscles and ligaments" in order to make its structure viable.[73] There is also little doubt that Alberti intended to appeal to his readers' understanding of horses—greater surely, in most cases, than their understanding of the art of building—when, reformulating Vitruvius's *utilitas, firmitas, venustas* for his public of Quattrocento *signori*, he writes that the parts of a building

> should be well-suited to the task for which they were designed and above all very serviceable; as regards strength and endurance, they should be sound, firm, and quite permanent; in terms of grace and elegance they should be groomed, ordered, garlanded, as it were, in their every part.[74]

While the requirements of serviceability and strength are applicable to horses and buildings alike, the metaphor of "grooming" and "garlanding" renders the third requirement, beauty, pointedly equine, recalling in this his advice in *De equo animante* about outfitting a warhorse for the celebration of a victory in battle.[75]

Alberti invokes the wholeness of the animal body as the exemplar for architecture several times in the course of his treatise. Yet despite the equine resonance of such directives, there is, in fact, only one occasion where he actually names the horse as the animal referred to. The circumstances that give rise to this single overt reference make it significant.

In chapter 2 of his sixth book, Alberti discusses the nature of beauty ("a great and holy matter") and how it differs from ornament, concluding that beauty is something inherent, suffused throughout the entire body of that which is beautiful, whereas ornament, "a form of auxiliary light or complement to beauty," is not inherent and "has the character of something attached or additional."[76] The chapter that follows presents an overview of the history of building, which began in Asia where in time, Alberti writes, sheer size outweighed all other concerns, eventually leading to the "folly of the pyramids." The Greeks who followed refined the lessons of their Asian forerunners but ultimately fell prey to an excessive preoccupation with good looks. Censure of oriental excess leads to praise of Italian restraint. This is where the horse comes in.

> In Italy, an innate sense of economy [*frugalitas*] demanded from the very start that a building be put together in the same way as a living creature. Consideration of the horse brought with it the realization that it was rare to praise the shape of the animal's individual parts unless they were perfectly adapted to their purpose and led to the conclusion that grace of form could never stand alone or be separated from suitability to intended use.[77]

With world conquest came lessons in embellishment learned from the conquered Greeks, he continues.[78] These, together with the insatiable enthusiasm for building Romans inherited from their Etruscan forebears, led to a depth of understanding and an architectural expertise that raised their achievements to ever higher levels of refinement and magnificence, so that in time "Italy's dominion over the world, already famous for every other virtue, was by her ornament made still more impressive."[79] Alberti's grand imperial narrative begins with the living horse, whose inherent beauty, a fusion of grace and utility, informs the core principle—the "great and holy matter" fundamental to the art of building—which the splendor of ornament brings to light.

Latent in this assignment of an equine foundation to the architecture of Roman power is the suggestion that beauty in the art of building shares with the well-trained warhorse a similar potential for unrivaled expression of a prince's will. To abandon, as Alberti did, the body of the well-shaped man and replace it with the body of the living horse as the perfect embodiment of "the absolute and fundamental rule of nature" he calls *concinnitas* was to give Vitruvius's corporeal paradigm a new shape, deliberately tailored to the preoccupations of his fifteenth-century milieu. In this, as in much else, Alberti was both a subtler theoretician and a far abler courtier than others who, like Filarete and Francesco di Giorgio, read Vitruvius less critically.

Alberti's architectural career began in Ferrara not with a building but with an equestrian monument and an essay on horses. Unlike the other northern Italian cities where he worked during the years that followed—Rimini, Mantua, Urbino, Florence—there is in Ferrara not a single built project attributable to his authorship.[80] But his courtship of the Este nobility and the architectural treatise its prince, Leonello, asked him to write remained neither unacknowledged nor without issue.

The Palazzo Schifanoia, one of several Este family villas known as *delizie* or "delights," was originally a suburban hunting lodge at the edge of the city. Leonello's brother and successor Borso d'Este enlarged it in the mid 1460s with an expansion that included an immense reception room (25 by 11 by 7.5 meters high) known as the Salone dei Mesi or "hall of the months," named for the frescoes painted on its walls by various hands between 1468 and 1469.[81] Each of the twelve months, separated from its neighbors by giant painted Corinthian pilasters, is presented in a tripartite rubric that conforms to an elaborate iconographical program thought to have been devised by Pellegrino Prisciani, court astrologer and secretary to the duke.[82]

The top register of each month represents the triumph of a presiding Olympian deity: Venus for the month of April, for instance. Below this, in the narrow middle register, is the corresponding astrological sign (Taurus for April) accompanied by personifications of three attending decans.[83] The bottom, terrestrial register is the most prominent, taking up nearly half the height of the wall to celebrate the duke, who features repeatedly in each of the seven surviving months engaged in two princely activities, to the virtual exclusion of all others: government and hunting.

The twelve months, five of them no longer legible, unfold counterclockwise, beginning in the westernmost corner of the south wall of the room, where January is preceded by a section of wall which, like six other such segments, is not subdivided into three. The seven undivided panels document historical events against the background of real, mainly Ferrarese, landscapes, with none of the encomiastic theatricality of the calendar months where Borso's rule parades as the perfect sublunary reflection of cosmic order governed by Olympian gods and the twelve heavenly signs.[84]

The undivided panel to the right of January is a prelude to the entire calendar, representing Borso's anticipated investiture as duke of Ferrara by Pope Paul II, which in fact did not take place until 14 April 1471, after the frescoes were completed.[85]

Being formally granted the title he had coveted for twenty years was the pinnacle of Borso's political career. Dukedom gave him sovereignty independent of the will of the people and obviated the need to acknowledge the authority of communal structures on which the right to govern, at least in principle, continued to depend.[86] A duke did not need popular acclaim as a condition of signiorial power, something required of every Este ruler since Obizzo II was elected lord of Ferrara two hundred years earlier. As duke, Borso d'Este was sovereign and answerable only to himself. This, above all, was what the Salone and its calendar of months were meant to celebrate.[87]

The calendar that progresses from right to left around the room concludes with the month of December on the far left of the western wall, at right angles to the investiture panel with which the sequence began. The top, Olympian register features the triumph of Vesta, chaste goddess of the hearth. Capricorn, the sea goat whose head has here been replaced with that of a unicorn, Borso's personal emblem, presides over the winter solstice in the middle, astrological register.[88] The image below in the terrestrial register has almost entirely disappeared, but a rendering of what was left of it at the end of the nineteenth century when damage was less extensive shows it dominated by the front of the Palazzo di Corte, the Este ancestral residence at the city center.[89] To the right of the archway known as the *volto del cavallo*, the bronze equestrian statue of Borso's father, Niccolò III d'Este, commissioned by Leonello d'Este and erected by Borso himself, attested to Borso's dynastic legitimacy and further vindicated his right to rule. There is little doubt that the now illegible foreground of the painting once included Borso d'Este with his courtiers and, most likely, their horses.

For everywhere in the Salone dei Mesi, the walls teem with horseflesh. So numerous and so repetitive are the horses that the artists who painted them are thought, at times, to have resorted to the use of horse templates.[90] Indeed, there is not a single surviving episode of this prodigious epideictic narrative that lacks a substantial equestrian component.

The Este, identified by Armelle Fémelat as *une maison hippophile* exceptionally given to equestrian representations of its members, were major contenders in the competitive culture of horses, as I mentioned earlier.[91] Hence, most obviously and in general, the ubiquity of horses in these paintings, notably the inclusion in the month of April of the St. George's Day palio, over which Borso on horseback presides from a height. Specifically relevant to the overall theme of the frescoes, however, is the prominence given to scenes of the hunt, which gravitate around the central figure of the duke who rides out, surrounded by mounted huntsmen, in every one of the seven surviving months. The overall theme here, as noted, is Borso d'Este's sovereignty, and hunting on horseback had ever been a sport of kings.

According to Plato's *Laws*, hunting on horseback was the only permissible kind of hunting, reflecting a "divine" kind of courage, which fishing, trapping, or hunting on foot did not.[92] For Plato's contemporary Xenophon, as indeed for many later authors, hunting was an analogue for warfare, whose challenges hardened a man, trained him for power, and proved his worth as a leader. "It is not easy to find any quality required in war that is not required also in the chase," Xenophon wrote in his *Cyropaedia*, a work concerning the education of the sixth-century BCE Persian monarch Cyrus the Great which was widely read in the Renaissance.[93] Moreover, the horses chosen for hunting, coursers usually, were generally the same breed as the ones used in warfare, and trained to perform for their riders with the same perfect tractability.[94]

According to contemporary accounts, Borso's sole diversion from the tasks of government, which they say he undertook with unflagging devotion, was the "honest pleasure" of hunting. This he avidly pursued because the bodily fatigue of the sport kept him chaste: he is said to have considered sexual relations beneath his dignity, and was concerned about keeping hereditary bloodlines pure, this last perhaps in reaction to his father's tireless womanizing whose fallout in illegitimate births led to the endlessly contested Este succession.[95] Be that as it may, Borso remained a lifelong bachelor. Deference to his birth sign, Virgo—he was, after all, a devotee of astrology—may have contributed to his alleged preoccupation with his own virginity, which is reflected in his adoption of the unicorn, emblem of chastity and continence, as a personal device.[96] This no doubt is what led to having the unicorn's head replace that of the notoriously randy goat in the representation of Capricorn that presides in the astrological register of December. A relief on the marble surround of Borso's renovated main entrance to the Palazzo Schifanoia has a unicorn bending down to dip its horn into a pool in order, as legend had it, to purify the water and rid it of poison.[97] In 1453, following his investiture as duke of Modena and Reggio, a triumphal pageant celebrating the event included a chariot drawn by two artificial unicorns.[98]

The month of March, one of the three panels by Francesco del Cossa that take up the east wall of the room, is among the best preserved of the frescoes in the Salone. There, two unicorns pull the triumphal car of Minerva, who rules the Olympian register. The unicorns are of interest not only in drawing attention to the presiding virgin goddess of wisdom as to a mythical mirror of the duke himself. They also draw attention to the man standing just behind them, their curved necks tracing a pair of milk-white arches that underscore his presence and elevate his portrait with the suggestion of a marmoreal pedestal or base. The person thus spotlighted is Leon Battista Alberti, who thirty years earlier had concluded his treatise on painting with a request that painters reward his labors by including his portrait in their *istorie* or stories.[99] All well and good. But what is he doing in *this* particular story and not, say, in the month of May, also by Cossa, at the other end of the well, where the presiding deity is Apollo, patron of the arts?

Bareheaded and solemn, Alberti stands a little apart from a group of prominent Ferrarese jurists and other learned disciples of Minerva, whom he faces as if instructing them. Unlike him, all wear head coverings that reflect their rank; some hold documents or books. Among them are men whose portraits identify them as Borso d'Este's councilors.[100] Below, at the right of the terrestrial register of the month, these same men or their homologues appear as advisers to the duke, who stands at the entrance of a small arcaded *all'antica* pavilion, to hear the pleas of three indigent petitioners: two men and a woman with a child. Behind Borso and his entourage, the word IUSTICIA is spelled out in Roman capitals on the lintel of an opening in the rear wall of the

Francesco del Cossa, *The Triumph of Minerva*, upper register of the month of March, 1469 (detail). Salone dei Mesi, Palazzo Schifanoia, Ferrara. Bridgeman Images.

Francesco del Cossa, lower register of the month of March, 1469. Salone dei Mesi, Palazzo Schifanoia, Ferrara. Scala / Art Resource, NY.

pavilion. Above the inscription, a circular medallion presents the duke in profile, Roman style as the portrait of justice itself.[101]

Assuming Alberti is there in some advisory capacity, what kind of guidance is he imparting to the high-ranking jurists he addresses in the Olympian register of Francesco del Cossa's month of March? Why has he been made part of their conversation? Marco Folin's answer (and it strikes me as very much the right one) is that counting Alberti among the prince's councilors points to the political dimension of his teaching, whose "practical operative value made it a tool of government potentially no less effective than other, more traditional forms of knowledge such as jurisprudence."[102]

As I said, the overriding theme of these frescoes is Borso d'Este's sovereignty, played out in the terrestrial register of the cycle through the performance of two interrelated princely activities: government and hunting. Thus, while the rightmost third of this register for March has Borso rendering justice, in the remaining two thirds he participates in a hunt. Twice over, as a matter of fact: once in the foreground, riding out, and then again on a distant promontory leading a group of fellow hunters. At the upper left, a small vignette of agricultural workers tying up vines is ancillary to the display of signiorial power as an illustration of its benefits. Similarly subordinate to the prevailing narrative are other seasonal activities of daily life: the palio in April, a cherry harvest in May, threshing in August, grapes being pressed in September. In the foreground of the lower left of July, you see a trio of buxom young washerwomen. Riders from yet another installment of the duke's sempiternal hunt loom up behind them as they kneel at a stream, attending to their laundry. One of the women turns to look at the huntsmen as they close in.

The same one-third to two-thirds proportion allocated in March to government and hunting respectively is repeated in each of the other surviving months. As in March, Borso's governmental duties are invariably performed standing with his entourage in the ennobling framework of *all'antica* architecture—scenographic aedicules which vary in size and ornateness according to the nature of the lordly task at hand. The complex vaulting and rich ornament of the pavilion where, in the month of September,

Borso receives a Venetian ambassador are vehicles of grandeur meant to telegraph the importance of the event. In April, on the other hand, where he presents his court jester Scoccola with a gratuity, the transaction takes place in the trabeated opening of a relatively plain kiosk, whose noble restraint reflects the simplicity of the duke's kindly gesture while also, of course, calling attention to its princeliness. Truth to tell, a well-designed *all'antica mise en scène* could make almost any activity look princely.

The choice of décor had, not coincidentally, to do with the architectural principle Vitruvius called *decor*, the appropriateness he defined as "the perfect appearance of a work using the correct elements in keeping with accepted practice."[103] The Latin verbs *decoro* (to ornament) and *decet* (it is fitting) are cognates, as is the noun *decus* (ornament, honor, dignity). Vitruvius's older contemporary Cicero wrote that "in an oration nothing is more difficult than to see what is fitting [*quid deceat*]," adding that this key principle, which the Greeks called *to prepon*, is called *decorum* in Latin.[104] The Ciceronian notion of *decorum* underwrote Alberti's understanding of the principle, and led to his virtually identical assertion that "the greatest glory of the art of building is to have a sense of what is appropriate [*quod deceat*]."[105]

Rhetorical categories had been used to formulate the terms of architectural discourse since antiquity, by Vitruvius as well as by Alberti whose theories and vocabulary Cicero did much to shape.[106] That is not the issue here. My purpose, as it has been from the start, is to look at how the architectural theory of Vitruvius and his Renaissance heirs, Alberti among them, is reflected in the replacement of communes by signories during the century and a half that followed the cultural rebirth Petrarch is said to have inaugurated in the mid fourteenth century.

In this, Alberti's revival of the principle of *decor* is particularly relevant, for through the appeal to *decorum*, he makes what he calls "fitting" or "appropriate" in architecture a vindication of a sociopolitical hierarchy he considers at once desirable, naturally founded, and moral.[107] Having established, at the beginning of book 4, that the men who govern should be wise, skillful, and wealthy, he then sets out to "discuss what is appropriate [*quid conveniat*] for the people as a whole, what for the few important citizens and what for the many less important ones."[108] Book 5, on the works of individuals, opens with the assertion that the man who rules alone is to be most highly honored, and the proposal to consider what is appropriate to his case. There follows the discussion I reviewed in chapter 3 concerning the legitimate "king" versus the illegitimate "tyrant," and the dwelling appropriate to each. "It is seemly [*condecet*]," he writes, "that a royal palace [*regum aedes*] be sited in the city center, easy of access, elegant and refined, rather than ostentatious."[109]

It is most fitting (*commodissime*) that such a city be divided by a wall, he explains, for wealthy citizens would be happier separated from the workshops and market stalls at the city center, where "that rabble, as Terence's Gnatho calls them, of poulterers, butchers, cooks and so on, will be less of a risk and a nuisance if they do not mix with important citizens." According to Festus, Alberti continues, Servius Tullius, legendary king of Rome in the sixth century BCE, "ordered all the patricians to live in a district where any rebellion could be instantly put down from a hilltop."[110] In a later chapter, he cites Virgil with approval for having understood it "to be fitting [*convenire*] for leading citizens to have houses well away from the base-born masses and the hubbub of working men."[111] It is, Alberti intimates, in keeping with the wisdom of ancient authority (Terence, Festus, Virgil) that the decorum of creating what we would call gated communities for housing elites is to be advocated. The issue of a hierarchical city receives further consideration in the opening chapter of book 7, where Alberti presents as alternatives the "dignity" of having the nobility's residential quarters far from "any contamination of the common herd" and the "utility" of having every district of the city contain all requirements such as shops and so on in addition to "the houses of the most important citizens."[112]

Book 9, on the ornament of private buildings, begins with praise for the *frugalitas* of ancestral builders—their prudent sense of economy or thrift, which Alberti invokes as a time-tested model of decorum. "The best of later generations were faithful to this frugality in works both public and private, as far as the maintenance of decent custom would allow," he continues, adding that "everything is best when it is tempered to its own importance."[113]

This same *frugalitas*, according to Alberti, had prompted ancestral builders to recognize in the horse a model of how to put a building together, which led in turn to the conclusion that "grace of form could never stand alone or be separated from suitability to intended use [*expetita usus commoditate*]."[114] Alberti's stress on suitability (*commoditas*), rather than on use as such, is also evident in his reformulation of the Vitruvian triad at the beginning of his treatise, where his rendering of Vitruvius's *utilitas* (use) as *ad usum commoda*, "suited to the task," betrays a similar shift in emphasis. The account of "grace and elegance" (Vitruvian *venustas*) that concludes the passage ends it on a decidedly horsey note, as I observed earlier.[115]

What Alberti's dual appeal to the exemplary frugality of ancestral builders seems to imply is that decorum, like *concinnitas*, is grounded in an equine paradigm. Or, at the very least, that the suitability to use which gives beauty to a horse and the fitness to importance which contributes to the grace and elegance of a building are comparable iterations of the same principle, one that the frugal ancestors of Alberti's aetiology were the first to recognize as fundamental in the art of building. "In our theory of building," he writes elsewhere, "we do not distinguish between what is fitting [*commoda*] and what is necessary."[116]

In the Schifanoia frescoes that showcase Borso d'Este's sovereignty, the duke is either on horseback or standing. When he is standing, ennobling architectural décor makes up for his lack of a mount through the deployment of *all'antica* pavilions "tempered," as Alberti would have it, according to the importance of the princely task at hand, whether it is greeting an ambassador, remunerating a faithful retainer, or, as in March, rendering justice at the entrance of a soberly arcuated structure where his portrait in the medallion behind him is labeled IUSTICIA.

The monument Borso raised to himself fifteen years before these frescoes were painted had also made him a manifestation of justice, for the identification was a favorite trope, as Charles Rosenberg has shown.[117] While his father Niccolò III's monument was, of course, equestrian, Borso's monument, which had no horse, had him sitting atop the elaborate multitiered entablature of a giant Composite column that was—as the painted pavilions at Schifanoia would later be—architectural affirmation of his authority in matters of government. Not just government, but *good* government. For that of course is the point of representing Borso's sovereignty in an epideictic that hammers home with unfailing grace and elegance the inherent, cosmically sanctioned desirability of one man's rule and the ancillary benefits thereof.

A comparison with Lorenzetti's allegory of good government seems unavoidable and gives the measure of how much has changed in the intervening century and a half. Needless to say, it would be absurd to cast the famously affable Borso d'Este as a Tyrammides, the horned demon Lorenzetti made the personification of one-man rule in his fresco cycle of the 1330s, discussed in earlier chapters. Yet there is absolutely no doubt that he, Borso, reigns alone in the Ferrarese murals where the common good (if indeed that is what is signified by the vignettes of threshing, vine-trimming, laundry, and the like confined to small corners of the pictorial space) devolves from the beneficence of the smiling prince you are expected to see as Justice personified. The prince, in other words, is the source, not the subordinate, of the Common Good, the personification who of course is the presiding force in the Sala dei Nove in Siena. There, government by the Sienese themselves, guided by a transcendent Justice, administers its benefits which occupy the whole east wall of the room. The "hubbub of working men," which Alberti would later advise leading citizens to distance themselves from, resonates throughout this idealized Siena as its very *raison d'être*.

The entire panorama includes the city proper and the countryside beyond its walls. Among countless ordinary people standing, walking, or seated on benches, there are just six horsemen and one horsewoman, all minor players in the overarching narrative. Given their horses, the riders are probably aristocrats, but there is no suggestion that they rule the city, in which there is, of course, no evidence at all of architecture *all'antica*, nor indeed of any kind of structure meant as scenographic enhancement of any one man's importance. In Lorenzetti's mid-Trecento rendering of the well-governed city, it is the whole community's importance that is enhanced, and not by a building or buildings but by the light that emanates from the shared public space of the *platea communis* at the city center.

Borso d'Este died in August 1471, just four months after his investiture as duke of Ferrara. His younger half-brother Ercole who inherited the title would rule for 34 years and change the face of the city. By the beginning of the next century the duke had made all of Ferrara, now greatly expanded, not just a fictional *mise en scène* for the enhancement of his importance, but a veritable citywide grandstand for his uncontestable sovereignty.

Alberti, who died in 1472, did not advise the new duke in person, of course. But his councilor, the court librarian, astrologer, and general polymath Pellegrino Prisciani did. Prisciani, who was something of a fixture at the Este court and admired Alberti greatly, had also advised Ercole's predecessor. The acknowledgment Alberti receives in the Schifanoia frescoes whose iconographic program Prisciani developed for Borso d'Este was almost certainly at Prisciani's instigation.[118] Similarly if, as has been claimed, *On the Art of Building* became Ercole d'Este's *livre de chevet*, this was also undoubtedly with the scholar's encouragement.[119]

Sometime between 1490 and the duke's death in 1505, Prisciani wrote a short treatise called *Spectacula* for Ercole, whom he addresses in a Latin preface where he directs his dedicatee's attention to the benefits scholars can bring to those who govern.[120] The work itself is written around a collation of passages from Vitruvius and Alberti, translated into Italian and taken for the most part from the authors' respective chapters on the theaters and other places of public entertainment Alberti calls *spectacula* ("show buildings"), which no doubt gave Prisciani his title.[121]

His opening paragraphs dwell on the importance of spectacle in cities, not only as a form of celebration and for the pleasure it gives to the people, but above all for the great service it renders to the state.[122] In this Prisciani follows Alberti, but with greater immediacy, reformulating what his model advises in general terms as counsel addressed to the duke in person. Thus, he writes,

> I cannot help but praise Your Highness for having
> organized so many great spectacles that have brought

your gentle and most devoted people together, to delight them, improve their way of life, encourage them to study and become learned men so as to honor and be of no small benefit to the entire state. In this way has Your Most Illustrious Lordship obliged me to seek out ancient records of such spectacles and games and the buildings they require.

For even as Plato advised, he continues, games and theatrical performances should be held every year as necessary for the ornament and well-being of the city.[123]

Although Vitruvius is as much an authority for Prisciani as Alberti is, the Ferrarese's insistence on the public benefit of spectacle derives entirely from the latter. In all of the relevant chapters of *De architectura* there is not a single mention of public shows being necessary for the honor and well-being of the state. Nonetheless, it is worth recalling that it was in imperial Rome that the political strategy of what, a century and a half after Vitruvius, Juvenal would famously indict as "bread and circuses" was best understood and most effectively deployed. The loss of civic autonomy Juvenal deplores is arguably no less deplorable in the decline of the medieval commune's civic institutions, with the *spectacula* Prisciani presents as a benefit to the entire state a late Quattrocento iteration of the Roman satirist's *panem et circenses*.[124] At Rome, a hundred years before Juvenal, the reign of Augustus Caesar had marked the end of the 500-year Republic and inaugurated the period of one-man rule known as the Empire. Nobody before Augustus, writes his biographer Suetonius, "had ever provided so many, so different, or such splendid public shows [*spectacula*]," following up his claim with a long and detailed list of the emperor's lavish entertainments.[125] In this as much as anything else, Augustus was Ercole d'Este's model.[126]

The work on spectacle Prisciani prepared for his prince as a digest of Vitruvius and Alberti tends to channel all of their writing on architecture, and indeed all of architecture itself, in the direction of that single (spectacular) purpose, with implications far beyond acknowledgment of Ercole d'Este's well-known predilection for spectacle and the revival of ancient theater.[127] In the frescoes of the Salone dei Mesi, representations of cosmic order, horses, and architecture-as-décor had all contributed to the creation of a showcase for Borso d'Este's sovereignty and, concomitantly, for the benefits of this one man's good government. The showcase for his successor Ercole's sovereignty became the entire city, with the principal benefit of his rule nothing less nor more than the show itself. The importance of Prisciani's insistence on the service spectacle renders to the state resides in its theoretical vindication of precisely that intention.

Though Pellegrino Prisciani's debt to his sources was great, he was more than just their unreflective intermediary, as Danilo Aguzzi Barbagli has shown.[128] The attention he pays to the Colosseum, whose elliptical *relevé* he drew based on personal survey, contests Alberti's claim that amphitheaters consist of "two theaters, their tiers linked in a continuous circle," and is a case in point.[129] His assessment of his authorities is judicious, as he weighs them one against the other and also, as with the Colosseum, against his own experience. But the most significant body of firsthand knowledge to inform the treatise—the awareness to which it owes its very existence—is its author's eyewitness to the changes under way in his native city during the rule of his prince and patron Ercole d'Este. This is particularly evident in the extended range of buildings he includes under the rubric of *spectacula*. It is worth repeating that *spectacula* were interchangeably both shows and the places where shows were held.

The work begins with an account of theaters, drawn principally from Vitruvius and Alberti but accompanied by Prisciani's own explanatory plans and sections, which were something of a first at a time when available sources did not yet include drawings.[130] Chapters on amphitheaters and circuses follow.[131] After that Prisciani strikes out on his own with a chapter somewhat cryptically entitled *Del portico xysto o vero ambulatione*: roughly, "On the portico or covered walkway." Alberti also discusses these so-called *ambulationes*, but for him such porticos are not *spectacula* but *publica opera*, "public works," as indeed they were for Vitruvius who discusses them in his chapter on palaestrae.[132] Prisciani is specific and unequivocal: the *portico xysto* or *ambulatio*, he writes, is "another kind of show building [*una altra facta de spectacolo*]."[133]

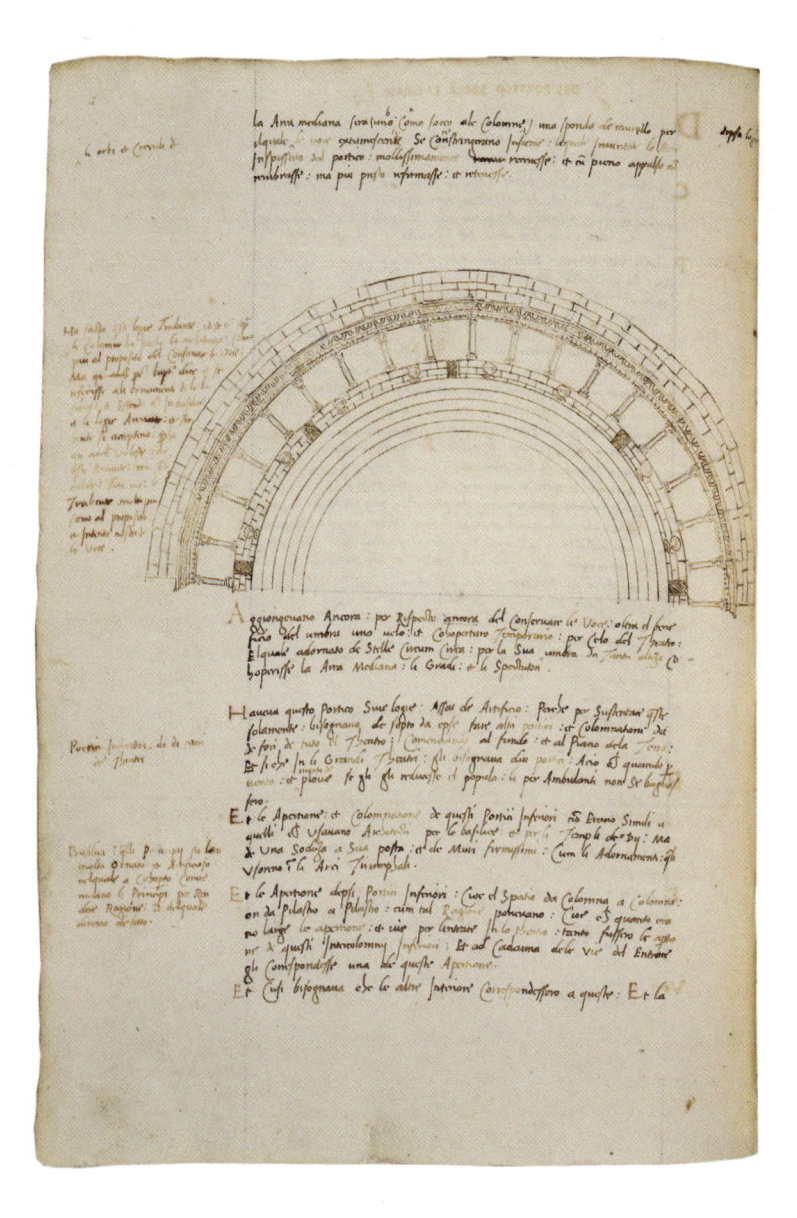

Pellegrino Prisciani, *Spectacula*, c. 1500. Biblioteca Estense, Modena, Ms. Lat. 466=alfa X.1.6, fol. 23v. By permission of the Ministero della Cultura—Gallerie Estensi, Biblioteca Estense Universitaria.

Next come chapters on the architectural orders, the Doric, Ionic, and Corinthian, with the proportions and ornaments of their respective column shafts, bases, capitals, and entablatures, all with accompanying illustrations. Prisciani's account of the Corinthian capital includes Vitruvius's story about its origin—the girl, her tomb, the basket, and so on—which Alberti omits.[134] In *De architectura*, the orders or "kinds" of columns are treated in books 3 and 4, the two books Vitruvius devotes to temples. Alberti follows suit, giving his own account in book 7 of his treatise under the title "Ornament to sacred buildings." The extent to which the orders would become the undisputed, virtually exclusive focus of writing about architecture in the course of the next two centuries tends to obscure the significance of Prisciani's displacement of them from the sacred to the spectacular, not to mention the significance of his concern, complete with explicative graphics, for getting the look exactly right as a guarantee of the *all'antica* authenticity of the spectacle.

Most remarkable of all by far is Prisciani's inclusion of, as he puts it, the "forum or what we call a piazza" among his *spectacula*.[135] This Alberti does not do, nor does Vitruvius. Nonetheless, Prisciani's unnamed authority here ("some have rightly written") is in fact book 5 of *De architectura*, on public works, which begins with a discussion of fora and a mention, which the Ferrarese has obviously seized upon, concerning the ancient Roman custom of staging gladiatorial shows in them, with what Vitruvius calls *spectacula* ("tiered seating" or "bleachers" in this instance) temporarily arranged on the perimeter to accommodate spectators.[136] But his principal authority in this is Ercole d'Este, duke of Ferrara.

A frenzy of architectural activity, which continued unabated until his death in 1505, followed his accession in August 1471 to what had become, with Borso d'Este's investiture four months earlier, a hereditary title independent of popular approval. It was a situation Ercole appears to have recognized as being not entirely without risk. Within weeks of taking power, in a move which closely followed Alberti's advice on the matter, he was building a fortified corridor that would give him a secure escape route, should the need arise, from his residence in the Palazzo di

Corte at the city center to the garrisoned fortress, the Castel Vecchio, to the north.[137]

The Palazzo di Corte was located on the west side of the *piazza comunale*, also known as the *piazza maggiore*, an L-shaped public square, which ecclesiastical, communal, and signiorial authorities had, exceptionally if at times uneasily, held in common since the inception of Este rule in the mid thirteenth century.[138] The cathedral and palazzo faced each other across the short leg of the L. Its long leg, which flanked the south side of the cathedral, was a market square, surrounded by communal government buildings such as the Palazzo della Ragione, which housed the commune's law courts, and a mixture of workshops and commercial establishments. The building projects Ercole undertook during the early years of his reign ultimately converged on the transformation of this shared public place into the prince's personal parade ground, with the mongrel confusion of the original piazza reconfigured in keeping with Alberti's directives as just the kind of "forum" Prisciani would later classify as a *spectaculum*.

When in 1454, four years after Borso d'Este became lord of the city, he had his statue enthroned on the summit of a Composite column as a manifestation of justice, he raised the monument in front of the Palazzo della Ragione on the long south side of the *piazza maggiore*. At the time, Borso's chosen location was at once a tacit nod to the dependence of his position on communal ratification and a reminder of the commune's dependence on *him*. Duke Ercole withdrew this acknowledgment of civic interdependence a year after his accession when he removed his half-brother's monument to the front of the Palazzo di Corte, where he installed it to the left of the palace entrance.[139] There, paired with the equestrian monument to their father Niccolò III d'Este on the opposite, right-hand side, the two monuments together made an unequivocal declaration of dynastic power and transformed the palace entrance, henceforth the *volto del cavallo*, into what was in effect a triumphal arch, whose position also made it the entry from the palace courtyard into the *piazza maggiore*, or "forum," of Ferrara. "The greatest enhancement to a forum ... is the arch" Alberti wrote in the chapter that furnished Pellegrino Prisciani with his own account.[140]

Asymmetrical, with few of the forms, proportions, and ornaments Alberti prescribes, the *volto del cavallo* is a lopsided, cobbled-together affair, and a poor excuse, relatively speaking, for an Albertian, Roman-style triumphal arch (Vitruvius does not discuss triumphal arches). But as an archway that is unquestionably triumphal, it qualifies nonetheless—if not in canonical detail, in intent and general morphology at the very least. Circumventing the shortfalls inevitable in any such ad hoc assembly of preexisting parts would require starting from scratch, which Ercole d'Este, with the advice among others of Pellegrino Prisciani, would soon undertake to do.

In the meantime transformation of the *piazza maggiore* and of the adjacent Palazzo di Corte, on which public life was to become wholly dependent, proceeded apace.[141] In the course of the 1470s, communal agencies—taxation offices, the wheat control board, law courts, and the municipal council known as the *Savi*, among others—were removed to offices in the refurbished palace courtyard, which became the de facto seat of government.[142] Although Ercole's courtyard looked nothing like a cortile on the Florentine model, his intentions made it yet another iteration of the trend, endorsed by Alberti, whereby, beginning with Cosimo de Medici in the mid 1450s, the atrium of a prince's house became a locus of power.[143]

Commercial and artisanal activity was banished from the piazza along with governmental functions.[144] Market stalls, kennels, bakeries, and a lumber yard were all swept away. The venerable *loggia dei calegari* or shoemakers' loggia that had occupied the eastern end of the piazza for over 200 years became a school for humanistic studies in the early 1480s. Alberti's disdain for "base-born masses and the hubbub of working men" was entirely in tune with the tenor of the times, and perfectly synchronous with Pope Sixtus IV's simultaneous banishment of the market from the Capitol at Rome in 1477, as well as with projects of urban *renovatio* under way elsewhere.[145]

As at the Campidoglio, but completed with lightning speed, comparatively speaking, clearance of the Ferrarese piazza was accompanied by major changes in décor.[146] Commercial establishments allowed to remain henceforth did dignified business in the porticoes of new marble colonnades: the cloth merchants in a long arcade against the south side of the cathedral where, now hidden from view, the statutes promulgated by the commune of Ferrara in 1173 were inscribed; the cobblers (until they were displaced by the humanists) in an identically refurbished loggia at the end of the square; moneychangers, tailors, and building contractors in similarly elaborated ground-floor loggias of the three superimposed tiers of marble arcades added to the front of the Palazzo di Corte, whose top two levels were accessible from the palace interior.[147]

Decorated with relief portraits of twelve Roman emperors, the topmost level projected over the others under a protective roof and was Ercole d'Este's personal reviewing stand. From this imperial box, his *regium cubiculum*, the duke could be observed high above the crowd watching *spectacula* unfold in the forum below: feats of arms and celebrations of all kinds but most especially jousts and tournaments for which, as a condottiere and expert horseman, he had a special proclivity. When it was renovated, the façade of the Palazzo della Ragione was repainted, as was the front of the former cobblers' loggia, with chivalric scenes in keeping with such contests. "Chivalry," from the French *cheval*, was by definition all about men on horses. The *chevaliers* inevitably prominent in these painted images were, perhaps more than anything else in the radically altered décor of the piazza, an indicator of how much had changed in the city, their fictional presence as horsemen, on the front of the Palazzo della Ragione above all, having little to do with the previous life of the square and everything to do with its present one. In 1481, in what was by then a needlessly redundant gesture of signiorial appropriation, the fountain installed at the eastern end of the erstwhile *piazza comunale* was made in the shape of a diamond, the duke's personal emblem.

Ercole d'Este's inauguration of what has been called the great era of Ferrarese theater followed the renovation of the *piazza maggiore*.[148] It began in 1486 with the performance in the vernacular of a comedy by the ancient Roman playwright Plautus called *The Menaechmi* in the courtyard of the Palazzo di Corte, at the west end of the piazza. During the next fifteen years this and other

Roman comedies were performed in different parts of the same palace where they were presided over by the duke, seated in an elevated tribunal, whose virtues were celebrated on stage during the *intermezzi*. The labors of Hercules, Ercole's mythical namesake, were a favorite subject.[149]

Another constant was the inclusion, whatever the play, of a scenographic feature known as the *città ferrarese*—a "Ferrarese city" of painted wood that was the play's *mise en scène*.[150] "We saw," writes the poet Battista Guarini in an eyewitness account of the inaugural 1486 performance, "we saw the city raised with towers and walls / and dwellings arranged along magnificent broad avenues."[151] The plays varied but the décor never did.

In February of 1502, five Plautus comedies were staged not in the ducal palace, as had until then been the custom, but exceptionally and for the first time in the Palazzo della Ragione, seat of the commune's civic administration until the 1470s when, as mentioned earlier, Ercole d'Este had the law courts, municipal council, and taxation offices moved to the courtyard of his palace. Also for the first time the theater, located on the upper floor of the Palazzo della Ragione, was built with a semicircular *cavea*, as described by Vitruvius and represented in Prisciani's *Spectacula*.[152]

The *mise en scène* of a *città ferrarese* remained unchanged and provided the same urban setting for all five plays. Also unchanged, of course, was the sovereign presence of the duke, of exceptional consequence on these occasions, since the theatrical performances were among the entertainments marking the marriage of his son and heir, Alfonso, to Lucrezia Borgia. An overpass led from the ducal palace to the new venue and gave Ercole and his retinue elevated, red carpet access to the theater.[153]

It would be difficult to overstate the significance of this confluence of events. Through its transformation into a *spectaculum*, not only was the original civic purpose of the Palazzo della Ragione usurped by the requirements of spectacle. The overpass that linked it to the Palazzo di Corte effectively assimilated this erstwhile seat of communal government to the ducal residence and reduced it to just another room in the palace. Another feature of the princely décor.

Pellegrino Prisciani, the *piazza maggiore*, Ferrara, as redesigned in the late 1470s. From *Historiae Ferrarienses liber IX*, Archivio di Stato, Modena, ms. 133, fol. 19r (detail). By permission of the Ministero per i Beni e le Attività Culturali e per il Turismo—Archivio di Stato di Modena prot. no. 2710.

As I said, one of Ercole d'Este's closest advisers in these undertakings was Pellegrino Prisciani, who included a perspective drawing of the refurbished *piazza maggiore*, viewed from the west, in his never-published *Historiae Ferrarienses* written in Latin between the late fifteenth and early sixteenth centuries.[154] In the fourth of the manuscript's nine surviving books, the chapter called *Descriptio urbis Ferrariae*, there is a *pictura* where, he writes,

> readers can apprehend what is written in the text, embracing it at a glance, at a distance as it were from above. In this way my representation will show—through a properly proportioned and accurately measured drawing—the city of Ferrara, its suburbs and buildings and the Po that glides past it, presenting clearly the previous circuit walls of the city as well as the enlargements [*ampliationes*] I spoke of.[155]

The *pictura* here referred to is an ink and wash drawing, spread over the next two folios of Prisciani's manuscript. As Marco Folin has shown, this innovative and extremely precocious orthogonal projection of Ferrara, seen "as it were from above," was drawn in 1494–1495, and predates even the much-vaunted plan of Imola Leonardo da Vinci drew in 1502.[156] Drawn to a scale of 1:8,000, as its author notes in the right-hand margin, its principal interest in the present context is as an accurate and very early representation of the *ampliatio* or "enlargement" of Ferrara known as the Herculean Addition: the famous expansion which more than doubled the city's size and five hundred years later would qualify it as an "ideal city," earning it the title of World Heritage Site.[157]

It is generally agreed that Ercole d'Este's decision to extend the boundary of Ferrara northward was originally dictated by concern to strengthen the city's defenses against the possibility of renewed attack from the north, after his two-year-long war with Venice ended in 1484.[158] The project had other motivations as well. When his enemies objected to what they saw as a threat, Ercole insisted that his aims were wholly peaceful. Indeed, from the outset, the undertaking had included plans for nonmilitary urban development within the territory known as the Barco to

Pellegrino Prisciani, plan of the Herculean Addition, 1494–1495, with south at the top. From *Historiae Ferrarienses liber IV*, Archivio di Stato, Modena, ms. 130, fols. 20v–21r. By permission of the Ministero per i Beni e le Attività Culturali e per il Turismo—Archivio di Stato di Modena prot. no. 2710.

be encompassed by a new, six-kilometer fortification wall.[159] Yet despite the duke's avowal of none but peaceful intentions, during the decade and more of its implementation, the venture continued to display the character of a military operation. The 250 hectares of the Addition were hardly ancient Gaul, of course, but the unswerving resolve with which the condottiere prince attacked his project brings to mind the speed and determination Julius Caesar was famous for and claimed as the key to his success, in Gaul as elsewhere. Vitruvius, who had been with Caesar during his Gallic campaign, writes that an architect must be equipped with the right kind of knowledge so that, "fully armed," he may reach his goal "swiftly and with authority."[160] Architecture is war waged by other means.

Ercole's first recorded visit to the site with a view to its enclosure and eventual urbanization took place on 14 December 1484 when, as the chronicler Ugo Caleffini reports, "the duke mounted into a carriage and, accompanied by crossbowmen on horseback, peasants, and his engineer, went out to the Barco to see about making it bigger than it was."[161] The engineer in question must have been Biagio Rossetti, long (and, as it now appears, wrongly) credited as sole author of the entire Addition.[162] That Rossetti designed the new fortification wall remains undisputed, however, and would account for his having been part of that initial expedition. The presence of armed crossbowmen as outriders was overt confirmation of military intent, and a reminder that the recently concluded peace with Venice was a fragile one. Peasants, there no doubt because they lived in the area, may have been concerned, if so justifiably, about their possible displacement. Although part of the Barco—or, as it would become known, the Terra Nuova—was the duke's private hunting park, much of it was agricultural land, which would be irretrievably compromised during the years to come.

Ground was not broken for another seven and a half years, with excavation of the deep, 30-meter-wide moat following the trace of the new wall, marked out in late August 1492.[163] Construction of the wall itself began three years later, with development inside the new perimeter going forward in tandem—all of this, the chronicles record, under the close supervision of the duke in person. If, as certain scholars have claimed, the real author of the Addition was Ercole d'Este himself, he was nothing like the hands-off *concepteur* Alberti famously defines as an architect, who never actually visits a building site, as in fact Alberti never did.[164]

Apart from his first exploratory visit in a carriage, Ercole's trips to the Barco during the 1490s were invariably on horseback, carried out in the manner of a general mustering his troops. His secretary Siviero Sivieri records how almost every morning he would mount his horse and spend the entire day riding tirelessly from one end of the immense site to the other, directing proceedings from his saddle and examining every detail of work in progress, even missing mealtimes.[165] In those days, Caleffini confirms, Ercole took interest in nothing else.[166] What Marco Folin has called Ercole's fundamentally irrational obsession did not escape criticism. "The duke of Ferrara," writes another chronicler, one Hondedio di Vitale, "does nothing but build palaces, make music, stage jousts, and ride from one place to another, and never thinks of governing."[167] Good government—or indeed any government at all—seems to have been of minimal concern to the prince who, Hondedio goes on to lament, refused to listen to his people.[168] The cost of the Addition—in forced labor, massive decline in agricultural production, and ever-increasing taxes—was astronomical. The benefits to the *popolo* who mostly underwrote it were nil, while investors, speculators, and unscrupulous entrepreneurs profited greatly.[169]

Commissioned around this time, possibly by Ercole himself, and perhaps after a drawing by Pellegrino Prisciani, a well-known bird's-eye view of Ferrara from the south presents it, explicitly, as the *spectaculum* of current signiorial predilection.[170] Located at the exact geometrical center of the image, its stage is the hugely overscaled, short leg of the L-shaped *piazza maggiore*—the section of the square in front of the ducal palace. Completely occluded from view is the much larger, long leg of the L whose erasure strikes all recollection of the communal administration formerly located there from its visual record, and with it any reminder of the concessions to communal authority once demanded of the city's lord. Around it, the rest of the city figures as the architectural *mise en scène* for this nexus of power with no visible occupant. The

View of Ferrara, woodcut, 1498. Biblioteca Estense, Modena. Photo: A. De Gregorio. © DeA Picture Gallery / Art Resource, NY.

empty stage is a constant in contemporary renderings of what are taken to be "ideal cities"—those in the famous panels now in Baltimore, Berlin, and Urbino most notably. Like Ferrara in this late fifteenth-century woodcut they are cities without people. In the Ferrarese view there is a noteworthy exception, however.

At the top of the image at the north of the city, you see the Herculean Addition, still under construction, with its newly completed fortification wall and some of the buildings that preexisted the area's development: the Palazzo della Certosa, for instance, an Este palace the duke enlarged, and the church of Santa Maria degli Angeli, which gave its name to the Addition's broad new north-south thoroughfare. By the time Ercole died in 1505 the Via degli Angeli (now the Corso Ercole I d'Este) would be lined with some twenty new aristocratic *palazzi*, including the spectacular Palazzo dei Diamanti, built for Ercole's younger brother Sigismondo and designed by Biagio Rossetti: a brilliant tour de force of stone-cutting with its cladding of diamond-pointed white marble, which, with the diamond a family emblem, made it another affirmation of Este sovereignty.[171]

The sole human occupants of the otherwise deserted city represented in this idealized view appear in the middle distance at the rear of what may be one of the new palaces on the Via degli Angeli. As large as the *palazzo* behind him, and isolated against the background of an undeveloped field, the duke of Ferrara sits on horseback a little ahead of a retinue of somewhat smaller courtiers, also on horseback.[172] Standing in front of Ercole's horse, cap in hand, a man reaches up to present him with what looks like a document; a plan perhaps for which the duke's approval is required, or some other proposal connected with the site where, paradoxically, no construction is visibly under way, nor any worker present. Whatever the exact nature of the exchange between the two men, the deferential posture of the man on foot spotlights the horseman's elevated position of authority.

While the image is graphic affirmation of what the chronicles say about Ercole's constant presence on the site, it also repeats the refrain that his visits were always on horseback. *Il duca monto a cavallo...* ; *Sua Excellentia ha cavalcato da ogni die* ... The wildly ambitious project of doubling the size of the city the woodcut presents

View of Ferrara, woodcut, 1498: detail of Duke Ercole on horseback. Biblioteca Estense, Modena. Photo: A. De Gregorio. © DeA Picture Gallery / Art Resource, NY.

as a stage for display of its ruler's power is, perforce, a project for the simultaneous, directly proportional magnification of that power. The architect prince here pictured as the man in charge is also, let us not forget, a warrior prince and a man on a horse. If his horse, as I suggested earlier, is (as indeed a war horse must be) the emanation of its rider's will, so too is the new city that here springs up around him, as if by his sole fiat, in an unrivaled expression of his dominance and (as both Vitruvius and Alberti would have recognized) its lasting proof.

At the upper right-hand edge of the open field that surrounds the duke and his party, the sketch of a small arcade signals what would be the ceremonial center of the new city: the Piazza Nuova, as it was known, built *ex novo* on farmland purchased from one Niccolò Zermia in 1493.[173] Unhampered by the preexisting conditions that had complicated the makeover of the *piazza maggiore* in the old city, the duke and his architects could exploit this uncompromised vacant (or at least vacated) site to lay out an ideal "forum," twice the size of the piazza at the city center, in perfect keeping with Alberti's advice on the matter: a double square (100 by 200 meters, in this case), surrounded by porticoes, of which only two sections were ever completed.[174]

The single recorded mention of what the immense square might have been for is Ugo Caleffini's diary entry for 9 May 1494, where he writes that the duke was having a new piazza "made for a marketplace [*da fare mercato*]."[175] Charles Rosenberg has supposed that the square was to be a venue for a variety of military and civilian activities, including those of a market.[176] It is obvious, however, that the main reason for its development was to create precisely the kind of antique forum-as-*spectaculum* Pellegrino Prisciani favors, meant above all for the spectacle of the Ferrarese lord's magnificence.[177]

The unrivaled dominance to which the Herculean Addition testified, and of which the figure of the prince on horseback was the consummate epitome, would have received unequivocal ratification in the equestrian monument of Ercole that was to have occupied the center of the piazza clearly intended as a setting for the monument.[178] According to the anonymous author of the *Diario ferrarese*, in December 1498 foundations were being laid in the Piazza Nuova for a base "on which," he writes, "the commune intends to place a large marble column, and on top of it they are going to put a gilded bronze statue of the duke Ercole on horseback to commemorate that his lordship had had the Terra Nuova built, and the fortifications."[179] Ercole, close to seventy by then, went out every day *a cavallo* to supervise, the diarist continues. But the project was never completed in the duke's lifetime and was ultimately abandoned by his successors.

The proposed equestrian monument would have been grandiose. The Ferrarese artist and architect Ercole de' Roberti was put in charge of the project in about 1493. Two surviving images, one an ink drawing, the other a woodcut, record its projected appearance, with the woodcut, published in an album by one Alfonso Maresti in 1672, considered the more accurate of the two representations.[180]

Although they differ somewhat in their details, both images agree on the essentials: a two-tiered base supporting not one but two columns with the duke, helmeted and in full armor, riding as if into battle on top of their crowning entablature. The twin columns recall, no doubt intentionally, the pillars of Hercules that were one of Ercole d'Este's emblems, for the trope of the duke as a mirror of his mythical namesake had been current for decades, as a well-known bronze statuette of Hercules on horseback dating from early in his reign attests, as well as many other representations, including coins.[181]

Like the ideal forum whose centerpiece it was meant to be, Ercole's monument would have been designed and assembled *ex novo*, differing in this from the one of his father, Niccolò III, in the old city, which it was obviously intended to outdo. Ercole's perfectly matched marble columns were monoliths, each measuring nine meters (30 feet) in height, with a diameter of one and a half meters.[182] This proportion of 1:6 is consistent with those of Vitruvius's "manly" Doric order, but being destined, according to the surviving images, for a kind of hybrid Composite or Corinthian capital, the columns were unusually thick for their height, which was twice that of the mismatched columns under Niccolò's statue. Not surprisingly, the size of these monoliths made for difficulties in transport. One of them sank into the Po as it was being

Equestrian monument to Ercole I d'Este (project), c. 1490. From Alfonso Maresti, *Teatro geneologico dell'antiche et illustri famiglie di Ferrara* (Ferrara: Stampa Camerale, 1672), 2:152. Biblioteca Comunale Ariostea di Ferrara.

unloaded from a barge, never to be recovered. The other reached its destination but could not be raised, and lay abandoned on the site until 1639, when a fireworks explosion split it in two.[183]

A seventeenth-century drawing of the monument's two-tiered base shows the lower tier, a few fragments of which survive, with a frieze of ducal emblems, military trophies, and the garlanded monogram HER. DU.[184] The taller top tier is divided into rectangular panels meant to carry a lengthy inscription, of which there are several surviving transcriptions.[185] A preamble in Italian declares the area within a 20-foot radius of the monument an asylum, with any violation punishable as a crime of *lèse majesté*. There follow seven stanzas in Latin cataloguing Ercole d'Este's achievements. It was in recognition of his great deeds, the text concludes, that the "senate" of Ferrara named him "Augustus" and conferred on him the title of *Pater patriae*.

It would be neat but sadly impossible to attribute the source of Ercole's text to that of Augustus Caesar's own, autobiographical *Res gestae* (Achievements) which it closely resembles, in both form and content, especially given the duke's known adulation of the Roman emperor. Though Ercole's text is shorter, it touches all the same bases, and concludes with the bestowal of precisely the same titles, Augustus and *Pater patriae*, as the Augustan text.[186] But the text of the original *Res gestae* was unknown in Ercole's day. Initially discovered late in the sixteenth century inscribed in Greek on the walls of the early first-century CE Temple of Augustus in what is now Ankara, it was not transcribed until 200 years after that, and only published in the nineteenth century.[187]

Suetonius's lives of the Caesars were well known, however, and at the end of the final chapter of his life of the "divine" Augustus, he writes of a scroll, included with the emperor's will, that contained an account of what he had accomplished (*rerum a se gestarum*), which he "desired to have inscribed on bronze tablets and set up at the entrance to his mausoleum."[188] The preamble to the *Res gestae* inscribed on the temple wall in Ankara refers to these tablets, explaining that what follows is a copy whose original is "engraved on two bronze pillars set up in Rome."[189] It was undoubtedly Suetonius's mention of them that suggested to Duke Ercole, or more probably to his scholarly entourage who then suggested it to him, how much such an epigraphic memorial of his achievements would contribute to the grandeur of his towering monument. And it was also Suetonius's life of Augustus that gave the author(s) of Ercole's inscription the thematic structure on which to model their account of the duke's achievements. These, with remarkable success, the court epigraphers distilled into the lapidary formulation "in memory of the Divine Ercole d'Este, second Duke" so uncannily similar in tone and outline to the imperial *Res gestae* "engraved on two bronze pillars at Rome" which they clearly wished to emulate but had obviously never seen.¹⁹⁰

Ercole's military successes are given pride of place in the opening two stanzas of his inscription. His architectural undertakings, detailed in the four stanzas that follow, take up almost all of the remaining text and are ultimately what prevail as the most memorable of his accomplishments. "From the time he succeeded to the *Imperium* he planned and perfected much for the ornament [*ornatum*] of the *Urbs*," this section of the Ferrarese inscription begins. The *Imperium* here is Ercole's dukedom, of course, and the *Urbs* not Rome but the city of Ferrara.¹⁹¹ The source is not difficult to pinpoint.

"The *Urbs*, whose ornament [*ornatum*] was not in keeping with the majesty of empire [*maiestas imperii*], Augustus so perfected," writes Suetonius, "that, as he rightly boasted, he was leaving clothed in marble the city he found as brick."¹⁹² A standard reference for virtually every princely builder of the Renaissance and beyond, this well-known passage introduces Suetonius's account of Augustus's extensive building programs, which were reflected not only in Ercole d'Este's inscription but in the frenetic aedilatory activity the inscription records.

Ercole's inscription also recalls the dedication of *De architectura*, where Vitruvius's language, as John Oksanish has observed, anticipates precisely the terms Suetonius would later adopt to describe Augustus's architectural ambitions.¹⁹³ "When I realized," Vitruvius writes addressing the emperor,

> that you had care not only for the common life of all
> men ... but also for the fitness of public buildings—so that
> even as through you [Rome] was increased with provinces,

> so public buildings were to provide eminent guarantees for the majesty of empire [*maiestas imperii*]—I decided ... to set out for you my writings on these matters. ... It is because I noticed how much you have built and are now building, both public and private buildings in keeping with the greatness of your achievements [*pro amplitudine rerum gestarum*] so that these might be transmitted to the memory of posterity ... that in these scrolls I have ... laid out all the principles of the discipline.[194]

Building is more than just a great achievement. Unlike a victory in battle, which refers only to itself, building also *testifies* to great achievements of whose memory it is the unrivaled repository.[195] Of this Vitruvius, not Suetonius, who in any case was not writing principally about architecture, was for the princely builders of the day the ultimate validation. In the Renaissance, the epitome of the achievements so recorded—the epitome, you could say, of architecture itself—became a warrior prince on horseback: here, had Ercole d'Este's monument been completed, a horseman on the summit of a fifty-foot architectural support with its equestrian builder's for the most part architectural *res gestae* inscribed on its base in sovereign affirmation of the work's entire significance.

But what record, if any, is there of the bronze statue meant to crown the monument? What, in particular, of the horse? Ercole de' Roberti, the monument's original designer, died in 1496, which is why, five years later, with his statue still without a sculptor, Ercole d'Este wrote to Giovanni Valla, his ambassador at Milan, then occupied by the French. In Milan, Ercole wrote, there was, he knew, the mold for the horse Ludovico Sforza had planned to have cast in bronze, made by *uno maestro Leonardo* skilled in such things, which, since it would now be of no use in Milan, would be most suitable for casting his own horse—the one he planned to raise *suso la piaza qui de terre nova* in Ferrara. Would Ambassador Valla ask Georges d'Amboise, the French king Louis XII's representative at Milan, if he might have it?[196]

The horse in question is the best-documented of Leonardo da Vinci's commissions.[197] There are, to begin with, Leonardo's own detailed record in what is known as the Codex Madrid II and the many studies he made for the project.[198] Literary evidence includes extensive correspondence, a description by Leonardo's friend, the mathematician Luca Pacioli, in his *De divina proportione*, and ecstatic encomia penned by court poets in awe of the *stupendo cavallo*.[199] Of the *stupendo cavallo* itself, however, there remains no trace.

The earliest record of Leonardo's involvement is the offer of services he addressed to Ludovico (il Moro) Sforza in the mid 1480s, where he presents himself as a military engineer with exceptional knowledge of *instrumenti bellici*, concluding his itemized list of the kind of strategic "secrets" (*secreti*) he would be willing to impart with the claim that he could also take in hand "the bronze horse ... which is to be to the immortal glory of the prince your father of happy memory, and of the illustrious house of Sforza."[200] As Leonardo intimates, the horse was to be part of a dynastic monument meant to honor the warlord Francesco Sforza who seized Milan by force in 1450. Galeazzo Maria, Ludovico's older brother and Francesco Sforza's heir, first conceived the project in 1473 as a life-sized equestrian statue, but the project came to a halt when Galeazzo Maria was assassinated in 1476. In a series of maneuvers as devious as they were murky, Ludovico usurped the dukedom from his dead brother's young son, the rightful heir Giangaleazzo.[201] And when, as de facto ruler of Milan, he took the project up again some ten years later with Leonardo as his *maestro*, it had become focused almost entirely on the horse, whose dimensions, in what looks very much like hyperbolic insistence on the usurper's legitimacy, had swelled to three times life-size.[202] The setting, never realized, for display of the colossus was to have been a vast piazza Ludovico planned to clear in front of the Castello Sforzesco, the fortress at the city's edge his father Francesco had had rebuilt in the 1450s to affirm his sovereignty.[203] Its reaffirmation was the horse, and, like the Piazza Nuova in Ferrara, the huge city square Ludovico projected as its *mise en scène* in Milan was a new kind of civic space entailing architectural erasure of any lingering memory of the erstwhile communal city.[204] Leonardo made a sketch of the piazza showing where, directly in front of the fortified entrance to the castle, the monument was meant to stand.[205]

In November 1493, Leonardo's finished clay model of the horse was on view in the courtyard of the Corte Vecchio at the city center for the appreciation of guests attending the wedding of il Moro's niece, Bianca Maria Sforza, to Emperor Maximilian. The "stupendous" size of the horse, which had excited admiration even before anyone had seen the model, was by far the principal focus of enthusiasm. How big exactly was it? Leonardo records that his model measured 12 *braccia*, a measurement corroborated by Luca Pacioli, who specifies that the horse was 12 *braccia* from the ground to the nape of its neck, adding that 200,000 *libbre* of bronze had been stockpiled for its casting.[206] According to Virginia Bush's calculations, this means that the height of the clay model was 7 meters, or nearly 23 feet, with a bulk 27 times the bulk of a living horse and the requisite bronze weighing 65,360 kilograms, or 71.5 tons.[207] It was, to put it mildly, gigantic.

Filarete, who some twenty-five years earlier wrote his treatise on architecture for the warlord the horse was meant to celebrate, had been an enthusiast for precisely such gigantism, as the overscaled buildings of his "ideal" city of Sforzinda and its port repeatedly bear out. Size, he argued, was a determinant of what he called *qualità*, "qualities" applicable interchangeably to classes of people and their social rank and to classes of objects and their relative value.[208] In book 21 of his *architettonico libro*, a drawing often invoked as background for the Sforza monument has a fictional King Zogalia (an anagram for Galeazzo, then the Sforza heir) sitting astride a rearing horse on the top of a five-story revolving tower that in turn stands on a monumental triumphal arch.[209] The horseman in this image, clearly larger than life and obviously meant as a celebration of signiorial power, epitomizes the sense of this (yet another) absurdly outsized building while again underscoring the view that on the scale of relative worth bigger is quite literally better. The towering equestrian monument Ercole d'Este planned to raise *suso la piaza ... de terre nova* in Ferrara would not have been out of place in such a context.

In a treatise on sculpture published in Florence in 1504, Pomponio Guarico adopts a similar position, assigning a hierarchical scale of "quality" to different sizes of statues, from life-size for men of *virtù*, through one and a half times for kings and emperors, to twice for heroes such as Hercules, and finally *colossi* three times life-size for gods (*divi*) like Jupiter, Mars, and Minerva.[210] Virginia Bush has connected Guarico's hierarchy with the colossal dimensions of the Sforza horse, suggesting that its triple life-size may have been chosen as a deliberate sculptural reflection of the qualifier *divus* often attached to Francesco Sforza's name in the encomiastic literature of the period, as indeed it was to Ercole d'Este's.[211]

The model displayed for Ludovico's wedding guests to marvel at in 1493 had almost certainly been completed earlier, for by May of 1491 Leonardo's attention was shifting from the clay colossus itself to the even greater challenge of having it cast in bronze.[212] This he hoped to achieve in a single pour rather than in separate pieces, as was customary, and using other hitherto untried casting techniques, which he documents, along with sketches, in his notebooks.[213] By 1494 the mold, or *forma* as Leonardo called it, appears to have been complete, and the horse ready for casting.[214] This was the mold Ercole d'Este wrote to ask for in 1501, because, as he told his ambassador, it was now of no use in Milan.

Why of no use? To begin with, the bronze was gone, sent in 1494 by il Moro to Ercole, who was his father-in-law, for casting cannon to defend against the invading French. By 1499, il Moro himself was gone, driven from his city by the armies of Louis XII, then captured and imprisoned in France, where he died in 1508. In 1499, the clay horse was also gone, or almost, irreparably damaged by French crossbowmen using it for target practice. All that was left was the mold, now useless in Milan, obviously, but possibly useful in Ferrara. Whether or not it was ever transferred there, or what became of it, is not known.[215] Perhaps Ercole changed his mind about it after he or one of his advisers did the math and realized that the columnar support of his projected monument was, in all likelihood, both structurally inadequate for, and proportionally out of keeping with, a statue 7 meters high, weighing some 70 tons. And that was just the horse, without a rider.

The rider, needless to say, was the project's raison d'être. At some point, probably before Leonardo's involvement, the rider received particular prominence in two studies for the monument by the Florentine artist Antonio Pollaiuolo, one now in New York, the other in Munich.[216] In these drawings, the artist has made every effort to render the horseman's identity as Francesco Sforza unmistakable, not only by representing him in a recognizable likeness, but through deliberate emphasis on the details of his armor, his control over his rearing mount, and the authority of the raised right hand extending his warlord's baton in a gesture of unchallengeable command.

Rendered with comparable attention to detail, the naked woman who lies howling in terror under the horse in the New York drawing lifts her left arm in a vain attempt to fend off the rampant stallion, its sheath well in evidence, about to trample her to death.[217] In the Munich version, where the violence lacks the sexual dimension, the figure under the less obviously male horse is a man armed as an ancient Roman. Like his female counterpart, he lifts his left arm to ward off attack. In both drawings the artist has included this clearly futile gesture of self-defense to provide support for the otherwise unsupported front quarters of the horse.

In Pollaiuolo's rendering, the equestrian monument is an incisive three-part discourse on power, in which the horse, its crucial middle term, is the emanation of the horseman's will on the one hand and the inexorable agent of its effect—the trampled foe—on the other. If you remove both the rider and the victim from the equation, the riderless horse becomes an impersonal exaltation of power *tout court*.[218] A more fitting ornament for the deserted public places of "ideal" Renaissance cities is hard to imagine.

When Leonardo first took on the project, he also planned to feature a rearing horse, and in a drawing made at that time, he even gave it a rider identifiable as Francesco Sforza, though rendered more freely than by Pollaiuolo.[219] But a tree stump, not a fallen enemy, provides support for the horse's front legs in this small, early study. Later, there was the thrilling drawing of spectacular dynamism where the three elements—rider, rearing horse, and prostrate victim—are all present.[220] But the horseman, sitting far back on his unsaddled mount, is abbreviated in an animated nude outline with no identity at all, while the presence of a victim, prone with (his? her?) right arm raised, is even more sketchily intimated in a scramble of horizontal lines under the animal's front hoofs. The drawing, more than anything else, concerns the

Antonio Pollaiuolo, study for an equestrian monument to Francesco Sforza, c. 1482–1483. Pen and brown ink and wash on paper. Robert Lehman Collection, 1975 (1975.1.410), The Metropolitan Museum of Art, New York. Image copyright © The Metropolitan Museum of Art. Image source: Art Resource, NY.

Leonardo da Vinci, study for an equestrian monument to Francesco Sforza, metalpoint on blue prepared paper, c. 1487. Royal Collection Trust © Royal Collection / Royal Collection Trust © Her Majesty the Queen; cleared and granted permission by the Royal Family. Elizabeth II 2021 / Bridgeman Images.

horse, for whose greater enhancement both the rider and the victim perform in secondary roles.

When the horse grew to three times life-size, the rampant pose ceased to be a statically viable option and had to be given up. The alternative, settled on by 1490, was a pacing horse like the one in the equestrian portraits of Sir John Hawkwood, Niccolò III d'Este, Gattamelata, and Bartolomeo Colleoni. This last was by Andrea del Verrocchio, in whose Florentine workshop Leonardo had been employed before going to Milan. The apprenticeship could well have something to do with his confidence in assuring il Moro of his competence to take in hand "the bronze horse … which is to be to the immortal glory of the prince your father." For Leonardo, taking him at his word, the project had been all about the horse from the very beginning.

Leonardo drew horses throughout his working life, from the 1470s as an apprentice in Verrocchio's studio, to 1519, the year of his death in France where he had been living as a guest of the French king, Francis I. The countless drawings that survive are thought to represent only a fraction of his original output.[221] There are well over a hundred in the Windsor collection alone. Of these at least a quarter, drawn in Milan around 1490, can be directly linked to the Sforza project. They often include the horses' proportions and measurements, sometimes even their innards—detailed studies of living animals, for the most part, whose draftsman seems intent on uncovering, as it were, an essence of horsiness that would animate his gigantic, now sedately pacing model and infuse it with the dynamism inherent in the abandoned rampant pose. *De equo animante*.

The focus on living horses had a significant exception, however: a bronze horse that was neither that of the *Gattamelata*, nor indeed of the *Colleone*, both of which Leonardo aimed to surpass, but the ancient equestrian statue in gilded bronze Petrarch had admired over a hundred years earlier, where the horse, as the poet wrote to his friend Boccaccio, "seems to be just on the point of reaching, with a spirited bound, the summit of an eminence": the *Regisole*, so-called, at Pavia.[222] Leonardo made a tiny pen and ink sketch of this statue, just over an inch square (2.8 by 3.6 centimeters).[223] The drawing, now at Windsor, was cut from a folio in the manuscript collection in Milan known as the Codex Atlanticus, where the artist also recorded his thoughts on the horse.[224] The *Regisole* did have a rider, of course, for the name, "sun king," referred not to the horse but to the royal personage, possibly the Ostrogothic king Theodoric, seated on its back. But no one, from Petrarch on, least of all Leonardo, was particularly interested in the horseman. Leonardo's notes read as follows.

> What is to be praised above all in the horse at Pavia is the movement. It is more praiseworthy to imitate ancient things than modern ones. Can there not (in a horse) be the same beauty and utility as appear in fortresses and men? The trot has almost the same quality as that of a free horse. Where natural vivacity is lacking, it must be made by artificial means.[225]

The repeated emphasis on the liveliness of the Pavia horse in these somewhat elliptical observations highlights the chief preoccupation of Leonardo's own horse studies and points to the lessons to be learned from the ancient statue: that artifice is required to restore a lack of "natural vivacity" and that in this the *Regisole* is an exemplary confirmation of the quintessentially Renaissance conviction that it is better to imitate the ancients than the moderns. The direct bearing on this of his cryptic note concerning the beauty and utility of horses, comparable, he intimates, to that of fortresses and men, is elusive, however. The notion of the horse as a paradigm of beauty and utility had already been put forward by Alberti who, for this very reason, assigned an equine foundation to the architecture of Roman power, and indeed, as I argued earlier, to architecture itself.[226]

But Leonardo's seemingly random remark was not part of any systematic argument. It may have originated with Alberti, but that the best horses were, in equal measure, both beautiful and useful would in any case have hardly been news to horsemen of the late Quattrocento—or indeed of any century. Martin Kemp has pointed to the possible relevance of a passage in *The City of God*, which Leonardo owned in vernacular translation, where St.

Augustine writes of use and beauty in the bodies of men.²²⁷ But what did fortresses have to do with it?

Leonardo sketched the *Regisole* horse and jotted down his thoughts about it sometime in late June of 1490 when he visited Pavia with the Sienese architect and engineer Francesco di Giorgio Martini to study the *tiburio* (lantern) of the cathedral there. Francesco, an assiduous reader of Vitruvius and his first translator, had recently completed a treatise on architecture, written in Italian, the first of the two discussed in chapter 4.²²⁸ Leonardo owned a version of it, acquired after Francesco's death.²²⁹ Like most artists of his day, Francesco had many areas of expertise, but his greatest claim to fame was as a designer of fortresses, which accounts for the military bias that prevails in much of his theoretical work. His first treatise begins with a chapter on *città, fortezze e castelli*, whose members he argues, citing Vitruvius as his authority, must relate to one another with perfect proportions, just as they do in the human body. Next to the text, there is a drawing of the naked boy discussed earlier whose body parts have been made to correspond to the different parts of a fortified city: a *rocca* on his head, bastions at his feet and elbows, and a ravelin between his outspread legs.²³⁰ Fortified cities should be like the bodies of men.

As already mentioned, before concluding with the offer to take on the Sforza monument, Leonardo's letter to Ludovico Sforza had consisted almost entirely of an itemized list of devices, presented as testimonials to his (Leonardo's) exceptional gifts as an inventor of *instrumenti bellici*. Such instruments, obviously, were an interest he shared with his older contemporary, the foremost military engineer of the day. They also shared an intense interest in human proportions. For Francesco di Giorgio, as a reader of Vitruvius, this had to do with taking the corporeal referent as the bedrock of architectural meaning. Fortresses, along with almost everything else in architecture, were to be understood in terms of the proportions of the human body. Leonardo's Latin was rudimentary, which meant that his knowledge of Vitruvius was secondhand at best and, at the time he met Francesco di Giorgio, his interest in human proportion, based, he writes, on measurement of "the most graceful" living models, was only marginally connected with architecture, if at all.²³¹ Though self-styled as an expert in the machinery of war, he was unlikely before then to have thought of a man's body as underwriting fortress design. The notion struck a chord, apparently.

When he visited Pavia with Francesco, the horse project was at the top of Leonardo's mind. Horse studies, sometimes with measurements and proportions, proceeded in tandem with studies of human proportion, which occasionally appear on the same sheet as the drawings of the horses.²³² "Can there not in a horse be the same beauty and utility as appear in fortresses and men?" Leonardo asks, as if interpellating his colleague to wonder if the connection between the male body and the architecture of fortification might not extend to include an equine component. He seems to have thought it should.

Leonardo's *stupendo cavallo* would, after all, have been little more than a much-admired, probably very lifelike if absurdly overscaled sculptural representation of a horse until, or unless, it found its proper place. Only in the vast city square il Moro was planning to clear for it in front of his fortified *castello* would the gigantic horse fulfill its role as the exaltation of signiorial power it was meant to be. And only with the horse in place would the piazza so conceived come into its own as a site of sovereign control. In the end, it mattered little who actually sat in the saddle.

If Leonardo's knowledge of Francesco di Giorgio's first treatise in whose opening folios his fortress man appears is, for the most part, a matter of scholarly consensus, it is not because of the fortress man, whose possible relevance to the issue at hand remains, as far as I know, unremarked. Rather, it is because of a drawing that appears a little later in the same manuscript at the beginning of a chapter on cities where there is another naked youth, not armor-plated like the first, but standing gracefully poised with arms outstretched inside a circumscribing circle and square.²³³ Vitruvian man. Next to him at the bottom of the same folio, also unremarked and invariably cropped out of the picture, is a design for a perfectly symmetrical fortress whose template the graceful young man appears to be. Francesco di Giorgio's "fortress man" and his Vitruvian man are one and the same.

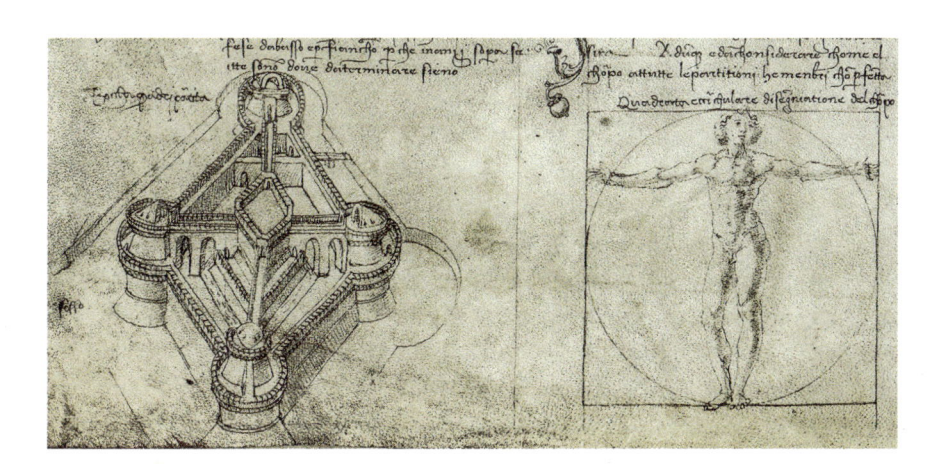

Francesco di Giorgio Martini, *Trattato di architettura I*, c. 1486. Biblioteca Reale, Turin, Codex Saluzziano 148, fol. 6v (detail). © MIC—Musei Reali, Biblioteca Reale di Torino.

It is generally agreed that Leonardo's appreciation of Vitruvius and his own, infinitely better-known rendering of the figure owe much to his familiarity with Francesco's treatise and the time they spent together in Milan and Pavia in June of 1490.[234] But if Leonardo's Vitruvian man can now, perhaps justifiably, be called "the world's most famous drawing," it was not always the case, for its celebrity is of relatively recent date.[235] It was only seventy years ago, after the publication of Rudolf Wittkower's *Architectural Principles in the Age of Humanism*, that the image acquired the emblematic status it has enjoyed among architects and historians ever since.[236]

It was Wittkower who first called the drawing a "Vitruvian figure" based, he said, on Leonardo's firsthand knowledge of *De architectura*; and Wittkower who was the first to qualify it as an *architectural* drawing, which transmitted what, in Vitruvius's text, he claimed was revealed as a "deep and fundamental truth about man and the world, [whose] importance for Renaissance architects can hardly be overestimated."[237] As the art historian Emanuele Lugli reminds his readers in a recent article, before Wittkower the then little-known drawing was understood simply as a proportional study. Thus, for the nineteenth-century Leonardo scholar Giuseppe Bossi the man was not "Vitruvian" at all, but an "uomo leonardiano." In Bernard Berenson's *The Drawings of the Florentine Painters* it is listed as "A man within a circle. Study for the proportions of the human figure."[238] The argument Lugli presents in his essay is a vindication of such earlier, comparatively low-key assessments.[239]

Close study of the drawing and its accompanying text—about a third of it fitted awkwardly around the circumference of the circle at the top of the image, the other two-thirds neatly transcribed below—leads to the provocative conclusion that the sheet began life as the frontispiece of a projected book on human proportion, which at first included only the man in the square and the text under it. The drawing's title, carefully centered, was taken not from Vitruvius but from Pliny's *Natural History*, which Leonardo owned in vernacular translation: *Tanto apre l'omo nele braccia, quanto ella sua altezza*—"The span of a man's arms is equal to his height."[240]

The circle with its center at the man's navel, as well as the outspread legs and raised arms, were added to the drawing later along with the text above the image, Lugli argues, perhaps after meeting Francesco di Giorgio. Only with the appended codicil, which begins at the top right-hand corner with "Vitruvius, the architect, sets down in his work on architecture that the measurements of man are arranged in the following manner," does Leonardo's arguably reworked drawing acquire its Vitruvian credentials.[241] That the Vitruvian proportions enumerated above the image do not correspond to the non-Vitruvian ones listed in the text below it, and that the length of the raised arms of the man *ad circulum* exceeds the length of the outstretched arms of the man *ad quadratum* by the width of two fingers corroborates the argument for a two-part execution of the drawing to which the man in the circle was added second, as a supplement.[242]

Moreover, aside from naming Vitruvius "the architect," Leonardo makes no mention of architecture in his account of the man's proportions, either above or below the image meant to embody them. Vitruvius's own Vitruvian man had been all about architecture, of course: "No temple can be coherently constructed unless it has symmetry and proportion; unless the way it is put together conforms exactly to the principle relating the members of a well-shaped man."[243] The directive appears at the beginning of *De architectura*, book 3, the first of Vitruvius's two books on temples, just before he sets down the very proportions Leonardo would later transcribe above his drawing, but with no suggestion that the well-shapedness of his ideally proportioned figure is to be taken as the referent for "bringing works of architecture to their proper completion," as Vitruvius instructs elsewhere.[244]

How much did Leonardo's Vitruvian man actually have to do with architecture? Or indeed with Vitruvius? Rather less, it would appear, than what Wittkower's *Architectural Principles* persuaded me, and generations of architecture students like me, that it did. In those days, it seemed that the entire sense of *De architectura* could, even should be abbreviated in that single, cosmically freighted figure; or at the very least that the image was to be taken as the transcription of a world picture whose "importance

All the King's Horses

for Renaissance architects can hardly be overestimated," as Wittkower claimed.

Whatever the importance of that picture in the history of ideas, which is where Wittkower and his followers thought Vitruvius, his treatise, and the history of architecture itself rightly belonged, its relevance to Vitruvius in an age of princes is questionable. For Vitruvius in the age of Vitruvius—the age, in other words, of Caesar and Augustus—the world picture embodied in the man he said could be circumscribed by a circle and square had been unequivocally Roman and imperial: a theoretical yet essentially operative template for architecture as the proof and guarantee of Roman world rule.[245] The thoroughness with which the figure's original purpose was embedded in the specific political and religious context of Vitruvius's own time made a Renaissance recovery of that purpose both unlikely and pointless.

But if Renaissance readers of *De architectura* failed to recognize the role of Vitruvian man as an emblematic vehicle for the deployment of a specifically Augustan imperial agenda, they could not fail to be struck by the work's imperial agenda *tout court* and by the role Vitruvius assigned to architecture for its advancement in a treatise that begins, "When your divine mind and power, Imperator Caesar, were seizing command of the world ..."[246] Petrarch, alleged father of humanism, was Vitruvius's first reader in this age of princes, and for Petrarch "renaissance" meant, above all, the revival of Roman military greatness, along with the attendant values of status, power, and personal glory embraced by the ambitious men whose patronage he cultivated: warlords who were everywhere wresting control of cities that had governed themselves as independent communes for (more or less) the previous two centuries in keeping with the ideal of a common good whose values were the antithesis of these would-be Caesars' own.

Such men were invariably horsemen, and during the century that witnessed consolidation of their power, horses—essential accomplices in the never-ending contest for dominance—became its consummate symbol, culminating at the end of the century in Leonardo's gigantic, if ultimately ephemeral, *stupendo cavallo*. His drawing of the figure known as Vitruvian man belongs to the same Milanese period: a study of the proportions of the human male that had nothing to do with such power struggles and, arguably, not much to do with architecture either. The horse, on the other hand, had to do with both.

Consolidation of signiorial rule also, invariably, entailed lavish building programs, guided by Vitruvian principles whose authority was vouchsafed by their imperial credentials. Alberti, who either in person or through his writings advised many of these princely builders and who, for all his reservations concerning *De architectura*, was Vitruvius's most penetrating interpreter, writes at one point that Roman world rule alone was reason enough to demand adoption of Roman architectural models.[247] In the cities ruled by princes, the architecture inspired by such models was proof of the sovereignty epitomized in a horseman's masterful control of his mount.

Among the Renaissance *trattatisti* discussed in these pages, Alberti was the only one to bypass the well-shaped man as the referent for the perfect correspondence of parts Vitruvius calls *symmetria* and replace him with the body of an *animans*, a living creature—paradigmatically the horse—as the embodiment of the harmonious correspondences that conferred on a work of architecture the character of what he called *concinnitas* and with it the beauty of an ideally unassailable whole.

The perceived alliance between horses and architecture does not originate with Vitruvius who, as I noted earlier, has nothing to say about horses. But his failure to discuss them is no reason to dismiss their relevance to the role his treatise played in the fifteenth century when, as I have tried to show, architects and their patrons grew to appreciate in this venerable Roman text something very like the same potential for dominance as was represented in the figure of a warrior prince on horseback. If you accept that Vitruvius wrote *De architectura* as a political work, and that its Renaissance interpreters grasped its purpose as the vindication of architecture as the ultimate vehicle of control, you must allow, in this age of princes, the living horse to contest the role of Vitruvian man as the ancient Roman author's best, most fitting representative.

All the King's Horses

Leonardo da Vinci, study for the Sforza monument after the *Regisole*, pen and ink, 1490. Royal Collection Trust © Royal Collection / Royal Collection Trust © Her Majesty the Queen; cleared and granted permission by the Royal Family. Elizabeth II 2021 / Bridgeman Images.

Epilogue

The equestrian statue of Marcus Aurelius now at the center of the Campidoglio at Rome is a copy. In 2005, the original gilded bronze was installed in the purpose-built Esedra di Marco Aurelio in the Palazzo dei Conservatori wing of the Capitoline Museums. In 2014, after further restoration of Ruggiero Bescapè's 1594 "restoration" of the original fragment, the marble sculpture of the lion attacking a horse was installed in the same space, to the right of the equestrian statue at a lower level. Wall texts of considerable length and detail document the entire history of the famous bronze. Information concerning the marble horse and its feline attacker is limited to the few lines of a label on the statue's base, where the sculpture is identified as Greek of the Hellenistic period, and Bescapè credited with its restoration. In keeping with prevailing indifference to recollection of Rome's communal period, there is no mention anywhere of the work's place during that time, or of the role it once played in the life of the city.

There is a certain inevitability in this dismissal. The immense authority which had emanated from the Hellenistic fragment when it presided *allo luogo del leone* on the Capitol during the Middle Ages is not only irrecoverable but almost impossible even to imagine now, embedded as it is in the polished perfection of the sculpture currently on display. Imperfect, the fragment had been all about the lion. In those days, the horse was a lifeless torso with no head, neck, legs or tail: little more than dead meat under the ravening teeth and claws of its assailant, fierce avatar of communal Rome's political aspirations. Regeneration of its missing parts in the Renaissance brought the horse back to life. Paired today with the horseman who rules the gallery from his cantilevered plinth, the sculptural group with its reconstituted horse has become both a repudiation, paradoxically enough, of Rome's communal past and an affirmation of the renewal to which Ruggiero Bescapè's restoration assimilated it. How could you, a sensitive museumgoer, not be moved by the struggle of the savaged horse whose head (noble, even in defeat) leads your gaze to the proud, remarkably similar head of the Roman emperor's mount that in the current installation rises beside the sculptural group to further discredit its original significance? The very horse which, it seems at least possible, inspired Bescapè to transform the Hellenistic fragment into the perfect whole that has supplanted virtually everything the ancient, ruined artifact once stood for.

Reverence for the bronze horseman and for the Renaissance princes whose ideal of rulership the statue came to represent has long eclipsed interest in the bold political experiment these princes dismantled as they presided over the renewal that remains ever vivid and unchallenged as a pinnacle of western cultural achievement. Political ambition was what fueled the antique revival embraced by *signori* who routinely appealed to Roman grandeur as justification for their own lust for power. But political ambition and the rebirth Petrarch was first to declare the means for its fulfillment demanded, as it were, a blank slate, and the political slate in fourteenth-century Italy was far from blank.

Lion attacking a horse, marble, Hellenistic, c. 300 BCE, restored by Ruggiero Bescapè, 1594. Capitoline Museums, Rome. Kim Petersen / Alamy Stock Photo.

Standing in the way of successful regime change were the communes whose erasure it required. Erasure not only of their well-established polities but erasure, quite literally, of the places that were the very condition of self-government and its ruling principle of the common good which took concrete shape in the measurable reality of a shared public realm. Refiguring these places as proof of one-man rule was where architecture, most notably Vitruvius and his impeccable imperial credentials, came in to create the "ideal" cities, so called, that left little or no surviving evidence of the real ones they displaced.

The village of Corsignano, refigured as Pienza by the pope who gave it his name. Mantua, wholly appropriated by the Gonzaga who demolished the medieval church of Sant'Andrea, erstwhile focus of a cult that affirmed communal solidarity, to make way for the great vaulted dynastic temple which, thanks to Alberti, became the ruling family's (and Alberti's) lasting memorial. Urbino, where the prince's residence grew into a *città in forma di palazzo* when the famous warlord Federico da Montefeltro poured his staggering profits as a mercenary captain into the palace that obliterated every trace of the city's communal past. Ferrara where, transformed into a *spectaculum*, the *piazza comunale* and eventually the entire city became the duke's personal parade ground.

So successful was these latter-day Caesars' *damnatio memoriae* of the communal past that theirs, the dominant narrative of renaissance, renewal, and the surpassing *virtù* of men who made it all possible has not only endured but received regular reinforcement. Marcus Aurelius, their emblematic representative, restored and newly honored in the Esedra di Marco Aurelio built just for him; the *piazza maggiore* in front of the palace at Urbino renamed Piazza Duca Federico in the early twentieth century; the Via degli Angeli in Ferrara christened Corso Ercole d'Este at about the same time; a few years later, in the same city, the reconstruction of the bronze statues of Borso d'Este and his condottiere father Niccolò III, to replace the ones melted down during the revolutionary upheavals of the late eighteenth century. The consecration of Pienza, Mantua, Urbino, and Ferrara as UNESCO World Heritage sites, all within the last 30 years.

It seems willfully insensible, in this the third decade of the twenty-first century, to imagine that the architects and theorists mentored by Vitruvius were not as complicit in advancing their patrons' political ambitions as they were in realizing the project of renewal that underwrote them. Acknowledgment of damage done is long overdue.

Acknowledgments

Twenty years ago, in my book *Vitruvius: Writing the Body of Architecture*, I concluded that imperial ideology informed the composition of *De architectura*, which Vitruvius wrote for Augustus Caesar, the first Roman emperor, as an argument for the necessary role of architecture in the Roman project of world dominion. This book is its sequel and concerns the political circumstances attending the recovery of Vitruvius's text in the Italian Renaissance.

During its long gestation, I have been the grateful recipient of generous support from the Graham Foundation for Advanced Studies in the Fine Arts, the Canadian Centre for Architecture, the Social Sciences and Humanities Research Council of Canada, and the J. Paul Getty Foundation, which financed research that included multiple trips to European sites, from Castiglione Olona to Hampton Court. My heartfelt thanks to all these institutions.

Public lectures given over the years and papers presented at various conferences have been privileged occasions for discussion. Special thanks to the School of Architecture at the University of Manitoba in Winnipeg for repeated invitations to lecture there as a guest speaker. Many of my ideas were first aired in Winnipeg. Courses given in the Art History department at Concordia University in Montreal were valuable opportunities for their further development.

First and foremost, among the many libraries I have relied on for my work, is the library at the Canadian Centre for Architecture, whose study room has been my home away from home for several decades. Welcome there has been unfailingly warm, and the collection remains incomparable. Its closure during the pandemic was especially hard to bear. I join countless students of architecture in expressing gratitude to the CCA's founding director Phyllis Lambert for the creation of this extraordinary institution.

Among the many brilliant scholars on whose work I have built my own, I am especially indebted to Anna Bedon, Patrick Boucheron, Paolo Carpeggiani, Marco Folin, Martin McLaughlin, Ingrid Rowland, and Joseph Rykwert for inspiration and guidance. Joseph Rykwert's interest in my work has ever been a source of encouragement.

The MIT Press has for a third time expertly brought my work into print, which demands expression of renewed appreciation. I owe special thanks, above all, to Thomas Weaver, Senior Acquisitions Editor, for taking me on and expertly shepherding *All the King's Horses* through the entire process, beginning with the engagement of three spirited readers to assess the manuscript. I am grateful for their stimulating, well-considered, and helpful reviews which have contributed significantly to the book's final shape—from the refinement of its subtitle to many details of structure and content. It has been a pleasure to work with Matthew Abbate who has, once again, edited my text with his accustomed rigor, discretion, and unfailing good judgment.

Acquiring images and the permission to use them is costly. I am grateful to the Bibliothèque nationale de France, the Rijksmuseum in Amsterdam, and the Technische Universität Berlin for waiving these costs. Very special thanks to architect Chris Bearman who kindly scanned the superb renderings he made of Sant'Andrea in Mantua over thirty years ago for inclusion in this book.

Three of its six chapters are revised and considerably expanded versions of previously published work. "Symmetry Takes Command" (chapter 2) appeared in the Hungarian journal *Symmetry: Culture and Science* in 2018. "Virtù-vious" (chapter 4) was first given as a seminar at the Canadian Centre for Architecture in 2008 and later published in the classics journal *Cahiers des études anciennes* (2011). "The Architectonic Book" (chapter 5), which began as a conference paper given in Berlin in 2011, later appeared in *Vitruvianism: Origins and Transformations* (Berlin: De Gruyter, 2016).

Notes

Prologue

1. Reception of Vitruvius (among others): Wittkower 1988; Zöllner 1987; Pellecchia 1992; Kruft 1994; Rykwert 1996; Rowland 1998; Payne 1999; Clarke 2002; Rowland 2005; Rowland 2014; Sanvito 2016; Rowland and Bell 2023.
2. Editions and translations: Rowland 1998; Tavares 2022.
3. Vitruvius 1535; cf. Mortimer 1964-1974, no. 535; Tavares 2022.
4. Plutarch *Fabius Maximus* 14 (Plutarch 1912, 1:278).
5. Cicero *In Catilinam* 2.11; cf. McDonnell 2006, 350-353, and below, chapter 4.
6. Cicero *Brutus* 23-24.

Chapter 1

1. Wilkins 1943; Regn and Huss 2009.
2. Regn and Huss 2009, 88.
3. Wilkins 1943, 159-162. But see Looney 2009.
4. Virgil *Georgics* 3.291-292; cf. Wilkins 1943; Wilkins 1955, 300-313; Godi 1970.
5. Laura and *laurea*: Wilkins 1943, 163; Bernardo 1962, 47-48; Regn and Huss 2009, 91-92.
6. Godi 1970, 17 for the Latin; trans. Wilkins 1955, 304.
7. Godi 1970, 18; Wilkins 1955, 304.
8. Regn and Huss 2009, 86.
9. Mommsen 2002. See his *Letter to Posterity*: "our own age has always repelled me," https://history.hanover.edu /texts/petrarch/pet01.html, visited 15 May 2018.
10. Mommsen 2002; McLaughlin 1988; Findlen 2002b; Burioni 2010. On Vasari's as the first use of the term *rinascita* ("renaissance") in 1550, and Vasari's influence in general, most recently Rowland and Charney 2017, 14.
11. Cicero *Pro Marcello* 8.25.
12. Cicero *Pro Archia* 10.24.
13. Godi 1970, 23; Wilkins 1955, 309.
14. Godi 1970, 23-27; Willkins 1955, 309-313.
15. On the *Africa* (inter alia), Mustard 1921; Bernardo 1962; Regn and Huss 2009.
16. Regn and Huss 2009, 97-98.
17. Petrarch *Africa* 9.216-267. Cf. Mustard 1921, 116-118; Regn and Huss 2009, 88-89.
18. Petrarch *Africa* 9.404-409.
19. Bedon 2008, 16.
20. Maire Vigueur 2010, 305; Boucheron and Menjot 2011, 292-333.
21. Boucheron and Menjot 2011, 297.
22. Miglio 1997.
23. Wilkins 1943, 191.
24. Usher 2009. Petrarch spent all of his teenage years studying law, initially in Montpellier (1316-1320), then in Bologna (1320-1325). Wilkins 1961, 4-7.
25. Suetonius *Divus Julius* 45.2.
26. Wilkins 1955, 300.
27. On the fresco cycle, most recently Boucheron 2013a.
28. Petrarch *Canzone* 237, stanza 5. On his hostility to cities, see especially his *De vita solitaria* (English trans. in Petrarch 1978) and his letter to posterity where he writes of his "deep-seated and innate repugnance to town life" (https://www.gutenberg .org/files/48776/48776-h /48776-h.htm, 70, visited 30 May 2018).
29. Translations of the texts that appear on the paintings follow Starn 1994, 99-101.
30. Skinner 1986.
31. See Boucheron 2013a, especially 156-176.
32. Boucheron 2013a, chapter 7: *Guernica en pays siennois*.
33. Hollingsworth 2021, 16.
34. Folin 2011b, 30.
35. Bernardo 1962, 6.
36. Petrarch 1906, 9; Ferraù 2006, 97-101.
37. Ferraù 2006, 53-101; McLaughlin 2009b, 338-339.
38. Fam. XVII.4, cited Andreoli Panzarasa 1975, 46: *optimum rei publicae statum esse sub unius imperio.*
39. Ferraù 2006, 55-56.
40. Kohl 1978; Ferraù 2006, 92-96.
41. Kohl 1978.
42. Petrarch 1978, 39.
43. Petrarch 1978, 42-66.
44. Petrarch 1978, 74-77.
45. Giovanni di Conversino da Ravenna 1980. Cf. Baron 1955, 1:114, whose translation I have cited; Folin 2006, 63-64.
46. Wilkins 1958.
47. Cited Dotti 1972, 52.
48. Cited Ferraù 2006, 73.
49. Wilkins 1958, 16.
50. Gordon 1991; Greenblatt 2012.
51. Eisner 2014.
52. Letter dated 16 June 1345, https://www.gutenberg .org/files/47859/47859-h

/47859-h.html (F. 24.3), visited 20 May 2018.

53. Ciapponi 1960, 59. Ciapponi thinks he may have found the manuscript in France (96). Cf. Pagliara 1986, 16.

54. Ciapponi 1960; Rowland 1997; Tosco 2011, 44–48.

55. Ms. Bodl. Auct. F. 5. 7. Cf. Ciapponi 1960, who dates the marginal notes to 1352–1353 (74).

56. Bodl. Auct. F. 5. 7, 4r. (Vitruvius 1.pref.1).

57. Petrarch 2017, 2:385 (S.7).

58. Vitruvius 6.1.

59. Bodl. Auct. F. 5. 7, 4v–5r (Vitruvius 1.1.1–11); 42v (Vitruvius 6.pref).

60. Zaccaria 1970, 511.

61. Vitruvius 1.1.1: "The knowledge of the architect is furnished with many disciplines and various kinds of learning. Judiciously exercised, it demonstrates everything the other arts achieve. It is brought into being by *fabrica* and *ratiocinatio*. *Fabrica* is the continuous and routine practice of the activity the hands accomplish out of matter; its offspring is a work whose form is in keeping with its intended purpose. *Ratiocinatio* is what can show how, and explain to what degree, things have been made with skill and calculation."

62. The term *ordini* (orders) was first used by Raphael and Angelo Colocci in their famous "Letter to Leo X" of 1519. Vitruvius uses the word *genus* or *genera* for the different "kinds" of columns. Rowland 1994, 98–99 and 103; Rykwert 1996, 4–6.

63. Petrarch 2017, 1:62–75 (F.6.2).

64. See the translator's notes in Petrarch 2017, 1:594–603. Also, inter alia, Weiss 1969, 32–35.

65. Patetta 1997, 167.

66. Petrarch 2017, 1:71.

67. Cicero *In Catalinam* 3; Cicero *Pro rege Deiotaro* 6. Cf. Vasaly 1993.

68. Letter dated 19 December 1345, http://www.gutenberg.org/files/47859/47859-h/47859-h.htm#Page_21 (F. 24.4), visited 7 June 2018.

69. Cicero *De finibus* 5.1.2.

70. Vitruvius 1.1.3.

71. Vitruvius 9.pref.17.

72. On the philosophical back story, McEwen 2003, 71–83.

73. Vitruvius 1.1.3; Bodl. Auct. F. 5. 7, 2, 4v.

74. Tuchman 1978, 240–241.

75. Boucheron 1998, 72–86; Boucheron 2003, 41–43.

76. Crouzet-Pavan 2003a, 21–26.

77. Black 2009, 1–2, 36–51.

78. Boucheron 1998, 114–129.

79. Fiamma 1938.

80. Cited Green 1990, 101.

81. Aristotle *Nicomachean Ethics* 1122b–1124a.

82. Fraser Jenkins 1970; Green 1990.

83. Green 1990, 102.

84. Gilbert 1977 for Giotto as the author of the murals.

85. Green 1990, 104.

86. Green 1990, 103.

87. Black 2009, 52.

88. Andreoli Panzarasa 1975, 48–50.

89. Petrarch 2017, 2:238–259, with translator's notes 2:649–652.

90. Vicini 1984, 9–12.

91. Tuchman 1978, 241.

92. Pellegrin 1955, 42.

93. Andreoli Panzarasa 1975.

94. Andreoli Panzarasa 1975, 59–60; Vicini 1984, 12.

95. https://archive.org/stream/petrarchfirstmod00petrrich/petrarchfirstmod00petrrich_djvu.txt, visited 26 June 2018.

96. Pellegrin 1955, 42.

97. Bologna 1986, 18.

98. Rovetta 1981, 9; Morresi 1988, 81. The manuscript, now in Paris (BN Ms. Lat. 7228), is listed in a catalogue of the Visconti library made in 1426 as *Virturbius de architretis instituendis*: cat. A254 in Pellegrin 1955, 130.

99. Godi 1970, 17 for the Latin; trans. Wilkins 1955, 304.

100. Vitruvius 1511; cf. Mortimer 1964–1974, no. 143. "This is the second time Vitruvius's *De architectura* has the honor of being dedicated to the greatest prince on earth." Vitruvius 1673, preface, unpaginated.

101. Ciapponi 1960, 98; Rovetta 1981, 9. For Cencio's letter to Francesco da Fiana in which the discovery is reported, Gordon 1991, 188.

102. Ciapponi 1960, 88–93; Weiss 1969, 51–52; Rovetta 1981, 9; Weiskittel and Reynolds 1983, 443; Tosco 2011, 47–48. http://www.treccani.it/enciclopedia/giovanni-dondi-dall-orologio_(Dizionario-Biografico)/; http://www.treccani.it

/enciclopedia/niccolo-acciaiuoli_(Dizionario-Biografico)/, visited 15 July 2018.
103. Vitruvius 1.2.3; Vitruvius 1521, fols. 14r–15v.
104. Rovetta 1981, 10; Morresi 1988, 85.
105. Foffano 1960; Pulin 1981; Morresi 1988, 91; Grafton 2002, 269–272; Elsner 2010.
106. Clarke 2002, 321–322.
107. Boucheron 1998 is the essential reference for this. See also Folin 2011b, 11, who singles out the Visconti court as the first of the great princely courts of the Renaissance.

Chapter 2

1. The statue that stands there now is a copy. Since 2005, the original has been displayed in the Esedra di Marco Aurelio, a purpose-built extension to the Capitoline Museum. For a brief history of the original and an account of the copy's creation, Mura Somella and Parisi Presicce 1997.
2. Tacitus *Historiae* 3.72
3. McEwen 2003.
4. McEwen 2003, 142–149. Thanks to Joseph Rykwert's *On Adam's House in Paradise*, first published over 40 years ago, this is among the best-known chapters in *De architectura*: Rykwert 1981.
5. Vitruvius 2.1.7. All translations from Vitruvius are my own. The Latin text used is that of the Belles Lettres edition: Vitruvius 1969–2000.
6. McEwen 2003, 130–154; Goldsworthy 2016; Virgil *Aeneid* 6.851–852.

7. Vitruvius 6.1.9–12; 1.pref.2.
8. Vitruvius 1.pref.2.
9. Vitruvius 1.2.4: "Symmetry is the fitting concord between members of the work and each other and the correspondence of individual elements to the form of the whole figure by means of a fixed part." On Vitruvian man, Vitruvius 3.1.1–3; Gros 2001; McEwen 2003, 156–183. The Leonardo drawing: Venice, Gallerie dell'Accademia no. 228 and below, chapter 6.
10. McEwen 2003, 111–112.
11. Cicero *De finibus* 3.74; Cicero *De oratore* 3.45.179.
12. Alberti 1988, 156 (6.2). I have emended the translation slightly. For the Latin, Alberti 1966a, 447.
13. Pearson 2011, 156–158; Boucheron 2012, 179: "je dirais ultimement que ce qu'il y a de plus éminemment politique dans l'implicite du signe architectural, c'est la valeur esthétique." See also Boucheron 2014, 3–4.
14. On the immutability of perfection in Alberti, Trachtenberg 2010, 77–79.
15. Alberti and Nicholas V (then Tommaso Parentucelli) had been friends at the University of Bologna in the 1420s. Gadol 1969, 5–6; Tavernor 1998, 3.
16. Manetti 2005, 123. Cf. Miglio 1996, 320–325.
17. Alberti 2007, 27.
18. Krautheimer 2000, chapters 12 and 14; Taylor, Rinne, and Kostof 2016, 222–231.
19. Krautheimer 2000, 192–197; Magnuson 2004,

86–100; Taylor, Rinne, and Kostof 2016, 188–195.
20. Maire Vigueur 2010, 305.
21. Magnuson 2004, 114–120; Maire Vigueur 2010; Wickham 2015.
22. Miglio 1997; Maire Vigueur 2010, 305.
23. Maire Vigueur 2010, 159–160; Wickham 2015, 127.
24. Christian 2010, 22–23.
25. Krautheimer 2000, 286; Bedon 2008, 9.
26. Brancia di Apricena 2000.
27. Rodocanacchi 1904, 9–40; Pietrangeli 1964, 191–194; D'Onofrio 1973, 71–121; Bedon 2008, 2–23.
28. Maire Vigueur 2010, 336–337.
29. Cited Saxl 1957, 208.
30. Brought to the Capitol possibly as early as 1144 (D'Onofrio 1973, 113). See further Ebert-Schifferer 1988, 144.
31. Pietrangeli 1964; Miglio 1981, 321–326; Jacks 1993, chapter 1; Bedon 2008, 10–16.
32. Michaelis 1891, 10; Miglio 1981, 326.
33. Ingersoll 1985, 71–74. On the route of the *possesso*, fixed in what became the *via papalis*, Taylor, Rinne, and Kostof 2016, 205–213.
34. Valla 2007, 181.
35. Valla 2007.
36. It was the humanist Bartolomeo Platina, Pope Sixtus IV's librarian, who first made the correct identification of the horse's rider as the emperor Marcus Aurelius in the late fifteenth century.
37. Valla 2007, 181.
38. Ingersoll 1985, 172.
39. Bedon 2008, 24–25.

40. Bedon 2008, 27–28.
41. Parisi Presicce 2000.
42. There is recent, convincing evidence that the wolf is not, as long assumed, an ancient Roman work, but a creation of Carolingian date (Carruba 2006). This late date of the eighth-ninth century would place the *lupa* squarely within the same time frame as the writing of the Donation, as well as that of concurrent affirmations of papal power already discussed.
43. D'Onofrio 1973, 125–129; Miglio 1982; Bedon 2008, 34; Christian 2010, 103–119 for a detailed discussion. The text on a panel posted on the front of the Museum reads, "The Capitoline Museums were born in 1471, when pope Sixtus IV donated to the people of Rome four great ancient bronzes ..."
44. Bedon 2008, 26.
45. Marcus Aurelius spent the last 12 years of his life (from 167 to 180 CE) waging war against the Germanic tribes of the empire's northeastern frontier. The campaign in all its relentless brutality is celebrated on the triumphal column of Marcus Aurelius in Piazza Colonna. On the ambiguities of *pax romana*, Goldsworthy 2016.
46. D'Onofrio 1973, 173–195; Bedon 2008, 51–80.
47. Fauno 1548, fol. 39r; Mezzatesta 1984.
48. Harprath 1985; Rebecchini 2007, 157–159; Bedon 2008, 56–57.
49. It can still be found there, on the grounds of the Villa Celimontana. The inscription on its base makes no mention of its original site or of its significance in communal Rome. I am grateful to Agnes Crawford, Roman tour guide *extraordinaire*, for helping me to find it.
50. Gamucci 1565, 18.
51. Bober and Rubenstein 1986, 219.
52. Ackerman 1986; Burroughs 1993; Bedon 2008, 205–272.
53. Bedon 2008, 183.
54. Tittoni 1996, 17; Bedon 2008, 163.
55. Bedon 2008, 205–272.
56. Parisi Presicce 1996, 102.
57. D'Onofrio 1973, 199; Bedon 2008, 205.
58. The Palazzo Nuovo was finally completed in 1663, during the reign of Pope Alexander VII Chigi. Pope Clement XII turned it into a museum along with the Palazzo dei Conservatori, opening both palaces (the Capitoline Museums) to the public in 1734.
59. Alberti 1988, 156 (6.2).
60. Maire Vigueur 2010, chapter 6.
61. Brice 1998.
62. Brice 1998, 230.

Chapter 3
1. The *torricini* as projecting the ideal entry to the city: Bruschi 2008, 59.
2. Cecini 1985, 125; Boucheron 2004, 249.
3. Castiglione 2003, 41.
4. Alberti's participation in the development of the Urbino palace: Miotto 2004; Bruschi 2008. On the date of *On the Art of Building*, most recently Modigliani 2013b. On *partitio*, or "compartition," Alberti 1988, 8 (1.2): "Compartition is the process of dividing up the site into yet smaller units, so that the building may be considered as being made up of close-fitting smaller buildings, joined together like the members of the whole body."
5. Alberti 1988, 23 (1.9).
6. "Omissions and shortcomings": Alberti 1988, 154 (6.1). On Alberti and Vitruvius, Krautheimer 1969a; Lücke 1994; Rykwert 1988; Patetta 2005, 104–114; McLaughlin 2016, 150–156; McLaughlin 2023, among others.
7. Alberti 2004, 586; see also the table in Krüger 2018, 15, where the tally of references is closer to 170.
8. On 13 December 1459, Ludovico Gonzaga, marquis of Mantua, wrote to Alberti, requesting the loan of his copy of *De architectura* for Pope Pius II, who was then his guest in the city leading the congress concerning a projected crusade against the Turks. Borsi 1989, 142, where the letter is cited; Cantatore 2003, 454. Why Pius did not address his request to Alberti directly remains a mystery.
9. McEwen 2003.
10. Vitruvius 1.pref.2–3.
11. Martines 1988, 102–110; Bonvini Mazzanti 1993, 14–16: "Tutti sono detentori di un potere che è un *monstrum* giuridico, al di fuori degli schemi ordinari codificati dalla lunga tradizione medioevale" (15); Boucheron 2009, 56–58; Rosenberg 2010b, 1–2; Folin 2011b, 8–10; Somaini 2011, 51–55.

12. Coleman 1999, 395.
13. Black 2009, 1–2, 36–51. See above, chapter 1.
14. Varanini 1994, 316–318.
15. Somaini 2011, 52; Folin 2015a, 3.
16. Folin 2010a, 585–587; Folin 2018.
17. Taylor, Rinne, and Kostof 2016, 251.
18. Tafuri 2006, 23–58; on Nicholas V's palace, most recently Cantatore 2015 with notes. Alberti and Nicholas V (then Tommaso Parentucelli) had been friends at the University of Bologna in the 1420s. Gadol 1969, 5–6; Tavernor 1998, 3.
19. Folin 2011b, 11.
20. There are two references to Vitruvius in his *Della pittura*, of 1435: Alberti 1991, 73 (2.37) and 84 (2.48). Cf. McLaughlin 2016, 160–162; McLaughlin 2023.
21. In his *Ludi mathematici* of about 1450, dedicated to Leonello's brother, the then-marquis Meliaduse, Alberti refers to "those books of mine on architecture which I wrote at the request of your most illustrious brother, my lord, Master Leonello" (Alberti 2010, 41). Cf. Grayson 1960, 153; Krautheimer 1969a, 328.
22. Alberti 1988, 257 (8.4); brick to marble: Suetonius *Divus Augustus* 28.3.
23. A draft of *On the Art of Building* shown to Nicholas V in 1452: Modigliani 2013b, 94–95; dedication to Federico da Montefeltro: Miotto 2004, 78.
24. Urb. Lat. 264. The manuscript entered the Urbino library in 1483, the year after Federico's death.

25. Boucheron 2007; Boucheron 2014, 6–7.
26. Alberti 1988, 4 (prologue).
27. Fraser Jenkins 1970; Green 1990; and above, chapter 1.
28. Alberti 1988, 5 (prologue).
29. Pearson 2011.
30. This according to Lorenzo Valla's account of 1440 (Valla 2007, 51–53). Valla is unequivocal in his condemnation of papal tyranny. See also Miglio 2005, 93.
31. Alberti 1890; Tafuri 2006, 34–35; Miglio 2009, 501–506; Modigliani 2013a.
32. Alberti 1890.
33. Manetti 2006a, 387–431.
34. Manetti 2006b, 477.
35. Westfall 1974 argued that the "plan" governing Nicholas's urbanism was Alberti's. But see, inter alia, Smith 2006, 225–254; Tafuri 2006, 23–58; Pearson 2011, 79–84.
36. Miglio 2009, 492–493; Modigliani 2013b, 94–95. The contemporary source cited is Mattia Palmieri's chronicle *Opus de temporibus suis ab anno 1449 ad annum 1482*. Palmieri and Alberti were colleagues in the papal curia (Miglio 2009, 498).
37. Pius II 2014, 263; see also Pius II 2003, 139 (1.28.3): "He erected magnificent buildings in his city, though he began more than he finished."
38. Müntz 1878–1882, 1:227.
39. Müntz 1878–1882, 1:227; Karmon 2011, 69–71.
40. Alberti 1988, 4 (prologue).

41. Adams 1989, 61–63; Chironi 2003, 172 n. 4; Pius II 2003, 7 (1.1.2).
42. Pius II 2003, 9 (1.2.3).
43. Mack 1987, 22–23; Coleman 1999, 375; Chironi 2003, 172; Tönnesmann 2013b.
44. Pius II 2003, 281–283 (2.20.3).
45. The UNESCO plaque, here in Italian only (my translation), hangs on a wall inside the loggia of the Palazzo del Comune which was completed in 1464.
46. Alberti 1988, 35 (2.1); Smith 1992, 128–130; Trachtenberg 2010, 395.
47. Mack (1987, 47) says Alberti "seems to have had an influence" on the design.
48. Pius II 1984, 2232 (11.22); cf. Cantatore 2003, 453.
49. Mack 1987, 43.
50. Mack 1987, 44–45.
51. Alberti 1988, 298–299 (9.4); Tavernor 1998, 83.
52. Mack 1987, 47–49; Tavernor 1998, 94–95; Fiore 2006, 104–108; Frommel 2009, who states that Rossellino's palace in Pienza lacks the elegance of its prototype, the Rucellai palace, which he attributes unequivocally to Alberti (78).
53. Cherubini and Finelli 1990; Tavernor 1998, 95; Tönnesmann 2013a; Ferretti 2015.
54. Fiore 2006, 99–100; Folin 2010a, 591–592; Folin 2015a, 10–11.
55. Pius II 2003, 317–319 (2.28.2–5).
56. Prodi 1987.
57. Pius II 1937–1957, 553; for the Latin, Pius II 1984,

2:1600 (8.8); cf. Prodi 1987, 42–43.
58. Fiore 2006, 99; cf. Girondi 2015, 166.
59. Vitruvius 6.3.1–4.
60. Alberti 1988, 146 (5.17); for the Latin, Alberti 1966a, 417. Pellecchia 1992, 387–389.
61. *In medio decus omne viae sunt Atria Cosmi / Atria quae a summis regibus apta putes*: Alberto Avogadro (d. 1465), "De religione et magnificentia Illustris Cosmi Medices Florentini" (in I. Lamius, ed., *Deliciae Eruditorum* 12, 1742), cited Bulst 1990, 98, and Tönnesmann 2013a, 22, 32 n. 37. See also Ferretti 2015, 271.
62. *Forum*: Pius II 1984, 2:1769 (9.24); Mack 1987, 101.
63. Pius II 1937–1957, 598; Pius II 1984, 2:1750 (9.23).
64. Vitruvius 6.5.2: *faciunda sunt vestibula regalia, alta atria et peristilia amplissima ...*
65. Clarke 2003, chapter 1. In December 1459, when he was in Mantua, Pius requested the loan of Alberti's copy of *De architectura*, of which he may have had a copy made. In any case, he obviously read the work with close attention. Borsi 1989, 142.
66. Pellecchia 1992.
67. Vitruvius 1511, fol. 4r–4v. See also Ciapponi 1984.
68. On the Cancelleria see inter alia Frommel 1995.
69. Vitruvius 1.2.2. On the absence of images in the original *De architectura*, McEwen 2003, 32–36, with references.
70. Pius II 1937–1957, 601–602; Pius II 1984, 2:1758–1766 (9.24: *Descriptio templi Pientini*).

71. On Alberti's "temples," Krautheimer 1969b.
72. Pius II 1937–1957, 546; Pius II 1984, 2:1576 (8.5).
73. Chironi 2003, 172.
74. Mack 1987, 76. Pius II died at Ancona on 14 August 1464.
75. Pius II 2003, 281 (2.20.2)
76. Trachtenberg 2010, who singles out Pienza as probably "the most stunning of the high velocity projects" initiated in the early Renaissance (124), points out that its piazza, "centered on an exceptional illusion ... replicated the look of the traditional Italian square assembled over generations" in what he calls the "simulacrum" of a communal piazza (395).
77. Vitruvius 1.4–7; Pearson 2011.
78. Pius II 1937–1957, 604; Pius II 1984, 2:1768 (9.25); Adams 1985; Adams 1989, 67–68; Mack 1987, 118–143.
79. Pius II 1937–1957, 604; Pius II 1984, 2:1768 (9.25).
80. Cited Mack 1987, 179; 178 for the Latin.
81. Chironi 2003, 175–176. A source of income as well as of control, *ius patronatus* entailed patronage rights obtained in exchange for an endowment: Humfrey 1993, 60–70.
82. Polverini Fosi 1990, 427; Chironi 2003, 179.
83. Chironi 2000, 23.
84. Mack 1987, 147.
85. Adams 1989, 69.
86. Adams 1989, 79 n. 47; patronage rights over cathedral chapter: Chironi 2000, 23.

87. Pius II 2003, 345–365 (2.35–2.40). Borso d'Este had been Duke of Modena since 1452; the dukedom of Ferrara was eventually conferred on him by Pope Paul II in 1471 shortly before he (Borso) died.
88. Bianchi and Carpeggiani 2006, 26.
89. Inter alia: Carpeggiani 1994; Tavernor 1998, 125–126; Calzona 2011.
90. Burns 1981, 29–30; Hollingsworth 1997; Calzona 2011, 33.
91. Cantatore 2003, 453; Calzona 2011 for the most detailed account to date.
92. Romani 1995.
93. Etruscan origins: Virgil *Aeneid* 10.197–204.
94. Golinelli 1985, 14–15; Signorini 1991, 13–17; Gardoni 2006, 194–196.
95. Capuzzo 2006, 304–306.
96. Capuzzo 2006, 333–334. Calzona (2011, 21) takes issue with the traditional account, claiming that the relic was never lost between 804 and its alleged rediscovery in 1048. See also Capuzzo 1991.
97. Capuzzo 1991, 65.
98. *De inventione et traslatione Sanguinis Domini*, in *MGH, Scriptores rerum Germanicarum*, 15:921–922, cf. Gardoni 2006, 194; Capuzzo 2006, 333–336, who gives the writing of *De inventione* a mid-twelfth-century date. Another, very brief record appears in the chronicle of the Benedictine monk Hermann of Reichenau (1013–1054).
99. Golinelli 1985, 19–20.
100. Marani 1974a; Carpeggiani 1987, 11; Capuzzo 2006, 333–336.

101. Calzona 2011, 21.
102. Vaini 1986, 24–26.
103. Vaini 1986, 211–220; Romani 1995, 64–66; Rodella 2003, 17–20.
104. Capuzzo 1991, 65–66 and n. 30.
105. Chambers 1981; Vaini 1986, 278–281; Bourne 2010.
106. Vaini 1986, 282–283.
107. Romani 1995, 82; Algeri et al. 2003; Calzona 2011, 26.
108. Togliani 2003, 89–92.
109. Cited Signorini 2003, 117; see also Signorini 1985; Arasse 1987; Cordaro 1992; Starn 1992. For the architecture, Rodella 1992.
110. Alberti 1988, 146 (5.17). For the Latin, Alberti 1966a, 417.
111. Johnson 1975a; Signorini 2003, 136. Alberti, who dedicated the Latin edition of his *On Painting* to Ludovico II's father Gianfrancesco in 1435, concludes the treatise with a request that painters reward his labors by including his portrait in their *historiae*—the stories they tell. In 1469, Francesco del Cossa did just that when he portrayed Alberti in one of the murals of the *Sala dei mesi* at the Palazzo Schifanaoia in nearby Ferrara, a fresco series commissioned by its ruling duke, Borso d'Este. Mantegna would have decided to include Alberti in his Gonzaga family portrait at just about the same time.
112. Tonni 2012, 277 identifies the horse as a "superb courser."
113. Signorini 2003, 126.
114. Virgil *Georgics* 4.6: *in tenui labor; at tenuis non gloria.* "The labor is slight, but not the glory." Bourne 2010, 159.
115. Alberti 1971, 214.
116. For the building history, Tavernor 1998, 127–142; Frommel 2001.
117. Reconstruction as a domed church: Tavernor 1998, 127–129, following a drawing made by Antonio Labacco in the sixteenth century. See also Wittkower 1988, 52–55; Carpeggiani 2005, 269–283.
118. Carpeggiani 1994, 182; Romani 1995, 105–107.
119. Calzona 2011, 31.
120. Calzona 2011, 39–40.
121. As for example, Alberti 1988, 262 (8.6): "Apart from being properly paved and thoroughly clean, the roads within a city should be elegantly lined with porticoes of equal lineaments, and houses that are matched by line and level." On Alberti's urbanism, Pearson 2011.
122. Carpeggiani 1994, 179.
123. Calzona 2011, 28–29.
124. Alberti 1988, 244–245 (8.1); cf. Calzona 2011, 32, 42–43.
125. Carpeggiani 2005, 285.
126. Carpeggiani 1987, 14–21; Bianchi and Carpeggiani 2006, 32–34.
127. Donesmondi 1613–1616, pt. 2, 15–19; cf. Signorini 1991, 43–44; Johnson 1975b, 6–7; Chambers 1977, 99; Carpeggiani 2005, 285.
128. Chambers 1977.
129. I have followed the text of the manuscript copy of the letter in the Mantua state archives as transcribed by Marani 1974b, 429, and the translations (with emendations) of Johnson 1975b, 8 and Bourne 2010, 155. This is what Alberti wrote in his letter, which is usually dated to 21 October 1470: *Ceterum io intesi a questi dì che la signoria vostra et questi vostri cittadini ragionavano de edificare qui a Sancto Andrea. Et che la intentione principale era per havere gran spatio dove molto populo capesse a vedere el sangue de Christo. Vidi quel modello del Manetti. Piaquemi. Ma non mi par apto alla intentione vostra. Pensai et congettai questo qual io ve mando. Questo sarà più capace, più eterno, più degno, più lieto. Costerà molto meno. Questa forma de tempio se nomina apud veteres etruscum sacrum. Sel ve piaserà darò modo de notarlo in proportione. Raccomandandomi alla vostra signoria. Servitor vostro Baptista de Albertis.*
130. Vitruvius 1.3.2. Cf. Carpeggiani 1987, 32.
131. Krautheimer 1969a, 327; Sfogliano Fallico 1974, 159; Van Eck 1998.
132. Alberti 1988, 155 (6.1).
133. Alberti 1988, 156 (6.2).
134. Vitruvius and *venustas*: McEwen 2003, 153–224.
135. Cicero *De officiis* 1.130; Lücke 1994.
136. Alberti 1988, 194 (7.3); for the Latin, Alberti 1966a, 545; Frommel 2001, 292.
137. Vitruvius 5.1.6–10.
138. Chambers 1977, 112–113 and 126–127, where the letter is reproduced.
139. Alberti 1988, 4 (prologue).
140. Boucheron 2010, 242 for the "municipalisation" of cathedrals.
141. Bruni 1741. The essay is dated 1418 (p. 229) and is available online at https://

ia802604.us.archive.org/18/items/leonardobruniaoopapegoog/leonardobruniaroopapegoog.pdf; cf. Bianchi and Carpeggiani 2006, 36.

142. Virgil *Aeneid* 10.197–204; Bruni 1741, 223.

143. See for example the dedication to Brunelleschi of his vernacular *Della pictura* (Alberti 1991, 34).

144. Alberti 1988, 194 (7.3).

145. Chambers 1977, 113.

146. Alberti 1988, 158–159 (6.3).

147. Alberti 1988, 197 (7.4); Vitruvius 4.7.1–2.

148. Krautheimer 1969b; Hersey 1994; Tavernor 1998, 159–178. See also Rowland 2006, 230–231.

149. As Krautheimer observed (1969b, 333), "The antique past, the present in which Alberti lives—both real and ideal—and the future he envisions are inextricably interwoven." The domed, Latin cross church you see in Mantua now is the result of much later extensions to Alberti's original "Etruscan" temple: Johnson 1975b, 23–42; Tavernor 1998, 165–169.

150. Carpeggiani 1987, 32; Bianchi and Carpeggiani 2006, 36.

151. Tavernor 1998, 179.

152. Saalman, Volpi, and Law 1992, 365.

153. Saalman, Volpi, and Law 1992, 371–376; Tavernor 1998, 179; Bulgarelli 2003, 16–18.

154. Bianchi and Carpeggiani 2006, 39.

155. Carpeggiani 2005, 291; Bianchi and Carpeggiani 2006, 39: "potremo affirmare che la combinazione di torri scalari et capella superiore si configura come une sorta di recupero del *Westwerk* altomedievale da Alberti rivisitato secondo i nuovi canoni morfologici dell'umanesimo, legittimati dall'antico." On *Westwerke* in general, Sapin 2002.

156. On Aachen, inter alia, Siebigs 2004; McClendon 2005, 105–127.

157. On the podium meant for the display of the relic: Bianchi and Carpeggiani 2006, 44–45, nn. 165, 186.

158. Alberti 1988, 261 and 265 (8.6).

159. Alberti 1988, 265–268 (265) (8.6); *via regia*: Alberti 1966a, 717.

160. Tavernor 1998, 179.

161. Romani 1995, 103–104; Pius II 2003, 373–377.

162. Shearer 1935; Willemsen 1953; Meredith 1994; D'Onofrio 1995; Pane 2000; Clarke 2003, 80–83.

163. Demolition of *borgo*: Pane 2000, 227.

164. Shearer 1935, 113–129; Scaglia 1981–1982, 203–206; Pane 2000, 238–246, 257. The Francesco di Giorgio drawing is one in a notebook of his drawings of Roman antiquities (Florence, Uffizi, Gabinetto dei Disegni n. 333 A recto). The anonymous early sixteenth-century drawing is in Vienna (National Bibliothek ms. 3228, fol. 5v).

165. On the statuary: Claussen 1995, 94–97; Fonseca and Pace 1995, cat. nos. IV.5, IV.6, and IV.7 (233–234). All the statues are now in the Museo Provinciale Campano in Capua.

166. Fonseca and Pace 1995, cat. no. IV.2.

167. Claussen 1995, 95 for the drawing (Biblioteca Apostolica Vaticana, Rome, Album of Séroux d'Agincourt).

168. Scaglia 1981–1982, 208.

169. Shearer 1935, 118.

170. Borsi 2006.

171. Bernich 1903; Hersey 1973, 7–8, 31; Di Battista 1998–1999, 16–17; Frommel 2008.

172. Panormita 1538, 15; Frommel 2008, 29–30.

173. http://www.treccani.it/enciclopedia/giovanni-antonio-campano_%28Dizionario-Biografico%29/, visited 9 April 2019. Campano's life of Federico da Montefeltro is in Urb. Lat. 1022, 67r–84v, where it follows a biography of Federico written by the humanist Francesco Filelfo (Zannoni 1901). The Urbino manuscript of Campano's biography of Braccio da Montone is Urb. Lat. 326 (Zannoni 1902–1903).

174. Campano 1929, 177: *Inter duas turres regium cubiculum, qua iter erat, supra caput altissima prominet testudine, marmoreis statuis vetustisque imaginibus distinctum atque ornatum* (my translation). Cf. Scaglia 1981–1982, 214 n. 20.

175. Scaglia 1981–1982, 206, 214 n. 20; Pane 2000, 238–241.

176. Lewis and Short 1988, s.v. *cubiculum*; McEwen 1995, 22; Pane 2000, 246. Pliny the Younger uses the term in this sense in his *Panegyricus* (51), a work Giovanni Aurispa

discovered in 1433, and which enjoyed considerable popularity (Clarke 2003, 29).

177. Carpegianni 1987, 32.

178. The image appears on the title page of a pattern book of pageant costume, armor, arms, and horse bits published in Mantua in 1554: Chambers and Matineau 1981, xvi and cat. 72.

179. https://whc.unesco.org/en/list/1287, visited 18 April 2019.

180. Bruschi 2008, 59.

181. Frommel 2004, 178–179. Federico was in Naples in the fall of 1466.

182. "… le cabinet devient une pièce de représentation, le lieu officiellement privé où se parachève l'image public du maître des lieux" (Arasse 1993, 248); Boucheron 2004, 277.

183. Arasse 1993; Tönnesmann 1994, 146. On the studiolo and its iconography (inter alia) Cheles 1986; Kirkbride 2008.

184. Searle 2010. Cf. N. J. Enfield, review in the *Times Literary Supplement*, 3 September 2010, 3.

185. Woods-Marsden 1989, for a discussion of popular attacks on castles in the fifteenth century.

186. Alberti 1988, 117 (5.1).

187. Alberti 1988, 121–122 (5.3).

188. Alberti 1988, 123 (5.4). Alberti's patrician antipathy to the turbulent multitude is everywhere in evidence in the political dinner pieces of book 10 of his *Intercenales*, written for the most part around 1440: Alberti 1987 (English trans. by David Marsh); Alberti 2003 with the introduction by Franco Bacchelli and Luca D'Ascia (lxxvi–lxxxi).

189. Alberti 1988, 156 (6.2). Cf. Boucheron 2013b.

190. For a recent biography, Stevenson 2021. See also, among others, Fiore 2011; Rossi and Brammanti 1995; Dennistoun 1909. Contemporary biographies, of which there were many, tended to hagiography. Among the latter, the *Vita* written by Federico's chancellor Pierantonio Palroni around 1470 is judged the least unreliable (Paltroni 1966). Cf. Falvo 1986, 120–124.

191. My account follows Modigliani 2004.

192. Inter alia, Tommasoli 1978, 35–42; Hollingsworth 2010, 333–334; Hollingsworth 2021, 133.

193. Westfall 1978, 22; Hollingsworth 2021, 133; Stevenson 2021, 67.

194. Modigliani 2004, 63.

195. Stevenson 2021, 67.

196. Peruzzi 1986, 228; cf. Tönnesmann 1994, 140.

197. *Pian di mercato*: Luni 1985, 23.

198. De Carlo 1970, 75–76; Luni 1985, 20–22; Benevolo and Boninsegna 1986, 41–54.

199. For a useful summary of the chronology of palace construction, Bruschi 2008, 55–58. See also Rotondi 1969; Frommel 2004.

200. Fiore 1994, 83.

201. Alberti 1988, 121–122 (5.3). On Federico's accessibility, inter alia Vespasiano da Bisticci 1997, 108, and Porcelio de Pandoni's 46-line verse description of the palace of 1474 (reprinted in Londei 1989, 116): *Hanc proceres ducesquque colunt populique frequentant* (l. 10). The description appears in book 7 of Porcelio's verse epic *Feltria*, commissioned by Federico in 1464. Cf. Hoffmann 2008, 55.

202. Ferretti 2015 and above.

203. Frommel 2004, 12–15, who identifies the model for the Composite column capitals of the courtyard as those of the Domus Flavia and the arch of Septimius Severus at Rome (15).

204. Alberti 1988, 4 (prologue).

205. See Ludovico's letter to his son Cardinal Francesco Gonzaga of 2 January 1472, cited above. Chambers 1977, 112–113 and 126–127, where the letter is reproduced.

206. Cited Cecini 1985, 127. Sulpicius's edition of *De architectura*: Vitruvius 1486.

207. Luni 1985, 19–22; Benevolo and Boninsegna 1986, 41–54; Luni 2009, 46–57.

208. Urb. Lat. 293 for the twelfth-century manuscript; Urb. Lat. 1360 for the fifteenth-century one; cf. Krinsky 1967, 65. Federico's crest with its black eagle appears on the illuminated first page of the fifteenth-century manuscript without the ducal crown or the monogram "FE DUX," which means the manuscript was made before Pope Sixtus IV made him a duke in 1474.

209. *qui ipsi Vitruvio nequaquam cedas*, cited Tocci 1958, 224. Cf. Cecini 1985, 125; Miotto 2004, 53.

210. Vitruvius 6.5.1. See further Louis Callebat's commentary in Vitruvius 1969–2009, 6:170–185.
211. Cicero *De officiis* 1.139: *Ornanda enim est dignitas domo.*
212. Vitruvius 6.5.2.
213. Vitruvius 2.8.1–6.
214. Volaterrano 1506, 399r; cf. Pagliara 1986, 30; Daly Davis 1989; Clarke 1996.
215. The text of the letter is published in Bruschi 1978, 19–22 (2l). I will discuss it in greater detail in the next chapter.
216. Fiore 2011, 286.
217. Höfter 2004 and Höfter 2006. Höfter's conclusions question those of Negroni 1993.
218. Bonvini Mazzanti 1993, 63; Stevenson 2021, 98.
219. Bonvini Mazzanti 1993, 57–154.
220. Bonvini Mazzanti 1993, 151.
221. *In civitate Urbini in platea magna dicte civitatis cuj platee a duobus sunt bona illustrissimi dominij nostrij a tertio et a quarto bona Episcupatus Urbini et alia alia latera* ... Cited Polichetti 1985, 163 and 358; cf. Luni 2009, 11.
222. Negroni 1993, 157–160; Höfter 2004; Höfter 2006.
223. Polichetti 1985, 163; Fiore 1989, 423; Tönnesmann 1994, 38; Boucheron 2004, 258–264.
224. Luni 2009, 11–13.
225. Volaterrano 1506, 400v–401r.
226. Luni 2009, 11.

Chapter 4
1. On the chronology of construction which is generally considered to have begun in 1464, Rotondi 1969; Bruschi 1978; Bruschi 2008, 55–58; Frommel 2004.
2. "Quelli uomini noi giudicamo dover essere onorati e commendati, li quali si trovano esser ornati d'ingegno e di virtù, e maxime di quelle virtù che sempre sono state in prezzo appresso li antiqui e moderni, com'è la virtù dell'architettura fundata in l'arte dell'arismetica e geometria, che sono delle sette arti liberali, e delle principali, perché sono in primo gradu certitudinis, e è arte di gran scienza e di grande ingegno, e da noi molto estimata e apprezzata." The Italian text is from Bruschi 1978, 18–22; my translation.
3. Liddell and Scott, s.v. *ageômetrètos* ("without geometry") for the sources.
4. Each regular solid corresponded to one of the four elements of the material world, with the fifth being the heavenly form of a "quintessence" that could contain them all. Tetrahedron (4 sides) = fire; octahedron (8 sides) = air; cube (6 sides) = earth; icosahedron (20 sides) = water; dodecahedron (12 sides) = quintessence. Cf. inter alia Pérez-Gómez 2004.
5. Wisdom 11:20.
6. The dedication reappeared in the 1509 print edition of *De divina proportione* (Pacioli 1509, fol. 1v): "De le vere commo afferma Aristotele e Averroís le nostre mathematici sonno verissime e nel primo grado de la certezza."
7. Zampetti 1981. Federico attended the school from 1434 to 1436. Pisanello's commemorative medal of Vittorino of c. 1446 has him in profile on the obverse, while on the reverse, the legend surrounding the salvific emblem of a pelican feeding her young with her own blood reads MATHEMATICUS ET OMNIS HUMANITATIS PATER ("mathematician and father of all the humanities"); https://www.metmuseum.org/art/collection/search/459775, visited 3 October 2018.
8. Fenucci and Simonetta 2007. "Most sainted preceptor" figures in the Latin inscription under Vittorino's portrait in the studiolo: Zampetti 1981, 258–259.
9. Miotto 2004, 46.
10. Cited Miotto 2004, 46.
11. There were two manuscripts of Vitruvius in the Urbino library: a twelfth-century one (Urb. Lat. 293) and a fifteenth-century one made for Federico (Urb. Lat. 1360). See above, chapter 3, n. 208. That *On the Art of Building* was still in progress at the time of Alberti's visits to Urbino is based on Modigliani 2013b, who argues that he was working on the manuscript until the day he died. Federico's copy of the work (Urb. Lat. 264) appears to have been commissioned well after Alberti's decease in 1472, only entering the Urbino library in 1483, a year after Federico's own death.

12. Alberti 1988, 156 (6.2); Alberti 1966a, 449 for the Latin. "Certain calculations of symmetries": Vitruvius 2.1.7 and above, chapter 2.

13. Alberti 1988, 317 (9.10); Vitruvius 1.1.3.

14. For Alberti, Sfogliano Fallico 1974, 157–163; Karvouni 1994. For Vitruvius, McEwen 2003, 40–49 and passim.

15. Vitruvius on music and architecture: 5.4–5; Alberti 1988, 305 (9.5). On *concinnitas*, Tavernor 1994.

16. Cosmic necessity: Vitruvius 5.5.5–6, 9.1.1–2, 10.1.4; Alberti 1988, 301–310 (9.5–7).

17. Bruschi 2008, 48.

18. Clough 1973.

19. This in Campano's funeral oration for Battista Sforza of 1472. Cited Charlet 1999, 96.

20. Paltroni 1966, 21–22.

21. *Tamburlaine the Great* 1.2.174–175. Marlowe's play was written in 1588. Machiavelli 1999, 79–82 (ch. 25). The chapter heading reads "How far human affairs are governed by fortune, and how fortune may be opposed."

22. In a chilling illustration of *virtù* in action Machiavelli relates how, in 1500, Cesare Borgia dealt with Remirro de Orca, the overly ambitious ruler of Cesena: "One morning, Remirro's body was found cut in two pieces on the piazza at Cesena, with a block of wood and a bloody knife beside it. The brutality of this spectacle kept the people of the Romagna at once appeased and stupefied [*satisfati e stupidi*]." Machiavelli 1999, 24 (ch. 7); for the Italian, Machiavelli 1995, 47.

23. Bernini Pezzini 1985; Wyatt 2014, 100–103.

24. Pacioli 1509, fols. 1v–2v, and above, n. 6 of this chapter.

25. The three parts of architecture: Vitruvius 1.3.1. *Gnomonice* (gnomonics), covered in book 9 of *De architectura*, was the construction of clocks. Cf. McEwen 2003, 25 and 229–250.

26. Designer of artillery: Vitruvius 1.pref.2; 10.10–12. Cf. Philippe Fleury's notes at Vitruvius 1969–2009, 1:59–61. Breathtaking speed: Caesar's own third-person account of his conquest of Gaul in *De bello gallico* makes repeated reference to how quickly and decisively he moved to annex the territory.

27. Above, chapter 1.

28. Chevalier 1985; McLaughlin 2009b.

29. Castiglione Olona: Pulin 1981, 30; Ferrara: Folin 2015b, 195; *camera picta*, above, chapter 3.

30. Foyle 2002, 149.

31. Which of the Gonzaga—Ludovico, or one of his sons—commissioned the work remains controversial. See Martindale 1979; Elam 1981; Campbell 2004 (91 for the citation). The *Triumphs* were purchased for Charles I of England in 1629, when the Gonzaga had fallen upon hard times, and have been located at Hampton Court ever since. For a detailed account, catalogue entry no. 66 in Chambers and Martineau 1981, 142–143.

32. Campbell 2004, 96 (fig. 6.10).

33. On the enmity between Federico da Montefeltro and Sigismondo Malatesta, recently Simonetta 2017.

34. Gaspare Broglio in Tonini 1882, 353–364, cited Helas 1999, 226–227. See also Bornstein 1988.

35. Gaspare Broglio, cited Helas 1999, 226–227; my translation.

36. Caesar *Bellum civile* 1.8; Lucan *Pharsalia* 1.235–245; Suetonius *Divus Julius* 32; cf. Campana 1933; Ravara 2006.

37. For the circumstances of Federico's seizure of power, above, chapter 3.

38. Ravara 2006, 72; http://www.treccani.it/enciclopedia/gaspare-broglio_(Dizionario-Biografico)/, visited 10 August 2019.

39. Bornstein 1988.

40. Petrarch 2003, 210 (20.10 in this edition, although earlier editions have the account in chapter 21).

41. Petrarch 2003, 211 (20.11). The account follows Suetonius *Divus Julius* 33, almost to the letter.

42. Pasquini 1933, 8.

43. Petrarch 1955.

44. Cited Gilbert 1977, 56.

45. Petrarch 1955, 218–219.

46. Textual evidence supports this hypothesis. Vitruvius's detailed description (2.9.15) of Caesar's construction of a siege tower while campaigning in the Alps at the beginning of the Gallic wars (59–58 BCE) bears all

the marks of a firsthand account (Vitruvius 1969–2009, 2:172–173, notes), as does his description (10.16.11–12) of the siege of Marseilles which took place from April to September of 49 BCE at the beginning of the civil war that immediately followed Caesar's crossing of the Rubicon in January of that year. These two descriptions imply that Vitruvius's attachment to Caesar covered the intervening ten years. See also Vitruvius 1969–2009, 10:289–293.

47. Vitruvius 1.pref.1.
48. Vitruvius 1.pref.2.
49. Cicero *Tusculanae disputationes* 2.43: *Appellata est enim ex viro virtus* ...
50. McDonnell 2006.
51. McDonnell 2006, 3.
52. McDonnell 2006, 142–149.
53. McDonnell 2006, 149–154.
54. McDonnell 2006, 385–389.
55. For examples of Roman imperial coins see Cohen 1955, vol. 2; Sutherland and Carson 1984.
56. Suetonius *Divus Julius* 61. Temple of Venus Genetrix: Steinby 1993–2000, s.v. *Venus Genetrix, aedes*; McEwen 2003, 204.
57. Janson 1973, 160 and 165.
58. Krinsky 1967; Ciapponi 1976; Brown 1976, 92.
59. Urb. Lat. 428, 442, and 882.
60. Brown 1976, 93.
61. Vitruvius 1486; Vitruvius 1511.
62. McEwen 2003, 35–38.
63. Vitruvius 1.1.1.

64. Filarete 1972, 432 (Ms. Magliabechiano, Florence, Bib. Naz. Magl. II.1.140, fol. 114v).
65. Vitruvius 1.1.3; Alberti 1988, 317 (9.10).
66. Vitruvius 1.1.5.
67. Vitruvius 1.1.6.
68. Callebat et al. 1984, s.v. *virtus*.
69. At 1.7.2, Vitruvius projects the contents of book 2 which, he says, will deal with materials, *quibus sint virtutes et quem habeant usum*. Cf. 2.pref.5, 2.1.6, 2.4.3, 2.5.2, etc. For book 8, see 8.pref.4, 8.2.1, 8.3.4, 8.3.12, etc.
70. Vitruvius 10.1.1, 10.1.2, 10.3.1, 10.3.6, etc.
71. See for example Vitruvius 1.1.17.
72. Vitruvius 10.16.12
73. Alberti 1966a, 11 (prologue); Alberti 1988, 4.
74. Vitruvius 1.1.1.
75. Vitruvius 3.pref.3.
76. Vitruvius 9.pref.3.
77. Vitruvius refers to the deified Caesar's "seat among the gods" in identical terms in his first preface (1.pref.2); Vitruvius 9.pref.3, with commentary at Vitruvius 1969–2009, 9:44–45.
78. Vitruvius 9.pref.4–18.
79. Vitruvius 2.pref.
80. Vitruvius 1.2.5.
81. Vitruvius 2.pref.4.
82. "King's double": McEwen 2003, 95–103. Alberti and Filarete both invoke Vitruvius's Dinocrates story in their treatises. See Alberti 1988, 12 (1.4), where the architect appears as "Polycrates," and 160 (6.4), where he is "Stasicrates or Dinocrates"; Filarete 1965, 18–19 (1972, 1:46), where he is called "Zenocrates."

83. Francesco di Giorgio Martini, *Opusculum de architectura*, Harley Ms. 3281, British Museum, Department of Prints and Drawings 197B21; cf. Popham and Pouncey 1950, 33. An English translation appears in Scaglia 1985, 42–44, where the author remarks on Francesco's poor Latin. See also Fiore 1998, 67–68; Adams 2004, 308.
84. Warnke 1985, 35, 135, and passim.
85. Vitruvius 1.pref.2–3.
86. Francesco di Giorgio Martini, Codex Magliabechiano II.1.141, 50v; Martini 1967, 2:427. For the dating of Francesco's treatises which remains controversial, Scaglia 1985; Mussini 1994; Merrill 2013; Riahi 2015, 13–14. On Francesco di Giorgio's collaboration with Federico da Montefeltro, Benelli 2010, 149–152.
87. For the map, Benevolo and Boninsegna 1986, 91; Adams 1994.
88. The translation, which dates from about 1485, has been preserved in fols. 103r–180r of the Codex Magliabechiano II.1.141, where it follows Francesco di Giorgio's *Trattato II*. See Scaglia 1985; Martini 2002.
89. Codex Magliabechiano II.1.141, fol. 27v; Martini 1967, 2:362.
90. Codex Saluzziano 148, fol. 3r; Martini 1967, 1:4.
91. Woods-Marsden 1989, 130.
92. Codex Magliabechiano II.1.141, fols. 46v–47v; Martini 1967, 2:414–417.
93. On the ubiquity of Francesco di Giorgio's

body images and their significance, Riahi 2015.

94. Its relevance to the design of temples is repeatedly stressed in the opening paragraphs of *De architectura*, book 3, the first of Vitruvius's two books on religious architecture. The only two other appeals to a body referent for the principle of commensurability in architecture occur in book 1: *De architectura* 1.2.2, 1.2.4.

95. Vitruvius 3.1.3.

96. McEwen 2003, 183–198. Cf. Price 1996. *Imperium sine fine* ("empire without end"): Virgil *Aeneid* 1.279.

97. McEwen 2003.

98. Codex Saluzziano 148, fol. 6v; Martini 1967, 1:20; and below, fig. 6.21.

99. High-mindedness: Vitruvius 1.1.7.

100. McDonnell 2006, 105–128.

101. McDonnell 2006, 332–335.

102. Cicero *In Catilinam* 2.11; cf. McDonnell 2006, 350.

103. McDonnell 2006, 353.

104. Pevsner 1942.

105. Panofsky 1930, 150–170; Mommsen 1953.

106. Panofsky 1930, 153.

107. Grafton 2002, 32–33.

108. Alberti 1960, 5–6; trans., Alberti 1971, 29.

109. Alberti 1960, 9; trans., Alberti 1971, 32.

110. Inter alia, Gadol 1969; Grafton 2002, 8–29.

111. Burckhardt 1990, 102–104. For the autobiography, Alberti 1972, English translation in Alberti 1989. Alberti was identified as the author of the work in 1843 (Fubini and Menci Gallorini 1972, 23).

112. Alberti 1989, 7; Alberti 1972, 68 for the Latin.

113. McLaughlin 2009a, 78.

114. Grafton 2002, 41.

115. Cicero *Brutus* 23–24.

116. Alberti 2003, 41–57; Alberti 1987, 23–27 for the English.

117. Alberti 1966a, 51 (1.6); Alberti 1988, 18. Cf. Lücke 1975, s.v. *virtus*.

118. Alberti 1966a, 11 (prologue); Alberti 1988, 4.

119. Alberti 1966a, 359 (5.6); Alberti 1988, 126.

120. Alberti 1966a, 457 (6.3); Alberti 1988, 159.

121. Cited Helas 1999, 226.

122. Gobbi 1982, 56–68; Ettlinger 1990 (133 for "Tempio Malatesiana" which the author considers misleading); Hope 1992; Tavernor 1998, 51–77; Turchini 2000; Paolucci 2010.

123. Above, chapter 3.

124. Gobbi 1982, 14.

125. Gobbi 1982, 14. The bridge was completed under Tiberius in 20 CE.

126. Above, n. 36 of this chapter.

127. Folin 2010d, 18; Hollingsworth 2021, 69.

128. Folin 2010d, 24–27; Hollingsworth 2021, 89–90.

129. Pius II 2003, 326–335 (2.32).

130. Pius II 2003, 327 (2.32.1).

131. Antonio Paolucci (2001, 41) calls 1450 "l'anno di Sigismondo."

132. https://neolatin.lbg.ac.at/research/basinio-da-parma-hesperis, visited 3 September 2019. Ettlinger 1990, 139–140.

133. *Hesperis* 13, 343–348, cited Paolucci 2001, 44. For the inscription, Hope 1992, 52 and n. 5, where it is translated; Folin 2010d, 37. Cf. Tavernor 1998, 58.

134. Alberti 1988, 117 (5.1). On the castle, Gobbi 1982, 56–59; Ianucci 1972; Turchini 2003; Folin 2009, 21–23.

135. Covini 2003, 59.

136. Turchini 2003, 21–22.

137. Gobbi 1982, 37–46.

138. Folin 2010d, 33.

139. Filarete 1965, 3; Filarete 1972, 5 (ms. fol. 1r).

140. Tigler 1963, 2; Onians 1971; De Keyser 2019.

141. Beltramini 1996.

142. Filelfo, Ms. Ambrosiano G 93, Milan, fol. 218v, cited Beltramini 1996, 121.

143. Vitruvius 1.pref.2.

144. Beltramini 1996, 120.

145. Martines 1988, 140–148; Robin 1991, 85–88.

146. Ianziti 1988; Hollingsworth 2021, 48–51.

147. Machiavelli 1999, 5 (ch. 1), 21 (ch. 7); Machiavelli 1995, 7, 40.

148. Robin 1991.

149. Filelfo 2009.

150. Filelfo 2009, 3–5.

151. Boucheron 1998, 207–214.

152. Filelfo 2009, 104–117.

153. Filelfo 2009, 181.

154. Filelfo 2009, 183.

155. Firpo 1954, 33; Lang 1972, 391; Scotti 2015, 139–140.

156. Cuzin et al. 2000, cat. no. 41. The bronze statuette, now in Dresden, measures 37 centimeters high by 36 centimeters in length.

157. Seymour 1973; Spencer 1979 (550 for the medal of Julius Caesar); Glass 2015.

158. Firpo 1954; Onians 1988, 158–170.
159. Filarete 1965, 119; Filarete 1972, 262 (ms. fol. 68v).
160. Filarete 1965, 246–247; Filarete 1972, 532–535 (ms. fol. 143r).
161. Diamond as Sforza emblem: Menges Nogueira 2018, 38–39. On diamonds and precious stones: Filarete 1965, 52; Filarete 1972, 74–75 (ms. fol. 17v). On their properties, Pliny *Natural History* 20.1.2 and 37.15.4. On Pliny as a source for Filarete's treatise, Fane-Saunders 2009.
162. Filarete 1965, 15–16; Filarete 1972, 39–43 (ms. fol. 7v). Cf. Tönnesmann 2009, 9.
163. Pfisterer 2009, 99–103.
164. On their collaboration, also Onians 1971, 104–113; Onians 1988, 159–162.
165. Warnke 1985, 135 and passim.
166. Boucheron 1998, 335–377.
167. Filarete 1965, 199–200; Filarete 1972, 430–433 (ms. fol. 114r–v).
168. On the medal: Firpo 1954, 34–35; Boucheron 1998, 335–336.
169. Vitruvius 1.pref.3: "Thus, bound to you by the benefice that freed me from fear of want for the rest of my life, I began to write this work for you."
170. Vitruvius 1.pref.2: ... *et cum eis commoda accepi.*
171. Boucheron 1998, 356.
172. Filarete ms. fols. 144r and 145r.
173. Filarete 1965, 245–259; Filarete 1972, 531–562 (ms. fols. 142v–151r).

174. Filarete 1965, 256; Filarete 1972, 557 (ms. fol. 150r).
175. Filarete 1965, 180–181; Filarete 1972, 389–390 (ms. fol. 102v).
176. Filarete 1965, 293–294; Filarete 1972, 633–635 (ms. fol. 172r).
177. Filarete 1965, 293 n. 4.
178. Filarete 1965, 179; Filarete 1972, 179 (ms. fol. 102r).
179. Filarete 1965, 181; Filarete 1972, 393 (ms. fol. 103r–v).
180. Filarete 1965, 183; Filarete 1972, 398 (ms. fol. 104v).
181. On the appeal to precedent, recently Price and Thonemann 2010.
182. Inter alia, Grassi 1985; Giordano 1998, 64–65; Whittemore 2009.
183. Ianziti 1988, 20–30; Martines 1988, 140–148.
184. Ianziti 1988, 61–64; Ianziti 2019.
185. Cited Ianziti 2019, 107.
186. Ianziti 1988, 103–127.
187. Vulpi 2001 336–337; Whittemore 2009.

Chapter 5
1. https://it.wikisource.org/wiki/Le_vite_de%27_pi%C3%B9_eccellenti_pittori,_scultori_e_architettori_(1568)/Antonio_Filarete_e_Simone.
2. Martines 1988, 140–148; Robin 1991, 85–88.
3. Filelfo 2009, 81 (*Odes* 1.10.93–110); cf. Robin 1991, 89–97.
4. Filelfo 2009, 104–105 (*Odes* 2.2).
5. Filelfo 2012, 99–301; Hankins 2019, 386–392; Humble 2019, 157–164.

6. Filelfo 2012, 101–106; cf. Hankins 2019, 390–391.
7. Alberti 1966b, 195. Cf. Grafton 2002, 337.
8. Patrizi 1567, bk. 1, fols. i–xlv; cf. Hankins 2019, 398–416.
9. Patrizi 1567, bk. 1, fols. xl–xliiii.
10. Codex Magliabechiano II.1.141, fols. 46v–47v; Martini 1967, 2:414–417.
11. Codex Saluzziano 148, fol. 3r; Martini 1967, 1:4.
12. Corio, *Storia di Milano*, 1335–1337, cited Woods-Marsden 1989, 130.
13. Onians 1973; Onians 1988, 162–170. See also Firpo 1954, 22–25; Hollingsworth 2021, 59.
14. Filarete 1965, 10; Filarete 1972, 24 (ms. fol. 4v).
15. Vitruvius 2.1.1–7, and above, chapter 2.
16. On diamonds and precious stones, Filarete 1965, 52; Filarete 1972, 74–75 (ms. fol. 17v). On their properties, Pliny *Natural History* 20.1.2 and 37.15.4. On Pliny as a source for Filarete's treatise, Fane-Saunders 2009.
17. The term "orders" did not become current until the mid sixteenth century. See Rowland 1994.
18. Filarete 1965, 18; Filarete 1972, 18 (ms. fol. 3r).
19. Filarete 1965, 94–96; Filarete 1972, 214–215 (ms. fol. 55v).
20. Filarete 1965, 256; Filarete 1972, 557 (ms. fol. 150r).
21. Filarete 1965, 8; Filarete 1972, 18 (ms. fol. 3v). In his treatise on painting, Alberti also chose the head as a unit of measurement over Vitruvius's choice of the

foot, to which he explicitly objects: Alberti 1991, 73 (2.37).

22. Filarete 1965, 96–98 (ms. fols. 56r–57v). See ms. fol. 57v for the drawing of Filarete's three *qualità*.

23. Filarete 1965, 12; Filarete 1972, 28 (ms. fol. 5v).

24. Filarete 1965, 84 (ms. fol. 48v). The drawing strongly resembles Filarete's relief portrait of Caesar on a large steel plaquette he made c. 1445, now in the Bargello museum in Florence; see *Giulio Cesare* 2008, cat. no. 155, as well the portrait bust of Caesar on a medal Filarete made (above, chapter 4, n. 157).

25. McEwen 2003, 142–145 and n. 221.

26. Onians 1988, 159; Giordano 1998, 157.

27. Yates 1975, 5.

28. Kantorowicz 1931, 435–438, 448; Cammarosano 1995; Guarducci 2003. The ox-drawn *carroccio*, mounted with civic standards, religious symbols, and sometimes a bell and/or a tower—emblematically, the self-governing commune itself—was the rallying focus of a patriotic zeal on the battlefield: Volmer 1994; Ogliari 2005.

29. Powell 1971, xxvi.

30. Powell 1971, 48–49.

31. Powell 1971, 3; cf. Kantorowicz 1931, 223–227.

32. Powell 1971, 4; cf. Burdach 1913–1928, 296–320; Kantorowicz 1957, 115–116.

33. Yates 1975, 5–9.

34. Jellinek 1893; Kantorowicz 1931, 258–266; Kantorowicz 1957, 468–475.

35. Yates 1975, 8. There were two copies of Dante's *De monarchia* in the ducal library at Pavia: Pellegrin 1955, A367 and A453.

36. The diamond was adopted by Francesco Sforza's father Mucio Antendolo Sforza as a family emblem in 1409 (Menges Nogueira 2018, 38–39).

37. Filarete 1972, 7 (ms. fol. 1v). The dedication to Francesco Sforza is reprinted in Filarete 1972, 8 n. 1.

38. Filarete 1965, 3.

39. Woods 1992.

40. Vitruvius 9.1.1.

41. Vitruvius 9.1.2.

42. Wittkower 1988, and below, chapter 6.

43. McEwen 2003.

44. Vitruvius 6.1.11

45. Vitruvius 1.1.1: *Architecti est scientia pluribus disciplinis et variis eruditionibus ornata*. The knowledge of the architect is furnished with many disciplines and various kinds of learning.

46. Aristotle *Metaphysics* 981a30–b5.

47. Aristotle *Metaphysics* 5, 1013a–b.

48. Aristotle *Nicomachean Ethics* 1094a.4.

49. Vitruvius 1.1.1. Cf. McEwen 2003, 319 n. 88.

50. Aristotle *Nicomachean Ethics* 1094a.1 (trans. W. D. Ross; Aristotle 1947, 308.)

51. Aristotle *Nicomachean Ethics* 1094a.25–29

52. Pevsner 1942, 559. See also Schuler 1999, 69–80; Tosco 2003.

53. Pellegrin 1955.

54. Onians 1971.

55. Zippel 1979, 232; Robin 1991, 50–51; Grendler 2002, 397.

56. Cetius Faventinus 2002, 49 n. 1.

57. *M. Ceti Faventini artis architectonicae privatis usibus abbreviatus liber*. Cf. Cetius Faventinus 2002, 4.

58. Biblioteca Ambrosiana, Milan, A137 sup. Cf. Ferrari 1984, 268–272; Cetius Faventinus 2002, introduction, xlvi.

59. Cetius Faventinus 2002, 42; trans. in Plommer 1973.

60. The Filarete manuscript, now in Venice (Biblioteca Nazionale Marciana Lat. VIII, 2 (= 2796): *Antoni Averulini florentini De Architectura libri viginti quinque*), was completed in 1488–1489. See Bonfini 2000, introduction; *Nel segno del Corvo* 2002, cat. no. 7. The Alberti manuscript, now in Modena, belongs to precisely the same time frame (*Nel segno del Corvo* 2002, cat. no. 21).

61. Fügadi 1990.

62. Lupescu 2008.

63. Bonfini 2000, 4; Bonfini ms. fol. 2r, my translation.

64. Karsay 1991; Mikó 1999.

65. Brandolini 2009.

66. Brandolini 2009, 139.

67. Brandolini 2009, 177.

68. Di Pietro Lombardi 2002.

69. Baker 2012.

70. Bonfini 2000, introduction, xix–xxiv; Beltramini 2003.

71. Bonaccorsi 1981, 304, 308; cf. Szörényi 1987.

72. Biblioteca Nazionale Marciana, Venice, Ms. Lat. VIII.2 (=2796), fol. 137v.

73. Di Pietro Lombardi 2002, 119.

74. Bonfini 2000, 6–7; Bonfini ms. fol. 4r.

75. *Opus igitur tibi dicatum libenter...*: Bonfini ms. fol. 5r; Bonfini 2000, 8.
76. Cuzin et al. 2000, cat. no. 41.

Chapter 6
1. Pope-Hennessy 1958; Janson 1973.
2. BN Ms. Lat. 6069. The manuscript dates from the mid fourteenth century. Cf. Pellegrin 1955, A835; Pellegrin 1961, 376–377.
3. The manuscript was in Padua until 1388 when, after deposing its original owner, Giangaleazzo Visconti seized the work and brought it to the Visconti library at Pavia. It is now in the Bibliothèque nationale in Paris.
4. Wells 1995; Raber and Tucker 2005b; Edwards and Graham 2012; Fratarcangeli 2014.
5. Leonardo da Vinci, Paris Ms. B, fol. 39r.
6. Tuohy 1996, 241; Chambers 1981, xix.
7. Malacarne 1995; Tobey 2005; Tonni 2012.
8. Chambers and Martineau 1981, cat. no. 78.
9. Tobey 2005, 76–78; Wind 2016.
10. Tobey 2005, 77.
11. Frontisi-Ducroux 1975, 103ff; McEwen 1993, 3–5, 116–118.
12. Alberti 1999. Alberti probably met Leonello in 1437 at the papal council held in Ferrara which he attended as a member of Pope Eugenius IV's entourage. In 1437, he dedicated an updated version of his early *Philodexios fabula* to the marquis, and in 1441 his treatise *Theogenius* (Rosenberg 1991, 42; Rykwert 1994, 158; Di Stefano 2010, 15). On Alberti's time in Ferrara in general, Grafton 2002, 189–224.
13. https://www.ferraranascosta.it/il-palio-di-ferrara/, visited 1 March 2020. On Este horse culture: Fémelat 2016.
14. http://www.treccani.it/enciclopedia/obizzo-d-este_res-c2d03a1b-87ec-11dc-8e9d-0016357eee51_%28Dizionario-Biografico%29/, visited 1 March 2020.
15. Alberti 1999, dedication, 202–206. For *De equo animante* as being principally concerned with "le cheval du prince," Fémelat 2015, 22.
16. Alberti 1999, 208–214.
17. Alberti 1999, 218–221.
18. Xenophon *De hippike* 11.1–9 (Xenophon 1925, 353–355). Cf. Wells 1995, 62. Xenophon appears as the first of Alberti's sources, listed at the end of the dedication of *De equo animante* (Alberti 1999, 206–207).
19. Alberti 1999, 206–207. Cf. Cecil Grayson's introduction, 199–200; Fratarcangeli 2014, 23–24; Bertelli 2016.
20. Alberti 1989, 7.
21. Pope-Hennessy 1958; Janson 1973.
22. Folin 2009, 273.
23. Horace *Carmina* 3.30.
24. The Gattamelata dates from 1446–1450, the Colleone from 1480–1488. Cf. Boucheron 1997, 439.
25. Sambin De Norcen 2009, 351.
26. Pliny *Natural History* 34.1–19.
27. Virgil *Aeneid* 6.846–853.
28. Virgil *Aeneid* 6.846: *excudent alii spirantia mollius aera.*
29. "Dans le désir de se mesurer à l'éternité du bronze, dont l'art antique s'était fait le maître, se jouait en somme l'idée même de Renaissance." Boucheron 1997, 421.
30. On the succession, Pius II 2003, 355–361 (ch. 39); Bestor 1996, 569–573; Rosenberg 1997, 50–53, 77–80; Folin 2007, 25–28; Folin 2018, ¶6–7; Hollingsworth 2021, 68.
31. For the dates, http://www.treccani.it/enciclopedia/leonello-d-este_(Dizionario-Biografico)/, visited 11 March 2020. On the legal issue, Bestor 1996.
32. Rosenberg 1997, 52–53 and 266 n. 16. On the papal *possesso*, above, chapter 2.
33. Rosenberg 1997, 68; Fémelat 2010, 201.
34. Rosenberg 1997, 80–82. Leonello had a son, Niccolò, who should have inherited.
35. Rosenberg 1997, 54; Folin 2009, 260; Sambin De Norcen 2009, 349 (who cites the passage in question); Fémelat 2010, 192.
36. Folin 2009, 263–264.
37. On Alberti as author of the statue's base, most recently Hollingsworth 2021, 79.
38. Folin 2009. For the traditional view, originally put forward in Venturi 1914, inter alia Gadol 1969, 118–119; Rosenberg 1997, 57–61.
39. Pliny *Natural History* 34.12: *Columnarum ratio erat attolli super ceteros mortales, quod et arcus significant.*

Cf. Sambin de Norcen 2009, 358–360.

40. Alberti 1988, 183 (6.13).

41. On the Borso monument: Rosenberg 1997, 88–109.

42. Rosenberg 1997, 70–74; Fémelat 2010, 293. The condottieri Francisco Sforza, Federico da Montefeltro, Ludovico Gonzaga, and John Hawkwood all wear versions of the same beret in their portraits.

43. Rosenberg 1997, 109.

44. Scardino 1991; cf. Fémelat 2016, 17.

45. The three drawings are as follows: "The inauguration of Obizzo d'Este as first lord of Ferrara," pen and ink on paper, in Pellegrino Prisciani, *Historiae Ferrarienses* (late fifteenth/early sixteenth century), Liber VII, Archivio di Stato, Modena, ms. 131, fol. 79v; "Equestrian monument to Niccolò III d'Este," in Anonymous, *Chroniche di Ferrara* (early seventeenth century), pen and ink and wash on paper, Biblioteca Apostolica Vaticana, Rome, Ms. Ott. Lat 2774, fol. 83r; "Equestrian monument to Niccolò III d'Este," pen and ink on paper, drawing on the verso of a letter addressed to Carlo Olivi in 1796, reproduced in Agnelli 1919, fig. u. Cf. Rosenberg 1997, 70–73; Fémelat 2010, 194–196.

46. Dean 1990, 14–15; https://www.ferrarana scosta.it/aldighiero-fontana/, visited 21 March 2020.

47. I am very grateful to Marco Folin, who kindly identified the horseman and his three sons for me.

48. Machiavelli 1999, 5–6 (ch. 2); Machiavelli 1995, 8–10.

49. Inter alia, Tuohy 1996; Folin 1997; Folin 2015b.

50. Folin 2010b.

51. In his *Ludi mathematici* of about 1450, dedicated to Leonello's older half-brother, Meliaduse, Alberti refers to "those books of mine on architecture which I wrote at the request of your most illustrious brother, my lord, Master Leonello" (Alberti 2010, 41). Cf. Krautheimer 1969a, 328; Morin 2010.

52. Callebat et al. 1984, s.v. *equus*; Vitruvius 9.4.3. Here, as elsewhere, I have followed the text of Vitruvius 1969–2009. Both Morgan (Vitruvius 1960) and Granger (Vitruvius 1983–1985) omit this paragraph from their translations. Schofield's more recent one (Vitruvius 2009) includes it, however.

53. Vitruvius 3.1.1–3.

54. Alberti 1988, 199 (7.5); Alberti 1966a, 559 for the Latin.

55. Vitruvius 3.1.3; Gros 2001; McEwen 2003, 150–183.

56. Cf. Westfall 1969, 78; Choay, introduction to Alberti 2004, 22.

57. On *De statua*, Gadol 1969, 76–81; Aiken 1980; Tavernor 1998, 40–41.

58. Cennino Cennini (1360–c. 1425) wrote his *Libro dell'arte* in about 1400. Chapter 70, headed "The proportions which a perfectly formed body should possess," begins as follows. "Take note that before going any further, I will give you the exact proportions of a man. Those of a woman I disregard because she does not have any set proportions." Cennini 1960, 49. On Cennini as one of Alberti's sources for *De statua*, Aiken 1980, 82.

59. McEwen 2003, 250–304.

60. "Italy's dominion over the world, already famous for every other virtue, was by her ornament made still more admirable. Thus did it [the world] submit itself entirely to her knowledge and tutelage, considering it shameful that Rome, citadel of the world and idol of all peoples, should see its glory rivaled by the works of those whom it surpassed in renown of every other virtue." Cf. Alberti 1988, 159 (6.3), whose translation I have emended slightly; Alberti 1966a, 457 for the Latin. See also Pierre Caye's postface in Alberti 2004, 543–545, as well as the French translation of this passage on p. 282.

61. Alberti 1988, 5 (prologue).

62. Alberti 1988, 5 (prologue); column orders: Alberti 1988, 201–203 (7.7) and 309 (9.7).

63. Alberti 1988, 156 (6.2). I have emended the translation slightly; Alberti 1966a, 447 for the Latin.

64. Tavernor 1998, 43; see also Tavernor 1985; Tavernor 1994.

65. Alberti 1988, 302–303 (9.5) whose translation I have emended; Alberti 1966a, 817 for the Latin. See also Alberti 2004, 440.

66. Alberti 1988, 186 (6.13); cf. McLaughlin 2023.

Notes to Chapter 6

67. Cicero *Orator* 44.149.
68. Plato *Phaedrus* 264c: "Every discourse ought to be a living creature [*zôon*], having a body of its own"; Cicero *De oratore* 3.45.179.
69. Lewis and Short 1988, s.v. *animo*.
70. Alberti 1988, 2–3 (prologue).
71. *On the Art of Building* written at Leonello d'Este's request: above, n. 51 of this chapter; Alberti 1988, 4–5 (prologue).
72. Alberti 1988, 318 (9.11); translation emended slightly. Alberti 1966a, 865 for the Latin.
73. Alberti 1988, 81 (3.12); see also the glossary in this edition under "Bones and paneling / *os et complementum*" (421).
74. Alberti 1988, 9 (1.2); translation emended slightly. See Alberti 1966a, 25 for the Latin.
75. Alberti 1999, 210–211; cf. Morin 2010, 183.
76. Alberti 1988, 156 (6.2).
77. Alberti 1988, 158 (6.3). I have altered the translation somewhat. For the Latin, Alberti 1966a, 455. See also the French translation in Alberti 2004, 281–282. The passage draws heavily on Cicero *De oratore* 3.45.179, discussed earlier.
78. Cf. Horace *Epistles* 2.1.156–157: "Captive Greece took captive her savage conqueror and brought the arts to rustic Latium." Here, as in his view of the excesses and general uselessness of Greek and Asian architecture, Alberti conforms to received opinion as transmitted for example in Pliny *Natural History* 36.75, Frontinus *De aquaeductu* 16, and Martial *Spectacula* 8.36. 1–4.
79. Alberti 1988, 159 (6.3).
80. Both his involvement in the design of the base of the equestrian monument and in that of the cathedral bell tower in Ferrara have been discredited by, inter alia, Rykwert 1994; Tavernor 1998, 9; Folin 2009; Folin 2010b.
81. Settis and Cupperi 2007, 2:58.
82. Warburg 1999; Settis and Cupperi 2007, 1:29.
83. Aby Warburg was the first to decipher the astrological program and identify its sources in 1912 (Warburg 1999).
84. Folin 2007.
85. For the biographical details, http://www.treccani.it/enciclopedia/borso-d-este-duca-di-modena-reggio-e-ferrara_(Dizionario-Biografico), visited 9 May 2020.
86. Folin 2015b, 193.
87. Folin 2007, 19.
88. Milosavljević-Ault 2012, 65.
89. Varese 1989, figs. 36–38; Folin 2007, 25; Milosavljević-Ault 2012, 66–68.
90. https://artsandculture.google.com/exhibit/il-salone-dei-mesi-di-palazzo-schifanoia-musei-civici-di-ferrara/3gLCfZgiGsJhIA?hl=en, visited 13 May 2020.
91. Fémelat 2016 (*maison hippophile*, 15).
92. Plato *Laws* 7.824a.
93. Xenophon *Cyropaedia* 1.2.11 (Xenophon 1960, 1:18). As noted in chapter 5, Francesco Filelfo translated the *Cyropaedia* into Latin in the mid 1460s. Other classical sources with passages that stress the political dimension of the hunt include Dio Chrysostom's *Third Oration on Kingship* (*Orations* 3.133–138) and Pliny the Younger's *Panegyricus* (81.1–2); cf. Manolaraki 2012. Dio's *Orations* were well known in fifteenth-century Italy (Swain 2000; Hankins 2019, 392). In 1433, the humanist Giovanni Aurispa discovered a manuscript of Pliny's *Panegyricus* in Mainz and brought it to Ferrara. See also Galloni 1993, 11; Antonioli 2003; Pavan 2010, 34–35.
94. Gennero 2011.
95. Bestor 1996.
96. The contemporary sources include C. da Sangiorgio, *Storia del tradimento verso il duca Borso da Giovanni Lodovico Pio ed Andrea da Varegana* (1469), published in A. Capelli, "La congiura del Pio signori di Carpi contro Borso d'Este," *Atti e Memorie della R. Deputazione di Storia Patria per le Provincie Modenesi e Parmensi* 2 (1864): 367–416 (cited Folin 2007, 17, 39–40), and the Ferrarese panegyrist Ludovico Carbone. For the latter, see A. Lazzari, "Un dialogo di Ludovico Carbone in lode del Duca Borso," in *Atti e Memorie della Deputazione Ferrarese di Storia Patria* 28 (1929): 127–149 (145), and Folin 2007, n. 96. There is speculation that Borso may have been gay.

97. On Borso's renovation of the Palace, including the marble entrance, Tuohy 1996, 332.

98. Gardner 1968, 75; cf. Milosavljević-Ault 2012, 67.

99. Alberti 1991, 95 (3.63); Varese 1985.

100. Folin 2010b, 299–303.

101. Rosenberg 1979, 381; Rosenberg 1997, 101–102.

102. Folin 2010b, 303; my translation.

103. Vitruvius 1.2.5, Schofield trans. in Vitruvius 2009, 17 (emended). On *decor*, inter alia Onians 1988, 36–39; Payne 1999, 35–37; Courrént 2011, 228–235.

104. Cicero *Orator* 70.

105. Alberti 1988, 315 (9.5); Alberti 1966a, 855 for the Latin. See especially Anstey 2006.

106. Callebat 1994; Van Eck 1998; Rykwert 1998; McEwen 2003, 79–82, 140–144; Gros 2006; and most recently Oksanish 2019, among others.

107. Anstey 2006, argues that the Ciceronian/Albertian notion of *quod deceat*, being rhetorical and intended primarily to persuade, is "apparently *amoral*" (136–137). But this, of course, has no bearing on Alberti's defense of social hierarchy as both natural and ethical.

108. Alberti 1988, 94 (4.1); Alberti 1966a, 271 for the Latin.

109. Alberti 1988, 121 (5.3); Alberti 1966a, 347 for the Latin.

110. Alberti 1988, 118 (5.1); Alberti 1966a, 335–337 for the Latin. Cf. Folin 2006, 95.

111. Alberti 1988, 125–126 (5.6); I have emended the translation somewhat. For the Latin, Alberti 1966a, 357.

112. Alberti 1988, 192 (7.1); Alberti 1966a, 537 for the Latin. On Alberti and the "rabble," Pearson 2006.

113. Alberti 1988, 291–292 (9.1); Alberti 1966a, 779–781 for the Latin.

114. Alberti 1988, 158 (6.3); Alberti 1966a, 455.

115. Vitruvius 1.2.2; Alberti 1988, 9 (1.2); Alberti 1966a, 25; Morin 2010, 183.

116. Alberti 1988, 119 (5.1); Alberti 1966a, 337–339 for the Latin.

117. Rosenberg 1979; Rosenberg 1997, 88–109.

118. Warburg 1999; Folin 2010b, 299–303.

119. Tuohy 1996, 280, 293; Rosenberg 1997, 128–129, 137–138; Folin 2010b, 296.

120. Prisciani 1992, 33 (*Prohemium*). Cf. Cicero *De officiis* 1.44. There is a more recent edition of the *Spectacula* available online (Prisciani 2012), which appeared in print with an introductory essay by Elisa Bastianello three years later (Prisciani 2015). In her introductory essay Bastianello argues for a date no earlier than 1498, because the text of *De architectura* Prisciani cites appears to be based on that of an early print edition of Vitruvius of 1497. Moreover, the work includes a measured drawing Prisciani made of the Colosseum, most probably after a visit to Rome in 1501, which points to an even later date of composition (Bastianello 2015, 11–12).

121. Vitruvius 5.3–9. Alberti 1988, 268–282 (8.7–8); Alberti 1966a, 724–769. Danilo Aguzzi Barbagli concludes his edition of *Spectacula* with a useful concordance that matches Prisciani's text with the relevant passages in Vitruvius and Alberti (Prisciani 1992, 93–115). See also Bastianello 2015 and Torello-Hill 2015.

122. Prisciani 1992, 35–36 (ms. 18r-v); cf. Alberti 1988, 268: in spectacle "there lies a sure and certain way to enhance the well-being and honor of the fatherland [*ad patriam salutem et decus*]"; Alberti 1966a, 725 for the Latin.

123. Prisciani 1992, 36–37 (ms. 18v, my translation); cf. Alberti 1988, 269: show grounds cater to both diversions and contests "such as Plato recommended should be held each year because of their extraordinary benefit to the well-being of the state and the honor of the city [*ad reipublicae salutem et urbis decus*]" (8.7); Alberti 1966a, 729 for the Latin.

124. Juvenal *Satires* 10.77–81 (Juvenal 1954, 120):

For since their votes have been no longer bought
All public care has vanished from their thought;
And those who once with unresisted sway
Gave armies, empire, everything away,
For two poor claims have long renounced the whole,
And only ask the Circus and the Dole [panem et circenses].

For a definitive study, Veyne 1990.

125. Suetonius *Divus Augustus* 43 (Suetonius 1979, 78).

126. Ercole and Augustus: Gundersheimer 1972, 75, 86; Gundersheimer 1973, 212; Liebenwein 1984; Manca 1989, 530; Rosenberg 1997, 169–170.

127. Aguzzi Barbagli, introduction to Prisciani 1992, 12; Tuohy 1996, 234–276; Bastianello 2015, 11.

128. Aguzzi Barbagli, introduction to Prisciani 1992, 9–30.

129. Prisciani 1992, 56–57 (ms. 27r-v); Aguzzi Barbagli, introduction to Prisciani 1992, 27–28; Bastianello 2015, 12; Alberti 1988, 178 (8.8).

130. Prisciani 1992, 35–53 (ms. 18r–26r). The first illustrated Vitruvius was the Giocondo edition of 1511 (Vitruvius 1511). Nonetheless, there is an illustrated, partial manuscript of *De architectura*, originating in Ferrara and known as the *Vitruvio Ferrarese*, which dates from about the same time as Prisciani's *Spectacula* and whose text is a transcription of the same 1497 Vitruvius edition as Prisciani used, which suggests that Prisciani may also have been the author of the illustrated Vitruvius manuscript in question (Rykwert in Sgarbi 2004, 7; Bastianello 2015, 13). But the work's date and the question of its authorship remain inconclusive. Claudio Sgarbi, who discovered the manuscript, argues that its author was a friend of Leonardo's, one Giocomo Andrea da Ferrara (Sgarbi 2014). See Gros 2005, and Pizzigoni 2007, who thinks that the author was someone close to Bramante, if not Bramante himself; also Lester 2011, 201–206 and Schofield 2016, who does not commit himself. The first illustrated edition of Alberti's *De re aedificatoria* did not appear until 1550 (Alberti 1550). On Prisciani's drawings in the *Spectacula*, Torello-Hill 2015, 233.

131. Prisciani 1992, 53–59 (ms. 26v–29v).

132. Alberti 1988, 269, where *ambulationes* is translated as "parades" (8.8); Alberti 1966a, 755 for the Latin. Vitruvius 5.11.

133. Prisciani 1992, 59.

134. Vitruvius 4.1.9–10; Prisciani 1992, 68–70 (ms. 34r).

135. Aguzzi Barbagli, introduction to Prisciani 1992, 22–24; Folin 2010b, 305.

136. Prisciani 1992, 83 (ms. 40r); Vitruvius 5.1.1–2. Vitruvius also mentions shows (*munera*) offered by magistrates in the forum and elsewhere in the preface to book 10 (10.pref.3).

137. Alberti 1988, 121–122 (5.3); Folin 2015b, 194. Above, chapter 3.

138. Folin 1997, 363; Folin 2015b, 187.

139. Rosenberg 1997, 107–109.

140. Alberti 1988, 265 (8.6); Prisciani 1992, 85 (ms. 40r), where the chapter heading reads *De li arce ali boche de le piaze* (On arches at the entrances of piazzas).

141. Tuohy 1996, 52–63, 88–89, and passim; Rosenberg 1997, 110–123.

142. Folin 1997, 365–367; Folin 2015b, 198.

143. Alberti 1988, 146 (5.17); Fiore 2006, 99–100; Folin 2010a, 591–592; Folin 2015a, 10–11.

144. Folin 1997, 365–366; Folin 2015a. All of the changes discussed in these paragraphs are documented in contemporary accounts: cf. inter alia Zambotti 1949; Gundersheimer 1972; Caleffini 2006.

145. *Vulgi ignobilitate et fabrorum tumultu*: Alberti 1988, 126 (5.6). I have emended the translation somewhat. For the Latin, Alberti 1966a, 357. On the Capitol, Bedon 2008, 26, and above, chapter 2. See also Pearson 2006; Pearson 2011, 106–109.

146. Rosenberg 1997, 114–117. The speed with which "tyrants" can carry out urban improvements is one of Giovanni di Conversino da Ravenna's reasons for defending one-man rule in his *Dragmalogia* of 1404, where he points to the activities of Ercole's grandfather Niccolò II d'Este and Francesco da Carrara by way of example (cited Baron 1955, 112–113). Cf. Folin 2006, 63.

147. Tuohy 1996, 87–89, 252–253.

148. Torello-Hill 2010, 2015.

149. Torello-Hill 2015, 243.

150. Povoledo 1975; Torello-Hill 2015, 241–242.

151. Cited in Latin, Povoledo 1975, 398; my translation.

152. Povoledo 1975, 400–401; Torello-Hill 2010, 5–6; Torello-Hill 2015, 232–233.

153. Povoledo 1975, 400.

154. *Historiae Ferrarienses liber IX*, Archivio di Stato, Modena, ms. 133, fol. 19r (cf. Folin 1997, 360).

155. *Historiae Ferrarienses liber IV*, Archivio di Stato, Modena, ms. 130, fol. 20r, cited in Latin in Folin 2010c, 115 n. 31, and in Italian translation on p. 109; my translation.

156. Folin 2010c; for the date, which is based on internal evidence, p. 103. On Leonardo's plan of Imola, inter alia Pinto 1976, 35–40; Ballon and Friedman 2007, 682–683, 689. Prisciani may have known Alberti's *Descriptio urbis Romae* of the mid 1440s (Alberti 2007 and above, chapter 2), but Alberti's work was a table of polar coordinates for drawing a plan of Rome, and not a drawing as such.

157. On the Addition, Zevi 1971; Tuohy 1996, 124–141; Rosenberg 1997, 130–152, and for an exceptionally fine-grained study, Folin 2006.

158. Tuohy 1996, 124; Rosenberg 1997, 131; Folin 2006, 74.

159. Folin 2006, 73–75.

160. Caesar *Bellum Gallicum* 2.3, 5.51, 6.3, and most famously the *Veni, vidi, vici* of his Pontic victory in 47 BCE; Vitruvius 1.1.2; McEwen 2003, 26–28.

161. Caleffini *Croniche*, Biblioteca Apostolica Vaticana, Rome, Vat. Lat., 9263, fol. 223v (14 December 1484), cited Folin 2006, 72 (my translation).

162. Zevi 1960; Zevi 1971. But see Tuohy 1996, 277–283;

Rosenberg 1997, 148–152; Folin 2006, 130–147.

163. Tuohy 1996, 124; Rosenberg 1997, 131; Folin 2006, 74.

164. Ercole as architect: Tuohy 1996, 277–283; Rosenberg 1997, 148–152; cf. Folin 2006, 131–132; Alberti 1988, 3 (prologue) and 318 (9.11). On Alberti's "authorial figure of the architect," Trachtenberg 2011.

165. Siviero Sivieri, in letters to Ercole's wife, Eleanor of Aragon, early in 1493: ASM, ASE, Cancelleria; Cartegio Referendarii, Consiglieri, Cancellieri et Segretari, b. 4; cited Rosenberg 1978, 64–65, nn. 35, 36; Folin 2006, 81–87.

166. Caleffini, *Croniche*, 13 February 1493, cited Folin 2006, 82.

167. Hondedio di Vitale, *Cronaca*, Biblioteca Ariostea, Ms. Antonelli, n. 257, fol. 14v, cited Folin 2006, 128.

168. Hondedio di Vitale, *Cronaca*, fol. 16r; cited Folin 2006, 128.

169. On the economics of building the Addition, Rosenberg 1997, 132–134; Folin 2006, 116–129.

170. *Il disegno di Ferrara del 1490*, woodcut, Biblioteca Nazionale Estense, Ferrara, Ms. It. 429 (alpha H.5.3), fol. 18. The date of 1490 in the title (lower right) is misleading. Given the details included in the image, it must have been made several years later.

171. Very useful drawings detailing the sequence, extent, and nature of the development (preexisting buildings; churches, palaces,

convents, and small *cassette* built as rental properties) appear at the end of Marco Folin's study (Folin 2006, 164, 169–174).

172. Folin 2006, fig. 7 (p. 163).

173. On the Piazza Nuova, Tuohy 1996, 339–341; Rosenberg 1997, 140–142; Folin 2006, 82–84.

174. Alberti 1988, 265–266 (8.6); Prisciani 1992, 83–85 (ms. 40r–v).

175. Caleffini, *Croniche*, 9 May 1494; cited Kehl 1992–1993, 184–186; Tuohy 1996, 340 n. 236; Folin 2006, 84.

176. Rosenberg 1997, 141–142.

177. Kehl 1992–1993, 188; Folin 2006, 84.

178. For the most detailed account of the monument, Rosenberg 1997, 153–181. Also Manca 1989, 530–535; Kehl 1992–1993; Folin 2006, 83–84; Fémelat 2016, 22–30.

179. *Diario ferrarese*, December 1498, cited in translation Rosenberg 1997, 153 and in Italian 280 n. 3. I have emended the translation slightly.

180. Pen and wash drawing, Biblioteca Apostolica Vaticana, Rome, Ms. Ottobuoni 2774, fol. 125; for the woodcut, Alfonso Maresti, *Teatro geneologico et istoria dell'antiche et illustri famiglie di Ferrara*, vol. 2 (Ferrara, 1672), 152. Rosenberg 1997, 157–164, dates both images to the seventeenth century, and considers the Maresti woodcut more accurate. Folin 2006, 84, says they are both sixteenth-century in

Notes to Chapter 6

origin. See also Kehl 1992–1993; Fémelat 2016, 22–23.

181. Bertoldo di Giovanni, *Hercules on Horseback*, bronze, 1473, Gallerie Estensi, Ferrara, 2265. Draper and David 1992, 147–148; cf. Fémelat 2016, 23. On Ercole's portaiture in general, Manca 1989. Ercole represented as Hercules, Grierson 1959, 41–43; pillars of Hercules, Kehl 1992–1993, 187; Tuohy 1996, 289–290.

182. Kehl 1992–1993, 187; Rosenberg 1997, 154. The overall height of the monument, including the base but without the statue, would have been about 18 meters—the height of a six-story building.

183. Rosenberg 1997, 172.

184. Biblioteca Apostolica Vaticana, Ms. Ottobuoni Latina 2774, fol. 127; cf. Rosenberg 1997, 162. The frieze fragments are at the Casa Romei, Ferrara, c. 1499. Folin 2004, 232.

185. One, by Lorenzo Schrader, appears in *Monumentum Italiae* (Helmstadt, 1592), fol. 53r-v; the other one, virtually identical, in Marc'Antonio Guarini, *Compendio historico* (Ferrara, 1621), 202–203. Cf. Rosenberg 1997, 165–168 where it is translated, and 287–288 n. 44 for the Latin (after Guarini). See also Liebenwein 1984, 13.

186. Augustus 1967, 54–55 (*Res gestae* 33–34).

187. Güven 1998, 34.

188. Suetonius *Divus Augustus* 101.4 (Suetonius 1979, 112).

189. Augustus 1967, 18 (*Res gestae*, preamble).

190. Dio Cassius's *Roman History*, known in Italy in the fifteenth century, also includes an extensive biography of Augustus (books 45–56). Ercole's Latin inscription begins, *Memoriae Divi Erculis Estensis Ducis secundi*: Guarini transcription, cited Rosenberg 1997, 287, translated 165.

191. *Multa, Imperium adeptus, ad Urbis ornatum excogitavit, perfecitque...*: Guarini transcription, cited Rosenberg 1997, 287; my translation.

192. Suetonius *Divus Augustus* 28.3; my translation.

193. Oksanish 2019, 60.

194. Vitruvius 1.pref.2–3.

195. McEwen 2003, 71–88.

196. Ercole d'Este's letter to Giovanni Valla, dated 19 September 1501: Grierson 1959, 45; Bush 1978, 61; Rosenberg 1997, 162–163; Boucheron 1997, 486–487 where the letter, published in Pedretti 1953, 151, is cited (n. 179).

197. Ahl 1995, 25. See also Spencer 1973; Bugnoli 1974; Bush 1978; Boucheron 1997.

198. Codex Madrid II, fols. 141–157; cf. Reti 1968; Leonardo da Vinci 1974; Bugnoli 1974; Bush 1978, 47, with references. On the drawings, inter alia Kemp 1995.

199. Bush 1978; Boucheron 1997, whose appendices, 492–499, are particularly useful. *Stupendo cavallo*: the Milanese poet Matteo Bandello, cited Bush 1978, 66.

200. Biblioteca Ambrosiana, Milan, Codex Atlanticus, folio 391r; Richter and Bell 1970, 2:295–298. Cited in English Reti 1974, 7. See also Bush 1978, 49; Boucheron 1997, 495; Vecce 2006, 78–79. The conventional date assigned to this undated letter has been 1482–1483 (Kemp 1995, 67), but other evidence strongly suggests a later date (1485–1486): Schofield 1991, 113–115 and Boucheron 1997, 457–458.

201. Among many accounts, Santoro 1968, cf. Boucheron 1997, 423 n. 5; Bologna 1986, 88–96; Hollingsworth 2021, 171–173. See also Bush 1978 and Bush 1995.

202. Bugnoli 1974, 92; Bush 1978, 56.

203. Bush 1978, 58; Patetta 1993, 46. A decree for clearance of the square was issued in August 1492, reprinted Beltrami 1904, 17–22; Boucheron 1997, 429–433. On the *castello*, above, chapter 4.

204. Boucheron 1997, 429.

205. Codex Atlanticus 95r: Beltrami 1904, 11; cf. Boucheron 1997, 431, and his reconstruction of Leonardo's plan on the following page (432).

206. Leonardo, Codex Madrid II, fol. 151v, cited Boucheron 1997, 497; Pacioli 1509, fol. 1r.

207. Bush 1978, 56.

208. Above, chapter 5.

209. Filarete 1965, 293–294; Filarete 1972, 633–635 (ms. fol. 172r); and above, fig. 4.10. Filarete's translator, John Spencer, was the first to invoke the image as

background for the Sforza horse (Spencer 1973, 27).

210. Guaricus 1969, 102–105; cf. Bush 1978, 57.

211. Bush 1978, 57; Boucheron 1997, 471–472.

212. Bush 1978, 47; Boucheron 1997, 469

213. Codex Madrid II, fols. 141–157. Fol. 157v, dated 17 May 1491, is the first page of the account (Leonardo wrote from right to left). Bugnoli 1974; Bush 1978, 47–48; Boucheron 1997, 469–470, 489–491.

214. Boucheron 1997, 481.

215. Grierson 1959, 46.

216. Antonio Pollaiuolo, *Study for the Equestrian Monument to Francesco Sforza*, pen and brown ink and wash; Metropolitan Museum of Art, New York, Robert Lehman Collection, 1975.1.410. Antonio Pollaiuolo, *Study for the Equestrian Monument to Francesco Sforza*, black chalk, pen and brown ink and wash, Staatliche Graphische Sammlung, Munich, Inv. 1908: 168 Z. For a recent detailed study of the drawings, which belonged at one time to Giorgio Vasari, Menges Nogueira 2018, who thinks the Munich drawing is later than the other. See also Spencer 1973; Bush 1978.

217. Vasari identified the prostrate woman in the New York drawing as a personification of Verona, but since Verona was never one of Francesco Sforza's conquests, the reference to a conquered state or territory is more probably generic (Menges Nogueira 2018, 38).

218. "La statue équestre représente un prince, mais c'est l'idée même du pouvoir princier qu'elle exalte." Boucheron 1997, 474.

219. Leonardo da Vinci, study for the Sforza monument, The Royal Collection at Windsor, RCIN 912357. The entire collection is available for consultation on line: https://www.rct.uk/collection/search#/page/1. See also Spencer 1973; Bush 1978; Boucheron 1997.

220. Leonardo, study for the Sforza monument, RCIN 912358.

221. Kemp 1995, 74.

222. https://archive.org/stream/petrarchfirstmod00petrrich/petrarchfirstmod00petrrich_djvu.txt, visited 26 June 2018; and above, chapter 1.

223. Leonardo, study for an equestrian monument, RCIN 912345. Müller-Walde 1899; Kemp 1995, 70; Boucheron 1997, 471. Trip to Pavia with Francesco di Giorgio: among others, Vecce 2006, 127–129; Lester 2011, 193–200.

224. Codex Atlanticus, fol. 147r. Cf. Pedretti 1957.

225. Codex Atlanticus, fol. 147rb: *Di quel di Pavia si lauda piu il movimento che nessun altro cosa. L'imitation delle cose antiche è piu laudabile che quelle delle moderne. Non puo essere bellezza e utilità come appare nelle fortezza e nelli uomini. Il trotto è quasi di qualità di cavallo libero. Dove manca la vivacità naturale, bisogna farne una accidentale.* Richter and Bell 1970, 2:434. Cf. Kemp 1995, 70, whose translation I have followed in part; Boucheron 1997, 471 n. 128.

226. Alberti 1988, 158 (6.3).

227. Augustine *De civitate dei*, 22.24, cited Kemp 1995, 70–71. See also Vecce 2019, 37.

228. Codex Saluzziano 148; Martini 1967, vol. 1.

229. Biblioteca Medicea Laurenziana, Florence, Codex Ashburnham 361, ms. 282; Vecce 2019, 39.

230. Codex Saluzziano 148, fol. 3r; Martini 1967, 1:4.

231. Rudimentary Latin: Shi 2019; most graceful living models: Codex Atlanticus 160r, cited Lugli 2019, 73, who dates the note to 1490.

232. As for example the Windsor drawings RCIN 912304 and RCIN 912319.

233. Codex Saluzziano 148, fol. 6v; Martini 1967, 1:20. An all but identical drawing also appears in the Codex Ashburnham 361, which Leonardo owned.

234. Vecce 2006, 127–128; Lester 2011, 197–200; Lugli 2019, 70–72.

235. Lester 2011 calls it "the world's most famous drawing" in the subtitle of his book.

236. Zöllner 1987, 8–22; Zöllner 1995, 331–334; Payne 1994; Lugli 2019, 78–79.

237. Wittkower 1988, 22.

238. Berenson 1903, 2:122, no. 1099. The same listing reappeared in later editions. Cf. Lugli 2019, 76.

239. Lugli 2019, 79–87.

240. Pliny *Natural History* 7.17.

241. *Vetruvio, architetto, mette nella sua opera d'architectura, chelle misure*

dell'omo sono dalla natura disstribuite in quessto modo. The translation follows Kemp 1989, 309; cf. Lester 2011, 207–208.

242. Lugli 2019, 85–87.
243. Vitruvius 3.1.1.
244. Vitruvius 1.2.4. See also 1.2.2, 3.1.3, 3.1.4, 3.1.9.
245. McEwen 2003, 156–183, 275–298, and above, chapter 2.
246. Vitruvius 1.pref.1.
247. Alberti 1988, 457; Alberti 1966a, 457.

References

Ackerman, J. 1986. *The Architecture of Michelangelo*. Harmondsworth, UK: Penguin Books.
Adams, N. 1985. "The Acquisition of Pienza 1459–1464." *Journal of the Society of Architectural Historians* 44.2 (May), 99–110.
Adams, N. 1989. "The Construction of Pienza (1459–1464) and the Consequences of *Renovatio*." In S. Zimmerman and R. F. E. Weissmann, eds., *Urban Life in the Renaissance*, 50–79. Newark: University of Delaware Press.
Adams, N. 1994. "L'Architettura militare di Francesco di Giorgio." In Fiore and Tafuri 1994, 114–150.
Adams, N. 2004. "Knowing Francesco di Giorgio." In Fiore 2004, 1:305–316.
Agnelli, G. 1919. "I monumenti di Niccolò III e Borso d'Este in Ferrara." *Atti e Memorie della Deputazione Ferrarese di Storia Patria* 23, 1–52.
Ahl, D. C., ed. 1995. *Leonardo da Vinci's Sforza Monument Horse: The Art and the Engineering*. Bethlehem, PA: Lehigh University Press.
Aiken, J. A. 1980. "Leon Battista Alberti's System of Human Proportions." *Journal of the Warburg and Courtauld Institutes* 43, 68–96.
Alberti, L. B. 1485. *De re aedificatoria*. Florence: N. di Lorenzo.
Alberti, L. B. 1550. *L'architettura di Leonbatista Alberti tradotta in lingua fiorentina da Cosimo Bartoli . . . con la aggiunta de disegni*. Florence: Lorenzo Torrentino.
Alberti, L. B. 1890. "De porcaria coniurazione epistola." In Alberti, *Opera inedita e pauca separatim impresa*, ed. Hieronymo Mancini, 257–266. Florence: J. Sansoni.
Alberti, L. B. 1960. *Della famiglia*. In Grayson 1960–1973, vol. 1. Bari: Laterza.
Alberti, L. B. 1966a. *L'architettura (De re aedificatoria)*. 2 vols. Trans. G. Orlandi, introduction and notes by P. Portoghesi. Milan: Polifilo.
Alberti, L. B. 1966b. *De ichiarchia*. In Grayson 1960–1973, 2:187–288.
Alberti, L. B. 1971. *Della famiglia*. In *The Albertis of Florence: Leon Battista Alberti's* Della famiglia, trans. G. A. Guarino. Lewisburg, PA: Bucknell University Press.
Alberti, L. B. 1972. *Leonis Baptistae de Albertis vita*. In Fubini and Menci Gallorini 1972, 68–78.
Alberti, L. B. 1987. *Dinner Pieces*. Trans. D. Marsh. Binghamton, NY: Medieval and Renaissance Texts and Studies.

Alberti, L. B. 1988. *On the Art of Building in Ten Books*. Ed. and trans. J. Rykwert, N. Leach, and R. Tavernor. Cambridge, MA: MIT Press.

Albert, L. B. 1989. "The Life of Leon Battista Alberti by Himself." In Watkins 1989, 7–17.

Alberti, L. B. 1991. *On Painting*. Trans. C. Grayson, introduction by M. Kemp. Harmondsworth, UK: Penguin Books.

Alberti, L. B. 1999. *De equo animante*. Latin text, introduction and notes by C. Grayson, French trans. by Y. Boriaud. *Albertiana* 2, 191–235.

Alberti, L. B. 2003. *Intercenales*. Ed. and trans. F. Bacchelli and L. D'Arcia, preface by A. Tenenti. Bologna: Pendragon.

Alberti, L. B. 2004. *L'art d'édifier*. Ed. and trans. P. Caye and F. Choay. Paris: Seuil.

Alberti, L. B. 2007. *Leon Battista Alberti's Delineation of the City of Rome* (Descriptio urbis Romae). Ed. M. Carpo and F. Furlan, critical edition by J-Y. Boriaud and F. Furlan, English trans. by P. Hicks. Tempe: Arizona Center for Medieval and Renaissance Studies.

Alberti, L. B. 2010. *Ex ludis rerum mathematicarum (Ludi mathematici)*. In Williams, March, and Wassell 2010, 9–70.

Algeri, G., et al., eds. 2003. *Il palazzo ducale di Mantova*. Mantua: Sometti.

Andenna, G., et al., eds. 2006. *Le origini della diocesi di Mantova e le sedi episcopali dell'Italia settentrionale (IV–XI secolo)*. Trieste: Editreg SRL.

Andreoli Panzarasa, M. P. 1975. "Il Petrarca e Pavia viscontea." *Archivio Storico Lombardo* 100, 42–65.

Anstey, T. 2006. "The Dangers of Decorum." *Architectural Research Quarterly* 10.2 (June), 132–139.

Antonioli, G. 2003. "La caccia nel pensiero degli umanisti della corte estense (XV secolo)." *FD Bolletino della* Ferrariae Decus, 31 December, 36–48.

Arasse, D. 1987. "Il programma politico della Camera degli sposi, ovvero il segreto dell'immortalità." *Quaderni di Palazzo Te* 6, 45–64.

Arasse, D. 1993. "Frédéric dans son cabinet." *Nouvelle revue de psychanalyse* 48, 239–257.

Aristotle. 1947. *Introduction to Aristotle*. Ed. R. McKeon. New York: Modern Library.

Augustus Emperor of Rome. 1967. *Res gestae divi Augusti / The Achievements of the Divine Augustus*. Trans. P. A. Brunt and J. M. Moore. London: Oxford University Press.

Avesani, R., et al., eds. 1984. *Vestigia: studi in onore di Giuseppe Billanovich*. Rome: Edizioni di storia e letteratura.

Baker, P. 2012. "La trasformazione dell'identità nazionale d'Ungheria nelle *Rerum ungaricarum decades* di Antonio Bonfini." *Studi Umanistici Piceni* 32, 215–223.

Balbo, F., et al., eds. 1954. *Studi in memoria di Gioele Solari*. Turin: Edizioni Ramella.

Ballon, H., and D. Friedman. 2007. "Portraying the City in Early Modern Europe: Measurement, Representation and Planning." In Woodward 2007, 680–704.

Baron, H. 1955. *The Crisis of the Early Italian Renaissance: Civic Humanism and Republican Liberty in an Age of Classicism and Tyranny*. 2 vols. Princeton: Princeton University Press.

Bastianello, E. 2015. "Una costellazione di fonti antiche e di disegni architettonici: Pellegrino Prisciani sotto il segno de Vitruvio." In Prisciani 2015, 7–26.

Bedon, A. 2008. *Il Campidoglio: storia di un monumento civile nella Roma papale*. Milan: Electa.

Beltrami, L. 1904. *Il decreto per piazza del Castello di Milano: 22 agosto 1492*. Milan: Umberto Allegretti.

Beltramini, M. 1996. "Francesco Filelfo et il Filarete: nuovi contributi alla storia dell'amicizia fra il letterato e l'architetto nella Milano sforzesca." *Annali della Scuola Normale Superiore di Pisa*, s. IV, Quaderni 1–2, 119–125.

Beltramini, M. 2003. "Filarete in toga: la latinazzione del Trattato d'architectura." In A. Rovetta and G. Hajnoczi, eds., *Lombardia e Ungheria nell'età dell'Umanesimo e del Rinascimento*, special issue of *Arte Lombarda* 139.3, 14–20.

Beltramo, S., F. Cantatore, and M. Folin, eds. 2015. *A Renaissance Architecture of Power: Princely Palaces in the Italian Quattrocento*. Leiden: Brill.

Benelli, F. 2010. "Diversification of Knowledge: Military Architecture as a Political Tool in the Renaissance. The Case of Francesco di Giorgio Martini." *RES Anthropology and Aesthetics* 57/58, 140–155.

Benevolo, L. 1978. *The Architecture of the Renaissance*. 2 vols. London: Routledge & Kegan Paul.

Benevolo, L., and P. Boninsegna. 1986. *Urbino*. Rome: Laterza.

Bentini, J., ed. 2004. *Gli Este a Ferrara: una corte nel Rinascimento*. Exh. cat. Milan: Silvana Editoriale.

Berenson, B. 1903. *The Drawings of the Florentine Painters*. 2 vols. London: J. Murray.

Bernardo, A. S. 1962. *Petrarch, Scipio and the* Africa: *The Birth of Humanism's Dream*. Baltimore: Johns Hopkins University Press.

Bernich, E. 1903. "Leon Battista Alberti e l'Arco trionfale di Alfonso d'Aragona." *Napoli Nobillissima* 12, 116–117.

Bernini Pezzini, G. 1985. *Il fregio dell'arte della guerra nel Palazzo Ducale di Urbino*. Rome: Istituto poligrafico e Zecca dello Stato.

Bertelli, S. 2016. "La 'Mascalcia' di Giordano Ruffo nei più antichi manoscritti in volgare italiano conservati in Emilia Romagna." *Pallas, Revue d'études antiques* 101, 293–321.

Bestor, J. F. 1996. "Bastardy and Legitimacy in the Formation of a Regional State in Italy: The Estense Succession." *Comparative Studies in Society and History* 38.3, 549–585.

Bianchi, M., and P. Carpeggiani. 2006. "Ludovico Gonzaga, la città, l'architettura. Uno scenario per Andrea Mantegna." In Signorini 2006, 20–45.

Bianchi, P., and P. Passerin d'Entrèves. 2011. *La caccia nello Stato sabaudo.* Turin: Silvio Zamorani editore.

Black, J. 2009. *Absolutism in Renaissance Milan: Plenitude of Power under the Visconti and the Sforza 1329–1535.* Oxford: Oxford University Press.

Bober, P. P., and R. Rubenstein. 1986. *Renaissance Artists and Antique Sculpture: A Handbook of Sources.* Oxford: Oxford University Press.

Bologna, G. 1986. *Il castello di Milano.* Milan: Federico Motta editore.

Bonaccorsi, P. 1981. *Callimachi experientis carmina.* Ed. F. Sica, with an introduction by G. Paparelli. Naples: Fratelli Conte.

Bonfini, A. 1488–1489. (Bonfini ms.) Biblioteca Nazionale Marciana Lat. VIII, 2 (= 2796): *Antoni Averulini florentini De architectura libri viginti quinque.*

Bonfini, A. 2000. *La latinazzione del trattato d'architettura di Filarete (1488–89).* Ed. M. Beltramini. Pisa: Scuola normale superiore.

Bonvini Mazzanti, M. 1993. *Battista Sforza Montefeltro, una "principessa" nel rinascimento italiano.* Urbino: Quattroventi.

Borgo, F., ed. 2019. *Leonardo e Vitruvio: Oltre il cerchio e il quadrato.* Venice: Marsilio.

Bornstein, D. 1988. "The Wedding Feast of Roberto Malatesta and Isabetta da Montefeltro: Ceremony and Power." *Renaissance and Reform* 24.2, 101–117.

Borsi, F. 1989. *Leon Battista Alberti, the Complete Works.* New York: Rizzoli.

Borsi, F. 2006. *Leon Battista Alberti e Napoli.* Florence: Edizione Polistampa.

Boucheron, P. 1997. "La statue equestre de Francesco Sforza: Enquête sur un memorial politique." *Journal des savants*, 421–499.

Boucheron, P. 1998. *Le pouvoir de bâtir: urbanisme et politique éditilaire à Milan (XIVe-XVe siècles).* Rome: École française de Rome.

Boucheron, P. 2003. "De l'urbanisme communal à l'urbanisme seigneurial. Cités, territoires et édilité en Italie du Nord (XIIIe-XVe siècles)." In Crouzet-Pavan 2003b, 41–77.

Boucheron, P. 2004. "*Non domus ista sed urbs*: Palais princiers et environnement urbain au Quattrocento (Milan, Mantoue, Urbino)." In Boucheron and Chiffoleau 2004, 249–284.

Boucheron, P. 2007. "L'architettura come linguaggio politico: cenni sul caso lombardo nel secolo XV." In Gamberini and Petralia 2011, 3–53.
Boucheron, P. 2009. "Les laboratoires politiques de l'Italie." In P. Boucheron, ed., *Histoire du monde au XVe siècle*, 53–72. Paris: Fayard.
Boucheron, P. 2010. "Politisation et dépolitisation d'un lieu commun." In Lecuppre-Desjardin and Bruaene 2010, 237–251.
Boucheron, P. 2012. "L'implicite du signe architectural: notes sur la rhétorique politique de l'art de bâtir entre le moyen âge et la renaissance." *Perspective* 1/2012, 173–180. (Open edition journals.)
Boucheron, P. 2013a. *Conjurer la peur: Essai sur la force politique des images, Sienne 1338*. Paris: Seuil.
Boucheron, P. 2013b. "Résumé de la conférence de Patrick Boucheron tenue à Francfort le 23 mai 2012." *Revue de l'IFHA* 4, 64–67, uploaded 14 February 2013. http://ifha.revues.org/395, visited 2 October 2016.
Boucheron, P. 2014. *De l'éloquence architecturale*. Paris: Éditions B2.
Boucheron, P., and J. Chiffoleau, eds. 2004. *Les palais dans la ville: Espaces urbains et lieux de la puissance publique dans la Meditérranée médiévale*. Lyon: Presses universitaires de Lyon.
Boucheron, P., and M. Folin, eds. 2011. *I grandi cantieri del rinnovamento urbano: Esperienze italiane ed europee a confronto secoli xiv–xvi*, Rome: École française de Rome.
Boucheron, P., M. Folin, and J-P. Genet, eds. 2018. *Entre idéel et matériel: Espace, territoire et légitimation du pouvoir (v. 1200–v. 1641)*. Paris: Éditions de la Sorbonne. Available at http://books.openedition.org/psorbonne/40783.
Boucheron, P., and D. Menjot. 2011. *La ville médiévale*. Paris: Seuil.
Bourne, M. 2010. "The Art of Diplomacy: Mantua and the Gonzaga, 1328–1630." In Rosenberg 2010a, 138–195.
Brancia di Apricena, M. 2000. *Il complesso dell'Aracoeli sul Colle Capitolino (IX–XIX secolo)*. Rome: Quasar.
Brandolini, A. L. 2009. *Republics and Kingdoms Compared*. Ed. and trans. J. Hankins. Cambridge, MA: Harvard University Press.
Brice, C. 1998. *Monumentalité publique et politique à Rome: le Vittoriano*. Rome: École française de Rome.
Brown, V. 1976. "Caesar." In Cranz and Kristeller 1976, 3:87–139.
Bruni, L. 1741. "De origine urbis Mantuae." In *Leonardi Bruni arretini epistolarum libri VIII*, 217–229. Florence: ex typographia B. Paperinii.
Bruschi, A. 1978. "Federico da Montefeltro, Patente a Luciano Laurana." In Bruschi et al. 1978, 1–22.
Bruschi, A. 2008. "Luciano di Laurana. Chi era costui? Laurana, fra Carnavale, Alberti a Urbino. Un tentativo di revisione." *Annali di Architettura* 20, 37–81.

Bruschi, A., et al., eds. 1978. *Scritti rinascimentale di architettura*. Milan: Polifilo.

Bugnoli, M. V. 1974. "Il cavallo." In Reti 1974, 89–109.

Bulgarelli, M. 2003. "Alberti a Mantova. Divagazione intorno a Sant' Andrea." *Annali di architettura* 15, 9–36.

Bulgarelli, M., A. Calzona, M. Ceriani, and F. P. Fiore, eds. 2006. *Leon Battista Alberti e l'architettura*. Cinisella Balsamo: Silvana Editoriale.

Bulst, W. A. 1990. "Uso et trasformazione del Palazzo Mediceo fino ai Riccardi." In Cherubini and Finelli 1990, 98–120.

Burckhardt, J. 1990. *The Civilization of the Renaissance in Italy*. Harmondsworth, UK: Penguin Books.

Burdach, K. 1913–1928. *Rienzo und die geistige Wandlung seiner Zeit, vom Mittelalter zur Reformation*. Berlin: Weidmannsche Buchhandlung.

Burioni, M. 2010. "Vasari's *Rinascita*: History, Anthropology or Art Criticism?" In Lee, Péporté, and Schnitker 2010, 115–137.

Burns, H. 1981. "The Gonzaga and Renaissance Architecture." In Chambers and Martineau 1981, 29–39.

Burroughs, C. 1993. "Michelangelo at the Campidoglio: Artistic Identity, Patronage and Manufacture." *Artibus et Historiae* 14.28, 84–111.

Bush, V. 1978. "Leonardo's Sforza Monument and Cinquecento Sculpture." *Arte Lombarda* 50, 47–68.

Bush, V. 1995. "The Political Contexts of the Sforza Horse." In Ahl 1995, 79–86.

Calabi, D., ed. 1997. *Fabbriche, piazze, mercati: La città italiana del Rinascimento*. Rome: Officina.

Calabi, D., and E. Svalduz, eds. 2010. *Luoghi, spazi, architetture: il Rinascimento italiano e l'Europa 6*. Treviso: Angelo Colla-Fondazione Cassamarca.

Caleffini, U. 2006. *Croniche 1471–1494*. Ed. F. Cazzola. Ferrara: Deputazione provinciale ferrarese di storia patria.

Callebat, L. 1994. "Rhétorique et architecture dans la *De architectura* de Vitruve." In Gros 1994, 31–46.

Callebat, L., et al. 1984. *Vitruve. De architectura. Concordance*. Hildesheim: Olms-Weidmann.

Calzona, A. 2011. "'*Illis civium nostrorum petitionibus. . . :*' Ludovico II Gonzaga e le strategie urbane a Mantova al tempo dell'Alberti." In Boucheron and Folin 2011, 17–44.

Calzona, A., et al., eds. 2003. *Il sogno di Pio II et il viaggio da Roma a Mantova*. Florence: Olschki.

Calzona, A., et al., eds. 2009. *Leon Battista Alberti: architetture e committenti*. 2 vols. Florence: Olschki.

Cammarosano, P. 1995. "Federico II e i communi." In Fonseca and Pace 1995, 29–33.
Campana, A. 1933. *Il cippo riminese di Giulio Cesare*. Rimini: La libreria Arnaud.
Campano, G. A. 1929. *Braccii Perusini vita e gesta ab Anno MCCCLXVIII ad MCCCCXXIV ab auctore Johanne Antonio Campano* (1458). Ed. Roberto Valentini. Rerum Italicarum Scriptores XIX, 4. Bologna: Nicola Zanichelli.
Campbell, S. J. 2004. "Mantegna's Triumph: The Cultural Politics of Imitation '*all'antica*' at the Court of Mantua 1490–1530." In S. J. Campbell, ed., *Artists at Court: Image-Making and Identity 1300–1550*, 91–105. Boston: Isabella Gardiner Stewart Museum.
Cantatore, F. 1994. "Biografia cronologia di Francesco di Giorgio architetto." In Fiore and Tafuri 1994, 432–433.
Cantatore, F. 2003. "Leon Battista Alberti e Mantova: Proposte architettoniche al tempo della Dieta." In Calzona et al. 2003, 443–455.
Cantatore, F. 2015. "The Palace of Nicholas V: Continuity and Innovation in the Vatican Palaces." In Beltramo, Cantatore, and Folin 2015, 290–319.
Capuzzo, R. 1991. "Note sulla tradizione e sul culto del Sangue di Cristo nella Mantova medievale." *Storia e arte*, 61–72.
Capuzzo, R. 2006. "Le *inventiones* del precioso Sangue di Cristo: Eventi e significati in rilettura delle Fonte." In Andenna et al. 2006, 293–381.
Carpeggiani, P. 1982. "Corte e città nel secolo dell'Umanesimo. Per una storia urbana di Mantova, Urbino e Ferrara." *Arte Lombarda* 61, 32–42.
Carpeggiani, P. 1987. *Sant'Andrea in Mantova: un tempio per la città del principe*. Mantua: Publi-Paolini.
Carpeggiani, P. 1994. "*Renovatio urbis*: strategie urbane a Montova nell'età di Ludovico Gonzaga." In Rykwert and Engel 1994, 178–185.
Carpeggiani, P. 2005. "Alberti a Mantova. Una città per il principe." In Grassi and Patetta 2005, 263–307.
Carruba, A. M. 2006. *La lupa Capitolina: Un bronzo medieval*. Rome: De Luca editori d'arte.
Caruso, C., and A. Laird, eds. 2009. *Italy and the Classical Tradition: Language, Thought and Poetry 1300–1600*. London: Duckworth.
Castiglione, B. 2003. *The Book of the Courtier*. Trans. G. Bull. London: Penguin Books.
Cecini, N. 1985. "Memoria e mito del Palazzo Ducale di Urbino nei testi letterari dal XV al XX secolo (appunti per un' antologia)." In Polichetti 1985, 125–134.
Cennini, C. 1960. *The Craftsman's Handbook*. Trans. D. V. Thompson, Jr. New York: Dover.

Cerboni Baiardi, G., G. Chittolini, and P. Floriani, eds. 1986. *Federico di Montefeltro: lo Stato, le Arti, la Cultura*. 3 vols. Rome: Bulzoni.

Cetius Faventius, M. 2002. *Abrégé d'architecture privée*. Ed. and trans. M-T. Cam. Paris: Belles Lettres.

Chambers, D. S. 1977. "Sant'Andrea of Mantua and the Gonzaga Patronage 1460–1472." *Journal of the Warburg and Courtauld Institutes* 40, 99–127.

Chambers, D. S. 1981. "Mantua and the Gonzaga." In Chambers and Martineau 1981, xvii–xxiii.

Chambers, D. S., and J. Martineau, eds. 1981. *Splendours of the Gonzaga*. Exh. cat. London: Victoria and Albert Museum.

Charlet, J-L. 1999. "Le lexicographe et le prince: Federico d'Urbino dans le *Conucopiae* de Niccolò Perotti." In Secchi Tarugi 1999, 87–99.

Chastel, A. 1961. *Art et humanisme à Florence au temps de Laurent le Magnifique: études sur la Renaissance et l'humanisme platonicien*. Paris: Presses Universitaires de France.

Cheles, L. 1986. *The Studiolo of Urbino: An Iconographic Investigation*. University Park: Pennsylvania State University Press.

Cherubini, G., and G. Finelli, eds. 1990. *Il Palazzo Medici Riccardi in Firenze*. Florence: Giunti.

Chevalier, R., ed. 1985. *Présence de César: actes du colloque des 9–11 décembre 1983: hommage au doyen Michel Rambaud*. Paris: Belles Lettres.

Chiaroni, L., and G. Ferlisi, eds. 2001. *Leon Battista Alberti e il Quattrocento. Studi in onore di Cecil Grayson e Ernst Gombrich*. Florence: Olschki.

Chironi, G. 2000. *L'Archivio Diocesano di Pienza*. Rome: Ministero per i beni e le attività culturali.

Chironi, G. 2003. "Pius II and the Formation of the Ecclesiastical Institutions of Pienza." In von Martels and Vanderjagt 2003, 171–185.

Christian, K. W. 2010. *Empire without End: Antiquities Collections in Renaissance Rome*. New Haven: Yale University Press.

Ciapponi, L. A. 1960. "Il De architectura di Vitruvio nel primo umanesimo." *Italia medioevale e umanistica* 3, 59–99.

Ciapponi, L. A. 1976. "Vitruvius." In Cranz and Kristeller 1976, 3:399–409.

Ciapponi, L. A. 1984. "Fra Giocondo of Verona and His Edition of Vitruvius." *Journal of the Warburg and Courtauld Institutes* 47, 72–90.

Ciotta, G., ed. 2003. *Vitruvio nella cultura architettonica antica, medievale e moderna: atti del convegno internazionale di Genova, 5–8 novembre 2001*. Genoa: De Ferrari.

Clarke, G. 1996. "The Palazzo Orsini in Nola: A Renaissance Relationship with Antiquity." *Apollo* 144, 144–150.

Clarke, G. 2002. "Vitruvian Paradigms." *Papers of the British School at Rome* 70, 319–346.
Clarke, G. 2003. *Roman House—Renaissance Palaces: Inventing Antiquity in Fifteenth-Century Italy*. Cambridge: Cambridge University Press.
Claussen, P. C. 1995. "Scultura figurativa federicana." In Fonseca and Pace 1995, 93–102.
Clough, C. H. 1973. "Federigo da Montefeltro's Patronage of the Arts, 1468–1482." *Journal of the Warburg and Courtauld Institutes* 36, 129–144.
Cohen, H. 1955. *Description historique des monnaies frappées sous l'Empire romain communément appelées médailles impériales*. 8 vols. Graz: Adademische Druck-u. Verlagsanstalt.
Coleman, E. 1999. "The Italian Communes: Recent Work and Current Trends." *Journal of Medieval History* 25.4, 373–397.
Colocci, F., ed. 2006. *Contribuiti e richeche su Francesco di Giorgio nell'Italia centrale: simposi di studi*. Urbino: Edizione Comune di Urbino.
Cordaro, M., ed. 1992. *Mantegna. La Camera degli sposi*. Milan: Electa.
Courrént, M. 2011. "*Tenuitas cum bona fama*: éthique et architecture dans le De architectura de Vitruve." *Cahiers des études anciennes* 48, 219–236.
Covini, N. 2003. "Aspetti della fortificazione urbana tra Lombardia e Veneto alla fine del medioevo." In Turchini 2003, 59–77.
Cranz, F. E., and P. O. Kristeller, eds. 1976. *Catalogus translationum et commentariorum*. Washington, DC: Catholic University Press.
Crouzet-Pavan, E. 2003a. "'Pour le bien commun': à propos des politiques urbaines dans l'Italie communale." In Crouzet-Pavan 2003b, 11–40.
Crouzet-Pavan, E., ed. 2003b. *Pouvoir et édilité: Les grands chantiers dans l'Italie communale et seigneuriale*. Rome: École française de Rome.
Cuzin, J. P., et al., eds. 2000. *D'après l'antique*. Exh. cat. Louvre: Paris.
Daly Davis, M. 1989. "'*Opus Isodomum*' at the Palazzo della Cancelleria: Vitruvian Studies and Archaeological Antiquarian Interests at the Court of Raffaele Riario." In Danesi Squarzina 1989, 442–457.
Danesi Squarzina, S., ed. 1989. *Roma, centro ideale della cultura dell'antico nei secoli XV e XVI. Da Martino V al sacco di Roma 1417–1527*. Milan: Electa.
Dean, T. 1990. *Land and Power in Late Medieval Ferrara: the Rule of the Este 1350–1450*, Cambridge: Cambridge University Press.
De Carlo, G. 1970. *Urbino: The History of the City and Plans for Its Development*. Trans. L. S. Guarda. Cambridge, MA: MIT Press.
De Keyser, J., ed. 2019. *Francesco Filelfo, Man of Letters*. Leiden: Brill.
Dennistoun, J. 1909. *Memoirs of the Dukes of Urbino*. London: J. Lane.
Di Battista, R. 1998–1999. "La Porta e l'arco di Castelnuovo a Napoli." *Annali di architettura* 10–11, 7–21.

Di Lorenzo, A., ed. 1991. *Le muse e il principe: Arte di corte nel Rinascimento padano*. Modena: Panini.

Di Pietro Lombardi, P. 2002. "Mattia Corvino e i suoi emblem." In *Nel segno del Corvo* 2002, 117–128.

Di Stefano, E. 2010. "Il *De equo animante* di L. B. Alberti: una teoria della bellezza." In Furlan and Venturi 2010, 1:15–26.

Donesmondi, I. 1613–1616. *Dell'istoria ecclesiastica di Mantova*. 2 parts. Mantua: Aurelio & Lodovico Osanna fratelli.

D'Onofrio, C. 1973. *Renovatio Romae: storia e urbanistica del Campidoglio all'EUR*. Rome: Edizioni mediterranee.

D'Onofrio, M. 1995. "La Porta di Capua." In Fonseca and Pace 1995, 230–232.

Dotti, U. 1972. *Petrarca e Milano*. Milan: Ceschina.

Draper, J. D., and J. David. 1992. *Bertoldo di Giovanni, Sculptor of the Medici Household: Critical Reappraisal and Catalogue Raisonné*. Columbia: University of Misouri Press.

Ebert-Schifferer, S. 1988. "Ripandas kapitolischer Freskenzyklus und die Selbstdarstellung der Konservatoren um 1500." *Römisches Jarhbuch für Kunstgeschichte* 23/24, 75–218.

Edwards, P., and E. Graham. 2012. "Introduction: The Horse as a Cultural Icon." In Edwards et al. 2012, 1–36.

Edwards, P., et al., eds. 2012. *The Horse as a Cultural Icon: The Real and Symbolic Horse in the Early Modern World*. Leiden: Brill.

Edwards, S. 2011. "*La Scala Elicoidale*: The Spiral Ramps of Francesco di Giorgio." In Hub and Pollali 2011, 107–132.

Eisner, M. 2014. "In the Labyrinth of the Library: Petrarch's Cicero, Dante's Virgil and Historiography of the Renaissance." *Renaissance Quarterly* 67.3 (Fall), 755–790.

Elam, C. 1981. "Mantegna at Mantua." In Chambers and Martineau 1981, 15–25.

Elsner, J. 2010. "Image and Site: Castiglione Olona in the Early Fifteenth Century." *RES: Anthropology and Aesthetics* 57/58, 156–173.

Esch, A., and C. L. Frommel, eds. 1995. *Arte, committenza ed economia a Roma e nelle corti del Rinascimento (1420–1530)*. Turin: Einaudi.

Ettlinger, H. S. 1990. "The Sepulchre on the Façade: A Re-evaluation of Sigimondo Malatesta's Rebuilding of San Francesco in Rimini." *Journal of the Warburg and Courtauld Institutes* 53, 133–143.

Falvo, J. D. 1986. "Urbino and the Apotheosis of Power." *Modern Language Notes* 101, 114–146.

Fane-Saunders, P. 2009. "Filarete's 'Libro architettonico' and Pliny the Elder's Account of Ancient Architecture." *Arte Lombarda* 155, 111–120.

Fauno, L. 1548. *Delle antichità della città di Roma*. 54 leaves. Venice: Michele Tramezzino.

Fémelat, A. 2010. "Alberti et le monument équestre de Niccolò III d'Este à Ferrare." In Furlan and Venturi 2010, 2:187–201.

Fémelat, A. 2015. "Des chevaux réels et un cheval idéal: naturalisme et idéalisation des chevaux des portraits équestres italiens des Trecento et Quattrocento." *In situ* 27 (November), 1–33.

Fémelat, A. 2016. "La Cavalcade des princes de Ferrare, de Modène et de Reggio. Une série d'effigies équestres du Quattrocento." *Seizième siècle* 12, 13–39.

Fenucci, F., and M. Simonetta. 2007. "The Studiolo in the 'Cube': A Visual Guide." In Simonetta 2007, 88–99.

Ferrari, M. 1984. "Fra I 'latini scriptores' di Pier Candido Decembrio e biblioteche umanistiche milanesi." In Avesani et al. 1984, 247–264.

Ferraù, G. 2006. *Petrarca: la politica, la storia*. Messina: Centro interdipartimentale di studi umanistici.

Ferretti, E. 2015. "The Medici Palace, Cosimo the Elder and Michelozzo." In Beltramo, Cantatore, and Folin 2015, 263–289.

Fiamma, G. 1938. *De rebus gestis ab Azone, Luchino et Johanne Vicomtibus ab anno MCCCXVII urque ad annum MCCCXLII*. Ed. C. Castignioni. Rerum Italicarum Scriptores, n.s., XII, 4. Bologna: N. Zanichelli.

Filarete. 1965. *Treatise on Architecture: Being the Treatise by Antonio di Piero Averlino known as Filarete*. Ed. and trans J. R. Spencer. New Haven: Yale University Press.

Filarete. 1972. *Filarete: Trattato di architettura*. Ed. A. M. Finoli and L. Grassi. Milan: Il Polifilo.

Filelfo, F. 2009. *Odes*. Ed. and trans. D. Robin. I Tatti Renaissance Library 41. Cambridge, MA: Harvard University Press.

Filelfo, F. 2012. *Traduzioni da Senofonte e Plutarco: Respublica Lacedaemoniorum, Agesilaus, Lycurgus, Numa, Cyri Paedia*. Ed. J. De Keyser. Alessandria: Edizioni dell'Orso.

Findlen, P., ed. 2002a. *The Italian Renaissance: The Essential Readings*. Malden, MA: Blackwell.

Findlen, P. 2002b. "Understanding the Italian Renaissance." In Findlen 2002a, 3–45.

Findlen, P., ed. 2019. *Leonardo's Library: The World of a Renaissance Reader*. Exh. cat. Stanford: Stanford University Libraries.

Fiore, F. P. 1989. "Interventi urbani in una signoria territoriale del Quattrocento a Urbino e Gubbio." In Maire Vigueur 1989, 407–437.

Fiore, F. P. 1994. "L'architettura civile di Francesco di Giorgio." In Fiore and Tafuri 1994, 62–113.

Fiore, F. P. 1998. "The Trattati on Architecture by Francesco di Giorgio." In Hart and Hicks 1998, 66–85.
Fiore, F. P., ed. 2004. *Francesco di Giorgio alla corte di Federico da Montefeltro*. 2 vols. Florence: Olschki.
Fiore, F. P., ed. 2005. *La Roma di Leon Battista Alberti*. Rome: Skira.
Fiore, F. P. 2006. "Leon Battista Alberti, palazzi et città." In Bulgarelli et al. 2006, 98–119.
Fiore, F. P. 2011. "Urbino and the Montefeltro and Della Rovere Families." In Folin 2011a, 284–305.
Fiore, F. P., and M. Tafuri, eds. 1994. *Francesco di Giorgio architetto*. Milan: Electa.
Firpo, L. 1954. "La città ideale del Filarete." In Balbo et al. 1954, 11–59.
Foffano, T. 1960. "La costruzione di Castiglione in un opuscolo inedito de Francesco Pizzolpasso." *Italia medioevale e umanisitica* 3, 153–187.
Folin, M. 1997. "Ferrara: 1385–1505: All ombra del principe." In Calabi 1997, 354–388.
Folin, M. 2004. "Framento della base del monumento a Ercole I." In Bentini 2004, 232.
Folin, M. 2006. "Un ampliamento urbano della prima età moderna: l'addizione erculea di Ferrara." In M. Folin, ed., *Sistole / diastole. Episodi di trasfomazione urbane nell'Italia delle città*. 51–174. Venice: Istituto Veneto di Scienze, Lettere e Arti.
Folin, M. 2007. "Borso d'Este a Schifanoia: Il Salone dei mesi come *speculum principis*." In Settis and Cupperi 2007, 1:9–50.
Folin, M. 2009. "La committenza estense, l'Alberti e il palazzo di corte di Ferrara." In Calzona et al. 2009, 1:257–304.
Folin, M. 2010a. "La dimora del Principe." In Calabi and Svalduz 2010, 583–603.
Folin, M. 2010b. "Leon Battista Alberti e Pellegrino Prisciani." In Furlan and Venturi 2010, 1:295–316.
Folin, M. 2010c. "La *Proportionalibus et commensurate designatio urbis Ferrariae* di Pellegrino Prisciani (1494–1495)." In M. Folin, ed., *Topografie urbane nell'Italia di Antico Regime*, 99–120. Reggio Emilia: Diabasis.
Folin, M. 2010d. "Sigismondo Pandolfo Malatesta, Pio II e il Tempio Malatestiana: la chiesa di San Francesco come manifesto politico." In Paolucci 2010, 17–47.
Folin, M., ed. 2011a. *Courts and Courtly Arts in Renaissance Italy: Art, Culture and Politics, 1395–1530*. Trans. C. Bolton et al. Woodbridge, UK: Antique Collectors Club.
Folin, M. 2011b. "Seignorial Courts in Renaissance Italy." In Folin 2011a, 8–31.

Folin, M. 2015a. "Princes, Towns, Palaces: A Renaissance 'Architecture of Power.'" In Beltramo, Cantatore, and Folin 2015, 3–17.

Folin, M. 2015b. "The Renewal of Ferrara's Court Palace under Ercole I d'Este (1471–1505)." In Beltramo, Cantatore, and Folin 2015, 188–213.

Folin, M. 2018. "Demeures des vivants, demeures des morts: Considérations comparatives sur les formes d'implantation urbaine des seigneurs en Italie aux XIVe et XVe siècles." In Boucheron, Folin, and Genet 2018. Available at http://books.openedition.org/psorbonne/41048.

Fonseca, C. D., and V. Pace, eds. 1995. *Federico II e l'Italia: percorsi, luoghi, signi e strumenti*. Exh. cat. (Rome, Palazzo Venezia, 22 December 1995–20 April 1996). Rome: De Luca Editalia.

Foyle, J. 2002. "A Reconstruction of Thomas Wolsey's Great Hall at Hampton Court Palace." *Architectural History* 45, 128–158.

Fraser Jenkins, A. D. 1970. "Cosimo de' Medici's Patronage of Architecture and the Theory of Magnificence." *Journal of the Warburg and Courtauld Institutes* 33, 162–170.

Fratarcangeli, M. 2014. "'La perfettione del Cavallo.' Trattistica e letteratura a uso e consumo di uno status symbol." In M. Fratarcangeli, ed., *Dal cavallo alle scuderie. Visioni, iconografiche e architettoniche*, 21–35. Rome: Campisano editore.

Frommel, C. L. 1995. "Raffaele Riario, committente della Cancelleria." In Esch and Frommel 1995, 197–212.

Frommel, C. L. 2001. "Il San Sebastiano e l'idea del tempio." In Chiaroni and Ferlisi 2001, 291–304.

Frommel, C. L. 2004. "Il palazzo ducale di Urbino e la nascita della residenza pincipesca del Rinascimento." In Fiore 2004, 1:167–196.

Frommel, C. L. 2008. "Alberti e la porta trionfale de Castel Nuovo a Napoli." *Annali di architettura* 20, 13–36.

Frommel, C. L. 2009. "La progettazione di Palazzo Rucellai." In Calzona et al. 2009, 1:49–80.

Frontisi-Ducroux, F. 1975. *Dédale: mythologie de l'artisan en Grèce ancienne*. Paris: F. Maspero.

Fubini, R., and A. Menci Gallorini. 1972. "L'autobiografia di Leon Battista Alberti. Studio e edizione." *Rinascimento*, n.s. 12, 21–78.

Fügadi, E. 1990. "A King for a Season." *New Hungarian Quarterly* 31.118, 75–82.

Furlan, F., and G. Venturi, eds. 2010. *Leon Battista Alberti: Gli Este e l'Alberti*. 2 vols. Pisa and Rome: Fabrizio Serra Editore.

Gadol, J. 1969. *Leon Battista Alberti: Universal Man of the Early Renaissance*. Chicago: University of Chicago Press.

Galloni, P. 1993. *Il cervo e il lupo: Caccia e cultura nobiliare nel medioevo.* Rome and Bari: Laterza.

Gambardella, A., ed. 2000. *Cultura artistica, città e architettura nell'età federiciana.* Rome: De Luca.

Gamberini, A., and G. Petralia, eds. 2011. *Linguaggi politici nell'Italia del Rinascimento.* Rome: Viella, 2011.

Gamucci, B. 1565. *Libri quattro dell'antichità della città di Roma.* Venice: Gio. Varisico, Compagni.

Gardner, E. G. 1968. *Dukes and Poets in Ferrara.* New York: Haskell House.

Gardoni, G. 2006. "Vescovi e città a Mantova dall'età carolingia al secolo XI." In Andenna et al. 2006, 183–246.

Garfagnini, G., ed. 1987. *Callimaco Esperiente poeta e politico del '400.* Florence: Olschki.

Gennero, M. 2011. "Il cavallo da cacci: razze e tipologie." In Bianchi and Passerin d'Entrèves 2011, 81–90.

Gianetto, N., ed. 1981. *Vittorino da Feltre e la sua scuola: umanesimo, pedagogia, arti.* Florence: Olschki.

Gilbert, C. 1977. "The Fresco by Giotto in Milan." *Arte Lombarda* 47–48, 31–72.

Giordano, L. 1998. "On Filarete's *Libro architettonico*." In Hart and Hicks 1998, 51–65.

Giovanni di Conversino da Ravenna. 1980. *Dragmalogia de eligibili vite genere* (1404). Ed. and trans. H. L. Eaker, with an introduction and notes by Benuamin Kohl. Lewisburg, PA: Bucknell University Press.

Girondi, G. 2015. "Patrician Residences and the Palaces of the Marquis of Mantua (1459–1524)." In Beltramo, Cantatore, and Folin 2015, 163–186.

Giuliano, A., ed. 2003. *Studi normanni e federiciani.* Rome: L'Erma di Bretschneider.

Giulio Cesare: l'uomo, le imprese, il mito. 2008. Exh. cat. Rome: Silvana editoriale.

Glass, R. 2015. "Filarete and the Invention of the Renaissance Medal." *The Medal* 66, 26–37.

Gobbi, G. 1982. *Rimini.* Rome: Laterza.

Godi, C. 1970. "La collatio laureationis del Petrarca." *Italia medioevale e umanistica* 13, 1–27.

Golden, L., ed. 2001. *Raising the Eyebrow: John Onians and World Art Studies.* Oxford: British Archaeological Reports.

Goldsworthy, A. K. 2016. Pax Romana: *War, Peace and Conquest in the Roman World.* New Haven: Yale University Press.

Golinelli, P. 1985. "Dal santo del potere al santo del popolo. Culti mantovani dall'alto al basso medioevo." *Quaderni Medievali* 19, 12–34.

Gordon, P. W. G., ed. 1991. *Two Renaissance Book Hunters: The Letters of Poggio Bracciolini to Nicolaus de Nicolis*. Translated from the Latin and annotated. New York: Columbia University Press.

Grafton, A. 2002. *Leon Battista Alberti, Master Builder of the Renaissance*. Cambridge, MA: Harvard University Press.

Grassi, G., and L. Patetta, eds. 2005. *Leon Battista Alberti Architetto*. Florence: Scala.

Grassi, L. 1985. "Sforzinda, Plusiapolis, Milano: città ideale, città del mito, città della storia nel trattato di Filarete." *Studi di letteratura francese* 11, 26–50.

Grayson, C. 1960. "The composition of L. B. Alberti's *Decem libri de re aedificatoria*." *Münchener Jahrbuch der bildenden Kunst* 11, 152–160.

Grayson, C., ed. 1960–1973. *Leon Battista Alberti opere volgari*. 3 vols. Bari: Laterza.

Green, L. 1990. "Galvano Fiamma, Azzone Visconti and the Revival of the Classical Theory of Magnificence." *Journal of the Warburg and Courtauld Institutes* 53, 98–113.

Greenblatt, S. 2012. *The Swerve*. New York: Norton.

Grendler, P. F. 2002. *The Universities of the Italian Renaissance*. Baltimore: Johns Hopkins University Press.

Grierson, P. 1959. "Ercole d'Este and Leonardo da Vinci's Equestrian Statue of Francesco Sforza." *Italian Studies* 14.1, 40–48.

Griffin, M., ed. 2009. *A Companion to Julius Caesar*. Chichester, UK, and Malden, MA: Wiley-Blackwell.

Gros, P., ed. 1994. *Le projet de Vitruve: objet, destinataires et reception du* De architectura. Paris: Boccard.

Gros, P. 2001. "La géométrie platonicienne de la notice vitruvienne sur l'homme parfait (*De architettura* III, 1, 2–13)." *Annali di architettura* 13, 15–24.

Gros, P. 2005. Review of Sgarbi 2004. *Annali di architettura* 17, 230–232.

Gros, P. 2006. "De la rhétorique à l'architecture." In P. Gros, ed., *Vitruve et la tradition des traités d'architecture: fabrica et ratiocinatio*, 281–287. Rome: École française de Rome.

Gros, P., and P. N. Pagliara, eds. 2014. *Giovanni Giocondo, architetto e antiquario*. Venice: Marsilio.

Guarducci, M. 2003. "Federico II e il monumento del caroccio in Campidoglio." In Giuliano 2003, 87–98.

Guaricus, P. 1969. *De sculptura* (1504). Ed. and trans. A. Chastel and R. Klein. Geneva and Paris: Centre de recherches de la IVe section de l'École pratique des Hautes Études, V.

Guillaume, J., ed. 1994. *Architecture et vie sociale à la Renaissance: l'organisation intérieure des grandes demeures à la fin du moyen âge et à la Rendaissance*. Paris: Picard.

Gundersheimer, W. 1972. *Art and Life at the Court of Ercole d'Este: the* De triumphis religionis *of Giovanni Sabadino degli Arienti*. Geneva: Droz.

Gundersheimer, W. 1973. *Ferrara: The Style of a Renaissance Despotism*. Princeton: Princeton University Press.

Güven, S. 1998. "Discovering the *Res gestae* of Augustus: A Monument of Imperial Image for All." *Journal of the Society of Architectural Historians* 57.1 (March), 30–45.

Hankins, J. 2019. *Virtue Politics: Soulcraft and Statecraft in Renaissance Italy*. Cambridge, MA: Harvard University Press.

Harprath, R. 1985. "La formazione umanistica di papa Paolo III." In M. Fagiolo, ed., *Roma e l'antico nell'arte e nella cultura del Cinquecento*, 63–85. Rome: Istituto della Enciclopedia italiana.

Hart, V., and P. Hicks, eds. 1998. *Paper Palaces: The Rise of the Renaissance Architectural Treatise*. New Haven: Yale University Press.

Helas, P. 1999. *Lebende Bilder in der italienischen Festkultur des 15. Jarhunderts*. Berlin: Akademie.

Hersey, G. 1973. *The Aragonese Arch at Naples, 1443–1475*. New Haven: Yale University Press.

Hersey, G. 1994. "Alberti e il tempio etrusco, postille a Richard Krautheimer." In Rykwert and Engel 1994, 216–223.

Hoffmann, H. 2008. "Literary Culture at the Court of Urbino." *Humanistica* 57, 5–59.

Höfter, J. 2004. *Der Palazzo Ducale in Urbino unter den Montefeltro (1376–1508). Neue Forschungen zur Bau- und Ausstattungsgeschichte*. Regensburg: Schnell & Steiner.

Höfter, J. 2006. "Nuove indagini sulla storia edilizia del palazzo ducale di Urbino: il primo palazzo dei Montefeltro sulla piazza grande." In Colocci 2006, 299–309.

Hollingsworth, M. 1997. "Alberti: A Courtier and His Patrons." In Mozzarelli and Oresko 1997, 217–224.

Hollingsworth, M. 2010. "Art Patronage in Renaissance Urbino, Pesaro, and Rimini, c. 1450–1550." In Rosenberg 2010a, 325–368.

Hollingsworth, M. 2021. *Princes of the Renaissance*. New York: Pegasus.

Hope, C. 1992. "The Early History of the Tempio Malatestiano." *Journal of the Warburg and Courtauld Institutes* 55, 51–154.

Hub, B., and A. Pollali, eds. 2011. *Reconstructing Francesco di Giorgio Architect*. Frankfurt: Peter Lang.

Hülsen, C., and H. Egger, eds. 1975. *Die römischen Skizzenbücher von Marten van Heemskerck im Königlichen Kupferstichkabinett zu Berlin*. 2 vols. Soest, Holland: Davaco Publishers.

Humble, N. 2019. "Erudition, Emulation and Enmity in the Dedication Letters to Filelfo's Greek and Latin Translations." In De Keyser 2019, 127–173.

Humfrey, P. 1993. *The Altarpiece in Renaissance Venice*. New Haven: Yale University Press.

Ianucci, A. M. 1972. "Il Castello, a decoro della città." In A. Donati, ed., *Il Sant'Andrea di Mantova e Leon Battista Alberti: atti del Convegno di studi organizzato dalla città di Mantova con la collaborazione dell'Accademia Virgiliana, nel quinto centenario della basilica di Sant'Andrea e della morte dell'Alberti, 1472–1972*, 82–88. Mantua: Edizione della Biblioteca comunale di Mantova.

Ianziti, G. 1988. *Humanistic Historiography under the Sforzas: Politics and Propaganda in Fifteenth-Century Milan*. Oxford: Clarendon Press.

Ianziti, G. 2019. "Filelfo and the Writing of History." In De Keyser 2019, 97–123.

Ingersoll, R. J. 1985. "The Ritual Use of Public Space in Renaissance Rome." PhD diss., University of California, Berkeley.

Jacks, P. J. 1993. *The Antiquarian and the Myth of Antiquity*. Cambridge: Cambridge University Press.

Janson, H. W. 1973. "The Equestrian Monument from Cangrande della Scala to Peter the Great." In Janson, *Sixteen Studies*, 153–169. New York: Abrams.

Jarzombek, M. 1989. *Leon Baptista Alberti: His Literary and Aesthetic Theories*. Cambridge, MA: MIT Press.

Jellinek, G. 1893. *Adam in der Staatslehre; Vortrag im Historisch-philosophischen Verein zu Heidelberg*. Heidelberg.

Johnson, E. J. 1975a. "A Portrait of Leon Battista Alberti in the Camera degli Sposi?" *Arte Lombarda*, 42/43, 67–69.

Johnson, E. J. 1975b. *Sant'Andrea in Mantua: The Building History*. University Park: Pennsylvania State University Press.

Juvenal. 1954. *Juvenal's Satires with the Satires of Persius*. Trans. W. Gifford, revised by J. Warrington. Everyman's Library. London: J. M. Dent and Sons; New York: E. P. Dutton.

Kantorowicz, E. 1931. *Frederick the Second 1194–1250*. Trans. E. O. Lorimer. New York: Ungar.

Kantorowicz, E. 1957. *The King's Two Bodies*. Princeton: Princeton University Press.

Karsay, O. 1991. "De laudibus Augustae Bibliothecae." *New Hungarian Quarterly* 121.32, 139–145.

Karvouni, M. 1994. "Il ruolo della matematica nel 'De re aedificatoria' dell'Alberti." In Rykwert and Engel 1994, 282–291.

Kehl, P. 1992–1993. "La Piazza Comunale e la Piazza Nuova a Ferrara." *Annali di Architettura* 4–5, 178–189.

Kemp, M., ed. 1989. *Leonardo on Painting: An Anthology of Writings by Leonardo da Vinci with a Selection of Documents Relating to His Career as an Artist.* Trans. M. Kemp and M. Walker. New Haven: Yale University Press.

Kemp, M. 1995. "Leonardo's Drawings for 'Il Cavallo del Duca Francesco di Bronzo': The Program of Research." In Ahl 1995, 64–78.

Kirkbride, R. 2008. *Architecture and Memory: The Renaissance studioli of Federico da Montefeltro.* New York: Columbia University Press.

Kirkham, V., and A. Maggi, eds. 2009. *Petrarch: A Critical Guide to the Complete Works.* Chicago: University of Chicago Press.

Kohl, B. J. 1978. "Francesco Petrarca: Introduction." In Kohl and Witt 1978, 25–34.

Kohl, B. J., and R. G. Witt, eds. 1978. *The Earthly Republic: Italian Humanists on Government and Society.* Philadelphia: University of Pennsylvania Press.

Krautheimer, R. 1969a. "Alberti and Vitruvius." In Krautheimer, *Studies in Early Christian, Medieval, and Renaissance Art*, trans. A. Frazer et al., 323–332. New York: New York University Press.

Krautheimer, R. 1969b. "Alberti's Templum Etruscum." In Krautheimer, *Studies in Early Christian, Medieval, and Renaissance Art*, trans. A. Frazer et al., 333–344. New York: New York University Press.

Krautheimer, R. 2000. *Rome: Profile of a City, 312–1308.* Foreword by M. Trachtenberg. Princeton: Princeton University Press.

Krinsky, C. H. 1967. "Seventy-eight Vitruvius Manuscripts." *Journal of the Warburg Institutes* 30, 36–70.

Kruft, H. W. 1994. *A History of Architectural Theory from Vitruvius to the Present.* New York: Zwemmer.

Krüger, M. 2018. "Contexto, subtexto, e intertextualidade no *De re aedificatoria*." *Albertiana* 21, 11–27.

Lang, S. 1972. "Sforzinda, Filarete and Filelfo." *Journal of the Warburg and Courtauld Institutes* 34, 391–397.

Lavin, M. A. 1972. *Piero della Francesca: The Flagellation.* London: Allen Lane the Penguin Press.

Lecuppre-Desjardin, E., and A-L. Bruaene. 2010. *De Bono communi: The Discourse and Practice of the Common Good in the European City (13th–16th C.).* Turnhout, Belgium: Brepols.

Lee, A., P. Péporté, and H. Schnitker, eds. 2010. *Renaissance? Perceptions of Continuity and Discontinuity in Europe c. 1350–1550*. Leiden: Brill.

Leonardo da Vinci. 1974. *The Madrid Codices*. 5 vols. Ed. and trans. L. Reti. New York: McGraw-Hill.

Lester, T. 2011. *Da Vinci's Ghost: The Untold Story of the World's Most Famous Drawing*. London: Profile Books.

Lewis, C. T., and C. Short. 1988. *A Latin Dictionary Founded on Andrews' Edition of Freund's Latin Dictionary*. Oxford: Clarendon Press.

Liebenwein, W. 1984. "Antikes Bildrecht in Michelangelos 'Area Capitolina.'" *Mitteilungen des Kunsthistorischen Instituts in Florenz* 28, 1–32.

Londei, E. 1989. "Lo stemma sul portale di ingresso e la facciata 'ad ali' del Palazzo ducale di Urbino." *Xenia* 18, 93–117.

Looney, D. 2009. "The Beginnings of Humanistic Oratory: Petrarch's *Collatio laureationis*." In Kirkham and Maggi 2009, 131–140.

Lücke, H-K. 1975. *Alberti Index*. Munich: Prestel.

Lücke, H-K. 1994. "Alberti, Vitruvio e Cicerone." In Rykwert and Engel 1994, 70–75.

Lugli, E. 2019. "In cerca della perfezione: nuovi elementi per l'Uomo vitruviano di Leonardo da Vinci." In Borgo 2019, 68–91.

Luni, M. 1985. "*Urvinum Mataurense* (Urbino), Dall'insediamento romano alla città medievale." In Polichetti 1985, 11–49.

Luni, M., ed. 2009. *Dal Forum di Urvinum Mataurense alla "Platea Magna" di Urbino in età ducale*. Urbino: Quattroventi.

Lupescu, R. 2008. "The Election and Coronation of King Matthias." In *Matthias Corvinus, the King* 2008, 191–195.

Machiavelli, N. 1995. *Il Principe*. Ed. G. Inglese, with an essay by F. Chabod. Turin: Einaudi.

Machiavelli, N. 1999. *The Prince*. Trans. with notes by G. Bull, introduction by A. Grafton. Harmondsworth, UK: Penguin Books.

Mack, C. R. 1987. *Pienza: The Creation of a Renaissance City*. Ithaca: Cornell University Press.

Magnuson, T. 2004. *The Urban Transformation of Medieval Rome, 312–1420*. Stockholm: Swedish Institute in Rome.

Maire Vigueur, J-C., ed. 1989. *D'une ville à l'autre: structures matérielles et organisation de l'espace dans les villes européennes (XIIIe–XVIe siècles)*. Rome: École française de Rome.

Maire Vigueur, J-C. 2010. *L'autre Rome: une histoire des Romains à l'époque des communes, XII–XIVe siècle*. Paris: Tallandier.

Malacarne, G. 1995. *Il mito dei cavalli gonzagheschi: alle origini del purosangue*. Verona: Promoprint.

Mallett, M. 1974. *Mercenaries and Their Masters: Warfare in Renaissance Italy.* London: Bodley Head.

Manca, J. 1989. "The Presentation of a Renaissance Lord: Portraiture of Ercole d'Este, Duke of Ferrara (1471–1505)." *Zeitschrift für Kunstgeschichte* 52.4, 522–538.

Manetti, G. 2005. *De vita ac gestis Nicolai Quinti summi pontifices.* Ed. A. Modigliani. Rerum Italicarum Scriptores 6. Rome: Sede dell'istituto Palazzo Borromini.

Manetti, G. 2006a. "Book Two of the Life of Nicholas V." Trans. and commentary by C. Smith. In Smith and O'Connor 2006, 361–469.

Manetti, G. 2006b. "The Life of Pope Nicholas V, Book 3: The Testament of Nicholas V." Trans. C. Smith. In Smith and O'Connor 2006, 471–483.

Manolaraki, E. 2012. "Imperial and Rhetorical Hunting in Pliny's *Panegyricus.*" *Illinois Classical Studies* 37, 175–198.

Marani, E. 1974a. "Tre chiese di Sant'Andrea nella storia dello svolgimento urbanistico mantovano." In *Il Sant'Andrea di Mantova e Leon Battista Alberti*, 71–115.

Marani, E. 1974b. "La lettera albertiana del 21 ottobre 1470." In *Il Sant'Andrea de Mantova e Leon Battista Alberti*, 427–431.

Martellotti, G., P. G. Ricci, E. Carrara, and E. Bianchi, eds. 1955. *Francesco Petrarca: Prose.* Milan and Naples: Riccardo Ricciardi.

Martels, Z. von, and A. Vanderjagt, eds. 2003. *"El più expeditivo pontifice": Selected Studies on Aeneas Silvius Piccolomini 1404–1464.* Leiden: Brill.

Martindale, A. 1979. *The Triumphs of Caesar by Andrea Mantegna in the Collection of Her Majesty the Queen at Hampton Court.* Foreword by Anthony Blunt. London: Harvey Miller.

Martines, L. 1988. *Power and Imagination: City States in Renaissance Italy.* Baltimore: Johns Hopkins University Press.

Martini, F. di G. 1967. *Trattati di architettura ingegneria et arte militare.* Ed. C. Maltese and L. Maltese Grassi. 2 vols. Milan: Polifilo.

Martini, F. di G. 2002. *La traduzione del* De architectura *di Vitruvio.* Ed. M. Biffi. Pisa: Scuola Normale Superiore.

Matthias Corvinus, the King: Tradition and Renewal in the Hungarian Royal Court, 1458–1490. 2008. Exh. cat. Budapest: Budapest History Museum.

McClendon, C. B. 2005. *The Origins of Medieval Architecture: Building in Europe, A.D. 600–900.* New Haven: Yale University Press.

McDonnell, M. A. 2006. *Roman Manliness*: Virtus *and the Roman Republic.* Cambridge: Cambridge University Press, 2006.

McEwen, I. K. 1993. *Socrates' Ancestor: An Essay on Architectural Beginnings.* Cambridge, MA: MIT Press.

McEwen, I. K. 1995. "Housing Fame: In the Tuscan Villa of Pliny the Younger." *Res: Anthropology and Aesthetics* 27 (Spring), 11–24.

McEwen, I. K. 2003. *Vitruvius: Writing the Body of Architecture*. Cambridge, MA: MIT Press.

McEwen, I. K. 2004. "Vitruvius, or the Hidden Menace of Theory." Fascicle in H. Frank and E. Sohn, eds., *Auf der Suche nach einer Theorie der Architektur*. Hamburg: Material-verlag.

McEwen, I. K. 2011. "*Virtù-vious*: Roman Architecture, Renaissance Virtue." *Cahiers des études anciennes* 48, 255–282.

McEwen, I. K. 2016. "The 'Architectonic Book.'" In Sanvito 2016, 101–112.

McEwen, I. K. 2018. "Symmetry Takes Command: The Case of the Roman Capitol." *Symmetry: Culture and Science* 29.3, 365–388.

McLaughlin, M. 1988. "Humanist Concepts of Renaissance and Middle Ages in the Tre- and Quattrocento." *Renaissance Studies* 2.2 (October), 131–142.

McLaughlin, M. 2009a. "Alberti and the Classical Canon." In Caruso and Laird 2009, 73–100.

McLaughlin, M. 2009b. "Empire, Eloquence and Military Genius: Renaissance Italy." In Griffin 2009, 335–355.

McLaughlin, M. 2016. "Tradizione letteraria e originalità del pensiero nel *De re aedificatoria*." In McLaughlin, *Leon Battista Alberti: La vita, l'umanesimo, le opere letterarie*, 145–162. Florence: Olschki.

McLaughlin, M. 2023. "Vitruvius and Alberti." In Rowland and Bell 2023.

Menges Nogueira, A. 2018. "Antonio Pollaiuolo's Designs for the Equestrian Monument to Francesco Sforza: Patronage and Portraiture at the Court of Milan." *Artibus et Historiae* 77, 31–56.

Meredith, J. 1994. "The Arch of Capua: The Strategic Use of Spolia and References to the Antique." In Tronzo 1994, 109–128.

Merrill, E. M. 2013. "The Trattato as Textbook: Francesco di Giorgio's Vision for the Renaissance Architect." *Architectural Histories* 1.1, art. 20. http://doi.org/10.5334/ah.at

Mezzatesta, P. 1984. "Marcus Aurelius, Fray Antonio de Guevara, and the Ideal of the Perfect Prince in the Sixteenth Century." *Art Bulletin* 66.4 (December), 620–623.

Michaelis, A. 1891. "Storia della Collezione Capitolina di antichità fino alla inaugurazione del Museo (1734)." *Mittleilungen des Kaiserlich Deutschen Archaeologischen Instituts, Römische Abteilung* 6, 3–27.

Miglio, M. 1981. "'*Et rerum facta est pucherrima Roma*.' Attualità della tradizione e proposte di innovazione." In *Aspetti culturali della società italiana nel periodo del papato avignonese: 15–18 ottobre 1978*, 311–369. Todi: Presso l'Accademia tudertina.

Miglio, M. 1982. "Il leone e la lupa. Dal symbol al pasticcio alla francese." *Studi Romani* 30, 177–186.

Miglio, M. 1996. "L'immagine del principe e l'immagine della città." In S. Gensini, ed., *Principi e città alla fine del Medioevo*. Pisa: Pancini.

Miglio, M. 1997. "Il senato in Roma medievale." *Il Senato nella Storia*, Vol. 2, 117–172.

Miglio, M. 2005. "Repubblica, monarchia e tirannide: cultura e società a Roma nel Quattrocento." In Fiore 2005, 90–101.

Miglio, M. 2009. "Restauri. Palmieri, Alberti e Manetti: opere a confronto." In Calzona et al. 2009, 2:489–512.

Mikó, À. 1999. "Matthias Corvinus, Matthias Augustus. L'arte antica al servizio del potere." In Secchi Tarugi 1999, 209–220.

Millon, H. A., and L. Nochlin, eds. 1978. *Art and Architecture in the Service of Politics*. Cambridge, MA: MIT Press.

Milosavljević-Ault, A. 2012. "A Finding on the Iconography of the Decans in the Month of December in the Sala dei mesi in Palazzo Schifanoia." *Godišnjak za društvenu istoriju* 19.1, 57–73.

Miotto, L. 2004. "L. B. Alberti e il Palazzo di Federico da Montefeltro." *Albertiana* 7, 41–78.

Modigliani, A. 2004. "Il consenso intorno nello Stato di Federico: i capitoli del 1444 con Urbino e Gubbio." In Fiore 2004, 1:49–79.

Modigliani, A. 2013a. *Congiurare all'antica: Stefano Porcari, Niccolò V, Roma 1453: Con l'edizione delle fonti*. RR inedita saggi 57. Rome: Roma nel Rinascimento.

Modigliani, A. 2013b. "Per la datazione del *De re aedificatoria*: Il codice e gli archetipi dell'Alberti." *Albertiana* 16, 91–110.

Moffatt, C. J., and S. Taglialagamba, eds. 2016. *Illuminating Leonardo: A Festschrift for Carlo Pedretti*. Leiden: Brill.

Mommsen, T. E. 1953. "Petrarch and the Story of the Choice of Hercules." *Journal of the Warburg and Courtauld Institutes* 16, 178–192.

Mommsen, T. E. 2002. "Petrarch's Conception of the 'Dark Ages'" (1942). In Findlen 2002a, 219–236.

Morin, P. 2010. "Beyond Measure: Equestrian Projects, Alberti and Ferrara." In Furlan and Venturi 2010, 1:177–185.

Morresi, M. 1988. "Humanistic Interpretations of Vitruvius in the Fifteenth Century." *The Princeton Journal: Thematic Studies in Architecture 3: Canon*, 81–100.

Mortimer, R. 1964–1974. *Harvard College Library Department of Printing and Graphic Arts, Catalogue of Books and Manuscripts*. Cambridge, MA: Belknap Press of Harvard University Press.

Mozzarelli, C., and R. Oresko. 1997. *La corte di Mantova nell'età di Andrea Mantegna, 1450–1550 = The Court of the Gonzaga in the Age of Mantegna, 1450–1550*. Rome: Bulzoni.

Müller-Walde, P. 1899. "Leonardo da Vinci un die antike Reiterstatue des Regisole." *Jahrbuch der Königlich Preussischen Kunstsammlungen* 20, 81–116.

Müntz, E. 1878–1882. *Les arts à la cour des papes pendant le XVe et le XVIe siècle*. 3 vols. Paris: E. Thorin.

Mura Somella, A., and C. Parisi Presicce, eds. 1997. *Il Marco Aurelio e la sua copia*. Cinisello Balsamo: Silvana Editoriale.

Mussini, M. 1994. "La trattatistica di Francesco di Giorgio: un problema critico aperto." In Fiore and Tafuri 1994, 378–395.

Mustard, W. P. 1921. "Petrarch's *Africa*." *American Journal of Philology* 42.2, 97–121.

Negroni, F. 1993. *Il Duomo di Urbino*. Urbino: Accademia Raffaello.

Nel segno del Corvo. 2002. *Nel segno del Corvo. Libri e miniature della biblioteca di Mattia Corvino re d'Ungheria (1443–1490)*. Exh. cat. (Biblioteca Estense Universitaria). Modena: Il Bulino.

Ogliari, F. 2005. *Milano e il carroccio: gli Svevi e la Lega lombarda*. Pavia: Selecta.

Oksanish, J. 2019. *Vitruvian Man: Rome under Construction*. New York: Oxford University Press.

Onians, J. 1971. "Alberti and φιλαρετη: A Study in Their Sources." *Journal of the Warburg and Courtauld Institutes* 34, 96–114.

Onians, J. 1973. "Filarete and the *qualità*, Architectural and Social." *Arte Lombarda* 38/39, 116–128.

Onians, J. 1988. *Bearers of Meaning: The Classical Orders in Antiquity, the Middle Ages, and the Renaissance*. Princeton: Princeton University Press.

Pacioli, L. 1509. *Diuina proportione: opera a tutti glingegni perspicaci e curiosi necessaria oue ciascun studioso di philosophia: prospectiua pictura sculptura: architectura: musica: e altre mathematice*. Venice: A. Paganius Paganinus.

Pacioli, L. 1982. *De divinia proportione*. Facsimile of the 1498 Ambrosiana manuscript. Introduction by A. Marinoni. Milan: Silvana.

Pagliara, P. N. 1986. "Vitruvio da testo a canone." In S. Settis, ed., *Memoria dell'antico nell'arte italiana*, vol. 3, 3–85. Turin: Einaudi.

Paltroni, P. 1966. *Commentarii della vita e gesti dell'illustrissimo Federico Duca d'Urbino*. Ed. with an introduction by Walter Tommasoli. Urbino: Accademia Raffaello.

Pane, G. 2000. "Nuove considerazione sulla Porta federiciana di Capua." In Gambardella 2000, 223–258.

Panofsky, E. 1930. *Hercules am Scheidewege und andere antike Bildstoffe in der neueren Kunst*. Leipzig: B. G. Teubner.

Panormita, A. 1538. *De dictis et factis Alphonsi Regis Aragonum*. Basel: Hevagiani.

Paolucci, A. 2001. "Anno Domini 1450." In A. Donati, ed., *Il potere, le arti, la guerra: lo splendore dei Malatesta*, 41–48. Exh. cat. Milan: Electa.

Paolucci, A., ed. 2010. *Il Tempio Malatesiano a Rimini*. Modena: Franco Cosimo Panini.

Papini, R. 1946. *Francesco di Giorgio architetto*. 3 vols. Florence: Electa editrice.

Parisi Presicce, C. 1996. "Il Campidoglio come memoria. Dall'*exemplar* di Michelangelo alla creazione del Museo." In M. Tittoni, ed., *Il Palazzo dei Conservatoi e il Palazzo Nuovo in Campidoglio*. Pisa: Pacini, 99–120.

Parisi Presicce, C. 1997. "Breve storia del Marco Aurelio." In Mura Somella and Parisi Presicce 1997, 16–26.

Parisi Presicce, C. 2000. "I grandi bronzi di Sisto IV dal Laterano al Campidoglio." In F. Benzi, ed., *Sisto IV: le arti a Rome nel primo rinascimento: atti del convegno internazionale di studi*. Rome: Shakespeare and Company, 189–200.

Pasquini, L. 1933. *Rimini e Giulio Cesare*. Rimini: Stabilimento tipografico Garattoni.

Patetta, L. 1993. "Milano dal XV al XVII secolo: la difficoltà di construire piazza." *Storia della Città* 54, 45–52.

Patetta, L. 1997. "Petrarca e l'archittetura delle città italiane." In Secchi Tarugi 1997, 161–180.

Patetta, L. 2005. "Teoria e practica. Appunti sul pensiero e sulle opere di Leon Battista Alberti." In Grassi and Patetta 2005, 91–152.

Patrizi, F. 1567. *F. Patritii Senensi de Regno et Regis Institione libri IX*. Paris: Aegidius Gorbinius.

Pavan, A. 2010. "Ercole Strozzi's *Venatio*: Classical Inheritance and Contemporary Models of a Neo-Latin Hunting Poem." *Humanistica Lovaniensa* 57, 29–54.

Payne, A. A. 1994. "Architectural Principles in the Age of Modernism." *Journal of the Society of Architectural Historians* 53.3, 322–342.

Payne, A. A. 1999. *The Architectural Treatise in the Italian Renaissance: Architectural Invention, Ornament, and Literary Culture*. Cambridge: Cambridge University Press.

Pearson, C. 2006. "Poulterers, Butchers and Cooks: Concepts of the Rabble in Leon Battista Alberti's *De re aedificatoria*." In P. Helas and G. Wolf, eds., *Armut und Armenfürsorge in der italienischen Stadtkulture zwischen 13. und 16. Jahrhundert*, 303–331. Bern: Peter Lang.

Pearson, C. 2011. *Humanism and the Urban World: Leon Battista Alberti and the Renaissance City*. University Park: Penn State University Press.

Pedretti, C., ed. 1953. *Documenti e memorie riguardanti Leonardo da Vinci a Bologna e in Emilia*. Bologna: Editoriale Fiammenghi.

Pedretti, C., ed. 1957. *Leonardo da Vinci: Fragments at Windsor Castle from the Codex Atlanticus*. London: Phaidon.

Pellecchia, L. 1992. "Architects Read Vitruvius: Renaissance Interpretations of the Atrium of the Ancient House." *Journal of the Society of Architectural Historians* 51.4, 377–415.

Pellegrin, E. 1955. *La Bibliothèque des Visconti et des Sforza, ducs de Milan au XVe siècle*. Paris: CNRS.

Pellegrin, E. 1961. "Manuscrits de Pétrarque dans les bibliothèques de France." *Italia Medievale e Umanistica* 4, 341–428.

Pérez-Gómez, A. 2004. "The Glass Architecture of Fra Luca Pacioli." In A. Pérez-Gómez and S. Parcell, eds., *Chora Four*, 245–286. Montreal: McGill-Queen's University Press.

Peruzzi, M. 2007. "The Library of Glorious Memory: History of the Montefeltro Collection." In Simonetta 2007, 28–39.

Peruzzi, P. 1986. "Lavorare al corte." In Cerboni Baiardi, Chittolini, and Floriani 1986, 1:225–296.

Petrarch. 1906. *Vie de César. Reproduction phototypique du manuscrit autographe (Ms. lat 5784) de la Bibliothèque nationale*. Introduction by Léon Dorez. Paris: Imprimerie Berthaud frères.

Petrarch. 1955. F. *De viris illustribus*. In Martellotti et al. 1955, 218–269.

Petrarch. 1978. "How a Ruler Ought to Govern His State." Trans. B. J. Kohl. In Kohl and Witt 1978, 35–78.

Petrarch. 2003. *De gestis Cesaris*. Ed. G. Crevatin. Pisa: Scuola normale superiore.

Petrarch. 2017. *Selected Letters*. 2 vols. Ed. and trans. E. Fantham. I Tatti Renaissance Library 76 and 77. Cambridge, MA: Harvard University Press.

Pevsner, N. 1942. "The Term 'Architect' in the Middle Ages." *Speculum* 17, 549–562.

Pfisterer, U. 2009. "I libri di Filarete." *Arte Lombarda* 155, 97–110.

Pietrangeli, C. 1964. "I palazzi Capitolini nel medioevo." *Capitolium* 39, 191–194.

Pinto, J. 1976. "Origins and Development of the Ichnographic City Plan." *Journal of the Society of Architectural Historians* 35.1, 35–50.

Pirotta, N., ed. 1975. *Li due Orfei. Da Poliziano a Monteverdi*. Turin: Einaudi.

Pius II (Aeneas Silvius Piccolomini). 1937–1957. *The Commentaries of Pius II*. 5 vols. Trans. F. A. Gragg. Northhampton, MA: Department of History of Smith College.

Pius II (Aeneas Silvius Piccolomini). 1984. *I commentarii*. 2 vols. Ed. and trans. L. Totaro. Milan: Adelphi.

Pius II (Aeneas Silvius Piccolomini). 2003. *Commentaries*. Vol. 1. Ed. and trans. M. Meserve and M. Simonetta. I Tatti Renaissance Library 12. Cambridge, MA: Harvard University Press.

Pius II (Aeneas Silvius Piccolomini). 2014. *Europe*. Trans. R. Brown, introduction and notes by N. Bisaha. Washington, DC: Catholic University of America Press.

Pizzigoni, V. 2007. "Un uomo, un'opera uno scopo: un'ipotesi sul manuscritto di Ferrara." *Annali di architettura* 18–19, 53–70.

Plommer, H. 1973. *Vitruvius and Later Building Manuals*. London: Cambridge University Press.

Plutarch. 1912. *Plutarch's Lives. The Dryden Plutarch Revised by Arthur Hugh Clough*. 3 vols. Everyman's Library. London: J. M. Dent and Sons; New York: E. P. Dutton.

Polichetti, M. L., ed. 1985. *Il Palazzo di Federico da Montefeltro. Restauri e richerche*. Urbino: Quattroventi.

Polverni Fosi, I. 1990. "Le diocesi de Pienza e Montalcino fra privilegi e riforme." In A. Cortonesi, ed., *La Val d'Orcia nel medioevo e nei primi secoli dell'età moderna*, 411–446. Rome: Viella.

Pope-Hennessy, J. W. 1958. "The Equestrian Monument in Italian Renaissance Sculpture." In Pope-Hennessy, *An Introduction to Italian Sculpture*, 3 vols., 2:62–72. London: Phaidon Press.

Popham, A. E., and P. Pouncey. 1950. *Italian Drawings in the Department of Prints and Drawings in the British Museum*. London: British Museum.

Povoledo, E. 1975. "La 'città ferrarese.'" In Pirotta 1975, 395–409.

Powell, J. M., ed. 1971. *The Liber Augustalis or Constitutions of Melfi Promulgated by the Emperor Frederick II for the Kingdom of Sicily in 1231*. Syracuse: Syracuse University Press.

Price, S. R. F. 1996. "The Place of Religion." *Cambridge Ancient History* 10, 812–847.

Price, S. R. F., and P. Thonemann. 2010. *The Birth of Classical Europe*. London: Allen Lane.

Prisciani, P. 1992. *Spectacula*. Ed. with an introduction by D. Aguzzi Barbagli. Modena: Cosimo Panini Editore.

Prisciani, P. 2012. "Biblioteca Estense Universitaria di Modena Ms. Lat. 466 = α X.1.6, cc. 17v–40v." Digital transcription with facing ms. pages. Ed. E. Bastianello. *La Rivista di Engramma* 85 (November).

Prisciani, P. 2015. *Spectacula*. Ed. E. Bastianello. Rimini: Guaraldi.

Prodi, P. 1987. *The Papal Prince. One Body and Two Souls: The Papal Monarchy in Early Modern Europe*. Trans. S. Haskins. Cambridge: Cambridge University Press.

Pulin, C. 1981. "The Palaces of an Early Renaissance Humanist." *Arte Lombarda* 61, 23–32.

Raber, K., and T. J. Tucker, eds. 2005a. *The Culture of the Horse*. New York: Palgrave Macmillan.

Raber, K., and T. J. Tucker. 2005b. Introduction. In Raber and Tucker 2005a, 1–41.

Ravara, C. 2006. "Il cippo riminese di Giulio Cesare. Omaggio ad Augusto Campana." *L'arco: Quadrimestrale di informazione culturale ed economia*, July-August, 68–79.

Rebecchini, G. 2007. "After the Medici: The New Rome of Pope Paul III Farnese." *I Tatti Studies: Essays in the Renaissance* 11, 147–200.

Regn, G., and B. Huss. 2009. "Petrarch's Rome: The History of the *Africa* and the Renaissance Project." *Modern Language Notes* 124.1 (January), 86–102.

Reti, L. 1968. "The Two Unpublished Manuscripts of Leonardo da Vinci in the Biblioteca Nacional of Madrid." *Burlington Magazine* 110, 10–22.

Reti, L., ed. 1974. *The Unknown Leonardo*. New York: McGraw-Hill.

Reynolds, L. D., ed. 1983. *Texts and Transmission: A Survey of the Latin Classics*. Oxford: Clarendon Press.

Riahi, P. 2015. *Ars et Ingenium: The Embodiment of Imagination in Francesco di Giorgio's Drawings*. Abingdon, UK: Routledge.

Richter, J.-P., and R. C. Bell, eds. 1970. *The Notebooks of Leonardo da Vinci*. 2 vols. New York: Dover.

Robin, D. 1991. *Filelfo in Milan: Writings 1451–1477*. Princeton: Princeton University Press.

Rodella, G. 1992. "Note sul Castello di San Giorgio e l'architettura della Camera picta." In Cordaro 1992, 221–231.

Rodella, G. 2003. "Le strutture architettoniche." In Algeri et al. 2003, 17–52.

Rodocanachi, E. 1904. *Le capitole romain antique et moderne: la Citadelle, les temples, le Palais sénatorial, le Palais de conservateurs, le Musée*. Paris: Hachette.

Romani, M. 1995. *Una città in forma di palazzo: potere signorile e forma urbana nella Mantova medievale e moderna*. Brescia: Centro di ricerche storiche e sociali Federico Odorici.

Rosenberg, C. M. 1978. "The Erculean Addition to Ferrara: Contemporary Reactions and Pragmatic Considerations." *ACTA: The Fifteenth Century* 5, 49–67.

Rosenberg, C. M. 1979. "The Iconography of the Sala degli stucchi in the Palazzo Schifanoia in Ferrara." *Art Bulletin* 61.3, 377–394.

Rosenberg, C. M. 1991. "Arte e politica alle corti di Leonello e Borso d'Este." In Di Lorenzo 1991, 39–52.

Rosenberg, C. M. 1997. *The Este Monuments and Urban Development in Renaissance Ferrara*. Cambridge: Cambridge University Press.

Rosenberg, C. M., ed. 2010a. *Court Cities of Northern Italy: Milan, Parma, Piacenza, Mantua, Ferrara, Bologna, Urbino, Pesaro and Rimini*. Cambridge: Cambridge University Press.

Rosenberg, C. M. 2010b. Introduction. In Rosenberg 2010a, 1–20.

Rossi, G. G., and V. Brammanti. 1995. *Vita di Federico di Montefeltro*. Florence: Olschki.

Rotondi, P. 1969. *The Ducal Palace of Urbino: Its Architecture and Decoration*. London: A. Taranti.

Rovetta, A. 1981. "Cultura e codici vitruviani nel primo umanesimo Milanese." *Arte Lombarda* 60, 9–14.

Rowland, I. D. 1994. "Raphael, Angelo Colocci and the Genesis of the Architectural Orders." *Art Bulletin* 76.1, 81–104.

Rowland, I. D. 1997. "Il Petrarca lettore di Vitruvio." In Secchi Tarugi 1997, 71–81.

Rowland, I. D. 1998. "Vitruvius in Print and in Vernacular Translation: Fra Giocondo, Bramante, Raphael and Cesare Cesariano." In Hart and Hicks 1998, 105–121.

Rowland, I. D. 2005. "From Vitruvian Scholarship to Vitruvian Practice." *Memoirs of the American Academy in Rome* 50, 15–40.

Rowland, I. D. 2006. "Bramante's Hetruscan Tempietto." *Memoirs of the American Academy in Rome* 51/52, 225–238.

Rowland, I. D. 2014. "Vitruvius and His Influence." In Ulrich and Quenemoen 2014, 412–425.

Rowland, I. D., and S. W. Bell, eds. 2021. *Companion to the Reception of Vitruvius*. Leiden: Brill.

Rowland, I. D., and N. Charney. 2017. *The Collector of Lives: Giorgio Vasari and the Invention of Art*. New York: W. W. Norton.

Rykwert, J. 1981. *On Adam's House in Paradise*. 2nd ed. Cambridge, MA: MIT Press.

Rykwert, J. 1988. Introduction to Alberti 1988, ix–xxi.

Rykwert, J. 1994. "Alberti a Ferrara." In Rykwert and Engel 1994, 158–161.

Rykwert, J. 1996. *The Dancing Column*. Cambridge, MA: MIT Press.

Rykwert, J. 1998. "Theory as Rhetoric: Leon Battista Alberti in Theory and Practice." In Hart and Hicks 1998, 32–50.

Rykwert, J., and A. Engel, eds. 1994. *Leon Battista Alberti. Catalogo della mostra Palazzo Te*. Milan: Olivetti and Electa.

Saalman, H., L. Volpi, and A. Law. 1992. "Recent Excavations under the 'Ombrellone' of Sant'Andrea in Mantua: Preliminary Report." *Journal of the Society of Architectural Historians* 51.4, 357–376.

Sambin De Norcen, M. T. 2009. "'*Attolli super ceteros mortals*.' L'arco del cavallo a Ferrara." In Calzona et al. 2009, 1:349–391.

Santoro, C. 1968. *Gli Sforza*. Milan: Dall'Oglio.

Sanvito, P., ed. 2016. *Vitruvianism: Origins and Transformations*. Berlin: De Gruyter.

Sapin, C., ed. 2002. *Avant nefs et espaces d'accueil dans l'église entre le IVe et XIIe siècle*. Paris: Éditions du CTHS.

Saxl, F. 1957. "The Capitol during the Renaissance, a Symbol of the Imperial Idea." In Saxl, *Lectures*, 2 vols, 1:200–214. London: Warburg Institute.

Scaglia, G. 1981–1982. "La 'Porta delle torri' di Federico II a Capua in un disegno di Francesco di Giorgio." *Napoli Nobilissima*, 20.5–6 (December 1981), 203–221, and 21.1–2 (March-June 1982), 123–134.

Scaglia, G. 1985. *Il "Vitruvio Magliabechiano" di Francesco di Giorgio Martini*. Florence: Edizioni Gonnelli.

Scardino, L. 1991. *Giacomo Zilocchi "valente rifaciatore delle statue de' principi Estensi." Il carteggio con Giuseppe Agnelli*. Ferrara: Liberty House.

Schofield, R. 1991. "Leonardo's Milanese Architecture: Career, Sources and Graphic Techniques." *Achademia Leonardi Vinci: Journal of Leonardo Studies and Bibiography of Vinciana* 4, 111–156.

Schofield, R. 2016. "Notes on Leonardo and Vitruvius." In Moffatt and Taglialagamba 2016, 120–134.

Schuler, S. 1999. *Vitruv im Mittelalter: die Rezeption von "De Architecura" von der Antike bis in die frühe Neuzeit*. Cologne: Böhlau.

Scotti, A. 2015. "The Sforza Castle of Milan (1450–1499)." In Beltramo et al. 2015, 134–162.

Searle, J. R. 2010. *Making the Social World: The Structure of Human Civilization*. Oxford: Oxford University Press.

Secchi Tarugi, L. R., ed. 1997. *Petrarca e la cultura europea*. Milan: Nuovi Orizzonti.

Secchi Tarugi, L. R., ed. 1999. *Cultura e potere nel Rinascimento: atti del IX convegno internazionale (Chianciano–Pienza, 21–24 luglio 1997)*. Florence: Cesati.

Il Senato nella Storia. 1997–1999. 3 vols. Rome: Istituto poligrafico e Zecca dello Stato.

Settis, S., and W. Cupperi, eds. 2007. *Il Palazzo Schifanoia a Ferrara = The Palazzo Schifanoia in Ferrara*. 2 vols. Modena: F. C. Panini.

Seymour, C. 1973. "Some Reflections on Filarete's Use of Antique and Visual Sources." *Arte Lombarda* 18.38/39, 36–47.

Sfogliano Fallico, R. 1974. "L'Alberti e l'antico nel *De re aedificatoria*." In *Il Sant'Andrea di Mantova e Leon Battista Alberti*, 157-170. Mantua: Biblioteca Comunale.

Sgarbi, C. 1993. "A Newly Discovered Corpus of Vitruvian Images." *Res* 23 (Spring), 31-51.

Sgarbi, C., ed. 2004. *Vitruvio Ferrarese, De architectura. La prima versione illustrate*. Preface by Joseph Rykwert. Modena: Franco Cosimo Panini.

Sgarbi, C. 2014. "Il *Vitruvio Ferarese*, alcuni dettagli quasi invisibili e un autore: Giacomo Andrea da Ferrara." In Gros and Pagliara 2014, 121-138 and 289-284.

Shearer, C. 1935. *The Renaissance of Architecture in Southern Italy: A Study of Frederick II of Hohenstaufen and the Capua Triumphator Archway and Towers*. Cambridge: W. Heffer and Sons.

Shi, V. S.-R. 2019. "*Omo (quasi) senza lettere*: Leonardo's Quest to Teach Himself Classical Latin." In Findlen 2019, 28-41.

Siebigs, H-K. 2004. *Der Zentralbau des Domes zu Aachen: Unerforschtes und Ungewisses*. Worms: Wernersche.

Signorini, R. 1985. *Opus hoc tenue: la Camera Dipinta di Andrea Mantegna: Lettura storica, iconographica, iconological*. Parma: Artegrafica Silva.

Signorini, R. 1991. "*Procumbe viator*: Papi nel mantovano e a Mantova e la disputa sul 'Preciosissimo Lateral Sangue N.S.G.C.'" In R. Signorini, ed., *Storia e arte religiosa a Mantova: Visite di Pontefici e la reliqua del Preciosissimo Sangue*, exh. cat., 7-54. Mantua: Casa del Mantegna.

Signorini, R. 2003. "La 'Camera dipinta' detta 'Degli sposi.'" In Algeri et al. 2003, 117-136.

Signorini, R., ed. 2006. *A casa di Andrea Mantegna: Cultura artistica a Mantova nel Quattrocento*. Cinisello Balsamo: Silvana Editoriale.

Simonetta, M., ed. 2007. *Federico da Montefeltro and His Library*. Exh. cat. (Morgan Library and Museum, New York, 8 June-30 September 2007). Milan: Y.Press SRL.

Simonetta, M. 2017. "Federico da Montefeltro e Sigismondo Malatesta: Ritratti di due nemini implacabili." In C. Colosimo, ed., *San Marino 1462-1463. I patti di Fossombrone e la bolla de Pio II*, 63-96. Villa Verrucchio: Ente Cassa di Faetano.

Skinner, Q. 1986. "Ambrogio Lorenzetti: The Artist as Political Philosopher." *Proceedings of the British Academy* 122, 1-56.

Smith, C. 1992. *Architecture in the Culture of Early Humanism: Ethics, Aesthetics and Eloquence 1400-1470*. New York: Oxford University Press.

Smith, C. 1995. "Piero's Painted Architecture: Analysis of His Vocabulary." In M. A. Lavin, ed., *Piero della Francesca and His Legacy*, 223-253. Studies in the History of Art, no. 48, Center for Advanced

Studies in the Visual Arts, Symposium XXVIII. Washington: National Gallery of Art.

Smith, C., and J. F. O'Connor. 2006. *Building the Kingdom: Giannozzo Manetti on the Material and Spiritual Edifice*. Tempe: Arizona Center for Medieval and Renaissance Studies.

Somaini, F. 2011. "The Political Geography of Renaissance Italy." In Folin 2011a, 36–61.

Spencer, J. R. 1973. "Il Progetto per il Cavallo di bronzo per Francesco Sforza." *Arte Lombarda* 38/39, 23–35.

Spencer, J. R. 1979. "Filarete, the Medallist of the Roman Emperors." *Art Bulletin* 61.4, 549–561.

Starn, R. 1992. "Room for a Prince: The Camera Picta in Mantua." In Starn and Partridge, 83–148.

Starn, R. 1994. *Ambrogio Lorenzetti: The Palazzo Pubblico, Siena*. New York: George Braziller.

Starn, R., and L. Partridge. 1992. *Arts of Power: Three Halls of State in Italy 1300–1600*. Berkley: University of California Press.

Steinby, E. M., ed. 1993–2000. *Lexicon topographicum urbis Romae*. 6 vols. Rome: Edizione Quasar.

Stevenson, J. 2021. *The Light of Italy: The Life and Times of Federico da Montefeltro, Duke of Urbino*. London: Apollo / Head of Zeus.

Stornajolo, C. 1902–1921. *Codices Urbinates Latini*. 3 vols. Rome: Vatican Press.

Suetonius. 1979. *The Twelve Caesars*. Trans. R. Graves, revised by M. Grant. Harmondsworth, UK: Penguin Books.

Sutherland, C. H. V., and R. A. G. Carson, eds. 1984. *The Roman Imperial Coinage*. London: Spink.

Swain, S. 2000. *Dio Chrysostom, Politics Letters and Philosophy*. Oxford: Oxford University Press.

Szörényi, L. 1987. "Callimacho Esperiente e la corte di re Matthia." In Garfagnini 1987, 105–118.

Tafuri, M. 2006. *Interpreting the Renaissance*. Ed. and trans. D. Sherer. Cambridge, MA: MIT Press.

Tavares, A. 2022. *Vitruvius without Text: The Biography of a Book*. Zurich: gta Verlag.

Tavernor, R. 1985. "Concinnitas in the Architectural Theory and Practice of Leon Battista Alberti." PhD thesis, University of Cambridge. https://doi.org/10.17863/CAM.16319.

Tavernor, R. 1994. "*Concinnitas*, o la formulazione della bellezza." In Rykwert and Engel 1994, 300–315.

Tavernor, R. 1998. *On Alberti and the Art of Building*. New Haven: Yale University Press.

Taylor, R., K. W. Rinne, and S. Kostof. 2016. *Rome: An Urban History from Antiquity to the Present*. Cambridge: Cambridge University Press.

Tigler, P. 1963. *Die Architekturtheorie des Filarete*. Berlin: De Gruyter.

Tittoni, M. 1996. "Il Campidoglio tra potere e potere." In M. Tittoni, ed., *Il Palazzo dei Conservatoi e il Palazzo Nuovo in Campidoglio*. Pisa: Pacini, 12–17.

Tobey, E. 2005. "The Palio Horse in Italy." In Raber and Tucker 2005a, 63–90.

Tocci, L. M. 1958. "I due manoscritti urbinati dei privilegi dei Montefeltro con una Appendice Lauranesca." *La Bibliofilia* 60, 206–257.

Togliani, C. 2003. "L'architettura da Fancelli a Giulio Romano." In Algeri et al. 2003, 89–116.

Tommasoli, W. 1978. *La vita di Federico da Montefeltro (1422–1482)*. Urbino: Argalia.

Tonini, L. 1882. *Storia civile e sacra riminese*. Vol. 5: *Rimini nella signoria de' Malatesti*. Rimini (reprint Rimini: Ghigi, 1971).

Tönnesmann, A. 1994. "Le Palais ducal d'Urbino. Humanisme et réalité sociale." In Guillaume 1994, 137–153.

Tönnesmann, A. 2009. "Il dialogo di Filarete, il principe e il potere." *Arte Lombarda* 155, 7–11.

Tönnesmann, A. 2013a. "Zwischen Bürgerhaus und Residenz zur sozialen typik des Palazzo Medici." In Tönnesmann, *Die Freiheit des Betrachtens*, 14–32. Zurich: gta Verlag.

Tönnesmann, A. 2013b. "Enea Silvio und die Architektur." In Tönnesmann, *Die Freiheit des Betrachtens*, 80–99. Zurich: gta Verlag.

Tonni, A. 2012. "The Renaissance Studs of the Gonzagas of Mantua." In Edwards et al. 2012, 261–278.

Torello-Hill, G. 2010. "Gli *Spectacula* di Pellegrino Prisciani e il revival del teatro classico a Ferrara." *La Rivista di Engramma* 85, 3–10.

Torello-Hill, G. 2015. "The Exegesis of Vitruvius and the Creation of Theatrical Space in Renaissance Ferrara." *Renaissance Studies* 29.2, 227–246.

Tosco, C. 2003. *Vitruvio in età gotica*. In Ciotta 2003, 306–316.

Tosco, C. 2011. *Petrarca: paesaggi, città, architetture*. Macerata: Quodlibet.

Trachtenberg, M. 2010. *Building-in-Time: From Giotto to Alberti and Modern Oblivion*. New Haven: Yale University Press.

Trachtenberg, M. 2011. "Ayn Rand, Alberti and the Authorial Figure of the Architect." *California Italian Studies* 2.1, unpaginated. Open access via escholarship.

Tronzo, W., ed. 1994. *Intellectual Life in the Court of Frederick II Hohenstaufen*. Washington, DC: Center for Advanced Studies in the Visual Arts.

Tuchman, B. 1978. *A Distant Mirror: The Calamitous Fourteenth Century*. New York: Knopf.
Tuohy, T. 1996. *Herculean Ferrara: Ercole d'Este and the Invention of a Ducal Capital*. Cambridge: Cambridge University Press.
Turchini, A. 2000. *Il Tempio malatestiano, Sigismondo Pandolfo Malatesta e Leon Battista Alberti*. Cesena: Il Ponte Vecchio.
Turchini, A., ed. 2003. *Castel Sismondo: Sigismondo Pandolfo Malatesta e l'arte militare del primo Rinascimento: atti del Convegno*. Cesena: Il Ponte Vecchio.
Ulrich, R. B., and C. K. Quenemoen, eds. 2014. *A Companion to Roman Architecture*. Oxford: Blackwell.
Usher, J. 2009. "Petrarch's Diploma of Crowning." In Caruso and Laird 2009, 161–192.
Vaini, M. 1986. *Dal Comune alla Signoria: Mantova dal 1200 al 1328*. Milan: F. Angeli.
Valla, L. 2007. *On the Donation of Constantine* (1440). Trans. with an introduction by G. W. Bowerstock. I Tatti Renaissance Library 24. Cambridge, MA: Harvard University Press.
Van Eck, C. 1998. "The Structure of *De re aedificatoria* Reconsidered." *Journal of the Society of Architectural Historians* 57.3, 280–297.
Varanini, G. M. 1994. "La propaganda dei regimi signorili: le esperienze veneta del Trecento." In P. Cammarosano, ed., *Le forme della propaganda politica nel Duecento e Trecento*, 311–343. Rome: École française de Rome.
Varese, R. 1985. "Un altro ritratto di Leon Battista Alberti." *Mitteilungen des Kunsthisorischen Instituts Florenz* 29, 183–189.
Varese, R. 1989. *Arte e copia tra Otto e Novecento: I mesi di Schifanoia nei dipinti e disegni di Giuseppe Mazzolani*. Florence: Centro Di.
Vasaly, A. 1993. *Representations: Images of the World in Ciceronian Oratory*. Berkeley: University of California Press.
Vecce, C. 2006. *Leonardo*. 2nd ed. Introduction by C. Pedretti. Rome: Salerno Editrice.
Vecce, C. 2019. "Leonardo e i suoi libri." In *Leonardo e i suoi libri*, exh. cat., 23–47. Rome: Bardi Edizioni.
Venturi, A. 1914. "Un opera sconosciuta di L. B. Alberti." *L'Arte* 17, 153–156.
Vespasiano da Bisticci. 1997. *The Vespasiano Memoirs. Lives of Illustrious Men of the XVth Century*. Trans. W. George and E. Waters, introduction by M. P. Gilmore. Toronto: University of Toronto Press.
Veyne, P. 1990. *Bread and Circuses: Historial Sociology and Political Pluralism*. Abridged with an introduction by O. Murray, trans. B. Pearce. London: Allen Lane.

Vicini, D. 1984. *Il Castello Visconteo de Pavia e i suoi musei*. Pavia: Logos International.

Vitruvius. 1486. *L. Victruui Pollionis ad Cesarem Augustum De architectura primus (-decimus)*. Ed. G. A. Sulpicio of Veroli. Rome.

Vitruvius. 1511. *M. Vitruvius per Jocundum solito castigator factus cum figures et tabula ut iam legi et intellegi possit*. Ed. G. Giocondo. Venice: Ioannis de Tridino.

Vitruvius. 1521. *Di Lucio Vitruvio Pollione De architectura libri dece: traducti de latino in vulgare affigurati*. . . . Trans. and commentary by C. Cesariano. Como: Magistro Gotardus da Ponte.

Vitruvius. 1524. *M. L. Vitruvio Polione De architectura tradocto di Latino in vulgare*. . . , Ed. F. L. Durantino. Venice: Ioanne Antonio & Piero Fratelli da Sabio.

Vitruvius. 1535. *M. L. Vitruvio Pollione Di architettura: dal vero esemplare latino*. Ed. F. L. Durantino. Venice: Nicolo de Aristotele detto Zoppino.

Vitruvius. 1673. *Les Dix Livres d'Architecture de Vitruve, Corrigez et Traduits en François, avec des Notes et des Figures*. Ed. and trans. C. Perrault. Paris: Jean Baptiste Coignard.

Vitruvius. 1960. *Vitruvius, the Ten Books on Architecture*. Ed. and trans. M. H. Morgan. New York: Dover.

Vitruvius. 1969–2009. *Vitruve. De l'architecture*. 10 vols. Ed. and trans. P. Gros et al. Paris: Belles Lettres.

Vitruvius. 1983–1985. *Vitruvius on Architecture*. 2 vols. Ed. and trans. F. Granger. Cambridge, MA: Harvard University Press; London: William Heinemann.

Vitruvius. 2009. *Vitruvius, On Architecture*. Trans. R. Schofield, introduction by R. Tavernor. London: Penguin Classics.

Volaterrano, R. M. 1506. *Commentatiorum urbanorum libri XXXVIII*. Rome: Johann Besicken.

Volmer, E. 1994. *Il carroccio*. Turin: Einaudi.

Vulpi, V. 2001. "Finding Filarete: The Two Versions of Filarete's *Libro architettonico*." In Golden 2001, 331–339.

Warburg, A. 1999. "Italian Art and International Astrology in the Palazzo Schifanoia (1912)." In Warburg, *The Renewal of Pagan Antiquity*, trans. D. Britt, introduction by K. W. Forster, 563–582. Los Angeles: Getty Research Institute for the History of Art and the Humanities.

Warnke, M. 1985. *The Court Artist*. Trans. D. McKlintock. Cambridge: Cambridge University Press.

Watkins, R. 1989. "L. B. Alberti in the Mirror: An Interpretation of the *Vita* with a New Translation." *Italian Quarterly* 30.117, 5–30.

Weiskittel, S. F., and L. D. Reynolds. 1983. "Vitruvius." In Reynolds 1983, 440–445.

Weiss, R. 1969. *The Renaissance Discovery of Classical Antiquity*. Oxford: Blackwell.

Wells, E. B. 1995. "Partners in Power: The Horses of Leonardo's Italy (1450–1550)." In Ahl 1995, 57–63.

Westfall, C. W. 1969. "Society, Beauty and the Humanist Architect in Alberti's *De re aedificatoria*." *Studies in the Renaissance* 16, 61–79.

Westfall, C. W. 1974. *In This Most Perfect Paradise: Alberti, Nicholas V, and the Invention of Conscious Urban Planning in Rome, 1447–1455*. University Park: Pennsylvania State University Press.

Westfall, C. W. 1978. "Chivalric Declaration: The Palazzo Ducale in Urbino as a Political Statement." In Millon and Nochlin 1978, 20–45.

Whittemore, L. 2009. "Città e territorio nel *Libro architettonico* del Filarete." *Arte Lombarda* 155, 47–55.

Wickham, C. 2015. *Medieval Rome: Stability and Crisis of a City 900–1150*. Oxford: Oxford University Press.

Wilkins, E. H. 1943. "The Coronation of Petrarch." *Speculum* 18.2, 155–197.

Wilkins, E. H. 1955. *Studies in the Life and Works of Petrarch*. Cambridge, MA: Medieval Academy of America.

Wilkins, E. H. 1958. *Petrarch's Eight Years in Milan*. Cambridge, MA: Medieval Academy of America.

Wilkins, E. H. 1961. *Life of Petrarch*. Chicago: University of Chicago Press.

Willemsen, C. A. 1953. *Kaiser Friedrichs II Triumphator zu Capua. Ein Denkmal Hohenstaufischer Kunst in Suditalien*. Wiesbaden: Carl Arnold.

Williams, K., L. March, and S. R. Wassell, eds. 2010. *The Mathematical Works of Leon Battista Alberti*. Foreword by R. Tavernor. Basel: Springer.

Wind, G. D. 2016. "Horseplay at the Te." *Notes on the History of Art* 35.1–2, 110–117.

Wittkower, R. 1988. *Architectural Principles in the Age of Humanism* (1949). London: Academy Editions.

Woods, L. 1992. *Anarchitecture: Architecture Is a Political Act*. London: Academy Editions.

Woods-Marsden, J. 1989. "Images of Castles in the Renaissance: Symbols of 'Signoria' / Symbols of Tyranny." *Art Journal* 48.2, 130–137.

Woodward, D., ed. 2007. *Cartography in the Early Renaissance*. Chicago: University of Chicago Press.

Wyatt, M. 2014. "Technologies." In M. Wyatt, ed., *The Cambridge Companion to the Italian Renaissance*, 100–138. Cambridge: Cambridge University Press.

Xenophon. 1925. *De hippike*. In *Scripta minora*. Ed. and trans E. G. Merchant, 353–355. Cambridge, MA: Harvard University Press; London: William Heinemann.

Xenophon. 1960. *Cyropaedia*. 2 vols. Ed. and trans. W. Miller. Cambridge, MA: Harvard University Press; London: William Heinemann.

Yates, F. 1975. *Astrea: The Imperial Theme*. London: Routledge and Kegan Paul.

Zaccaria, V. 1970. Review of G. Martellotti, ed., *F. Petrarca Laurea occidens—Bucolicum carmen X*. *Studi medievali* 11, 507–513.

Zambotti, B., ed. 1949. *Diario Ferrarese dall'anno 1476 al 1504*. Bologna: Zanichelli.

Zampetti, P. 1981. "Vittorino da Feltre e Federico da Montefeltro." In Gianetto 1981, 255–261.

Zampetti, P., and R. Battistini. 1985. "Federico da Montefeltro e il Palazzo Ducale." In Polichetti 1985, 51–66.

Zannoni, G. 1901. "Vita di Federico d'Urbino, scritta da F. Filelfo, pubblicata scondo il cod. Vatic. Urbin. 1022." *Atti e memorie della R. Deputazione di Storia Patria per le Province delle Marche* 5, 263–420.

Zannoni, G. 1902–1903. "Federico II di Montefeltro e Giovanni Antonio Campano." *Atti della Reale Accademia delle Scienze di Torino (Classe di scienze morali, storiche e filologiche)* 38, 108–118.

Zevi, B. 1960. *Biagio Rossetti, architetto ferrarese, il primo urbanisto moderno europeo*. Turin: Einaudi.

Zevi, B. 1971. *Sapere vedere l'urbanistica: Ferrara di Biagio Rossetti, la prima città moderna europea*. Turin: Einaudi.

Zippel, G. 1979. *Storia e cultura del Rinascimento italiano*. Padua: Antenore.

Zöllner, F. 1987. *Vitruvs Proportionsfigur: Quellenkritische Studien zur Kunstliteratur im 15. und 16. Jahrhundert*. Worms: Wernersche Verlagsgesellschaft.

Zöllner, F. 1995. "L'uomo vitruviano di Leonardo da Vinci: Rudolf Wittkower e l'*Angelus Novus* di Walter Benjamin." *Raccolta Vinciana* 26, 329–358.

Index

Aachen, 103
Acciaiuoli, Niccolò, 25
Adam, 182–184, 186–187, 195
Adelberto, 88
Aemilius Paullus, xiv
Aeneas, 19, 100, 218
Aesop, 191
Agostino di Duccio, 158
Aguzzi Barbagli, Danilo, 246
Alberti, Leon Battista, 34–35, 38, 44, 59, 64, 68, 70–71, 73–77, 81, 86, 93–96, 98–99, 101, 103–104, 107–108, 113, 115, 117, 119, 131–132, 142, 144, 154–157, 158, 162–163, 180–181, 194, 214–218, 220, 224–225, 229, 231–232, 236, 239–242, 244–250, 257, 260, 274, 281, 290
  De equo animante, 214–216, 229–231
  De ichiarchia, 181
  Della famiglia, 95, 155–156
  Descriptio urbis Romae, 35
  De statua, 226, 230
  Fatum et fortuna, 156
  Momus, 73
  On the Art of Building in Ten Books (*De re aedificatoria libri decem*), 34, 66, 69, 73, 96, 98, 113, 120, 145, 156, 162, 225, 227–228, 230, 244
  Vita (autobiography), 155
  and Vitruvius, 66, 69–70, 113, 122, 227–228, 232, 281
Albertus Magnus, 190
Alexander the Great, xii, 145–146, 150, 215
Alfonso V, king of Aragon (Alfonso I of Naples), 108, 174
all'antica architecture, 81, 86, 220, 239–240, 242–243, 248
Amazon, 140
Amboise, Georges d', 266
Ambrosian Republic, 164, 165, 171, 179, 181
amphitheaters, 246
analemma, 188
ancient theater, revival of, 245, 251–252
animans, animal, 226, 229, 281
Ankara, 264
Annunciation, 24
Anthropomorphism. *See* corporeal referent
antiquity, ancient splendor, 100–101
Apollo, 165, 236
Aquinas, St. Thomas, 190
Architect
  definition of, 257
  education of, 14, 16, 142
architecti scientia. *See* knowledge of the architect
architectonic, 187–192, 197–198
architectural legitimation, 175
architectural orders, 14, 183–185, 228, 248
architectural proof, 32, 34, 51, 58–59, 70, 84, 117, 131, 227–228, 280–281
architectural theory, 186–187, 225, 240, 291
architectural treatises, xi, 34, 66, 142, 147, 150, 156, 163, 166, 281
aretê, 152–153, 163–164, 166. *See also virtus*
Arezzo, Giovanni Antonio da, 96
Ariminum, 138. *See also* Rimini
Aristotle, 18, 130, 188–192, 197
  Metaphysics, 189–190
  Nicomachean Ethics, 18, 189–191
  Politics, 190
Arquà Petrarca, 11
Ascension, feast of, 89, 90, 103–104, 219
ashlar masonry, 122–125, 132, 134
Asia, 231
Aspertini, Amico, 41
astrology, 233–236

Athens, 15
atrium, palace courtyard, 77, 119, 250. *See also* cortile
Attila, 19
Augustine, St., 20, 130, 275
  City of God, The, 274
Augustus Caesar, xi, xii, 11, 13, 32–34, 56, 58, 66, 69, 82, 139–140, 146, 151, 158, 188–189, 215, 227, 245, 264–265, 280
  Res gestae, 264–266
Autocracy. *See* one-man rule
Averlino, Antonio. *See* Filarete
Averroes, 130
Avogadro, Alberto, 77

Baker, Patrick, 195
Baltimore, 259
Barbara of Brandenburg, 94
Barocci, Ambrogio, 134
Baroncelli, Niccolò ("Niccolò del Cavallo"), 219–220, 223
Basinio da Parma, 161
  Hesperis, 162
Battaglia (horse), 207
Beatrice of Aragon, 194
beauty, 10, 98–99, 228, 231–232
  power of, 34–35
Beltramini, Maria, 195
Berenson, Bernard, 278
  The Drawings of the Florentine Painters, 278
Berlin, 259
Bescapè, Ruggiero, 52, 287–289
Bible, 156
Biblioteca Ambrosiana, 192
Biondo, Flavio, 38
  Roma instaurata, 38
Boccaccio, Giovanni, 12, 21, 25, 273
Boccapaduli, Prospero, 58
Body. *See* corporeal referent
Bologna, 12, 86
Bonacolsi family, 89–91
  Giovanni, 90
  Pinamonte, 89–90
  Rinaldo ("Passerino"), 90

Bonfini, Antonio, 193–197
  Rerum ungaricarum decades, 195
Boniface IX, pope (Pietro Tomacelli), 36, 44
Boninus Mobritius, 192
Bonvesin della Riva, 17
  De magnalibus urbis Mediolani, 17
Borgia, Lucrezia, 252
Bossi, Giuseppe, 278
Boucheron, Patrick, 10
Bozzola, 94
Braccio da Montone, 108, 174
Bramante, Donato, 206
Brandolini, Aurelio Lippo, 194
  De comparatione rei publicae et regni, 194
bread and circuses, 245
bronze, 217–218, 268–269
Bruni, Leonardo, 100
  De origine urbis Mantuae, 100
Buda, 194
Budapest, 26
buon governo, 153. *See also* good government
Burckhardt, Jacob, 155
Bush, Virginia, 268–269
Bussolari, Giacomo, 19–20

Caesars, Renaissance rulers as emulators of, 5, 10–11, 14, 22, 69, 99, 135, 229, 280, 290
Cagli, 147
Caleffini, Ugo, 256–257, 261
Calixtus III, pope (Alfonso de Borgia), 73
Calvary, 88
camera degli sposi. See camera picta
camera picta (Mantua), 93–95, 135
Campano, Giannantonio (Giovanni Antonio), 84, 108, 110, 134, 174
Cancer, 158, 160
Cannae, xiv

Canossa family, 88–89
  Beatrice, 89
  Bonifacio, 88–89
  Matilde, 89
Capricorn, 234, 236
Capua gate, 107–110, 112–113, 186
Carrara family, 67
  Francesco da, 11, 206
carroccio, 186
Carthage, 5
Carya, 142
caryatids, 142, 169–170
Casa Areti, 167, 169–170
Cassano d'Adda, battle of, 214
Casteldurante, xii
Castiglione, Baldassare, 64, 94
  Book of the Courtier, 64, 94
Castiglione, Branda da, cardinal, 26, 135
Castiglione Olona, 26, 135
Castor and Pollux, 58
Catiline (Lucius Sergius Catilina), ii, 152–153
Cavalieri, Tommaso de', 55–56, 58
Cennini, Cennino, 226
  Craftsman's Handbook, 226
certainty, 130–131, 181
Cesariano, Cesare, xii, 26, 143
Cetius Faventinus, Marcus, 192, 197
Chambers, David, 97
Charlemagne, 19, 88, 103–104
Charles IV, Holy Roman Emperor, 20
Charles V, Holy Roman Emperor, 207
chastity, 235
Chironi, Giuseppe, 85
Christian I, king of Denmark, 94
Ciapponi, Lucia, 13
Cicero, Marcus Tullius, xiv, 4, 6, 12, 15–16, 32, 34, 99, 140, 145, 152–153, 155–156, 229, 240
  Brutus, xiv, 156
  De finibus, 15
circuses, 246

Cisalpine Gaul, 138
civilization, 32–33
Clarke, Georgia, 77
Colleoni, Bartolomeo, 217, 273
Colonna family, 3
  Giovanni, 15–16
common good, 8, 10, 19, 153–154, 171, 190, 243, 288
communal Rome, 6, 8, 35–40, 48, 59, 288–289
communal values, 8, 19, 280
communes, xi, 6–11, 17, 25–26, 67, 82, 89, 115–116, 117, 162, 186, 214–215, 249, 280, 288, 290
Composite order, 219, 223
concinnitas, 228–230, 232, 281
condottieri, 108, 132, 158, 164, 166, 194, 223. *See also* warlords
conquest, xii–xiv, 32–33, 58, 135, 141, 175, 232
Constantine (Flavius Valerius Constantinus), Roman emperor, 40, 43, 51
Constantinople, 74, 217, 220
Constantius II, Roman emperor, 47
Constitutions of Melfi, 186
Corinthian order, 44, 56, 101, 183–184, 207, 214, 248
Corio, Bernardino, 20, 182
corporeal referent, 33–34, 150–151, 225–228, 232, 275, 281
Corpus Christi, feast of, 76
Correggio, Azzo da, 11
Corsignano, 74, 76, 81, 84–86, 290
Cortenuova, battle of, 186
cortile, 76–77, 93
Corvinus, Matthias, king of Hungary, 193–197
cosmic order, 34, 94, 188–189, 233, 246
Cossa, Francesco del, 236–239
Costacciaro, 147
Cristoforo, Antonio di, 219

Crivelli, Lodrisio, 174–175, 179
  De vita rebusque gestis Francisci Sfortiae, 174
crossroads, 104, 120
Cyrus the Great, 235

Daedalus, 214
damnatio memoriae, 290
Dante Alighieri, 187, 191
  De monarchia, 187
Danube, river, 197
Dario (horse), 207, 209
De adamante Matthie, 195
De architectura, xi, xii, 12, 14, 17, 24, 26, 32, 66, 69, 77–78, 86, 98, 108, 113, 120, 122, 131, 135, 139, 141, 146–147, 151, 183, 187, 192, 195, 197, 226–227, 229, 248, 278–281. See also Vitruvius
De architectura, dedication, 13, 24–25, 32, 139–140, 280
De architectura, editions, xii, 1, 141, 352
  Cesariano (1521), xii, 26, 143
  Durantino (1524, 1535), xii–xv
  Giocondo (1511), xii, 25, 78–80
  Perrault (1673), 25
  Sulpicio (1486), 120
De architectura, manuscripts, 141
  BN Ms. Lat. 7228 (Paris), 22–25
  Ms. Bodl. Auct. F. 5.7 (Oxford), 13–14, 22, 296
  Petrarch's discovery of, 12–14
  Poggio Bracciolini's discovery of, 12, 25
  Vitruvio Ferrarese (Modena), 314 n. 130
Decembrio, Pier Candido, 26
décor, decorum, 96, 240–242, 250–252. See also mise en scène; scenography
De inventione Sanguinis Domini, 89
della Porta, Giacomo, 55–56

della Scala family, 67
  Cangrande I, 67, 90, 217
delle Vigne, Pier, 107
diamonds, 166–167, 187, 195, 197, 259
Diana, Roman goddess, 108
Diario ferrarese, 261
Dinocrates, 145–148, 150
Diodorus Siculus, 191
Donatello (Donato di Niccolò di Betto Bardi), 217
Donation of Constantine, 40, 43, 51
Dondi dall'Orologio, Giovanni, 25
Doric order, 146, 183–184, 248, 262
Dupérac, Étienne, 55–56
Durantino, Francesco Lucio, xii, xv
dynastic politics, 74, 84–86, 99–101, 219, 224, 234
dynastic succession, 94, 163

earthly paradise, 187, 197
Eastern Europe, 206
Easter Sunday 1341, 3
election of signori, 67, 214, 223–224, 234
eloquence, xiv–xv, 20, 156. See also rhetoric
Ennius, Quintus, 5
equestrian statues, 140–141, 204
  Bartolomeo Colleoni, 217, 273
  Bernabò Visconti, 217
  Cangrande I della Scala, 217
  Ercole d'Este, 261–266
  Francesco Sforza, 266–276
  Gattamelata, 217, 273
  John Hawkwood, 217, 273
  Justinian, 217, 220
  Marcus Aurelius, 31, 42–43, 48, 52, 55, 58, 141, 166, 198, 203–204, 287–288, 290
  Niccolò III d'Este, 215, 217–224, 234, 242, 273, 290
  Regisole, 21, 220, 273–275
  Victor Emmanuel, 59

Este family, 67, 197, 214, 233–235, 244
  Alfonso, 252
  Azzo VII Novello, 214
  Borso, 68, 86, 206, 218–220, 223, 234–236, 240, 242–244, 246, 249, 290
  Ercole I, 135, 223–224, 244–246, 248–252, 254, 256–257, 259–260, 262–266, 268–269
  Leonello, 69, 225, 233–234
  Niccolò, 93, 217–219, 221, 223–224, 234, 242, 249, 262, 273, 290
  Obizzo II, 214, 222–223, 234
  Sigismondo, 218
Etruscans, 88, 232
Etruscan temple, 100–101, 103–104
Euclid, 131
Eugenius IV, pope (Gabriele Condulmer), 68, 70, 116, 161
Europe, 8, 132
Ezzelino III da Romano, 214

Fabius Maximus, xiv
fabrica and *ratiocinatio*, 14, 142
Facio, Bartolomeo, 174
factuality of buildings, 113–114
family, preeminence of. See dynastic politics
Fancelli, Luca, 93, 96, 101
Fano, 99
Fauno, Lucio, 48
Federico da Montefeltro. See Montefeltro family: Federico
Feltre, Vittorino da, 131–132
Fémelat, Armelle, 234
Ferrante of Aragon (Ferdinand I of Naples), 108
Ferrara, 68, 85–86, 93, 135, 206, 214, 218, 223–224, 232, 234, 244, 248, 251, 254, 258–259, 264–266, 268–269, 290
  Barco, 254, 256–257

Index   357

Ferrara (*continued*)
   Corso Ercole I d'Este, 259, 290
   Corte Vecchio, 219 (*see also* Ferrara: Palazzo di Corte)
   Herculean Addition, 254–257, 259, 261
   Palazzo dei Diamanti, 259
   Palazzo della Certosa, 259
   Palazzo della Ragione, 249, 251–252
   Palazzo di Corte, 219, 223, 234, 249–251
   Palazzo Schifanoia, 233, 236, 242, 244
   Piazza Nuova, 260–262, 267
   Salone dei Mesi, 233–234, 246
   Santa Maria degli Angeli, 259
   Terra Nuova, 256
   Via degli Angeli, 259, 290
Festus, Rufus, 241
Fiamma, Galvano, 18, 21
Filarete (Antonio Averlino), 142, 163, 165–167, 169–171, 174–175, 179–180, 182–184, 187, 190–192, 195, 197–198, 225, 232, 268
Filelfo, Francesco (Francesco da Tolentino), 163, 165, 167, 170, 174, 179–181, 191, 197
   Ad Antonium Averlinum philaretum architectum, 164
   Odes, 180
   On Moral Doctrine, 191
   Sforziad, 174, 179
Florence, 5, 76, 85, 187, 217, 232, 268
   Palazzo Rucellai, 76, 78
   Palazzo Strozzi, 123
Folin, Marco, 162, 220, 239, 254, 257
Fontana, Aldighiero, 223
fortifications, 71, 147, 256, 259, 262, 276. *See also* fortresses
fortresses, 71, 92–93, 115, 147, 149–152, 162, 165–166, 249, 276

fortuna, 134, 154–155, 174
forum, 77–78, 82, 93, 104, 107, 120, 125, 137–139, 248–249, 251, 261–262
France, 33, 269, 273
Francesco di Giorgio. *See* Martini, Francesco di Giorgio
Francis I, king of France, 51, 206, 273
Franciscans, 36, 38
Frederick II Hohenstaufen, Holy Roman Emperor, 94, 107–108, 110, 123, 186, 216
   Liber Augustalis, 186

Galli, Federico, 122
Gaspare Broglio di Tartaglia. *See* Tartaglia, Gaspare Broglio di
Gattamelata (Erasmo da Narni), 217, 273
Gaul, 33, 135, 139, 141, 256
Genoa, 6
Ghibellines, 67
gigantism, 174, 192, 268–269
Giocondo, Fra Giovanni, xii, 25, 78, 107
Giotto di Bondone, 19
Giovanni di Conversino da Ravenna, 11
   Dragmalogia, 11
Giugni, Domenico, 194–195
Glorioso (horse), 207
glory, 4–5, 8, 13, 155, 174, 204–206, 215
gnomonics, 135, 187–188
God, 24, 88, 99, 100, 130, 154, 162, 181–182
Golden Book, 170–171
Gonzaga family, 67, 86, 90, 95–97, 112, 135, 137, 197, 206–207, 290
   Federico, 94
   Federico II, 207
   Francesco, cardinal, 94, 97, 99
   Gianfrancesco, 96, 100, 131
   Ludovico (son of Ludovico II), 94

   Ludovico II, 86, 93–94, 96–99, 101, 120, 131, 158
   Luigi, 90
   Vespasiano, 112
good government, 8–9, 17, 153–154, 243, 246, 257
Greece, 205
Greeks, 231–232
Guarico, Pomponio, 268
Guarini, Battista, 252
Guelfs, 67
Guernica, 10
guilds, 153, 167

Hampton Court, 137
Hannibal, xiv, 5
Harmony, 228. *See also concinnitas*; symmetry
Hawkwood, Sir John, 217, 223, 273
Hector, 19
Heemskerck, Maarten van, 42, 44, 46, 52–53
Henry III, Holy Roman Emperor, 89
Henry IV, king of England, 26
Henry VIII, king of England, 206
Herculean Addition. *See* Ferrara
Hercules, 19, 47, 134, 137–138, 145–146, 152, 207, 252, 262, 269
hierarchy, 82, 150, 167, 181–184, 186, 268
Holy Blood (Blood of Christ), 88, 90, 96–98, 103–104, 112
Holy See, 35, 47, 85
Homer, 5
   Iliad, 174
Hondedio di Vitale, 257
honey, 167–169
Horace (Quintus Horatius Flaccus), 217
horsemanship, 2, 206, 216
horsemen, 204, 251, 259, 280
horses, 2, 141, 155, 204, 206–217, 225, 230–232, 234–235, 242–243, 251, 257, 259–261, 266–273, 280–281

Giulio Romano paintings of, 207–217
Leonardo drawings of, 270–276, 282
house-city relation
Alberti on, 64–66
Mantua, 86, 90
Urbino, 64, 124, 290
House of Virtue (Sforzinda), 166
humanism, 35, 38, 51, 64, 96, 101, 154, 165, 166, 179, 250
human proportions, 33–34, 150–151. *See also* corporeal referent
Humphrey of Gloucester, duke, 26
Hungary, 26, 194–195
hunting, 233, 235, 239
Hunyadi, Janos, 194

Ianziti, Gary, 174
ichnographia, orthographia, scaenographia (plan, elevation, perspective), 26, 78–80
ideal cities, 75, 82, 84–85, 112, 125, 187, 191, 254, 259, 268, 290
Imola, 254
Imperator Caesar, 13, 16, 22, 24, 137, 139, 158
imperium, 138, 146–147, 151, 182, 265. *See also* sovereignty
ingenium, 146
Innocent VIII, pope (Giovanni Battista Cybo), 47, 73
Ionic order, 44, 56, 183–184, 248
Isidore of Seville, 191
Italy, 76, 82, 101, 125, 161, 194

Jacobins, 21
Janson, H. W., 141
Julius II, pope (Giuliano della Rovere), 123
Julius Caesar, xii, 4, 6, 8, 11, 13, 15, 33, 56, 58, 74, 82, 94, 120, 123, 135, 137–142, 144,
146, 158, 163–164, 166, 170, 175, 181, 184, 215, 256, 280
De bello gallico, 141
Jupiter, 269
justice, 8, 10, 40, 47, 107, 238–239, 242–243
Justinian I, Roman emperor, 217, 220
Justus van Gent, 7
Juvenal (Decimus Junius Juvenalis), 245

Kemp, Martin, 274
King Zogalia, 170–172, 268
knowledge of the architect (*architecti scientia*), 14, 22, 131, 142, 145–147, 189, 256
Krautheimer, Richard, 98

Latium, 5
Laura, 4
Laurana, Luciano, 117, 123, 129
laurel, xiv, 4–8, 11, 158, 220
legitimacy, 43–44, 70–71, 84, 115–116, 123, 135, 138–139, 161–164, 171, 175, 179, 194, 218–219, 234, 267
Leo III, pope, 43, 88
Leo IX, pope (Bruno von Egisheim-Dagsburg), 89
Leo X, pope (Giovanni di Lorenzo de' Medici), 48
Leonardo da Vinci, 33, 206, 254, 266, 267, 269–270, 272–276, 278–280, 282
Codex Atlanticus, 274
Codex Madrid II, 267
Libraries
Bibliotheca Corviniana (Buda), 194
Bodleian (Oxford), 13, 162
ducal library (Urbino), 69, 110, 120–122, 131, 141
Visconti library (Pavia), 22, 25–26, 191
lion, as symbol of communal Rome, 40
lion attacking horse, 40–41, 43, 52–54, 203, 287–289
Livy (Titus Livius), 5, 15, 100

Lombards, 186
Lombardy, 12
Longinus, St., 88
Lorenzetti, Ambrogio, 8, 10, 17, 19, 153–154, 243
The Well-Governed City, 9
Louis XII, king of France, 266, 269
Louis XIV, king of France, 25
Lucretius (Titus Lucretius Carus), 32, 145
Lugli, Emmanuele, 278–279
lupa (she-wolf), 47
Lusitania, 227

Machiavelli, Niccolò, 134, 164, 224
The Prince, 134
machinery (*machinatio*), 134–135, 144
of war, 134–135, 142, 144, 146, 276
Magliabecchiano codex, 147–148, 168, 172–173, 185, 197
magnificence, 18, 21, 70, 74, 77, 86, 88, 100, 120, 261
Maiano, Giovanni da, 137
Malatesta family, 162, 197
Carlo, 161
Galeotto Roberto, 161
Pandolfo, 161
Roberto, 137–138
Sigismondo Pandolfo, 137–138, 157–158, 161–163
Manetti, Gianozzo, 71
Manetti Ciaccheri, Antonio, 97
manliness, 99, 140, 142, 163, 206. *See also virtù; virtus*
Mantegna, Andrea, 92–94, 103, 135, 137
camera picta, 92–93
Triumphs of Caesar, 136–137
Mantua, 66, 69, 74, 85–87, 88–89, 93, 96, 100, 108, 111–112, 120, 131, 137, 206, 214, 232, 290
Casa del Mercato, 96
Castello di San Giorgio, 90, 92, 95–96
Ca' Zoiosa, 131

Index   359

Mantua (*continued*)
  civitas nova, 89, 93, 95, 100
  civitas vetus, 89–90
  Domus Magna, 90, 93
  Domus Mercati, 89
  Gonzaga Axis, 96, 104, 107, 113
  Palazzo della Ragione, 89, 96
  Palazzo del Podestà, 89, 96
  Palazzo Te, 207, 208–213
  Piazza Broletto, 96
  Piazza delle Erbe, 89, 95–96, 104, 107
  Porta Predella, 104
  Porta Pusterla, 95–96, 104
  San Pietro, 89, 100, 104
  San Sebastiano, 86, 95
  Sant'Andrea, 86, 88, 89–90, 96–100, 101–105, 112–113, 120, 157, 290
  Torre Salaro, 89
Marches, 63
Marcus Aurelius, Roman emperor, 31, 48–50, 52, 55, 58, 140–141, 166, 198, 203, 217, 287, 290
Marecchia, river, 158
Maresti, Alfonso, 262
marketplaces, 36, 44, 47, 117, 120, 261
Marlowe, Christopher, 134
Mars, 146, 216, 269
Martin V, pope (Otto Colonna), 68
Martini, Francesco di Giorgio, 107, 119–120, 134, 146–147, 150–152, 182, 206, 225, 232, 275–277, 279
  Opusculum de architectura, 146–147
  Trattato di architettura I, 149, 277
  Trattato di archittetura II, 148
mathematics, 130–132, 134–135
Maximilian I, Holy Roman Emperor, 268
McDonnell, Myles, 140
McLaughlin, Martin, 155

Medici, Cosimo de', 76–77, 86, 119, 250
Medici, Piero de', 187, 198
memory, 15–16, 36, 125, 140, 164, 266
Michelangelo Buonarroti, 48, 52, 55–56, 58
Michelozzo di Bartolomeo Michelozzi, 76
Middle Ages, 4, 35, 43, 48, 77, 117, 123, 125
Milan, 6, 12, 17–21, 25, 69, 86, 93, 129–130, 135, 163–167, 171, 174, 179–182, 190–192, 214, 217–218, 266–267, 269, 273–274, 278
  Biblioteca Ambrosiana, 192
  Broletto, 17–19
  Castello di Porta Giovia, 22, 165
  Castello Sforzesco, 22, 166, 267
  cathedral, 25
  Corte Vecchio, 268
  Sant'Ambrogio, 12
  military success, xii–xv, 134, 139, 145, 152–153, 156, 158, 161–162
Minerva, 236, 269
Mirabilia urbis Romae, 36
mise en scène, 240, 244, 252, 257, 265. *See also décor*; decorum; scenography
Modena, 68, 236
monarchy, 181, 187. *See also* one-man rule
Mondavio, 147
Montefeltro family, 123–124
  Antonio, 123, 124
  Buonconte, 123
  Federico, 63, 69, 86, 110, 113, 115–117, 119–120, 122–125, 129–132, 134, 137, 141, 146–147, 157, 162, 290
  Giannantonio, 115–116, 123
  Guidobaldo, 124
  Isabetta, 137
  Oddantonio, 116
  Taddeo, 123

Morel Favorito (horse), 207–208
Morin, Pauline, 225
Moro, il. *See* Sforza family: Ludovico
Mount Athos, 145
Munich, 269–270
music, 130, 132
Mussolini, Benito, 58, 139, 223

Naples, 25, 108, 113
  Aragonese gate, 113
  Castel Nuovo, 108
Narni, Erasmo da. *See* Gattamelata
natural order, 150, 181–182. *See also* cosmic order
Nature, 228–229
New York, 269–270
Nicholas V, pope (Tommaso Parentucelli), 35, 44, 47, 68–71, 73, 75, 86
North Africa, 206
Novate, Mabilio da, 64
Nuremberg Chronicle, 71
Nuvoloni, Ludovico, abbot, 97

obelisks, 36, 40, 46, 52
Oksanish, John, 265
Old Testament, 130
ombrellone, 103–104, 110–112
one-man rule, 8, 10–11, 181–182, 195, 243
Onians, John, 182, 191
opus caementicium, 122
ornament, 78, 99, 101, 104, 107, 122, 135, 182, 220, 231–232, 240–241, 265
orthogonal projection, 254
Ottoman Turks, 74, 194
Otto of Freising, 35
Ovid (Publius Ovidius Naso), 191
Oxford, 13–14, 16, 22, 162
  Bodleian Library, 13, 162

Pacioli, Luca, 130, 134, 267–268
  De divina proportione, 130, 135, 267

Padua, 11
palazzi, 115, 259
  ducal palace, Urbino, 63–66, 113, 117–125, 129, 132–133
  Palazzo dei Diamanti, Ferrara, 259
  Palazzo della Ragione, Ferrara, 249, 251
  Palazzo di Corte, Ferrara, 219, 223–224, 234, 248–251
  Palazzo Medici, Florence, 76
  Palazzo Piccolomini, Pienza, 75–76, 78, 84, 122
  Palazzo Rucellai, Florence, 76
  Palazzo Schifanoia, Ferrara, 233, 236, 242, 244
  papal palace, Vatican, 68, 71
palazzo comunale, 84
palio, 214, 235
Pannonia, 197
Panofsky, Erwin, 154
Panormita, Antonio, 108
papacy, papal power, 34–35, 40, 51, 58–59, 74, 203
papal Rome, 71–74
Papal States, 107, 161
Parma, 11
Parnassus, 4
Parthenon, 204
Pasti, Matteo de', 158
patriarchy, 181
Patrizi, Francesco, 181–182
  De regno et regis institutione, 181
patronage, 11–12, 86, 180
Paul II, pope (Pietro Barbo), 52, 181, 233
Paul III, pope (Alessandro Farnese), 48, 51, 56, 203
Pavia, 19, 20–22, 25, 129, 191, 217, 223, 273–276, 278
  Castello Visconteo, 22
  Certosa 25
Peace of Constance, 67
Perrault, Claude, 25
Persian prisoners, 143–144, 169–170
Petrarch (Francesco Petrarca), 3, 6–7, 10, 13–14, 16–17, 19–22, 24, 26, 31, 129, 138–140, 142, 154–155, 204, 206, 240, 273–274, 280, 288
  Africa, 3, 10–11
  coronation as poet laureate, 3–8, 15
  De gestis Cesaris, 10, 139
  De viris illustribus, 10, 139, 153, 204–206
Pevsner, Nikolaus, 190
piazza comunale, 124, 249, 251, 290. See also *platea communis*
piazza del comune, 74. See also *platea communis*
piazza maggiore
  Ferrara, 249–251, 254, 257, 261
  Urbino, 116, 125, 152
Piccolomini family, 84–85. See also Pius II
Pienza, 26, 75–76, 81–86, 290
  Palazzo Piccolomini, 75–77, 78, 84
  Santa Maria Assunta, 78
Pius II, pope (Aeneas Silvius Piccolomini), 26, 66, 72, 74, 76–77, 81–82, 84–86, 88, 93, 104, 108, 122, 161
  Commentaries, 74–77, 161
  De Europa, 73
Pius IV, pope (Giovanni Angelo Medici), 55–56
Pius V, pope (Antonio Ghislieri), 56
Pizzolpasso, Francesco, 26
platea communis, 17, 19, 68, 89, 107, 124, 244
Plato, 15–16, 26, 130, 145, 191, 229, 235, 245
  Laws, 191
  Republic, 191
  Timaeus, 130
Plautus, Titus Maccius, 251–252
  Menaechmi, 251
plebs, 165, 180
Pliny the Elder (Gaius Plinius Secundus), 78, 100, 191–192, 197, 217, 220, 278
  Natural History, 217, 220, 278
Pliny the Younger (Gaius Plinius Caecilius Secundus), 78
Plusiapolis, 171, 174, 190, 191
Plutarch (Lucius Mestrius Plutarchus), xiv, 100, 191
Po, river, 112
poets, 5, 14
Poggio Bracciolini, 12, 25
political ambition, 3–5, 24, 67, 71, 75, 107, 174, 288, 291
politics, 78, 152, 190, 197–198
Pollaiuolo, Antonio da, 269–271
Pompey the Great (Gnaeus Pompeius Magnus), xiv, 153
popolo, 6, 19, 43, 47, 93, 182, 204, 257. See also plebs
Porcari, Stefano, 70–71
portraits, 93–94, 126, 227, 236, 269
possesso, 40, 43–44, 56, 219
power, 8, 13, 45, 249–250, 270, 280. See also signorial power
  of architecture, 18, 214, 230, 274 (see also architectural proof)
primitive huts, 32, 183
Prisciani, Pellegrino, 223–224, 233, 244, 246, 249–250, 252, 261
  Descriptio urbis Ferarriae, 254
  Historiae Ferrarienses, 222–223, 253–255
  Spectacula, 244, 247, 252
proportion, 33, 225, 227. See also symmetry
public entertainment. See spectacle
public places. See *platea communis*
pulchritude. See beauty

Punic wars, 5, 117
Pythagoras, 131, 145

qualità, 182–184, 187, 268
Quattrocento, 68–69, 108, 134–135, 151, 191, 229, 231, 245, 274. *See also* Renaissance
Quintilian (Marcus Fabius Quintilianus), 192

Ravenna, 21, 117
rebirth and renewal, 4, 8, 25, 69, 288. *See also* urban renewal
Reformation, 51
Reggio, 236
Regisole, 21, 217, 220, 223, 273–275, 282
regium cubiculum, 110–113, 186, 251
Regnum Caesaris, 107
Renaissance, xi–xii, 4, 8, 11, 15, 31, 64, 75–77, 113, 141, 166, 187, 197, 235, 265–266, 274, 280, 288
  reception of Vitruvius in, xi, 66–70, 78–80, 120, 122–123, 135, 142, 163–164, 187, 197, 232, 275 (*see also* Alberti, Leon Battista: and Vitruvius)
Republic (ancient Rome), 138, 151–153
republics, 194–195
reverence for antiquity, 35
rhetoric, 240
Rimini, 117, 137–139, 157–158, 161–162, 232
  Arch of Augustus, 137, 157–158, 162
  bridge of Tiberius, 158
  Castel Sismondo, 158, 162
  Piazza Tre Martiri, 137
  San Francesco, 157–158, 161–162 (*see also* Rimini: Tempio Malatestiana)
  Tempio Malatestiana, 103, 157, 159
Robert, king of Naples, 3

Roberti, Ercole de', 262, 266
Roma (goddess), 140
Roman Empire, 66, 139. *See also* Augustus Caesar
Roman grandeur, 13, 35, 135, 186, 203, 207, 280
Roman house (*domus*), 122
romanitas, 163
Romano, Giulio, 207–214
  Sala dei Cavalli, 207, 208–213
Roman origins, 120, 123
Romans, 232
Rome, 3, 6, 16, 31, 34, 40, 48, 66, 68, 73–74, 88, 100, 108, 117, 123, 135, 137, 140–141, 189, 217, 219, 245, 264–265
  Arx, 31
  Aurelian wall, 59, 73
  Basilica of Maxentius/Constantine, 101
  Belvedere, 73
  Caelian hill, 52
  Campidoglio, 31, 34, 36, 48, 52, 54–59, 68, 71, 75, 161, 203, 250, 287
  Campo dei Fiori, 161
  Cancelleria, 78 (*see also* Rome: Palazzo Riario)
  Capitol, 3, 5, 15, 35, 38, 40, 44, 47, 51–52, 58, 59, 186, 203, 250, 288 (*see also* Rome: Campidoglio)
  Capitoline hill, 5, 31
  Capitoline Museums, 47, 287
  Colosseum, 44, 73, 246
  Esedra di Marco Aurelio, 287, 290
  Forum Julium, 141
  Forum Romanum, 6, 31, 44, 101
  Juno Moneta, temple, 31
  Jupiter Optimus Maximus, temple, 31
  Lateran, 35, 40, 42–44, 47–48, 68, 198, 204
  Monte Cavallo, 73
  Palazzo dei Conservatori, 44, 46–47, 52, 55, 58, 287
  Palazzo Nuovo, 58

Palazzo Riario, 123 (*see also* Rome: Cancelleria)
Palazzo Senatorio, 6, 15, 36–40, 44, 51–58, 203
Pantheon, 59, 73
Piazza dell'Aracoeli, 51–52
Piazza Termini, 59
Porta Pia, 59
sack of, 51
St. Peter's Basilica, 52, 68, 71, 161, 166, 170
St. Sylvester chapel, Santi Quattro Coronati, 43
Santa Maria in Aracoeli, 36, 38, 51, 63
Santa Maria in Capitolio, 36
Trajan's Column, 73
Vittoriano (Victor Emmanuel monument) 59, 62–63
Romulus, 10, 15, 139
Rosenberg, Charles M., 219, 242, 261
Rossellino, Bernardo, 75–76
Rossetti, Biagio, 256, 259
Rubino, 94
Ruffo, Giordano, 216
Rustici, Cencio de', 25

Sabbioneta, 112
sack of Rome, 51
Saggi, Zaccaria, 93
St. Andrew, 88
St. Gall, 25
St. George's Day, 235
Saluzziano codex, 149, 277
Saluzzo, Riccarda da, 218
San Leo, 147
Sassocorvato, 147
Savi, 219, 250
scenography, 239–240, 243–244, 252, 257. *See also* spectacle
Scipio Africanus the Elder, 5–6
Scoccola, 240
Searle, John R., 113
Servius (Maurus Servius Honoratus), 192
Servius Tullius, king of Rome, 241

Sessa, Taddeo da, 107
Sforza family, 171, 179, 195, 273
   Battista, 124
   Bianca Maria, 268
   Francesco, 86, 93, 164–167, 171, 174–175, 179–184, 187, 191, 194, 267, 269–270
   Galeazzo, 268
   Galeazzo Maria, 129, 184, 206, 267
   Giangaleazzo, 267
   Ludovico (il Moro), 130, 135, 206, 266–267, 269, 276
   Mucio Antendolo, 167
Sforzinda, 166, 170–171, 174, 179, 187, 190, 268
Shearer, Cresswell, 108
Sicily, 186, 206
   kingdom of, 107
Sidonius Apollinaris, 192
Siena, 8, 17, 74, 153–154, 243
   Palazzo Pubblico, 8, 19, 153
   Sala dei Nove, 8, 17, 153–154, 243
signification, 15–16, 22
signorial power, xi, 66–69, 82, 89–90, 95–98, 104, 107, 125, 239, 268, 270. *See also* power; sovereignty
Simonetta, Giovanni, 174
Sivieri, Siviero, 257
Sixtus IV, pope (Francesco della Rovere), 47, 97, 250
sollertia, 144–145
sovereignty, 146, 150, 182, 218, 234, 239, 246, 259, 281
Sparta, 144
spatial appropriation, 44–56, 96–97, 107, 112, 120, 124–125
spectacle, 244–246, 248, 261
spectacula, 244–245, 248–249, 251, 257, 288
Spencer, John, 170, 187
spider, 95
sprezzatura, 94
Statius, Publius Papinius, 191
statuary, 226–227. *See also* equestrian statues
Stevenson, Jane, 116
Stoics, 34

Suetonius (Gaius Suetonius Tranquillus), 8, 15, 141, 191, 245, 264–266
Sulla, Lucius Cornelius, xii
Sulpizio, Giovanni, da Veroli (Sulpicius Verulanus), 120
Sylvester 1, pope, 40, 45
symmetry, 31–34, 51, 58–59, 131, 135, 225–226, 228, 281

Tacitus, Publius Cornelius, 31
Tamburlaine, 134
Tartaglia, Gaspare Broglio di, 137–138, 157–158
   Cronaca universale, 137
Taurus, 233
Tavernor, Robert, 104
Temple of Augustus (Ankara), 264
temples, 99–103, 151
Terence (Publius Terentius Afer), 241
theaters, 246, 252
Theodoric, king of Ostrogoths, 274
three parts of architecture, 135, 187–188
Thucydides, 70
Timor, 8
Tolentino, Francesco da. *See* Filelfo, Francesco
triumphal arches, 103–110, 112–113, 157–158, 162–163, 220, 249–250
Turkey, 206
Tyrammides, 8, 243
tyranny, 8, 12, 115

Uccello, Paolo, 217, 223
UNESCO (United Nations Educational, Scientific and Cultural Organization), 64, 75, 112, 290. *See also* World Heritage Sites
universal man (Renaissance man), 155
urban renewal, 250
   Ferrara, 254–259
   Mantua, 86
   Pienza, 74–76, 82–85
   Urbino, 64–65

Urban V, pope (Guillaume de Grimoard), 13, 22
Urbino, xii, 13, 63–66, 69, 75, 85, 110, 114–118, 123–125, 129–133, 135, 137, 150, 206, 232, 259, 290
   Data (stables), 206
   Palazzetto della Jole, 123–124
   Piazza della Repubblica, 117
   Piazza Duca Federico, 125, 290
   Piazza Maggiore, 116 (*see also* Urbino: Piazza Duca Federico)
   Piazza Rinascimento, 123
   Porta Lavagine, 117
   Porta Valbona, 117
   studiolo, 113
Urbs, 265. *See also* Rome
Urvinum Mataurense, 117, 120. *See also* Urbino
usurpation, 10, 174, 186, 194. *See also* legitimacy

Valla, Giovanni, 266
Valturio, Roberto, 134
   De re militari, 134
Varro, Marcus Terentius, 145
Vasari, Giorgio, 4, 26, 179
Vatican, 68, 73, 170
Venice, 254, 256
Venus, 215, 233
Venustas. *See* beauty
Verona, 12, 90
Veronese, Guarino, 217
Verrocchio, Andrea del, 217, 273
Vesta, 234
Via Appia, 107
Via Flaminia, 117
Victor Emmanuel II, king of Italy, 59
Vigevano, 206
Vinci, Leonardo da. *See* Leonardo da Vinci
Virgil (Publius Vergilius Maro), 4, 15, 88, 94, 100, 151, 191, 218, 241
   Aeneid, 192

Virgin Mary, 24
Virgo, 235
virtù, 130–132, 134, 141, 144, 154–155, 158, 162, 164, 166–171, 174, 180, 183, 187, 194, 196–197, 288. *See also virtus*
virtue of architecture, 145, 152–154, 157, 171
Virtus (goddess), 140
virtus, xiv, 139–142, 145–147, 152–153, 155–158, 162–165, 174, 197, 206–207, 215. *See also virtù*
Visconti family, 12, 17, 20, 67, 214
    Azzo, 17–19, 21, 67
    Bernabò, 17, 19–20, 217
    Bianca Maria, 164
    Filippo Maria, 26, 164–165, 179, 181–182
    Galeazzo II, 17, 19–22, 25–26, 129
    Giangaleazzo, 25, 68
    Giovanni, 12, 17
    Matteo, 17
Viterbo, 76
Vitruvianism, 187–188
Vitruvian man, 33–34, 51, 151, 226–228, 281
    Francesco di Giorgio drawing, 151, 276–277
    Leonardo drawing, 278–280
Vitruvian triad, 98, 122, 231
Vitruvius (Marcus Vitruvius Pollio), xi–xii, xv, 12, 14, 16, 22, 25–26, 31, 33, 38, 58, 69–70, 77–78, 98–99, 108, 113, 120, 122–123, 131, 135, 139–142, 144–147, 150–151, 157–158, 163, 166, 169, 183–184, 187–189, 192, 195, 197, 224, 226–227, 229, 232, 240–242, 245–246, 248, 250, 252, 256, 260, 265–266, 275, 279–281, 290–291. *See also De architectura*
Volaterrano, Raffaele Maffei, 122–123, 125
    Commentatiorum rerum urbanorum, 122

De urbium aedificatio, 125
Volturno, river, 107

war, xiv–xv, 20, 131–132, 152, 235, 256
warhorses, 116, 232
warlords, 11–12, 26, 63, 110, 132, 142, 147, 165, 280. *See also* condottieri
Warnke, Martin, 146
well-shaped man, 33, 251, 226–227, 232, 279, 281
Westwork, 103–104
Windsor Castle, 273
Wittkower, Rudolf, 188, 278–280
    Architectural Principles in the Age Humanism, 278–279
Wolsey, Thomas, cardinal, 137
Woods, Lebbeus, 187
World Heritage Sites (UNESCO), 112, 125, 254, 290
    Ferrara, 254, 290
    Mantua, 112–113, 290
    Pienza, 75, 290
    Urbino, 64, 290

Xenophon, 181, 216, 235
    Cyropaedia, 181, 235
Xerxes, 142

Yates, Frances, 186–187

Zama, 5
Zermia, Niccolò, 261
Zilocchi, Giacomo, 223

© 2023 Indra Kagis McEwen

All rights reserved. No part of this book may be reproduced in any form by any electronic or mechanical means (including photocopying, recording, or information storage and retrieval) without permission in writing from the publisher.

The MIT Press would like to thank the anonymous peer reviewers who provided comments on drafts of this book. The generous work of academic experts is essential for establishing the authority and quality of our publications. We acknowledge with gratitude the contributions of these otherwise uncredited readers.

This book was set in Haultin by Jen Jackowitz. Printed and bound in Canada

Library of Congress Cataloging-in-Publication Data is available.

ISBN: 978-0-262-04761-6

10 9 8 7 6 5 4 3 2 1